PHILIP SELZNICK

Jurists: Profiles in Legal Theory

William Twining, General Editor

Philip Selznick

IDEALS IN THE WORLD

Martin Krygier

STANFORD LAW BOOKS

An Imprint of Stanford University Press

Stanford, California

Stanford University Press
Stanford, California
© 2012 by the Board of Trustees of the Leland Stanford Junior
University. All rights reserved.

Printed in the United States of America on acid-free, archival-quality
paper

Library of Congress Cataloging-in-Publication Data

Krygier, Martin, author.
    Philip Selznick : ideals in the world / Martin Krygier.
        pages cm. — (Jurists: profiles in legal theory)
    Includes bibliographical references and index.
    ISBN 978-0-8047-4475-1 (cloth: alk. paper)
        1. Selznick, Philip, 1919–2010. 2. Sociological jurisprudence.
3. Organizational sociology. 4. Social sciences—Philosophy.
I. Title. II. Series: Jurists—profiles in legal theory.

    K370.K794 2012

    306.2'501—dc23

                                                    2011036777

Typeset by Thompson Type in 10/13 Galliard

For Jonathan
My son and friend

Contents

Acknowledgments

Rudi Dutschke, a leader of the German student movement of the 1960s, advised his comrades that they were in for a "long march through the institutions." When Malcolm Feeley suggested I might write a book on the thought of Philip Selznick, one of the most interesting of institutional theorists, he didn't issue the same advice. But so it has turned out. On the way, I have accumulated many debts, both institutional and personal. There is no way to repay them, but they should at least be acknowledged.

I have been generously supported by my law school throughout this project. I have also benefited much from time spent at several stimulating and collegial intellectual centers. Among these were several periods at the Center for the Study of Law and Society, University of California Berkeley, which Selznick founded, where the suggestion for the book emerged, and where I have worked on it from time to time, given seminars and conference papers, and discussed work-in-progress with anyone who would listen.

I also gained from a visiting fellowship at the Humanities Centre, Central European University, Budapest, in 2003, in connection with a joint project with Princeton University's Law and Public Affairs Program, on "universalism and local knowledge in human rights." My chapter in the book that resulted was the product of seminars in Budapest and Princeton and was an attempt to discern and unveil Selznick's largely implicit theory of human rights. My special thanks to András Sajó for inviting me to join that project.

Concerted work on the book took place during my fellowship at the Center for Advanced Studies in the Behavioral Sciences, Stanford, in 2005–2006. That was true and fruitful fellowship. In 2009, I was Law

Foundation Distinguished Visiting Fellow at the five New Zealand Law Schools. I gave seminars on Selznick, inter alia, at them all. I am grateful for these opportunities and the valuable discussions they promoted.

As part of this project, I have also given seminars on parts of this book at the Regulatory Institutions Network, Australian National University; the Hertie School of Governance, Berlin; the Institute of Sociology, Jagiellonian University, Cracow; the Law and Society Center, University of Edinburgh; the Department of Sociology, Harvard University; the Julius Stone Institute of Jurisprudence, University of Sydney; and the Center for Legislative Studies, Tilburg University. Again I benefited from intellectual workouts and feedback at all these institutions.

Institutions aside, my personal debts are vast. At the Berkeley Center for the Study of Law and Society, which he founded, it is hard not to have conversations about Selznick, and I have had many. My conversational partners, sources of advice and inspiration, have included Meir Dan Cohen, Lauren Edelman, Malcolm Feeley, Sanford Kadish, Robert Kagan, David Lieberman, Charles McClain, the late Sheldon Messinger, Philippe Nonet, Robert Post, Jerome Skolnick, and Jonathan Simon. I gained much from their insights and their advice. Philip Selznick's widow, Doris Fine, deserves special mention. She was his soul mate and has been unfailingly generous in sharing her understanding and insights into the man she knew and loved so well.

From the very beginning, Selznick's long-time intellectual interlocutor, Kenneth Winston, undertook to read drafts of every chapter, and he gave me detailed commentary on them all. His generosity, wisdom, and encouragement have been boundless—and indispensable to me. At a late stage in the writing, James Rule read a draft of the book as a whole. His suggestions and criticism were both sharp and extremely helpful. So too were the suggestions of the two anonymous reviewers of the manuscript.

Roger Cotterrell, Arthur Glass, Ben Golder, Jonathan Krygier, Gianluigi Palombella, Gianfranco Poggi, Kim Lane Scheppele, Sanne Taekema, Robert van Krieken, Wibren van der Berg, and especially Paul van Seters have been happy to help at different times in the progress of the work; my wife, Julie Hamblin, at all times—even though in her case that meant very many times.

I owe special thanks to William Twining, who initially considered my proposal to the Press for a book on Selznick's legal sociology. He has been a kind, patient, and wise editorial advisor ever since, undaunted by the ballooning scope of the book or the time it took. The editors at the Press, first Amanda Moran and now Kate Wahl, who has also had carriage of the manuscript and its refinement, are exemplary professionals and a pleasure to work with.

My greatest debt in relation to this book is, naturally enough, to Philip Selznick himself. Though well disposed, he didn't seek the book, and he never interfered. But he gave as much of his time and reflections as I asked for, and then some. I believe the book gained enormously from our conversations and correspondence, as well as my interviews with him. Others will judge that, but I know *I* gained a great deal. I have sought to suggest the range and something of the measure of his intelligence in the book, but I also stress matters of character. Of course character is a large thing, beyond intellect. Philip's was admirable, and my respect for that, as well as for what he had to say, affects what follows.

My preoccupation with this work has lived with my family for a long time. What I owe them for their patience is the least of it, and in any event beyond measure or words.

Portions of this book build on ideas that first appeared in:
"Walls and Bridges: A Comment on Philip Selznick's *The Moral Commonwealth*," *California Law Review*, 82 (1994), 473–486;
"Selznick's Subjects," and "Philip Selznick, Normative Theory, and the Rule of Law," in Robert A. Kagan, Martin Krygier, and Kenneth Winston, eds., *Legality and Community: On the Intellectual Legacy of Philip Selznick* (Lanham, MD, and Boulder, CO: Rowman & Littlefield, 2002), 3–16 and 19–48;
"Human Rights and a Humanist Social Science," in Christopher L. Eisgruber and András Sajó, eds., *Global Justice and the Bulwarks of Localism: Human Rights in Context* (Amsterdam: Brill, 2005), 43–84;
"Philip Selznick: Incipient Law, State Law and the Rule of Law," in J. van Schooten and J. M. Verschuuren , eds., *International Governance and Law. State Regulation and Non-State Law* (Cheltenham, UK: E. E. Elgar, 2008), 31–55;
"Foreword" to Philip Selznick, *A Humanist Science* (Stanford, CA: Stanford University Press, 2008), vii–xv.

Apart from published sources, I have drawn on extensive conversations with Selznick and several of his colleagues, and conducted a series of structured interviews with him. Eight of these were videotaped and can be accessed at http://law.berkeley.edu/selznick.htm. Other useful resources can also be found at that site, including the transcript of Roger Cotterrell's interviews with Selznick for University of California, Berkeley's Bancroft Library's Oral History Project.

PHILIP SELZNICK

Introduction

Philip Selznick died in 2010, one of the last of a distinguished cohort of writers and intellectuals originally from New York who began their intellectual formation before World War II and who continued to be influential for decades. They included Irving Kristol, Gertrude Himmelfarb, Daniel Bell, Nathan Glazer, Seymour Martin Lipset, Irving Howe, and others.

Selznick spent a very long life engaged with large questions concerning society, politics, institutions, law, and morals. He contributed to numerous disciplines and subdisciplinary domains and was a major figure in each of the fields he entered and one of few to have been a participant, let alone eminent, in them all. Among these fields are general sociology, the sociology of organizations and institutions, management theory, political science, industrial sociology, the sociology and philosophy of law, political theory, and social philosophy grounded in what he came to call humanist science.

The present book discusses his contributions to these various subjects and domains. But it is haunted, *I* am haunted, by a remark of his former student and sometime collaborator, Philippe Nonet, that "those who look to Philip's work for contributions to this or that 'field'—'sociology of organization,' 'industrial sociology,' 'sociology of law,'—will doubtless find something, indeed a great deal, but they will miss all that matters."[1] The point might be phrased less dramatically; perhaps not *all*, just lots. Still, the observation resonates. This work seeks to vindicate my particular understanding of it, which may or may not be Nonet's.

I

Selznick's intellectual development began some years before World War II, with an intense period of activity and debate in that strangely fertile womb of intellectual productivity, the New York Trotskyist movement, its parties and party-lets, factions and fractions. Like many of his closest friends from that time, Selznick was intellectually formed, and formed as an *intellectual*, before and beside the academic disciplines he went on to profess. Their thought was spurred by several dramatic, indeed world-historical and world-shattering, events, specifically the Great Depression, the epochal competitions between liberal democracies and Nazism that culminated in World War II, and with communism, both before and after that war. These prompted urgent and large questions about public morality and about the worth of different sorts and arrangements of public institutions. Selznick didn't forget such questions, even as he wrote about many other things.

Out of that engagement came several writings read by a small number of clever would-be revolutionaries, later to become well known in American academic and public life, though rarely for that. Out of it, too, came Selznick's abiding concerns with the significance of institutions and the fate of ideals. These concerns animated all his subsequent work.

In his early political essays, and in *TVA and the Grass Roots*,[2] his first and classic contribution to organizational and institutional theory, he explored ways in which immanent organizational tendencies tend to undermine even the finest ideals, unless deliberately countered and mastered. He next explored what mastery might require. *The Organizational Weapon*[3] examined communist organizational strategy, designed to transform "recruits into deployable agents." *Leadership in Administration*[4] sought to generalize and systematize lessons learned, among other sources, from these first two works. The examination involved empirical research and sociological explanation, but it also led Selznick to reflect on large questions of normative social and political theory, among them the nature of politics and statesmanship, to an extent uncommon in works of this kind. He also wrote, with Leonard Broom, a major introduction to sociology[5] that, in seven editions over thirty years, was for a long time the leading sociology text in the United States. These early works had a great influence and probably remain the ones for which he is most widely known.

Thereafter Selznick moved to less populated domains and developed less fashionable preoccupations and commitments. In his second branch of work, beginning in the early to mid-1950s, he became one of the first, and one of very few, mainstream American sociologists to engage with the study of law; still fewer were engaged with jurisprudence. He published several important essays (particularly "Sociology and Natural Law"[6]) and books: *Law, Society, and Industrial Justice*;[7] *Law and Society in Transition*.[8] These works were notable for their explicit and pervasive interweaving of descriptive, analytic, normative, and policy-oriented concerns. Selznick sought to identify the particular character and basic ideals of legal order- ing, their range of variation, and the conditions that might allow them to be secured and, beyond that, to flourish.

These themes and views are developed in his writings, of course. But they also molded his institutional initiatives, which were substantial. In 1961, he founded the Center for the Study of Law and Society at UC Berke- ley, and later (1977) the Jurisprudence and Social Policy PhD program. The Center has drawn important scholars from several disciplines and faculties and ultimately from many countries. It grew from modest beginnings to become a major site of sociolegal research, which it remains. The JSP was the first interdisciplinary PhD program in law in the United States. It is the largest example of such sociolegal ecumenism, the only one based in a law school, and distinctive among pioneering law and society endeavors in its determination systematically to marry insights from humanist and social science disciplines with each other and with law. As Selznick put it at the time, its "stress on humanist scholarship distinguishes what we are about from recent precursors of JSP, including the law and society move- ment . . . I believe we can and should have a larger aspiration—the clarifica- tion of fundamental values. For this, we must rely heavily on philosophi- cal, cultural, and historical modes of inquiry."[9] In relation to all these, he did what he advocated in all his work: meld normative reflection, empirical research, and explanatory inquiry, with an eye to consequences.

His third group of writings, from the 1980s, coincided with his formal but nominal retirement. These works were more reflective than investiga- tive, more wide ranging in scale and scope than much of his earlier work, and explicitly concerned to communicate a large sociologico-philosophical vision. Their centerpiece is his magisterial *The Moral Commonwealth*,[10] a work of expansive range, ambition, erudition, and richness. Its overarch- ing concern is with challenges to and sources of "moral well-being"—of persons, institutions, and communities—in modern times; on the way there are few themes or thinkers left untouched. This was followed by two short books: *The Communitarian Persuasion*,[11] which extended the (liberal-) communitarian directions charted in *The Moral Commonwealth*, and his last work, *A Humanist Science*,[12] published two years before his death at 91, which sought to distill the methodological ecumenism and substantive humanism that had long underlain his thought and that make them available within but also beyond the academy.

II

Pursued through this large and various range of subjects, disciplines, and subdisciplines, Selznick's core themes are quick to state, though he approached them from many directions, and there has been considerable evolution in his ways of answering them. There are two: One is substantive; another, slower to evolve but also of long standing, has to do with the appropriate way to study the questions with which he has been concerned.

I start with substance. Selznick begins his magnum opus, *The Moral Commonwealth*, by recalling that in his "late teens and early 20s [he] went through an intense, fruitful and in some ways extraordinary experience" as an active and prominent young Trotskyist. At the same time he was "an eager student" of sociology and philosophy at City College of New York and then at Columbia University. He comments that "the two parts of my life did not fit very well."[13] That might be how it felt at the time, but it's not how the situation looks in retrospect. For Selznick already had a particular range of concerns recognizable throughout his varied life's works. As he recalled, "My youthful encounter with revolutionary socialism established a theme that influenced my work over many years . . . the fate of ideals in the course of social practice. Most of my specialized writings in the sociology of organizations and sociology of law have been preoccupied with the conditions and processes that frustrate ideals or, instead, give them life and hope."[14] That was his theme in 1992, but it was also his theme in the 1940s. He had a lot to say about it in the times in between and since.

Selznick wrote on many subjects, not self-evidently connected to each other. Most of his writings focus on large institutions, public and private, and on law, but he also wrote a good deal about persons and communities. All his particular subjects are treated with the "generalizing impulse" that in late-life reflections he saw as characteristic of all his thinking. His writings operate on several planes and exhibit several kinds of concern. They can all be read variously as well. Thus his first work, *TVA*, for example, has been understood primarily as an exposé of one particular organization and program or of the unanticipated consequences of an organizational strategy he made famous as "co-optation." These are not misreadings. However, Selznick was concerned both to explore larger theoretical implications of the particular case and to bring larger theoretical perspectives to bear on it. Again, those who read *The Organizational Weapon* as an examination of communist organizational strategy are right to do so, but they might not be aware of the broader implications for the character of organizational development, transformation, and leadership that also lie deep in the work. *Law, Society, and Industrial Justice* has typically been read as a work of analysis and advocacy in the fields of industrial relations, labor, and employment law. It is that, but there are in that work many larger, deeper, and I believe more enduring, things going on as well. *The Moral Commonwealth* teems with themes.

These layers of concern and significance are not piled on one another by accident. It doesn't take much reading into Selznick's works before one senses a strong and unifying temper—or better, perhaps, because the concept plays a significant role in the works, a coherent intellectual and moral *character*. That is revealed partly in enduring themes, arguments, exemplars, commitments. However, it also involves a distinctive if evolving sensibility, which is not merely a matter of emotional temperament but of moral and intellectual posture as well. Those who have read him on one subject or another, who know him in one period or from one classic contribution, might not immediately feel the general scope and force of this character, the extent to which his analysis of one thing is of a piece with, or a development of or from, his analysis of others and is driven and informed by continuing basic concerns. However, they are not far to seek.

These aspects of temper, character, and sensibility are not changeless. On the contrary, the scope of his interests, the focus of his passions, his particular judgments, and I believe his public mood and posture changed considerably over the years. His subjects are complex, as is his thought, and they have a complex coherence, too, not that of someone with just one thing to say. Still, I would stress that the continuities and coherence of which I speak are real, pervasive, and sustained. The fate of values and ideals in the world is his central theme.

Over time, his views about how one should go about exploring these questions also evolved. His earliest academic works largely conform to the disciplinary patterns of sociology of that era. However, he became restless over time, seeking a more encompassing (*ecumenical* is his term) way of doing social science. The terms he gave the mode of study to which he aspired have varied: *normative theory*, *normative science*, and the term on which he finally settled, *humanist science*. The key to humanist science (which many humanists and social scientists might consider a contradiction in terms, but Selznick regards as inescapable complements) stems from his substantive conviction that central to social understanding is the need to develop an appreciation of the role and play of values and ideals in the world: What are they, what do they do, what are they worth, what threatens them, what protects and sustains them, what enables them to flourish? These need to be acknowledged as proper objects of study, rather than mere epiphenomena of whatever is thought really to matter. This also requires identification of the values at stake in particular social processes, practices, and institutions; clarification of their nature; understanding what threatens them; exploring the conditions in which they might thrive.

Given this centrality of values, a social scientist should be informed by traditions of philosophical thought less chary of dealing with them than is typical of some of the more positivistic conceptions of behavioral (and legal) sciences. Moral philosophy is key here. On the other hand, because so much that is important about the play of values in the world is subject to variation and refracted through particular contexts, philosophical speculation needs anchoring in these matters of fact, contingency, and variety—and so social sciences. And because Selznick's concern is not with values applied to just anything but always ultimately as they affect human persons, the learning with which a normative theorist needs to be familiar—in aid of "genuine understanding of human frailty, suffering, and potentiality"[15]—will be informed by and contribute to traditions of humanism broadly conceived. The distinctive aim of humanist science, blending insights from these various sources so often separated, is "analytical and empirical study of ideals, understood as at once latent in and threatened by the vagaries of social life."[16]

These expansive ambitions are exemplified in the work. Selznick brings to whatever he writes, in whatever field, a distinctive combination of explanatory theory, empirical research, philosophical awareness, and normative engagement. Even the most fine-grained empirical analysis is not done merely for its own sake but to answer large questions of explanation and evaluation, and his normative reflection has always been anchored in sociologically derived observation and theory about the ways of the world.

His determination to blend the concerns of social research and moral philosophy is rare among empirical social scientists, and the depth of his philosophical knowledge and insight is rarer still. That is not the way most social scientists have been trained, or think, today. Relatively few share his ecumenical view of the discipline or would know what to do with it. On the other hand, Selznick is a great sociologist, and he is concerned with bringing to bear on normative, philosophical questions, close examination of social realities, and a disciplined understanding of the way that complex and large social and political institutions work, and vary, in the world.

III

There are many ways to write about thinkers and their thoughts. Common in the social sciences is piecemeal, discipline-centered citation. How an idea fits within a particular field is likelier to determine the interest it arouses than will its place in the development or illumination of its author's thoughts. If a particular contribution is fixed on in a particular literature, a writer will be associated with that contribution and literature. Contributions in other literatures tend to recede beyond the vision, even peripheral, of most disciplinarians. Members of specialized professions often have in mind highly specialized audiences, and no one else reads them. Sometimes that is a good idea.

Selznick moved more easily between subjects, disciplines, and literatures than do many who might have encountered him in one place and therefore not in another. He did so not because he was easily bored, but because he agreed with John Dewey that scholars should "learn how to think about ideas *in a practical way*, to be guided in . . . thinking by problems of life and practice, not academic disputes or disciplinary methods."[17] It is not surprising, nor is it simply a mistake, that his name is attached today to a particular work or idea as received in a professional academic domain, for his contributions to several such domains have been valuable. But recall Nonet's remark.

We treat the writings of certain authors differently: not retail, but wholesale; not primarily as framed by a particular academic discipline, but at large. Particular works and ideas are read in the light of an oeuvre, instances of a larger whole worthy of exploration. Interest comes to be focused on the writer's ideas taken in the round, and particular works are treated as outgrowths and evidence of those ideas. In such treatments, basic lines are clarified, connections and developments traced, informing values and underpinning commitments and ideas exposed. What is understood from one work is reassessed in the light of others. For we are as interested in the *way* a writer thought, in the flow, style, and pattern of argument, as much as in any specific detachable conclusion. "Classical" authors are often treated this way, and modish ones too.

Many authors, even of major works, will not repay holistic renditions, at least not with interest. Their best works are the ones we should read, and for the reasons one typically reads them: for what they say about their subjects. Reading all their works together one might learn more, without going deeper. One might find nothing much larger in the whole than appears in particular parts. One might even find less. They might not add up.

On the other hand, some authors not usually read holistically or by various publics deserve to be. One understands individual works better when one sees them in connection, and one gains insights from acquaintance with an overall cast of mind, sensibility, and point of view that can be missed if works are read on their own and for themselves or their disciplinary contributions alone. One learns not merely what a thinker thought about, or even what he or she thought, but what is involved in thinking that way. There are also matters of depth and complexity. There is the experience of discovering something new when you reread certain, but not just any, authors. Perhaps this is why such authors are read holistically and from different perspectives, in the search for clues to deeper themes and levels of meaning and significance.

I believe Selznick's thought requires and repays holistic treatment, though it has rarely received it. As might be surmised, his name is well known in and across a number of disciplines, through his books, through the work of his students, through the institutions he has generated and that flourish today. And yet his writings have retained neither the attention nor the influence they seem to me to warrant, nor have they been seen to form the cumulative and wide-ranging corpus that I believe they do. He is today likelier to be cited or recalled only in that truncated snapshot mode that diminishes the significance of his thought and misconstrues it.

There is no book-length treatment of Selznick's ideas taken in the round,[18] no monograph, no study of a distinctive mind at work, generating a sustained and cumulative body of writings developing over most of a century. The work is more respected than emulated and today more known about, I suspect, than known; cited rather than read. That seems to me a pity and, perhaps, to paraphrase Talleyrand, worse than a pity—a mistake.

For beyond his many particular insights into the nature and quality of institutional, legal, and social life and development, there is his cast of mind; *ways* of thinking, animating concerns and values, and a distinctive sensibility, that fuse humanist and scientific concerns, analytic and normative ones, without either embarrassment or false showmanship. These ways of thinking, concerns, values, and sensibility, this cast of mind, are the primary subjects of this book.

Because the explicit subjects on which he worked for the most part developed chronologically, this book generally deals with his writings in order of publication. Ultimately, however, my concern is less to summarize and locate Selznick's particular contributions on particular questions in particular disciplines and more, with Nonet's caution in mind, to convey his manner and style of thinking, what might be called, somewhat elusively but it's the best I can do, his moral-intellectual sensibility. The focus is on the character of his thought, as much as on what he chose to think about and what he thought about it. These characteristics of a mind at work, if that mind is distinguished, can have an importance that reaches beyond their specific "products," narrowly understood. They are easily passed over, however, in the hyperspecialized and discipline-generated and -framed orientations of many modern social scientists.

As will become clear, I admire Selznick's ambitions and his achievements, for reasons both intellectual and moral. Indeed, this book is an *appreciation* of his thought, in both senses of that word. According to one definition, to appreciate is "to estimate aright, to perceive the full force of." That, of course, is the primary task. But I have come to believe that appreciation is warranted in another sense as well: "to recognize as valuable or excellent; to find worth or excellence in."[19] That is another reason for writing this book. His thought warrants more appreciation, in either sense, than it now receives. Still, there are difficulties and risks attached to his singular enterprise, and he did not always surmount or evade them. There are also controversies over some of his commitments that find favor with me but not with everyone. I discuss several of these difficulties and controversies through the book, particularly in Chapters Five, Eight, Nine, and Twelve.

IV

As context for what follows, I should perhaps declare a personal reason for my now long engagement, and this particular sort of engagement, with Selznick's thought. It is a subtext of this book,[20] if largely subliminal in these pages. It has above all to do with what I have called his moral-intellectual sensibility.

I was born precisely thirty years after Selznick. My parents, his precise contemporaries, were politically engaged refugees from Nazism and Communism who had, largely fortuitously and wholly fortunately, ended up in a relatively sane and decent liberal democracy, Australia. I absorbed by inheritance political and moral concerns that Selznick's and my parents' generation confronted directly. In particular, concerns about the gulf between radically evil regimes, those we called totalitarian, and relatively benign ones. Those concerns went deep, and in my case had two relevant consequences.

First, confronted by hostile criticisms of liberal democracy, say from the student movement in the 1960s or critical legal studies in the 1970s and 1980s, I thought them insufferably light minded, frivolous, in light of the really existing alternatives on offer. My first question was always "compared to what?"—not a bad question, I still believe, but less of a conversation stopper than I once assumed. Secondly, my intellectual and moral formation had been one of sharp dichotomies: democracy and dictatorship, good and evil, friends and enemies, fears and hopes. One *chose*.

In Selznick I found a thinker who was light minded about nothing, well knew the comparisons that so concerned me, shared many of the same concerns, and didn't trivialize any of them. However I also learned a new language and way of speaking, as well as new thoughts and ways of thinking. These rejected the often polarized ways of thought that I had shared with both allies and opponents.

Selznick recognized evil and the importance of resisting it. However, he refused to let that realism douse idealism: A forced choice between the two, he insisted, was commonly a false choice. It was possible—it was right—both to acknowledge that things could be worse while at the same time seeking to make them better. Security against the first was crucial; aspirations for the latter equally so.

These are simple points to state but harder to appreciate and internalize, to *live*. They pull in different directions and typically appeal to people of different temperament. Selznick came to live them. He was that rare but distinguished type: a Hobbesian idealist, temperamentally and intellectually alert both to threat and to promise. For me his sustained combination of realism with idealism was a revelation: not so much a point in an argument as an outlook on the world. It went with his determination to accommodate complexity, his tolerance of ambiguity, suspicion of all-or-nothing choices, attention to variation and differences of degree, the interpretive charity he extended to arguments of so many thinkers with whom he disagreed—they might, he insisted, yet have something important to say. These matters, as much of sensibility as of argument, of style of thinking as much as particular thoughts, are central to what I have found lastingly attractive about Selznick's mind and have sought to convey.

There are thus many things this book is not, at least in its primary purpose. It is not a biography, not even an intellectual one. Nor is it an attempt to explain Selznick's thought sociologically, psychologically, or in any other way, except perhaps intellectually. Nor is its aim to estimate his influence in the academic fields to which he contributed. I say a fair deal about all these matters, and such books will be welcome, but it has not been my aim to write them. My primary goal has been to portray the character and workings of a distinguished mind, *cast* of mind, and way of thinking, as they emerge in Selznick's published writings; to expound the patterns and interrelationships among the ideas and ways of thought developed there; to explore and examine them; to make some claims for their significance; and to criticize them where that seems apt. Perhaps I am just trying to clarify for myself, as much as for whoever reads this book, why Selznick seems to me a thinker of real and abiding significance. I have satisfied my first audience. I now invite the opinion of a second.

PART I

First Thoughts

CHAPTER ONE

The "Tragedy of Organization"

The coincidence of political engagement, intellectual formation, and academic novitiate in Selznick's early years was both temporal and geographic. In 1936, Selznick commenced at City College New York, "a university which at the time," as Kim Lane Scheppele has recently written, "had a student body that was brilliant, poor, and deeply political."[1] The Great Depression of the 1930s and the threat of war, ideological passions and disputes, struggles over ends and means, all these were his subjects at City College. They emerged less from his classes, though, than from discussions in a student alcove—Alcove 1—adjoining the college cafeteria.

Of his classes, Selznick later recalled little with excitement. The philosopher Morris Cohen impressed him greatly, and some intensive reading of the culture and personality school in anthropology, for an honors program, also influenced him enduringly. Alcove 1, where students of the anti-Stalinist, prominently Trotskyist, Left met to "have discussions" was something else:

> We used to use a phrase, "having a discussion." "Having a discussion" meant something rather special in those days. It meant a fairly passionate interchange, arguing about some factual matter or an interpretation or what have you and doing it at the top of your lungs! That was a discussion![2]

In Alcove 2 were the Stalinists, who were forbidden to speak with their foes in Alcove 1, though it appears they abused each other often enough.[3] Other alcoves had been appropriated by other groups, but Alcove 1 housed a remarkable concentration of later prominent social scientists and intellectuals.

The engagements and disputes that began in the alcoves had an enormous impact on Selznick. It was not only a tumultuous but also an intellectually stimulating association, at the same time his political and intellectual awakening. His political activity continued after he enrolled at Columbia University in 1938 to begin graduate work in sociology. He joined the Trotskyist youth movement, the Young People's Socialist League (Fourth International), adopting Philip Sherman as his Party name. He was an active member and became organizer of its "Joe Hill Unit" in the Washington Heights section of Manhattan and, in 1938, a member of several executive committees, including the group's national executive.[4] Though he remained a Party member for only three years, part of them as he later recalled getting in, and part getting out, he often referred to what began in Alcove 1 as the most intense intellectual experience of his life.

Two significant, intertwined, contradictory yet also complementary, influences on his early thinking, Leon Trotsky and Robert Michels, shaped his early thought about politics and connected with his developing sociological concerns. To followers such as Selznick, Trotsky represented at once the incarnation and the failure of exalted ideals. He also identified a specific culprit for that failure: the Soviet bureaucracy. To an extent unprecedented and uncomfortable within orthodox Marxism, the concept and machinations of bureaucracy dominated the Trotskyist worldview by the time Selznick was initiated into it. The message from Michels, written well before Trotsky had even come near power let alone lost it, had a similar subject but broader implications. The propensity of bureaucracy to undermine cherished ideals was not, on his analysis, a conjunctural, tactical danger, a temporary backstep ultimately to be overcome. It was, as it were, ontological, written into the nature of political life and above all into the need for *organization* in politics. The juxtaposition of Trotsky and Michels, though it occurred somewhat fortuitously in Selznick's case, made a deep impression on him.

FROM TROTSKY TO MICHELS

Trotsky and Bureaucratic "Betrayal"

Leon Trotsky was a compelling figure, particularly for young idealists in the 1930s. He could easily, if not adequately, be portrayed as the personification of high ends, bloodied but unbowed by low means, at the same time the incarnation of the ideals of the Revolution (and pretty soon a martyr to them), and, in impotent and arguably therefore innocent exile, an explanation for why those ideals had become enmeshed in terror and worse. And that was roughly how he and his followers saw it. For a while Selznick was one of those followers. His immersion in the incessant intra-Party squabbles of that time was not merely a memorable moment in his life; it contributed deeply to the development of his thought.

In the context of economic depression at home, the threat of war against fascism looming, and the revolutionary alternative that the Soviet Union seemed to represent abroad, many young intellectuals throughout the world were drawn to communism in the 1930s. But after learning of the millions killed in the forced collectivization of agriculture in the early 1930s and the astonishing show trials and purges of the Party apparatus, the army, and the highest Party leadership itself from the mid-1930s, some were persuaded that, at least in its Stalinist phase, that experiment had become a catastrophe.

What options did that leave? One, which many of these young radicals including Selznick ultimately took, was to drop Marxism-Leninism, even to turn on it, altogether. But for many that did not happen at once. Instead, another option, which attracted a distinguished group for a time, was Trotsky. He had, after all, been second only to Lenin in making the Russian Revolution and had forged the Red Army that won the civil war. He was Stalin's most eminent Bolshevik rival (all the more after all other contenders had been broken and humiliated in the show trials and then liquidated). It also helped that he was a heroic larger-than-life figure, a charismatic orator, a brilliant writer, indisputably an idealist and an intellectual, but equally indisputably an activist, who had actually built and led revolutionary cadres, not merely talked about it. And as his power, and he, were relentlessly being destroyed by Stalin, he became more, not less, luminous in the eyes of the faithful.

He was squeezed out of power, first to internal exile, then expulsion from the Soviet Union, then to and from a series of countries pressed by Stalin to deport him. His final place of exile, from 1937 till his assassination on Stalin's orders in 1940, was Mexico City, relatively close at hand to the New York branch of the Socialist Workers' Party (SWP). He became much involved in the debates within that branch.

From the time he was forced from power by Stalin, and throughout his peripatetic exile from 1928 till his murder, Trotsky kept returning to one obsession: How had the ideals of Marxism, the mantle of Lenin, and control of the world's first "workers' state" been apparently eclipsed—and by *Stalin,* who, he was wrongly convinced, was not a worthy rival but a mediocre provincial of little significance?

Trotsky needed to explain, to his followers and to himself, his own defeat and what he took to be the betrayal of the movement to which he had given his life—quite literally, as it was to turn out. His mission became not merely to *represent* the failure of high Marxist ideals and prophecies but to account for it, in ways that both made theoretical sense within Marxism and allowed one to retain those ideals and not abandon the prophecies. His mode of analysis and his explanation, which quickly became compulsory orthodoxy among the faithful, deliberately denied primacy in Stalin's ascendancy to Stalin himself. That was probably a psychological necessity, and it was certainly a theoretical one. For apart from the terrible psychological challenge of defeat by such a "grey blur,"[5] Trotsky could not—as a Marxist—countenance an explanation that focused on individuals, rather than on underlying economically derived social forces.

For Marxists of Trotsky's vintage, certain fundamental "laws" were plain: It was not individuals who made history but social classes, rooted in the processes of economic production. In precommunist history, classes that owned the forces of production dominated, until the mode of production in which they ruled was exhausted; they would then (but only then) be replaced by classes hitherto excluded from ownership but connected with developing and ultimately more productive forces. Individuals were creatures of such processes, not their creators.

So, if Trotsky was to account for what threatened to be a world-historical calamity, he needed to find big battalions at work. However, in Russia, after the Revolution destroyed the aristocracy, peasantry, and nascent bourgeoisie, and after the workers had been "betrayed" by whatever Stalin represented, there were not many battalions left, least of all in power. By default, Trotsky found a culprit for his defeat: the Soviet bureaucracy.

And so "bureaucracy" came to attain a significance among Trotskyists that it very rarely, if ever, has had among Marxists. Indeed, Trotsky became distinctive among Marxists, particularly during his life in exile, in making of bureaucracy a concept with a social theory built into it.[6] "Class" was such a concept for Marx, but—and therefore—"bureaucracy" was not. It was almost always treated as a secondary phenomenon, overshadowed by the property-owning classes it was thought to serve, or the propertyless laboring classes it was taken to oppress.

Trotsky, by contrast, fulminated against bureaucracy for all the years of his exile with an intensity unmatched in Marxist writings, and his own writings were echoed by followers and even non- or ex-followers. For there was a logic involved, not merely a slogan. Anyone who flirted with Trotskyism in the 1930s had to master an esoteric discourse crafted to explain the vile doings of the bureaucratic "caste" or "clique" that had usurped power in the "degenerated workers' state" (that Trotsky had done so much to create).

Throughout the 1930s Trotsky insisted that the October Revolution had been "betrayed"[7] by a stratum of self-seeking bureaucrats who had succeeded in destroying the true "proletarian vanguard," the Bolshevik Party. Important though he claimed the bureaucracy was, however, Trotsky at the same time and for the same reasons insisted that its significance must not be exaggerated. In particular, he never stopped repeating that Soviet bureaucrats did not and could not constitute a new ruling class, for they did not "own" the nationalized Soviet state. The bureaucracy was a sort of classlike mutation, a venal "caste" or "clique" or "stratum"; like a class in many respects but fundamentally no class. And so, despite all, the Soviet Union was still fundamentally a workers' state, "degenerated" and "betrayed," to be sure, but not yet destroyed or replaced by a new ruling class.

These somewhat tortuous classificatory lessons had a sharp point, and Trotsky insisted on it with increasing desperation. Had the bureaucracy been a newly risen ruling class, the workers would be condemned to wait until the mode of production that gave it power was spent; time usually counted in centuries. Because it was only a "caste," a kind of parasite on the workers' state, however, the Revolution, though "betrayed," was not yet lost. There was still a chance that the workers—the true if somewhat bloodied ruling class—could snatch power back and thus redeem "their" revolution. And that possibility dictated how Marxists throughout the world should respond. Socialists must support the workers' state, even in war and, as happened, even if it joined the "imperialist" Nazis in such a war against the other imperialists. This caused trouble in New York.

Simmering disquiet over Trotsky's position came to a head with the outbreak of war and the revelation of the alliance between Soviet socialism and National Socialism. When the workers' state was revealed to be in cahoots with the fascists, a major faction fight developed within the SWP with a sizeable faction siding with James Burnham and Max Shachtman, the editors of the *New International*, the Party magazine, who rejected the official line. The dispute that erupted between this faction and the orthodox followers of James P. Cannon in turn led to another question about bureaucracy, altogether closer to home. This had local and practical significance, and it turned attention from social categorization of Soviet bureaucrats to *internal* bureaucratic tendencies. As one historian of the movement writes:

> Although the Russian question triggered the quarrel, when the Cannon clique closed ranks with Trotsky, shutting discussion out of the public press (the *Militant*) and declaring the matter closed, a new question surfaced, that of organization. Burnham and Shachtman, furious at the cloture of debate on this issue so central to Trotskyism, charged "bureaucratic conservatism," ossification in the party leadership structure, and leader-cultism against Cannon . . .
>
> At the April 1940 convention, both sides participated fully. Votes on the resolutions reaffirmed the Cannonite majority and thus suspended the Burnham-Shachtman minority. No one even mentioned the Russian question, which had set off the quarrel in the first place; the organizational question had eclipsed it altogether.[8]

Selznick left the SWP with the Shachtmanites, but he quickly began agitating for reform there, proclaiming "a major heresy, namely, the rejection of Bolshevism and of Leninism. He argued that Stalinism was rooted in Leninism."[9] He also proposed that Marxism no longer be taught as the party's official doctrine. A formal debate occurred between him and the still orthodox Irving Howe. At the meeting he met a slightly younger supporter from the floor, Irving Kristol. Not long afterwards, Selznick, Kristol, and a bevy of other talented young intellectuals set up their own fraction of the Shachtmanite faction of the Trotskyists. They were known as the Shermanites, led by "Philip Sherman."

The group was small but smart. It comprised a remarkable concentration of people later prominent both in American intellectual life, as academics and journalists, and in public life. They included Selznick's first wife, Gertrude Jaeger, whom he had met in 1938 and married in 1939; historian and polemicist Gertrude Himmelfarb and her husband, future neoconservative Irving Kristol (Party name, William Ferry); the sociologist Peter Rossi; political scientists Martin Diamond and Herbert Garfinkel; historian Marvin Meyers; and founder of the Free Press, Jeremiah Kaplan. Outside but friends with the group were Daniel Bell, Seymour Martin Lipset, Nathan Glazer, and other later luminaries of American academic life and public culture.

The Shermanites described themselves as "revolutionary anti-Bolshevik," and Selznick and Kristol drafted a letter of resignation from the Workers' Party. In the ensuing fracas, they issued a statement, "Defining a Tendency," in which they accused the Shachtmanite leadership of employing "the same bureaucratic organizational methods as Cannon." In 1941 they left the Workers' Party and joined the youth movement of Norman Thomas's Socialist Party, the Young People's Socialist League (YPSL). Though they had already resigned, the Shachtmanites proceeded to expel them with the special delicacy typical of such movements.

That was the end of Selznick's flirtation with Trotskyism, but the time had not been wasted. The "organizational question" can plausibly be said to have dominated the next ten to fifteen years of his life; the larger questions of the relations between ends and means remained with him to the end.

Michels and the "Iron Law of Oligarchy"

It was during this period of incessant debate about the "organizational question" that Selznick got hold of a copy of Michels's *Political Parties: A Sociological Study of the Oligarchical Tendencies of Modern Democracy*, first published in 1911. The English translation Selznick read was long out of print. It was republished only in 1949, by former Shermanite Jeremiah Kaplan's Basic Books. *Political Parties* spoke directly to many of the issues being debated in the Trotskyist movement in the 1930s and 1940s, for it was in origin and in effect "part of the academic critique of the Marxist belief that administrative and political problems of large-scale organization would be easily manageable under socialism."[10] Its primary focus was on European socialist parties, especially the German Social Democratic Party, at the beginning of the twentieth century the largest in the world. Michels had been a member until 1907.

Michels relentlessly piled up evidence and argument to show that no such party could avoid what he called the "iron law of oligarchy." In doing so, he challenged the Marxist insistence on the primacy of a logic of economically derived historical development, with another and independent logic, that of the bureaucratizing and oligarchic tendencies *immanent in the very fact, and necessity, of organization*. He also challenged the ultimate Marxist salvific fantasy, according to which *nothing* that today stood in the way of "truly human emancipation" would do so after the Revolution. For Michels insisted that oligarchic tendencies were not merely present but here to stay.

Michels had been a socialist, but it was not for that reason alone that he focused on socialist parties. Those parties were chosen specifically because of their strong commitment to democracy. Michels believed that the pursuit of democratic ideals concealed (and was undermined by) "immanent oligarchical tendencies." If one found that democracy was squeezed out even here, so Michels reasoned, one would have a more robust finding than one drawn from parties whose commitment to democracy was weak to begin with.[11]

Traditional Marxist explanations have little time for "immanent oligarchical tendencies," overwhelmed as they are thought to be by immanent progressive tendencies in processes of economic production that drove the relentless movements of social classes. Michels, by contrast, does not deny the significance of social class but insists that there are crucial imperatives in modern societies that it does not explain. And because it does not, he sees no reason to believe that a change in ruling class will of itself change those imperatives. In particular, he focuses on tendencies that allegedly apply whatever the pattern of social classes, as soon as people organize, which they will do, indeed must do, if they want to attain collective, particularly democratic, goals.

Unlike many enthusiasts for democracy (which, in a rather reserved and qualified way he was when he wrote *Political Parties*),[12] Michels did not believe it was any sort of antidote to the organizational forces he observed. On the contrary, democracy itself *impels* organization, which is "an absolutely essential condition for the political struggle of the masses."[13] This is all the more the case with a *fighting* party, for which "democracy is not for home consumption, but is rather an article made for export."[14] But whether or not an organization is built to fight, "who says organization, says oligarchy."[15]

What are the implications of that? For our purposes, five deserve mention. One is that the power of leaders increases with the extension of organization and with the associated indispensability of the organizational leadership.[16] Secondly, partly as a hydraulic counterpart to the rise of leaders, partly because of the incoherence of large numbers but partly also for intrinsic reasons to do with the character of mass publics, organization both derives from and produces mass impotence. Indeed the masses are not just impotent in an organized world; they are of their nature incompetent. This incompetence

> derives from the very nature of the mass as mass, for this, even when organized, suffers from an incurable incompetence for the solution of the diverse problems which present themselves for solution—because the mass *per*

se is amorphous, and therefore needs division of labor, specialization, and guidance.[17]

A third consequence is that to organize requires *an* organization, and in modern times a structured bureaucratic one.[18] Fourth, a standard tendency that accompanies the growth of organizational structures is what organization theorists (prominent among them Selznick) later came to identify as "goal displacement" in organizations. Michels describes it thus:

> from a means, organization becomes an end. To the institutions and qualities which at the outset were destined simply to ensure the good working of the party machine . . . a greater importance comes ultimately to be attached than to the productivity of the machine. Henceforward the sole preoccupation is to avoid anything which may clog the machinery.[19]

Finally, this transforms the party's relationship to its ideals:

> As the organization increases in size, the struggle for great principles becomes impossible. . . . The efforts made to cover internal dissensions with a pious veil are the inevitable outcome of organization based upon bureaucratic principles, for, since the chief aim of such an organization is to enroll the greatest possible number of members, every struggle on behalf of ideas within the limits of the organization is necessarily regarded as an obstacle to the realization of its ends, an obstacle, therefore, which must be avoided in every possible way.[20]

The cumulative result of these forces is the iron law of oligarchy.

A book's effects on readers often have as much to do with what is on their minds when they read it as with what it says. Michels's book came into Selznick's hands at a singular moment. It was, he later recalled,

> an important work of a kind of underground, out of print, passed around during the days of the faction fight of the Trotskyists . . . I don't think I bought the extreme version but the idea that there was some way of looking at the inner dynamic of leadership and organization that would result in the deflation and corruption of goals. And there was a strong sociological argument here that was compelling. . . . there were two strands going on at the same time: a political interest which focused people's minds on how it is that these dreams are being undone, but I personally was thinking more about the Trotskyist movement and what was happening to it, and its connections to Leninism, and so on. Michels's argument seemed to make human sense of it. A lot was brought out in the faction fight itself. A lot was about bureaucracy. There was also a lot of incidental talk, for example by Jim Cannon inveighing against the minority leaders, "these filthy office bureaucrats." A consciousness of bureaucracy was part of what I was thinking about here. Thinking about the Soviet Union as a kind of bureaucratic state, even if you didn't buy the idea of a "degenerated workers' state." So you had Michels who was really talking

about bureaucracy. All this came very much in our minds. We didn't need an academic impulse to take an interest in bureaucracy. But given my natural academic and analytical instincts it became easy for me to take an interest in bureaucracy in general. [21]

THE "TRAGEDY OF ORGANIZATION"

However one chose to characterize and explain it, the development of Stalinism in the Soviet Union represented to Selznick and his milieu the failure of vaunted ends and the triumph of those in control of organizational means. And even within the movement he had so intensely if briefly been part of, the "organizational question" loomed wherever he looked. That was true, of course, for many besides Selznick, and there are many ways one could and did respond to these calamities and disappointments. Selznick's response reveals his engagement with the particular historical problems they represented, but it was also an occasion, perhaps the first, for him to exercise his generalizing impulse on them. For him what was in play was not merely socialism or bureaucracy but means, ends, and "the fate of ideals."

I begin with some political/polemical writings from Selznick's youthful political engagements. They are not well known. They appeared in a genre of publication commonly called a "little magazine," in this case aptly so. Shortly after their expulsion from the Shachtmanites, Selznick/ Sherman and his friend, indeed comrade at the time, Irving Kristol/Ferry founded and edited *Enquiry: A Journal of Independent Radical Thought. Enquiry* was a *very* little magazine, which appeared, punctuated by the demands of war service, between 1942 and 1945. There were nine issues in all, each of twenty-four pages. Selznick published several unsigned editorials and six articles, several of them replies to angry critics of earlier articles.[22] His articles all had to do with the predicament of socialism in a time of disillusion and war.

In these pieces, all contributions to "the long, searching reappraisal which has turned the socialist movement in upon itself in recent years,"[23] some enduring lines of his thought were beginning to be drawn. The theme that dominates, on both a concrete and a more abstract plane, has to do with the "conditions that frustrate" ideals, and the need to approach the pursuit of ideals with those conditions firmly in mind. The problem appears most concretely as the "problem of bureaucracy" or the "organizational tragedy"; more abstractly considered, it is the interplay of ends and means.

In his first article, Selznick mentions "three factors which have been crucially operative in shaping our moral crisis." The first of them was "the broadening recognition of the frustration of ideal goals by the very fact of organization." Expanding on this theme, he writes:

> The tragedy of organization is profound and extensive. Many of us are only now coming to realize how thoroughgoing it is. We have long been accustomed to changes in the character of organizations, to the rise of bureaucracy, the introduction of conservatism, the general deflection of action and policy from the original goals for which organizations were constructed. But in the past we have damned particular men or special circumstances, confident that ideas, goodwill, and the needs of the masses would ultimately prevail. Most men have not felt that there was anything inherent in the character of the organizational process which cast a shadow over the future. But today that optimism is being tempered, where it is not buried in despair. For we now know that the very fact of organization produces consequences, wholly unintentioned and undesired, which thwart the will of those who initiate cooperative effort.[24]

He refers to Michels, who "in the field of political behavior . . . analyzes most clearly this phenomenon," but unlike Michels he does not root the problem in intrinsic qualities of human nature. He sees no reason to postulate that "the desire to dominate, for good or evil, is universal."[25] That, he believes, would falsely suggest that oligarchy really was inescapable.[26] Rather, he prefers a sociological interpretation:

> Organizational frustration is based on the relative inability of the mass of men to deal adequately with the tools of organized action. It is this basic incompetence which makes the mass-man—*who may be an intellectual as easily as a worker*—dependent upon his agents, who soon become his leaders. This process is conditioned by the cultural level of the participants, who are usually untrained in the procedures by which organizational control is retained in the body politic.[27]

On these matters, at least, Selznick finds more insight in Michels than in Marx, Engels, or Lenin, and he makes this clear. Thus, in an essay "On Redefining Socialism" he explains:

> It is necessary to definitely and positively reject the notion that the character of the political superstructure must be rooted in the economic foundations of society. It is difficult to avoid the conclusion that until we have plainly stated that there are some very important characteristics of political life which *are independent* of the way in which men make their living or of the productive

relations, our minds will continue to be subservient to that powerful principle of Marxist *Weltgeschichte*. . . . It is regrettable but true that the problem of bureaucracy, and an understanding of its general nature and profound implications for the limitations of human effort, is one set of notions over which Marxists of every stripe and political allegiance (Social Democrat, Communist, Trotskyist) seem inevitably to stumble and fall.[28]

Selznick returns to these themes frequently in the essays of this period.[29] He emphasizes that oligarchical tendencies are present whenever we organize to achieve. That has direct bearing on the possibility of achieving democratic ideals, but it also has another implication, of a sort that Selznick explores more closely in later work; for Selznick stresses that such tendencies are relevant, not merely to where we end up, but to how, and to what "we" are by the time we get there: "The problem of bureaucracy is crucially relevant to that of defining the basic commitments, self-image, and aspirations—in a word, the 'character'—of the organizational tools of action, whether of private associations or of the state."[30] We will meet the concept of "character" frequently in these pages. It is a key element in Selznick's thought.

So oligarchical tendencies are pervasive, just as Michels had argued. And yet Selznick insists on a distinction, between *predispositions* and concrete *outcomes*, that he believed Michels's absolutist predictions never acknowledged. Michels's thesis, he argues,

> does not tell us what we find in 85 out of 100 trade unions (or women's clubs, or political parties, or national states) studied; it does tell us about the *inherent predispositions* (hence about an aspect of the *nature*), of these organizations. We are told what must be taken account of in action; we are *not* told that nothing can be or is done to counteract these tendencies . . . *The predisposition ought not to be confused with the concrete reality;* at the same time, knowledge of inherent tendencies can prepare us for deviation from our ideals and for the need to protect democracy against even its "best" protagonists—ourselves.[31]

Michels had, then, rightly identified a "general tendency," but this, Selznick writes,

> is not an "iron law," though Michels considered it that. It is the way organizations will develop under present social conditions, if they are permitted to take the line of least resistance. This is a tendency which can be blocked, though it can probably never be completely controlled until the cultural level of the body of the participants is far higher than anything we know of today.[32]

There are objective tendencies to oligarchy, then, with which democrats need to cope, but there is no iron necessity. In this spirit Selznick advocated decentralization of power, factions, groups, a range of ways in which power might tame power, a phrase to which he frequently returns through his life. If we learn from Michels of the dangers of oligarchy, we should also learn "that the way of combatting this bureaucratic trend includes the development of counter-forces. Only power can check power, only new centers of strength, competing with the existing leadership, can be relied upon to defend the free institutions of a democratic society."[33] Or, as he wrote some forty years later:

> The Michels thesis has been troublesome to Marxists and to others who have hoped that humanist and democratic ideals might be fulfilled without taking personal and institutional recalcitrance into account. If there is recalcitrance, and if pressure to undo ideals is inevitable, then appropriate safeguards must be kept in place. For the prophets among us, this constraint is an irritation and a stumbling block. The vision of a perfect commonwealth is necessarily and permanently dimmed. There can be no appeal to millennial yearnings, no promise of a kingdom come. Above all, no movement or party can be trusted to impose its will in the name of "the people" or "history" without effective protection against abuse of power.[34]

This modified Michelsianism, Michels without the irresistible drama of iron and law, is a theme not only of Selznick's political writing but of his academic work as well. Thus he had already developed the same points in the same terms in his first academic publication, "An Approach to the Theory of Bureaucracy," a version of his master's dissertation at Columbia, written at the same time he was editing and writing for *Enquiry*. Here he develops a theme perhaps more immediately familiar to readers of *Enquiry* and the *Modern Review* than the *American Sociological Review*. This also has to do with the tragedy of organization, "the fact of organizational frustration as a persistent characteristic of the age of relative democracy . . . processes inherent in and internal to organization as such which tend to frustrate action towards professed goals."[35] There follows a discussion of a particular manifestation of the "tragedy," which is the generation of a gulf and an opposition between a bureaucratic leader and the rank and file "for which he is formally an agent."[36] This reworking of Michelsian themes ends with a reprise of the un-Michelsian nondeterministic nuance that occurred repeatedly in his political essays.[37] These qualifications have gone unnoticed by those, like his critics in *Enquiry* and Alvin Gouldner some ten years later,[38] who accused the young Selznick of a kind of disillusioned and overriding pessimism.

There is a pattern here that endures throughout Selznick's writings. It is the commitment to moral realism as a means to, rather than an alternative to, the striving for ideals. There is no doubt that in his early writings, the *tone* of realism outweighs that of idealism, and this is something that changes in important ways over time. But Selznick always resisted attempts to categorize his thought, or the thought appropriate to dealing with complex social problems, as *either* realistic or idealistic. It must be both.

Yet tone is important. We will return to it when discussing Gouldner's allegation of a pessimistic "metaphysical pathos" and when I discuss Selznick's sensibility. Selznick's early critics, to whom I refer in the following chapters, could be forgiven for mistaking the complexity of Selznick's position on the implications of Michels; notwithstanding his important caveats, Michels certainly *seemed* to be making most of the running here. And there was a certain youthful pleasure evident in debunking unrealistic idealists, from whom one was moving away politically. This can be found even more dramatically when Selznick lifts his vision from socialism and organizational constraints to the broader implications of these disappointments for our understanding of the fate of ideals in the world. Here too, however, and another mark of the tolerance for complexity in Selznick's thought, he rejected the often strong temptations of a "tragic view of the world."

It was obviously possible to share this analysis and restrict it to questions of organization. But Selznick generalized what he drew from Michels, in his critique of orthodox socialism. It was not merely a problem of bureaucratic tendencies compromising socialism and democracy; it was a deeper, more philosophical issue of means and ends. And Selznick enlisted his critique of bureaucratic tendencies to deal with those larger issues as well. As he later recalled,

> We were going through this whole political experience of trying to cope with what I called somewhere the moral ruin in the Soviet Union and giving it a larger significance about the relationship between means and ends, and things of that kind. So there was that effort always to connect up philosophical ideas with these issues of social practice. That's been a theme, I guess, that's stayed with me for a long time. I think it's been quite fruitful to do that.[39]

CHAPTER TWO

The Ideal and the Real

Selznick, it will be recalled, saw his youthful political encounters as the birthplace of his concerns with "the conditions and processes that frustrate ideals or, instead, give them life and hope." This description of his overarching preoccupation is interesting, not only for saying, more succinctly than is easy, what has animated a long life's work over a broad range. The sequence of its elements is also significant: first, what *frustrates* ideals, then what gives them life and hope.

Whether intentional or not, that way of putting things has point, both normatively and biographically. The normative sequence suggests a certain priority for dealing with threats over striving for aspirations;[1] not necessarily greater importance, but prior in the sense that one comes before, or is necessary for, the other. And secondly, whether or not for that reason, that is how his work developed. The early writings laid more emphasis on what might frustrate ideals than what they should be or how one might attain them. On the other hand, what gives them "life and hope" became a central concern of Selznick's writings from, roughly, the mid-1950s.

The early writings, addressed in the main to impatient idealists, are concerned with the dangers, and the self-defeating possibilities, of untempered idealism. In Selznick's later work, as we shall see, the emphasis, if not the argument, shifts considerably. One, not altogether misleading, shorthand way to evoke the shifts and tensions in his thought is to see them as reflecting differences in the prominence he gives to one or the other of two early, enduring, and contending influences on his understanding of the fate of ideals in the world: John Dewey and Reinhold Niebuhr.

By far the deepest and most enduring intellectual influence on Selznick was the American philosophy of pragmatism, particularly as it appeared in the works of John Dewey, though he was much influenced by the other pragmatists, particularly William James and George Herbert Mead, as well. Dewey's was a systematic philosophy, and Selznick followed and adapted it in many of its aspects, as will become clear throughout this book.[2] Indeed, so much of Selznick's work is a direct application of pragmatist tenets to his chosen fields of concern that I, who came to pragmatism only to understand Selznick, am repeatedly struck by how deeply he had internalized it. Someone should write a book about that.

Two elements in Selznick's engagement with Dewey, one positive and one critical, are of particular relevance here. On the one hand, Selznick accepted Dewey's insistence on the "continuum of means and ends" and its implications. On the other, Selznick was persuaded, particularly by Dewey's most trenchant critic, Reinhold Niebuhr, that there was a deep and systematic deficiency, a lack of balancing realism, in Dewey's idealism. One of the lasting, and most intriguing, aspects of Selznick's own work has been the pervasiveness of this dialog between realism and idealism. I deal first with means and ends, and then with the ideal and the real.

MEANS AND ENDS

Dewey rejected a host of what he called "pernicious dualisms" that set up and reify as dichotomies in thought phenomena that are not in fact dichotomous in life. The analytic distinction comes, he thought, to block appreciation of real-world connection. The point is a general one, but among the particular dichotomies that exercised Dewey were theory and practice, mind and body, individual and society, facts and values, and, of direct relevance here, means and ends. According to this last dualism, means and ends are qualitatively different, and the latter are key. Means are merely of derivative, instrumental significance, what one needs to achieve what one wants.

Dewey rejected the dichotomy on several grounds. One was that it is conceptually incoherent. First, it fails to capture the *interdependence* of means and ends. There are no serious ends-in-themselves, valuable quite irrespective of whatever it might take to achieve them. We evaluate both ends *and* means and compare them: "No case of notable achievement can be cited in any field (save as a matter of sheer accident) in which the persons who brought about the end did not give loving care to the instruments and agencies of its production."[3] Means must be evaluated in terms of their consequences for valued ends; ends can be criticized on the basis of what it would take to achieve them.

Dewey believed that there is no categorical qualitative difference between means and ends.[4] Means are valued as conditions for what we call ends and therefore, until attained themselves, serve as mediating ends. Those who fail to tend to them because they are concerned only with what they are means to, therefore, are not behaving "idealistically" but irresponsibly, and most probably impotently as well; "the contents of dreams and air castles are *not* ends-in-view, and what makes them fantasies is precisely the fact that they are *not* formed in terms of actual conditions serving as means of their actualization."[5] Ends are not self-sufficient *as* ends, just awaiting our recognition. On the contrary, what we do has manifold consequences. Our ends are chosen from among those, actual or hoped for.[6] Further, ends are in their turn means to further ends, and so it goes on: "Ends are, in fact, literally endless, forever coming into existence as new activities occasion new consequences. 'Endless ends' is a way of saying that there are no ends—that is no fixed self-enclosed finalities."[7] Whether something is considered means or end turns just on the moment and the context in which it is viewed, not on anything intrinsic in its nature.

Any attempt to drive a wedge between ends and means is not merely conceptually unsustainable; it is also "pernicious" in its social and political consequences. It betrays a deep, philosophically inspired and practically disabling, division between higher and lower realms: those of values, often spiritual, on the one hand, and a nether order of merely material means, on the other, beneath the consideration of exalted thinkers. This division, and the attendant "indifference to means" that it generates, has "borne corrupt and poisonous fruits," resulted in "the relative impotency of arts concerned with enduring human welfare. Sentimental attachment and subjective eulogy take the place of action. For there is no art without tools and instrumental agencies."[8] Conversely and paradoxically, the split between ethereal ends and practical means has left ordinary people to attend to practical affairs, unguided by longer-term reflection.[9]

In a lament that, some fifty years later, might have become the motto of the Jurisprudence and Social Policy Program, Dewey observes:

> Theory separated from concrete doing and making is empty and futile; practice then becomes an immediate seizure of opportunities and enjoyments which conditions afford without the direction which theory—knowledge and

ideas—has power to supply. The problem of the relation of theory and practice is not a problem of theory alone; it is that, but it is also the most practical problem of life. For it is the question of how intelligence may inform action, and how action may bear the fruit of increased insight into meaning: a clear view of the values that are worth while and of the means by which they are to be made secure in experienced objects. Construction of ideals in general and their sentimental glorification are easy; the responsibilities both of studious thought and of action are shirked.[10]

To justify purported means, then, one needs to examine their consequences and assess them in terms of one's "end-in-view." And it has to be real examination, not mere assertion. This has poignant exemplification in Dewey's response to Trotsky's account of the relations between means and ends. Dewey thought well of Trotsky from the time, 1936, that he agreed to travel to Mexico to chair an independent "commission of inquiry" into the crimes alleged in Stalin's "show trials" against his great rival. Dewey's commission cleared Trotsky of all charges, and in the process the two men came to respect each other. So when Trotsky published an essay, "Their Morals and Ours" in the *New International,* Dewey was asked to respond.[11]

Trotsky sought to repel the accusation that his own methods were indistinguishable from Stalin's because he too was committed to revolutionary and where necessary murderous means to attain his ends. As a Marxist, Trotsky rejected all forms of moral absolutism; nothing was *intrinsically* forbidden, for he insisted, in language close to that of pragmatism, on the interdependence of means and ends. Means could only be judged by the extent to which they served specified ends, themselves justifiable. The end for which Marxists fought was human liberation, and "that is permissible . . . which *really* leads to the liberation of mankind."[12] That was the master test; not the intrinsic character of the means used. *His* methods, deduced as leading to that end from the Marxist theory of class struggle, were thereby justified. Stalin's, which did not, were not.

Dewey, of course, also rejected absolutist morality. However, he pointed out that Trotsky did nothing to show empirically that revolutionary methods would lead to human liberation. What if, as Dewey believed, undemocratic means were almost certain to lead to undemocratic ends? In any event, what about unintended consequences? Trotsky claimed to *deduce* the need for such methods, by contrast, and their aptness for human liberation, from the alleged "laws" propounded in Marxist theory of class struggle; "means were deduced from a supposed scientific law instead of being searched for and adopted on the ground of their relation to the moral end of the liberation of mankind."[13] If the deduction is performed according to dogmatic, and axiomatic, postulates, "the means, the class struggle, does not need to be critically examined with respect to its actual objective consequences. It is automatically absolved from all need for critical examination."[14] Trotsky had lurched from one kind of absolutism, that of religion, which he rejected, just to end up with another—"scientific Marxism"—to which he was religiously devoted. Or to put it another way, the problem with the Marxist experiment was that there was nothing truly experimental about it.

DEWEY AND NIEBUHR

At the time he was reading Dewey, Selznick and his wife, Gertrude Jaeger, were also reading Freud and a number of contemporary theologians, including Paul Tillich and Dewey's most powerful American critic in the 1930s, the theologian and ethical realist Reinhold Niebuhr. In this theology, he sought not salvation but secular enlightenment. As he later reflected:

> To me, theology was a way of getting at certain truths about human nature and the human condition, which weren't being captured in other doctrines, and that's why we were attracted to it. Maybe Niebuhr was attractive because it was really so easy to translate into naturalist terms. He virtually did it himself. If you look at his discussions of the sin of pride, for example, he relates it to the ways people have of dealing with anxiety and tries to give a kind of psychological explanation of it and so on, with other things.
>
> So yes, I think this happened very early on. There's no question it was a very formative thing.[15]

From these writers came a picture of humanity and society altogether darker, less malleable, fuller of natural and human "recalcitrance" than could be found in Dewey. The point was most directly made by Niebuhr, in his several polemics with Dewey,[16] notwithstanding that on many matters they shared more than they allowed. Niebuhr situated Dewey within a larger critique of Enlightenment optimism, as grounded in the "belief that the growth of human intelligence would automatically eliminate social injustice."[17] Dewey served as Niebuhr's prime example of the naivete of that belief.

Dewey had a deep belief in progressive evolution—of knowledge, of values, of social and political arrangements—through reasoned conjecture, appraisal, and judgment, the application of controlled collective "intelligence," as he called it. This was not just a commitment but a faith, a secular democratic faith. By *intelligence* Dewey meant a way to knowledge that fused reason, experiment, and action:

> Concrete suggestions arising from past experiences, developed and matured in the light of the needs and deficiencies of the present, employed as aims and methods of specific reconstruction, and tested by success or failure in accomplishing this task of readjustment.[18]

Intelligence needed to be brought to bear on problems democratically, for democracy was not just a political, but also what might be called an epistemological, good. Through free and democratic discussion, hypotheses in all fields could be tested, confirmed, or rejected. Through the cumulative application of collective intelligence, we would come to know more and behave better, to understand what was the case, what was good for us, what worked, and what did not. The model was the procedures of hypothesis, testing, peer discussion, characteristic of scientific progress.

Dewey was fundamentally optimistic about the capacity of intelligence to generate social development. If the scientific method was consistently and conscientiously brought to bear on social problems, progress must occur. True, social understanding had not kept pace with the understanding of nonhuman nature, for the former was subject to a "cultural lag." Past prejudices and ignorance had not yet been overthrown; there were still people in thrall to prescientific ways of thought. Over time and with persuasion, however, the method of intelligence would prevail, problems would be resolved, and improvements would continue.

Niebuhr was profoundly skeptical of what he took to be the core assumptions of Dewey's whole worldview, perhaps more accurately the core blindnesses he attributed to it. The deepest such blindness was to natural and ineradicable forces—in human nature and in human societies as collective orders—that had and would continue to plague us. These flowed not just from ignorance, and they could not all be cured by application of "intelligence" but from interest, power, and indeed nature, red in tooth and claw. Humanity had elements of both spirituality and brutality, often they were intertwined, at times one flowed directly from the other, and brutality often triumphed. These are not just past truths; they are eternal. So too is the everpresence of social conflict, born of interest and passion. Where these are in play—and they can be counted on always to be somewhere in play—discussion and persuasion are often not to the point.

Having underestimated the forces with which pragmatic liberalism had to contend, modern moralists also misunderstood what was needed to deal with them, for that commonly involves power, not merely intelligence. Indeed, echoing Montesquieu, and in turn echoed by Selznick, Niebuhr frequently emphasized that "power must be challenged by power":[19]

> The selfishness of human communities must be regarded as an inevitability. Where it is inordinate it can be checked only by competing assertions of interest; and these can be effective only if coercive methods are added to moral and rational persuasion. Moral factors may qualify, but they will not eliminate, the resulting social contest and conflict.[20]

Niebuhr is a powerful, erudite and imaginative thinker, open to moral complexities, to the presence of good as well as evil in history. He does not denigrate idealism but insists that it must be married to realistic understanding of humanity and society. And that will not occur without an appreciation of evil, as—in either a religious or a secular rendition—original sin, that is, an ineluctable presence and temptation in human affairs. His complaint against Dewey (and "modern man," whose archetype Dewey is taken to be) is that in a deep sense he is blind to the ineradicable presence of evil in the world; hence his faith in the all-conquering power of reason and his invincible historical optimism. He does not appreciate "the basic paradox of history . . . that the creative and destructive possibilities of human history are inextricably intermingled."[21] Much of the critique is addressed to "modern man" and modern culture in general, but Dewey has, it appears, been delivered by central casting to exemplify them both.[22]

Both the democratic optimism of Dewey, and Niebuhr's assault on it, made profound and lifelong impressions on Selznick. He responds to more than their particular arguments. He absorbs their sensibilities, as it were, and, unlike most people affected by contrasting sensibilities, he responds to both. His thought is more than influenced by one or another; it is, to use a word he once used in conversation, *nourished* by them both, in ways deeper than by other thinkers who also influenced him profoundly, such as Weber and Durkheim. At different times he seems drawn to one more than the other, sometimes even drawn apart; but he never consciously abandons one for the other. They contend for his mind and his heart for the whole of his life. Wisdom for him involves not a choice between contradictory alternatives but recognition of the power of both and the enduring and fruitful tenacity of the very tension between them: recognition of the tension, but not resignation before it. Rather, he made a principled attempt to reconcile if possible, deal with if not, such enduring tensions, and he looked for productive consequences of them. In this, the confluence of Hegel, Marx, and Freud on the dynamic significance of conflict is also not a far stretch.

In his earlier writings, Selznick insisted that idealism must be tempered by Niebuhrian critique and particularly by Niebuhr's alertness to the permanence of evil in the world. Already in *Enquiry*, Selznick's wife Gertrude Jaeger had criticized Dewey and pragmatists more generally for lacking an awareness of evil. Dewey's "optimism amounts to a refusal to admit a social reality, however limited, which is not only permanent but recalcitrant to the morality of science. It denies what the theories of recalcitrance assert in various ways: that the requirements of societal organization have permanent, and limiting, consequences."[23] Selznick agreed in this estimation of the philosopher he most admired, for all his life. He was not always happy to dwell on it, and over time he came to develop, or at least seek reasons to display, a temperament closer to Dewey's than to Niebuhr's, not always to best effect.[24] But he never shed traces of either.

Selznick, then, began as a threat expert and never lost regard for that expertise. He is alert to fragility, vulnerability, and the need to guard against them. Moreover, his normative reflections are sustained and deepened by his understanding of social processes in general and of the dangers to which organizations and institutions, but also human personalities and groups, are susceptible. He has a lot to tell us about ways in which those dangers might be avoided. Hobbes, too, was a threat expert, and it is an honorable, if not always popular, profession. As we shall see, however, Selznick was not *only* a threat expert, and in later writings hope figures more prominently than fear. On his view at all times, however, wisdom requires due regard for both.

REALISTIC IDEALISM

In Selznick's first writings on ends and means and the fate of ideals, the focus was not primarily on the quality of ends themselves, either what they were or what they should be, but on the need, whatever the ends were, for their bearers to pay close attention to the means available to further them. Someone concerned with ideal goals, who did not do the serious work of understanding how we might reach them, was fated either to Utopianism or to opportunism or to a feckless oscillation between the two. Again and again, one is exhorted to take means seriously, to reckon with the fateful connections between them and ends, and to ponder their consequences. The sensibility here is tough minded and political, given to *seeing through* vague generalities and forcing people to take the measure of the real-world resources for, impediments to, and consequences of their realization. If you're fond of a temper skeptical of "unanalyzed abstractions," among them many professed ideals, then young Selznick is your man. And yet, even in these earliest provocations, as often they were, Selznick's views have a complexity that can be overlooked.

At their most general level, Selznick's writings make clear that it is no easy matter even partially to realize any important ideals, for so much in the world conspires against them. There are external forces that threaten the attainment of values, but, even more, there are forces internal to humans, social relationships, practices, organizations, which typically pose even greater threats. The need to be aware of them is a moral and political imperative, not merely an analytical one, because without meeting it we won't merely misunderstand the world but misbehave in it.

So one thing to learn, but which idealists find hard, is that they must be tough-minded realists. It is the height of irresponsibility to profess large ideals "without taking into account the forces and circumstances with which one has to deal."[25] Among the circumstances one needs to consider, some are local and contingent: the particular empirical balance of forces, strengths and weaknesses of particular parties, and so on. Others are the results of historical trends, such as the grim ones he saw around him in the 1940s. Still other things to consider, and fundamental, are perennial obstacles to the fulfilment of ideals. Among these are "dependable human failings,"[26] "the general recalcitrance of the human tools of action,"[27] "the low reliability of human benevolence,"[28] "the very fact of group life and purposive organization [that] can and does produce general phenomena which persist independently of the specific form of economic organization that happens to prevail."[29]

These are not small problems, and it is only if they are faced that they might be overcome. For "this is the bluntest challenge to the viability of social idealism: can the indispensible instruments of action be presented [sic] from turning into things alien and unclean, devouring, ultimately, ideal and idealist alike?" In context after context, social action faces such challenges. It is a paradox of unrealistic idealism that it lacks the resources to deal with them. Instead, "when ideals are taken as concrete goals, rather than as unrealizable judgments, we see each deviation as defeat, and feel that we live in a vale of unrelieved frustration."[30] Thus disappointed idealists often end up defeated and defeatist. This, however, is not because Michels had identified an "iron law," even of oligarchy, still less of the defeat of ends by means. Rather, he had identified a tendency which will win out *unless we take serious steps to counter it.*

Thus, Selznick insists:

> The sign and warrant of political wisdom (and in its inversion, the brand-mark of naivete) is the recognition of the resistant, recalcitrant, limiting nature of human personality and social institutions. . . . *action*—that kind, at least, which intervenes in events, which deals significantly with the primary stuff of social change, with classes and parties and governments—is always shaped and molded by the character of the institutions which it ventures to manipulate. The politically effective form of this impingement is the *limitation of alternatives,* or, put another way, the *presentation of historical choices.* The projected history of any given period may be infinitely various in the realm of fancy, but the real paths along which events may run are few and none too far apart. . . .
> The historical choice is the choice which is offered.[31]

There is a lot at stake in making the right choice. Understanding what is desirable in the light of what is possible not only helps you get where you might want to go, but also, again, affects crucially "the structure, the operative ideals, the habits, the alliances, in a word, the *character*"[32] of the movement to which you belong and that you hope will take you from here to there.

This emphasis on the need to weigh and temper ideals in the light of concrete circumstances, historical opportunities, and what might without too much distortion but no theological dressing be called original sin recurs in Selznick's work in a variety of contexts over the years. In the 1940s, the specific ideals that were in play were those of socialism, and the realities that needed to be taken into account were those that had so impressed Michels. But the point is larger.

Now someone who emphasizes such a catalogue of inescapable constraints is often dubbed in radical polemics a "conservative" and/or "pessimist" and/or "defeatist." On the Left, these labels were rarely used to compliment, and in his youth Selznick several times had one or another applied to him. Of course, Hobbesians might use these as terms of praise rather than blame, but Selznick's accusers usually have not, and it is characteristic of Selznick's taste for complexity that he can't fully avail himself of Hobbesian compliments. In the debates of the 1940s, charges of pessimism/conservatism were common. Thus the sociologist Lewis Coser, under his pseudonym "Louis Clair," dubbed Selznick "a radical in retreat,"[33] alleged that "the argument finally boils down to the age-old controversy between cultural optimism and cultural pessimism,"[34] and proclaimed that "while Selznick's theory can only stultify and break the will to action, revolutionary Marxism remains the theoretical embodiment of the will to progressive action."[35] Another critic complained that "the crowning disappointment in Selznick's approach is perhaps his bold embrace of outmoded and unscientific human nature concepts. . . . The text abounds with allusion to the permanence of man's corrupt character."[36] Marxists were confident that any such corruption was contingent on social circumstances and could be, would certainly be, transcended. Selznick did not share their confidence. Indeed, he thought it not merely misplaced but the source of a host of problems of its own.

On the other hand, Selznick resisted the charge that his position amounted to a defeatist or quietist pessimism, just as he resisted defeatism and quietism themselves. He was determined to hold onto both realism and idealism at the same time, for both analytical and normative reasons. This sour-sweet combination signals a crucial element of Selznick's intellectual and moral character that is easy to misconstrue, partly because it is uncommon and partly, too, because, while it is a stable feature of that character, at different times one and then the other element receives more emphasis.

A particular emphasis is not necessarily a general position, however, though it might be evidence of a state of mood or circumstance. Whether one emphasizes obstacles or ideals at different times over a long life will vary with one's appraisal of the objective balance of forces in particular situations, with tendencies among your interlocutors that you might be trying to correct, with your spirits, and many other things. Theoretically, however, it is also important what your general position requires and allows. In Selznick's work, though the emphases and the tone vary with circumstance and more generally change over time, they do so within a remarkably stable appraisal of the available options. They rarely contradict it.

The charge of a kind of predetermined pessimism is unlikely to be made against his later writings, as we shall see, because the balance between realism and idealism generally swings toward the latter. Even in these early and more apprehensive writings, however, the distance between realism and deterministic pessimism is frequently stressed.

In 1941 Selznick reviewed James Burnham's *Managerial Revolution*, for example, in which Burnham argued that a new ruling class of managers was coming to rule throughout the world. Selznick considered many of

Burnham's predictions plausible but denied that they were inevitable, or that they were a reason to give up.[37] A short time later, echoing Burnham, he says that "it must be expected . . . that some kind of statism will be the dominant political form for some time to come," but he immediately adds:

> Yet there is a curious fatalism which has developed in this connection: the notion that to thing [sic] in these terms is to predict the inevitable victory of a rigid, brutal fascist state. But history does not develop according to the rules of some immanent logic. Within this broad social trend, many variations are possible. The extent to which democracy prevails will depend upon many social conditions, not the least important of which will be the strength of those who are willing to organize and fight from below, depending upon and creating institutional mechanisms whose social fabric is consistent with and a part of democratic action. The dominant tide can be molded and it may one day be overcome. For here again it is a matter of empirical forces. A new outlook rooted in the *persistant* [sic] *and permanent* struggle for concrete democratic gains can mobilize strength for practical achievement.[38]

However realistic we need to be, he insisted a few years later, we must at the same time "avoid looking at the devil with fascinated eyes."[39]

How, then, to avoid the lure of an idealism that denies reality without surrendering to a realism that saps energy, or simply masks a failure of nerve? The answer is not to discard idealism per se. There is a place for it, and a crucial one, but it is easy, particularly in "progressive" movements, to mistake that place. Many idealists fail to distinguish ideals from operative and attainable goals. Both are important, but their roles are different and neither should be confused with the other. Ideals can motivate human strivings, but they are *of their nature* unattainable; that is why we call them ideal. Operative goals are values postulated *in the light of* realities that must be faced. If that is misunderstood, if we view abstract ideals as operative goals, then we will be multiply disappointed.

Most simply, we will be disappointed because our quest will fail. That is not a contingent matter. It is built into the logic of ideals *as* ideals:

> Ideals, we may say, are always abstract and utopian, defining aspirations which can never be fulfilled in history. They function as judgments upon us, and inform the concrete goals we set before us, but they ought not be confused with those goals. The Golden Rule, the classless society, and self-government are among such ideals; they are not situational, and in themselves do not help us to make the discriminations which are necessary in action. On the other hand, the concrete things to be desired, can be only partial renderings of ideal conceptions. This does not make them less valuable, for such deviations reflect the concreteness of life, including our multiple commitments and goals.[40]

Selznick often insists on this distinction between abstract ideals and operative goals in this period. He does not always express the distinction in the same terms, but it is clear enough and important to him:

> The distinction between ideals and concrete goals is no semantic sleight-of-hand. The Christian is not frustrated because he is not Christ. Nor do we long for "ideal["] pictures, houses, or governments. What we value must be of this world, able to survive in a world of other values and to function under conditions given in the situation at hand. Failing that, it can be of no use to us.[41]

If one mistake is to confuse ideals with prosaically attainable values, another is to sanctify prosaic instruments and tools, treating properly fungible means as unalterable ends, what later came among organization theorists to be known as "goal displacement." That is a mistake that bolshevism made, he argued, and with catastrophic consequences. Perhaps echoing Dewey's criticism of Trotsky, Selznick argues:

> The bolshevik revolution is in its nature *sacred*, generating an emotional emphasis which turns its adherents inward upon the apocalyptic image. This is hardly strange, for where objectives are vague and ill-defined, where the power of a given party (read: its leadership) is confused with the requirements of history, then the road to power absorbs the entire political agenda. . . .
>
> The tools of social and political action, devised with an eye toward what the world is really like, must be *profane* in character. As method, they must be secular, and therefore vulnerable to fact and logic, before the requirements of pragmatic evaluation and democratic dispute can come into effective play.[42]

So, dangers threaten from excessive elevation both of ultimate ends and of instrumental means, both where the former are understood as operative goals, and the latter are elevated to sacred ideals. But ideals are also threatened, and means easily triumph over ends, if we ignore or misunderstand the very tendency that means have to do just that. Selznick's "socialist" writings are all imbued with a passion to spell out administrative, organizational, and political imperatives that must be dealt with by any socialist movement (and were, Selznick believed, commonly and systematically understated by those with whom he was arguing). The point, he repeatedly insisted, was not to discourage such a movement but rather to persuade its partisans that "if these are indeed the facts, then it would seem far more in keeping with the spirit of democracy to recognize them explicitly, and to work out democratic controls within the framework presented by these facts, than to hold out gaudy hopes either to ourselves or to the workers which will have to be rescinded when living reality presents its cruel and limited alternatives."[43]

If ideals are not tempered by a sober grasp of real possibilities, constraints, opportunities, and a fashioning of instruments to deal with them, then not only will we be caught by surprise, but we will respond opportunistically and in ways that wound the very values that inspired our efforts. Thus:

> We know today of the evil consequences of being unprepared for the gap between hopes and reality. It is not only a matter of creating illusions: the real danger lies in the fact that events demand answers, and any organization will be forced to take that path dictated by expediency if it has not prepared itself along lines that will be helpful when propaganda alone will no longer suffice. In attempting to find political principles that will aid us in the embodiment of democratic values in social life, we are faced with the necessity of *taking into account* the facts about human life which exist today and are likely to persist in the period which confronts us.[44]

This is a point Selznick makes several times; it is a general one. It wasn't only Trotskyists who failed to appreciate the danger that ends will be "impotent" and means "tyrannous." As his next work, *TVA*, showed, this is a common failing. And, as his subsequent study, *The Organizational Weapon*, revealed, in many circumstances, particularly the building of party organizations, Communists could show exquisite awareness of such matters.

PART II

Organizations and Institutions

CHAPTER THREE

Organizations and Ideals

As we saw in Chapter One, no Trotskyist could avoid thinking about bureaucracy because Trotsky had elevated it to a role and importance scarcely ever before entertained by Marxists: that of key villain in the betrayal of the workers' revolution. Moreover, in the internal party feuds, "bureaucratism" was about as bad a charge you could hurl at anyone, and it was often hurled. It is thus no accident, as Marxists used to say, that bureaucracy quickly became the focus of Selznick's academic work as well.

Selznick was not the only ex-socialist sociologist to share that interest, but he is distinctive, in a way well captured by Webb:

> What is especially interesting about his career is the way he has used the burning issues of his radical past as the basis for his work as a professional sociologist. As a Trotskyist and Socialist, Selznick had been fascinated by the problems of bureaucracy and oligarchy and the dilemmas of organizational life. As an academic in the 1940s and 1950s, he turned these concerns into the cool language of scientific analysis and became in the process one of the most important organizational theorists of his generation.[1]

Until the mid-1950s Selznick's academic work, and the work for which he perhaps remains most widely known, continued to be primarily in organization theory. Several articles[2] and three books were foundational contributions to a particular way of thinking about organizations, which later came to be known as "institutionalism." The first two books were case studies, one of the TVA, the other of communist organizational strategy. The third was a more general exploration of institutional leadership, which, Selznick later observed, "began as an attempt to clarify a perspective I had brought to bear in [the] two previous books," seeking to draw out their underlying theoretical principles.[3] This chapter discusses *TVA and the Grass Roots* and *The Organizational Weapon*. The next will explore the larger theoretical presuppositions, concerns, and implications, of these and Selznick's other writings on organizations.

TVA

Selznick began graduate study at Columbia in 1938. His master's dissertation was on the theory of bureaucracy,[4] and a reduced and revised version of it became "An Approach to a Theory of Bureaucracy," his first academic publication. From 1941, he had a good deal to do with a young teacher fresh from Harvard, Robert Merton. He was much impressed by a class of Merton's on the analysis of social institutions, and when Merton fell ill during the course, Selznick became one of four participants asked to "'complete' the course. He lectured on 'organizational aspects of the Trotskyist party in New York.' In this non-Mertonian medley, Phil Selznick was the star."[5]

By 1942 he had become one of a number of Merton's doctoral students, followed in a couple of years by Peter Blau, Alvin Gouldner, and Lipset, whose dissertations and early work had to do with bureaucracy, on which Merton had already written briefly but suggestively.[6] These students were clearly inspired by Merton, and to some extent directed by him, but Selznick did not recall thinking of himself as a member of a group.[7] Indeed, at this stage his emotional and intellectual energies were still more politically than academically engaged. The university was more a fitfully visited "Shangri La," as he later put it, offering peace and libraries, than a source of intellectual direction. And though his respect for Merton was great, and he was without doubt significantly influenced by him, he does not appear to have been executing a Mertonian plan in choosing or writing the dissertation that became *TVA and the Grass Roots*. He later recalled of Merton's students that "everyone went his own way . . . We were on our own, and I'm sure everyone did the same as I did, floundering around looking for something. Lucky that what I thought of as an alternative didn't work out. I wanted to study a trade union. I went to a union official, someone gave me a letter of introduction, and he was so scornful I never went back."[8]

Instead, he became intrigued by claims that David Lilienthal, first chairman of the Tennessee Valley Authority, was making for its innovative "grassroots" ways of dealing with governance and administration. Selznick was confident that the reality must be different from the ideology (which he found to be the case, but not in ways he had expected). He began his fieldwork in Tennessee in 1942 and completed it by the time he was drafted in 1943. He wrote it up when he returned at the end of the war, after serving as a research analyst in the Philippines and in the occupation forces in Japan, until he was demobilized in 1946. It became *TVA and the Grass Roots*, published in 1949, and was soon acclaimed as a classic of organizational analysis.

In 1933, in the midst of the Great Depression, President Roosevelt called for legislation "to create a Tennessee Valley Authority—a corporation clothed with the power of government but possessed of the flexibility and initiative of private enterprise. It should be charged with the broadest duty of planning for the proper use, conservation, and development of the natural resources of the Tennessee River drainage basin and its adjoining territory for the general social and economic welfare of the Nation." Its responsibilities and significance were to be vast. They led "logically to national planning for a complete river watershed involving many States and the future lives and welfare of millions. It touches and gives life to all forms of human concerns."[9]

The Authority had responsibilities over the whole drainage basin of the Tennessee Valley, which cut across seven states. It was distinctive in its degree of autonomy and its powers; and "further, and in one sense most important, a broad vision of regional resource development—in a word, planning—informed the conception, if not the actual powers, of the new organization."[10] Though the specific powers granted to it were limited, it was given considerable discretion in how to exercise them and "there remained administrative freedom to devise methods of dealing with local people and institutions which would reflect the democratic process at work."[11]

Lilienthal claimed that the TVA was a unique experiment in developing a major federal administrative agency committed to grassroots administration and democracy.[12] He was not alone in thinking so. The TVA drew much interest specifically in its "techniques of democratic planning," not merely in the United States but abroad. Charles Perrow (himself an influential organization theorist and former student of Selznick's) called it "the first (and only) extensive flirtation in recent times with a socialist program in the United States."[13] Selznick later recalled it as "a major effort by the New Deal to test the efficacy—and the social value—of public enterprise."[14] Fresh from the faction fights, with a head full of Michels and a dawning theory of bureaucracy, Selznick was confident the truth must be more complicated and that it probably lay elsewhere. The reality turned out to confirm this expectation, and yet in ways that took him by surprise, as Roger Cotterrell's interview captures nicely:

> SELZNICK: While I was still casting about to decide on a project, I read an article by David Lilienthal, who was at that time the chairman of the TVA, who was touting this so-called grass-roots administration. He wrote many pieces on that subject, and this was one of his big talking-points. And so it struck me that this was a wonderful chance for me to study the relation between organization and ideology. You know, to just some smart-ass kid, from where I was sitting, I mean, this was clearly an ideological statement that probably needed to be punctured. I think I assumed that what we would really find is that informally, behind the scenes, TVA really dominated the other institutions. And I was wrong. But the idea that this would be a good subject for studying the connection between ideology and interests in administration, that turned out to be quite correct. . . .
>
> COTTERRELL: So you went into that project thinking that you would find the TVA in control of its constituency and managing things.
>
> SELZNICK: Right.
>
> COTTERRELL: And what you found was a complicated process of negotiation and compromise and so on.
>
> SELZNICK: Right, and, to a large extent, showing . . . the internal compromises that were made and the ways at least one important constitutency really got control of part of the TVA.[15]

TVA is a remarkable, and much-lauded, work. Like all Selznick's books, it operates on several levels. It is a case study of an important and innovative federal agency; if you want a rich and detailed description of the TVA, its objectives, and the ways it sought to pursue them, this is a good place to start. It is also a study of why certain strategies had profound, unanticipated, effects. That connected with a theme of Merton's, though it is not clear that Selznick's inspiration came from Merton rather than Alcove 1.[16] Most deeply, *TVA* is an occasion for expounding in general terms and exemplifying, through this case study, ways in which the inner, typically uncharted, informal, life of large institutions affects the interrelations between purported ends and adopted means and influences what occurs in the space between the two. Part of that exploration, its most enduring part, is an account of the behavior of organizations that takes the book far beyond a concern with its ostensible (real but not whole) subject matter: "It is TVA as an organization to which our attention is directed. Thus it is not dams or reservoirs or power houses or fertilizer as such, but the nature of the Authority as an ordered group of working individuals, as a living institution, which is under scrutiny."[17] Though it has been read, praised, and criticized at all these levels, it is that last one that was of most interest to Selznick.

Lilienthal distinguished between *government*, which often had to be centralized, and *administration*, which often did not have to be; "the hazards of managerial exploitation can be diminished by skillful efforts in the direction of decentralized administration of centralized authority."[18] The key to the democratization of which he boasted was his "grass-roots theory" of public administration. That meant that "managerial decisions should be made in the Valley, where the work was to be done, not in Washington."[19] It also meant working through "the people's institutions":

> It was felt that an imposed federal program would be alien and unwanted, and ultimately accomplish little, unless it brought together at the grass roots all the agencies concerned with and essential to the development of a region's resources: the local communities, voluntary private organizations, state agencies, and cooperating federal agencies. The vision of such a working partnership seemed to define "grass-roots democracy at work."[20]

This is not what Selznick expected to find, nor what he came to consider "the unavowed meaning of the official grass-roots policy,"[21] though that too was not what he expected to find.

Co-optation

The phrase *grassroots democracy* applied especially to the authority's agricultural programs. These required institutional mediation, and the institutions chosen to mediate the "people's voice" were the agricultural extension services of existing land-grant colleges[22] in the seven Valley states. That was a choice pregnant with consequence. For these services:

> became a close collaborator—virtually an operating arm—of the TVA in the agricultural field. The agency thereby accepted a number of commitments that reflected the character of the extension services in those days . . . a disposition to deal mainly with relatively prosperous elements of the local farm population, and a tendency to reflect dominant attitudes toward blacks and farm tenants. . . .
>
> Furthermore, the alliance created a group *inside* the TVA that vigorously defended the interests and perspectives of the extension services and exerted pressure on other TVA programs.[23]

This apparently innocent institutional choice led, Selznick argued, to a range of unintended consequences. In particular, these stemmed from the phenomenon he called "co-optation," *"the process of absorbing new ele-ments into the leadership or policy-determining structure of an organization as a means of averting threats to its stability or existence."*[24] He identified two forms: formal, "when there is a need to establish the legitimacy of authority or the administrative accessibility of the relevant public";[25] and informal, when "the problem is not one of responding to a state of imbal-ance with respect to the 'people as a whole' but rather one of meeting the pressure of specific individuals or interest groups which are in a position to enforce demands."[26] Most of the book explores the extent and signifi-cance of *informal* co-optation, in the process of which, Selznick argued, the Authority had given away some significant control of the store. Moves to increase *formal* local involvement in the Authority's activities, on the other hand, served less to increase citizen participation in the exercise of administrative power than to legitimize the administration and extend the power of leaders.

Selznick interpreted the Authority's grassroots policy as a "protective ideology,"[27] an attempt to accommodate local and national interests that might "wreck the program if moved to resistance."[28] Whatever the strat-egy chosen, something would have had to be done to accommodate "the iron necessities of continuing to exist and work in that area,"[29] especially because the TVA was not a response to local demand but a federal initia-tive that needed to counter potential sources of local resistance from those many in the South committed to states' rights and suspicious of federal intervention and from powerful and dominant interests in the Valley, who could only with some naive optimism be taken to represent "the people."

The need to accommodate these "iron necessities" meant that the dem-ocratic impulse of the policy would be systematically compromised. Not everyone was a beneficiary of the Authority's democratic impulses, but, rather, powerful people and institutions that might block the Authority's activities and therefore had to be wooed. Above all, these were the power-ful owners of larger and more prosperous farms.[30] As one extended review of *TVA* quipped, "It would be more accurate to speak of them as grass-tops than grass-roots organizations."[31] This resulted not simply in uneven distribution of favors but also in commitments that restricted the activities of the Authority itself.

These commitments meant that the Authority became wedded to the social status quo, and to elite "agriculturalist" interests rather than oth-ers, by "freezing" the social arrangements and social interests that it had blessed with its recognition. They also locked the Authority into its des-

ignated "administrative constituencies" and tied it to their side in controversies both local and national. They had other unanticipated effects as
well. They inhibited direct approaches to local citizens, over the jealous
and well-placed heads of the co-opted agencies. They allowed well-placed
beneficiaries to create a conservative lobby within the organization. And
they led to particular and consequential policy choices being made in line
with interests that had become parts of the organization. Thus, planners
within the TVA sought to preserve public ownership over public lands to
be used for public purposes, particularly conservation. They lost to the
"agriculturists," however, who demanded and were granted private ownership. Again, richer, larger farmers were consistently favored over poor
ones. Whites won against blacks, both because the TVA excluded "Negro"
institutions as grassroots participants and because "an attempt to carry
forward a policy of nondiscrimination (as against Negroes) will not proceed very far when the instrument for carrying out this policy—usually
as an adjunct of some broader program—has traditions of its own of a
contrary bent."[32] Serious frictions developed between the TVA and other
relevant federal agencies, which in turn led to attempts to block the propa-
gation of such organizations, "a fact which is consequential for the future
of the Authority itself."[33]

Above all, these tactical accommodations had profound and fateful consequences for the *character* of the organization as a conservation
agency. *Character* is a technical term in Selznick's organizational theory,
one borrowed from Dewey. As Selznick explained in *TVA*, "'Consequences,' writes Dewey, 'include effects upon character, upon confirming
and weakening habits, as well as tangibly obvious results,' . . . these considerations from the social psychology of the individual provide us with tools
for organizational analysis."[34] And though character is

> a vague and ill-defined quality . . . unacknowledged and often poorly under-
> stood, [it] represents a fundamental prize in organizational controversy. . . .
> What are we? What shall we become? With whom shall we be indentified?
> Where are our roots? These questions, and others like them, are the special
> responsibility of statesmen, of those who look beyond the immediate context
> of current issues to their larger implications for the future role and meaning
> of the group.[35]

The TVA was light on statesmanship. Its character was allowed to be re-
molded by "the TVA agricultural group, reflecting local attitudes and interests."[36] In all, as Selznick later put it, "Something more than simple com-
promise was involved: there was also a kind of organizational surrender."[37]

Apart from the more important informal sort, there were also examples of formal co-optation. Here too there is systematic slippage between the "democracy" in the name of which these initiatives are made and their results. This time, and as Michels might have predicted, it is

> primarily for the convenience of the administration. It is easy enough for administrative imperatives which call for decentralization to be given a halo; that becomes especially useful in countries which prize the symbols of democracy. But a critical analysis cannot overlook that pattern which simply transforms an unorganized citizenry into a reliable instrument for the achievement of administrative goals, and calls it "democracy."[38]

If most of the book, then, displays deformations of "democratic planning" where the adjective compromises the noun, in formal co-optation the direction is reversed. In this particular case, however, informal rather than formal co-optation dominated.

In neither case—formal or informal—do we understand the deeper meaning of the TVA's innovations if we take its leaders at their word. But this is not because they intended these deformations, could easily have done otherwise, or were lying. Many of these consequences were unanticipated, and, Selznick insists, they were not simple or easily corrected errors. They were responses to real and urgent necessities: "The choice, indeed, may often lie between adjustment and organizational suicide";[39] "the operation of this cooptative process probably did much to enhance the stability of the TVA within its area and especially to make possible the mobilization of support in an hour of need. In this sense, one cannot speak of the decisions which led to this situation as mistakes."[40] Moreover, that the TVA did not always live up to its press releases was not a matter of the insincerity or ill will of its leaders, whose values and achievements Selznick admired on the whole. On the contrary, it was precisely because the TVA was an admirable institution led by men with admirable goals that the distortions of those goals in the everyday workings of the organization were so revealing. Just as Michels had concentrated on the most ostensibly (and sincerely) democratic of institutions to show how inexorable oligarchic pressures were, so too, in conscious or unconscious imitation of Michels, Selznick concludes his book by observing:

> No one is surprised when a weak or corrupt governmental agency does not fulfill its doctrinal promise. When, however, a morally strong and fundamentally honest organization is subject to the kind of process we have described, then the pervasive significance of that process becomes materially enhanced. In a sense, it is just because TVA is a relatively good example of

democratic administration that the evidences of weakness in this respect are so important. . . .

For the things which are important in the analysis of democracy are those which bind the hands of good men. We learn that something more than virtue is necessary in the realm of circumstance and power.[41]

Here, then, is a case study of unanticipated consequences, unexpected and often intransigent realities that derailed the pursuit, even well-meaning and diligent pursuit, of deliberately chosen ends. Many of these derailing features had to do with organizational imperatives that could not be wished away, however pure or honorable the ideals of those subject to them.

Organizations and Ideals

The Michelsian tone of *TVA*—skeptical, critical, unmasking—is unmistakable. And there is, indeed, no controversy over the Michelsian flavor of Selznick's early academic writings. He wrote directly about Michels in two of his earliest academic publications, seeking to systematize and qualify the "iron law."[42] He saw his investigation of the TVA as "entering a field of inquiry which probes at the heart of the democratic dilemma," which was that "[a] faith in majorities does not eliminate the necessity for governance by individuals and small groups. Wherever there is organization, whether formally democratic or not, there is a split between the leader and the led, between the agent and the initiator."[43] And though Michels is not mentioned in the first edition of *TVA*, Selznick stressed his influence in the preface to its 1965 reissue, and it has been widely noted.[44]

However, if Michels's influence on *TVA* is clear, it also needs some specification, for influence comes in many forms and operates at various levels. In his earliest writings, Selznick was much impressed by the substantive core of the iron law—oligarchy—even while he insisted it was neither iron nor a law. In this work, however, the core finding contradicts Michels's prediction and Selznick's initial expectation. Moreover, given his central thesis that the leaders of the Authority had *ceded* real organizational power to structurally and economically significant outsiders, one can detect a quasi-Marxist theme that sits uneasily with Michels's "iron law."

On the other hand, Selznick generalized three of Michels's central insights in particular, well beyond the "iron law." These themes distinguished all Selznick's work on organizations and reflected Michels's ideas: the crucial place of *organization* and *organizations* in modern societies; the importance of *leadership*; and, as always, the relationship between means and ends.

The first two go naturally together in Selznick's thought, as they did in Michels's. If Selznick did not agree that "he who says organization, [necessarily] says oligarchy," he certainly believed that modern societies are dependent on organization and organizations, that organizations need leaders, and that both organizations and their leaders, and the relations between them, are of crucial importance: for each other, and for everyone in large and complex societies.

When reintroducing *TVA* on its republication several years later, Selznick recalls, in language redolent of his *Enquiry* essays:

> The TVA mythology is scrutinized in several ways. Most important is the critique of official TVA doctrine as a screen for covert, opportunistic adaptation. Here the mode of analysis used by Robert Michels in his still-remarkable *Political Parties* . . . is especially relevant. Indeed, I had that book very much on my mind during the years just prior to 1942–43, when this research was done. Michels taught that ideals go quickly by the board when the compelling realities of organizational life are permitted to run their natural course. . . . In his quest for insight into the forces that frustrate idealism, . . . he chose to show . . . how difficult it is for even radical idealists to avoid the tyranny of means and the impotence of ends. Means tyrannize when the commitments they build up divert us from our true objectives. Ends are impotent when they are so abstract and unspecified that they offer no principles of criticism or assessment.
>
> Sociological realism . . . can be an exercise in skepticism and an apology for passively accepting things as they are. But it is also a way of taking ideals seriously. If ideals *are* to be taken seriously there must be genuine concern for their embodiment in action, and especially in the routines of institutional life. We cannot be content with unexamined formulae, no matter by whom expressed. We cannot forego a look behind the facade—even if it is our own.[45]

The Michels effects that so concern Selznick in these passages are the effects of means chosen on values, ideals, ends that they are supposed to serve. Indeed, organization is mentioned in these passages only in relation to the tendency of particular organizational means to overwhelm ideals. Otherwise Michels is generalized, quite beyond his specific conclusions. The argument applies to organizations, to be sure, but it can be read more broadly, even if the results it illuminates are contrary to those that Michels would predict. Whatever the concrete result, *TVA*, like the German Social Democratic Party (SDP) that Michels had analyzed, displayed the difficulty of avoiding "the tyranny of means and the impotence of ends," and the need for realism as "a way of taking ideals seriously." More broadly still, both cases illuminate "the fate of ideals in social practice," in particular "the conditions and processes that frustrate ideals." In combination, they allow Michels to travel, far beyond the "iron law."

The lesson Selznick had already absorbed in his Trotskyist debates, and that he confirmed in *TVA*, is that "the problem of means is vital, [but] it is also the most readily forgotten." People's imaginations are gripped by visions, ideologies, ideals; "methods are more elusive." And yet, while "no democratic program can be unconcerned about . . . objectives . . . the crucial question for democracy is not what to strive for but by what means to strive. And the question of means is one of what to do now and what to do next—and these are basic questions in politics."[46]

At this general level, then, Michels is confirmed even while he is challenged in his specific predictions. In Selznick's next book, *The Organizational Weapon*, confirmation is both general and particular. That book, even more than its predecessor, echoes Michels in detail as well as in its general lines; it is above all concerned with the capacity of communist leaders to fashion an organization that ensures their own power and pursuit of their own objectives, even as they speak in the name of "the workers of the world."

THE ORGANIZATIONAL WEAPON

In 1946–1947 Selznick took his first academic appointment, as an instructor in sociology at the University of Minnesota, Minneapolis. In 1947, he left to join UCLA, where he stayed until 1952. He met there another pragmatist, the philosopher Abraham Kaplan, with whom he became good friends. A course they taught together in 1950 or 1951, on "ethical problems of social organization," was important for Selznick:

> A lot of what I later came to emphasize was developed in at least a rudimentary way in that course. It was an opportunity for me to take seriously and define my position on a number of issues. It led to this more general and more positive view of things. . . . I remembered thinking of myself as a Hobbesian, but that is only one aspect. This is something you start with and then you have to look at these larger possibilities.[47]

Kaplan also had a serendipitous influence on Selznick's career. He was connected with "this psychological warfare bunch," which became the core of the social sciences division of the RAND Corporation. He introduced Selznick to the group in 1948, and between 1948 and 1952 Selznick was a research associate of the social sciences division of RAND. In that capacity, and in the early and some of the most dramatic years of the Cold War, he wrote a book on communist organization strategy, which became *The Organizational Weapon*. Like many of his former comrades, Selznick had become staunchly anticommunist by this time, and like many former Bolsheviks he had learned a lot about communist strategies. The book penetratingly examines the specific challenges that communist leaders face in their bid to take power in a hostile environment and the distinctive ways in which they dealt with such challenges. Moreover, as we shall see, it had other, more theoretical, dimensions as well.

Like *TVA*, Selznick's second book was also a case study, but it differed markedly in subject matter and method from the first. First of all, it was concerned with a very different kind of organization from the TVA: the Marxist-Leninist "combat party" seeking to gain power in noncommunist states.[48] Secondly, it was not a study of any particular case but of a *type*. It was an attempt to develop, drawing on a large array of sources from around the world:

> a model that will effectively expose a *central* pattern of motivation and action, applicable in its basic features to the bolshevik movement in all countries and throughout its history. We have therefore emphasized what the record shows to be *general*, recognizing that there can be and are deviations in detail from one country or period to another, but that there *is* a persistent underlying pattern.[49]

The model focused on a particular but crucial part of communist strategy: its organizational component. It was common observation that Communist Parties behaved differently from most organizations, indeed from most political parties. Not only outsiders noticed it, but "'Our Party,' the Bolshevik leaders tell their ranks, 'is not like other parties.'"[50] Selznick agreed. Conventional democratic political parties, formed to contest other parties of different commitments but similar type, are "committed to electoral victory in the short run, decentralized, capable of absorbing new ideas and social forces, incapable of making many demands upon a weakly involved party membership."[51] Communist Parties differed in ways Selznick considered to be systematic, and he sought to theorize those ways.

Some differences were empirically observable, such as "the remarkable persistence of the communist core membership despite great fluctuations and turnover, and the persistence of strategies and tactics of power aggrandizement despite significant shifts in political 'line.'"[52] The job of sociological theory was to *interpret* these observable traits, looking for "latent structures" and "latent commitments" that underlay their most distinctive attributes and enabled the theorist to explain not merely what *did* occur and why, in organizations of a particular type, but what tendencies were *immanent* in such organizations, given that they were of this type. That explanation would not without more guarantee specific predictions, or displace the need for factual observation, because it dealt with only one aspect of communist strategy. In any event, like Michels's less-than-iron law, it had to be understood as a distillation of systematic *tendencies*. What was revealed was a logic, not a law. Specific behaviors were never the result of this logic standing alone because in reality it never did stand alone. Instead, oligarchical tendencies were always encountered in particular circumstances, were offered specific and variable opportunities, and met with specific and variable obstacles. What actually happened was a result of the combination of logic and circumstances, which often included other, frequently contending, logics and many varied circumstances. Here, too, there were no iron laws, but that did not mean that all was random or haphazard, defying analysis or predictions of suitably qualified sorts.

The "operational code" of communist parties, Selznick argued, consists of:

> . . . distinctive modes of group membership and distinctive modes of social control. A system is created capable of making very large demands upon totally involved members. It is a system marked by *a distinctive competence to turn members of a voluntary association into disciplined and deployable political agents*.[53]

It is this *distinctive competence*, a concept of central importance in Selznick's understanding of institutions more generally, that Selznick seeks to understand. An organization of this sort "could be built only over a long period and with great effort."[54] It required the transformation of a voluntary organization into a "managerial structure" by which *adherents* are converted into *cadres* of *"deployable personnel."*[55] That in turn depended on an organization developing a specific competence to effect such transformations because they do not occur naturally or even commonly in organizations but have to be formed. Selznick's interest was in how that competence was established and sustained, often over long periods of time, in circumstances that were rarely welcoming or easy, indeed *because* circumstances were neither welcoming nor easy.

Other organizations that seek to convert adherents into "deployable agents," terrorist organizations for example, might well furnish suggestive contemporary parallels, for "no group has a monopoly on the use of organizational weapons."[56] Wherever people seek to develop "deployable agents" in hostile circumstances, they will require specific organizational strategies and competences: "Such a view is characteristic of groups which seek to catapult themselves out of obscurity into history when, as it seems to them, all the forces of society are arrayed in opposition."[57] Marxist-Leninists made an art form of this, but it can be emulated, put to other uses, and re-created, doubtless in differing forms and in service to different gods.

This is true because Communist Parties were a species of "combat party." Most organizations are not "weapons," but that is precisely what Communist Parties were. As such, they were not fashioned to compete routinely in open elections within constitutionally established constraints and rules of the game, in the hope of winning control of government for a limited period of time. Rather they were forged for an in-principle unrestrained struggle for total hold on power.

As we already learned, first from Philip Sherman and then from *TVA*, professed goals and ideals are never enough. To have the distinctive competence for these and allied activities, such competence must be built into the apparatus itself, into its *means*, not merely its ends. Selznick explains it thus:

> We cannot truly determine the aims of an institution without knowing what it is as a social system—how it is held together, what resources it can muster and what it can do with them, and what its posture is in relation to other groups. The interdependence of strategy and distinctive competence is especially important; hence the study of institutional capabilities is a vital phase of institutional assessment. Only in this way can we distinguish effectively between merely verbal aims, or such as may be derived solely from doctrine, and aims that truly guide behavior because they are embodied in and supported by the social structure of the group.[58]

An army displays some similar competences, but it has the backing of the state and law, and it commonly keeps its troops in barracks separate from nonmilitary communities. Until they succeed, Communist Parties never have the backing of their own state (though they often were backed by external communist states); indeed, they commonly started as ideologically suspect groups, often illegal, hiding their activities, in whole or in part, from hostile police and security services. Moreover, communist organizational strategies were intended to combat such attention and often persecution, not simply to survive and/or propagate the faith (as might be true of, say, the Falun Gong or Baha'i) but to gain power. This combination of aims led to an "inherent tension":

the combat party must continuously guard against certain characteristic dangers: excessive isolation on the one hand and liquidation on the other. To build and sustain the system requires a heavy emphasis on the withdrawal of members from society and upon ultimate doctrinal purity; at the same time the members must be deployed in the political arena. The first carries the risk that the party will be transformed into an isolated sect, the second that members will place the interests of target groups, such as trade unions, above those of the party itself. The working out of this inner conflict not only summarizes a considerable portion of communist history but also helps us to identify what the necessities of the system are, what has to be done in order to maintain its peculiar integrity.[59]

Party cadres have at the same time to be steeled against a world of temptations and ready to infiltrate it without losing their primary characters as party operatives. They have to become *insulated* from outside loyalties, ways of thought, and temptations and *absorbed* into the Party and its work to an extent that is uncommon.[60] They have to be trained for conspiratorial activity, and nerved for it, in "the continuous and systematic search for 'pieces of power.'"[61] They need to neutralize opponents, and for much of the time even more, rivals for their common constituency;[62] they need *access* to target groups and institutions to do what is required of them, they need to seek legitimacy, they need to mobilize support, but they must maintain at all times their identity and integrity as Party operatives, independent of the groups and institutions they seek to penetrate and able to exploit them for the Party's purposes.[63] For those who do not meet these stringent requirements, there are highly elaborated organizational means of dealing with "betrayal."[64]

In all this, the party must sustain and communicate to the faithful a clear understanding of the distinctive *character* of the party that they serve. Otherwise they might dissolve into the waters in which they are supposed to swim purposefully and to feed. The character of the party must constantly be guarded against myriad sources of corruption, to sustain and guard the kinds of commitments that enable the leadership "to mobilize and 'hurl' the organization against strategic targets in the struggle for power."[65]

None of this comes easily or quickly. On the contrary, such transformations cannot be "simply *resolved* into existence: a long process of indoctrination and action is required to inculcate methods of organization and work so deeply that they select and create congenial personality traits,"[66] and "the reorientation . . . is not simply one of technical organization, but of restructuring the *attitudes and actions* of the membership."[67]

Selznick constantly probed the "hidden organizational meaning of seemingly straightforward propaganda activities,"[68] whose ostensible targets seemed to lie outside the organization but whose real importance may be "not to spread communist symbols, but simply to create an atmosphere conducive to the free use of the combat party and its agencies. Similarly, we speak of the organizational relevance of ideology when it performs internally oriented morale functions."[69] Again, "Communist 'theory' cannot be understood solely as a guide to action. It is partly that, but doubtless of equal significance is the managerial function Marxist-Leninist doctrine fulfills."[70] The "cults of personality" that typically develop in communist states are also not simply due to the peculiar vanity of communist leaders. Rather they are part of a much more widespread endeavor of Communist Parties, in power and striving for it, to convert loyalty to the party to "loyalty to the party *organization*. A halo is raised over party leaders, party organs, party decision."[71] In all this, Lenin appeared to have recognized those more general truths about organizations of all sorts, outlined in Selznick's earliest work and not always observed by the leaders of the TVA: "that proximate, operational goals are more important in the struggle for power than abstract, ultimate goals";[72] "institutional loyalties are fostered as a way to give abstract ideals a content that can effectively summon psychological energies."[73]

Much of *The Organizational Weapon* focuses on how to develop the "vanguard," but of course there is "the mass." Communist Parties are not, as the naive might imagine, transparent tribunes of the masses; nor, however, are they putschists or saboteurs, for whom the people are mere bystanders to their explosive activities. Bolshevik writings and actions embody a highly differentiated and complex analysis of the masses, who are key because "they are the font of power."[74] So they are indispensable, though in a curious way not central, and the Party's relationship to them is of a special sort. For the Leninist Party is a kind of caricature or logical reduction of Michels's iron law:

> Thousands of words have been written by bolshevik leaders to hammer home the thesis that the thoughts of the workers are sources of power for the party *if* manipulative control is established. Least of all are the thoughts of the workers to be taken as guideposts for the party . . . It is the party, not the workers, which is the arbiter of these historical interests. The workers are continually susceptible to "reactionary prejudices," to being misled, deceived, betrayed, corrupted. The party is the great stabilizer which holds the class to the course fixed by history. It is the cleanser and the purifier, the teacher, the judge, and, at the inevitable hour, the jailer.[75]

Communist Parties must *lead*, and ensuring such leadership is the primary goal of communist organizational work. The Party seeks "access" to the masses, "legitimation" before them, targeted "mobilization" of some of them, elimination or at least "neutralization" of rivals and opponents. Apathy is often useful to the leadership, but it must also be able to muster support. That requires mastery of tactics of penetration and infiltration. They all were "primarily means of creating power for the leaders."[76] Communists are particularly good at such activities because:

> The tactical advantage which the communists gain in the course of unity maneuvers is not based on episodic or "clever" manipulation. It derives from the fundamental increment of power offered by the combat party. The latter creates a corps of disciplined cadres dedicated to the ubiquitous pursuit of power. In this sense the basis of communist influence is real and not illusory. The ability to deploy forces in a controlled and systematic way makes possible minority control in large organizations, especially in an environment of general apathy and in the absence of competing power centers.[77]

Not only were communists devoted students of organizational weaponry, but contemporary mass society was full of what today might be called soft targets. For in the penultimate chapter of the book,[78] Selznick ventures some "frankly preliminary" hypotheses as to sources of social vulnerability to political manipulation and penetration. He emphasizes that these sources are available for exploitation not only by communists but by any outside political forces, whether of the left or right. For they amount to weakened capacities of self-defence, whatever the source of attack. The key issue is "the capacity of institutions to meet, within their own terms, the requirements of self-maintenance. Self-maintenance, of course, refers to the preservation of central values and purposes as well as to the bare continuity of organizational existence."[79] That, in turn, depends on the ability of culture-bearing elites to defend the character of their institutions. That ability, however, depends on them understanding that character and being committed to it and its defence. Such understanding and commitment, however, are eroded by the pressures of "mass society":

> The strength of cultural values depends on the ability of key agencies to transmit them without serious attenuation and distortion. But this in turn requires that these institutions be secure, that the elites which man them be able to maintain their distinctive identities. This becomes increasingly difficult as powerful solvents—science, technology, industrialization, urbanization— warp the self-confidence of the culture-bearers and, at the same time, expose them to the pressures of an emergent mass.[80]

In his preface to the book's 1960 reissue, Selznick observes that "the vulnerability considered here is not uniquely a vulnerability to communism. The McCarthy episode in American life during the early 1950's reflected the same exposure of institutions to political assault. The diagnosis has to do with a lowering of resistance in specific ways. The attack may come from a number of different quarters."[81] This is a good point. Unfortunately, what Selznick fails to do is explain why no successful *Bolshevik* revolution ever occurred in modern massified societies. They all occurred in societies far less developed. Barrington Moore made the point well:

> so far as Communism is concerned, it is quite clear that this doctrine focusses attention on the wrong end of the horse. Communism has not gained a strong foothold in those advanced industrial countries where the processes alleged by Selznick to exist have supposedly been going on for the longest time. Instead, the Communist variety of totalitarianism has flourished best in peasant societies that for one reason or another were having difficulty in making the transition to an industrial order.[82]

This is not a refutation of Selznick's analysis of vulnerabilities of mass societies, but it is a significant gap in an attempt to explain the successes of communism.

We will return to the theory and implications of mass society later because these tie in with Selznick's understanding of culture and of community. For the present, they are also a key component of his understanding of institutions and what is involved in leading, rather than merely managing them. For the key to institutional self-maintenance is leadership that sustains the institution's character; in a sense, leadership that understands what communists understand:

> Vulnerability can be controlled only by the affirmation in practice of the moral ideals which define the character of an organization. This affirmation requires, above all, the shaping of individuals so that they become competent to apprehend those threats, from within and without, which endanger the institution's self-image. It is the failure to do this that leaves the door open to *effective* penetration. . . . Unions, universities, and other agencies which embody values have most to fear when they become bound to the moment, to the technical job at hand, to limited views of their social function. They are then softened for ideological and organizational manipulation: they will become unable to distinguish between those who defend treasured aspirations and those who corrupt them.[83]

In Selznick's next book, these observations on leadership and the key importance of institutionalizing values beyond "the moment" were generalized as key ways to distinguish institutional leaders from organizational managers. Today, long after the collapse of communism, denizens of many of our furiously managed and too rarely led institutions, among them universities, might learn from the analysis.

The Organizational Weapon doubtless had an activist, or "awakening" component. Written by a man confident he "knew the score" about Bolshevism, it was conceived in part as an exposé intended to guide people seeking to oppose communism. Indeed, in the introduction to the book, Selznick suggests that "because of its stress on action rather than on ideological analysis, this volume may be used as an advanced-training manual for anti-communist forces."[84] But it would pay those forces to be sophisticated, lest they misunderstand two central and interrelated features of what they read—its qualified political significance and its scientific novelty.

Politically, it is important not to miss or misapprehend a point Selznick makes several times: Even a successful organizational strategy is only a piece in the complex of assault and defence that compete within any society that contains (and seeks to contain) wielders of organizational weapons. Thus he emphasizes

> the *subordinate* role of organizational activity in the struggle against totalitarianism. . . . To speak of organizational strategy and tactics is to define a special sphere of interest and action. It must not be forgotten that this sphere is limited, providing special increments of power to political elites whose fundamental sources of weakness and strength must be looked for elsewhere. . . .
>
> In the long view political combat plays only a tactical role. Great social issues, such as those which divide communism and democracy, are not decided by political combat, perhaps not even by military clashes. They are decided by the relative ability of the contending systems to win and to maintain enduring loyalties. Consequently, no amount of power and cunning in the realm of political combat, can avail in the absence of measures which rise to the height of the times.[85]

Scientifically, and in explanation of this focus on a self-confessedly subsidiary—if crucial—matter, it is necessary to grasp the precise concern of Selznick's analysis and its novelty, for this is the work of a theorist of, and self-consciously a study of, *organization*, who argues for the significance of this particular domain but does not consider it all important. In particular, the book is concerned not so much with how communists solve, or attempt to solve, the many political problems that face them. Rather it is concerned with an at once fundamental but second-order issue: how they create and sustain organizational means *capable* of dealing with such problems. This, of course, was precisely the issue that he found the TVA had failed to confront successfully.

Selznick's late colleague, Sheldon Messinger, made the point well.[86] He distinguished between two levels of problem-solving engagement that a Communist Party must engage in. At the first level, such a party works in a context where its goals of achieving "total power" are held illegitimate, as are the means they use to reach that goal. That presents them with a "level-one problem": what a party must do to overcome this predicament. The novelty of Selznick's approach is that it concentrates on a deeper level of issues, what Messinger calls "level-two problems," that is *"what must we do to construct and maintain an organizational means which will fill the requirements at level one"*:

> Michels revealed to us that administrators in carrying out day-to-day pursuits came to be guided by considerations specific to the means of action. He phrased this negatively . . . by telling us that ultimate goals tended to be lost sight of in the bureaucratic life. Selznick might be said to have drawn a profound lesson from this, namely, that one set of problems seldom enough considered is what one must do, from day-to-day, in order to have in hand a means appropriate to goal-achievement. Since TVA administrators were not especially cognizant of this problem, their means of action became ill-suited to pursuit of ultimate goals posited at the outset of their activities. The bolsheviks, on the other hand, *are* cognizant of this problem: thus it is possible for Selznick to view the construction of their means as illuminating "those aspects of organization most important in the power process."
>
> More important . . . is the implication of this point of view for research. It constitutes a directive . . . to make the leap from consideration of what one must do to achieve a given goal, to what one must do to construct and preserve means of action appropriate to a given goal.

It might be said that Selznick's next book, *Leadership in Administration*, seeks to generalize the "leap" that Messinger identifies. In this respect, *TVA* could be viewed as a study of well-intentioned failure while *The Organizational Weapon* studied ill-intentioned success. The subsequent volume draws from these and other exemplary organizational histories to analyze some of the ingredients of failure and success in institutional leadership, more generally conceived.

Leadership in Administration represents a dramatic departure in ambition and tone from the *TVA* and *The Organizational Weapon*. If they took the form of exposés, as Perrow says the "old institutionalists" generally tended to,[87] this has an altogether different, more constructive, concern. It might be recalled that Selznick had said in 1950 that the study of techniques "for blocking the bureaucratic drift" was "one of the most pressing tasks of our time." However, only *Leadership in Administration*, of his early organizational writings, was clearly devoted to such a task. But if the ambition was different, and the sensibility was beginning to change, the theoretical project was coherent. It drew on and extended a distinctive understanding of the social character of organizations and institutions, and it did so with a view to exploring, as always, the role and fate of ideals in the world.

CHAPTER FOUR

Institutional Leadership

In a suggestive essay on *Leadership in Administration*, Hugh Heclo observes that:

> As many students of public administration realized at the time, Selznick's 1949 *TVA and the Grassroots* was much more than just another case study. Among other things, it showed how political and bureaucratic realities could chip the luster off high-minded, progressive plans intended for the common good. Twenty years later, the intellectual critics known as neo-conservatives (who were mostly ex-Cold War liberals) would develop this theme of unintended consequences into a devastating bludgeon against the Sixties' Great Society programs. It was not hard work. The harder job was to look squarely into the shadows that come between thought and deed, intent and results, and see the mishaps as a challenge to figure out how one might do better.[1]

There is a lot in this passage. Selznick had begun as a master unmasker, ready to reveal the underside of the finest plans. He had, to be sure, always insisted that realism and idealism should be understood as complementary rather than zero-sum alternatives, but his distinctive contribution had been to the realist corner. Show him what appeared to be the case, tell him what should be, and he would typically respond by revealing what, notwithstanding appearances, in the face of the best intentions, really and often stubbornly was.

In *Leadership*, however, he began to explore not merely the inevitable challenges to ideals but what might yet be done to vindicate them. Long before he and some of his friends of the 1940s grew apart politically from the 1960s, as they cleaved rightwards and he to a complex position to their left, Selznick's work had begun to augment his expertise on "the shadows . . . between thought and deed, intent and results," with attempts to "figure out how one might do better." As I mentioned in the Introduction, the combination is simpler to state than accomplish. Unmaskers are often temperamentally suspicious of idealists, and the reverse is also true. That attempt to blend realism and idealism, to recognize their frequent tensions but also seek to respect the demands of them both and at once, has become nevertheless one of the central characteristics of Selznick's thought. Again, Heclo captures the distinctiveness of what was being undertaken in *Leadership*, which represents, though he does not pursue it, a significant and later sustained change of emphasis in the development of Selznick's work:

> That exertion in a positive direction lay behind the writing of *Leadership in Administration* only a few years after the *TVA* volume. . . . the important point is not that the case study method was left behind in favor of broader sociological generalizations. What matters more is that Selznick sought to think through the problem of maintaining ideals amid grubby organizational realities. The experience of TVA's directors became the material, not for bashing, but for elevating the concept of leadership.[2]

That is precisely true of *Leadership*, and it illuminates all of Selznick's subsequent work. Challenges to the realization of ideals were at the center of his youthful polemics and *TVA*; one apparently successful response to them had been explored in *The Organizational Weapon*. But each was only an example of a larger set of issues that Selznick sought to address in *Leadership in Administration*.

FORMAL AND INFORMAL SYSTEMS

One way to understand Selznick's distinctive contribution to the study of modern organizations is to contrast his approach with that of their most famous student, Max Weber. That contrast is instructive less because it was uppermost in Selznick's own mind (it was not),[3] or because Selznick was the only writer to differentiate his ideas from Weber's (Weber is such a dominating ancestral presence in organization theory that such differentiation has become almost a rite of passage),[4] than because it underlines the specific implications of Selznick's concern with what is *characteristic* of the workings of modern large-scale organizations, implications that Weber might be said to have underplayed in favor of what *distinguishes* them from other organizational types.

Weber and Bureaucracy

Our understanding of large organizations, and specifically of the peculiarly modern organizational form that he called bureaucracy, owes its greatest debt to Weber. It was he who emphasized the novelty and increasing pervasiveness of modern hierarchical organizations, made up of full-time, trained professionals, masters of "the files," working in unprecedentedly large numbers, handling unprecedented flows of administrative work, unprecedentedly penetrating domain after domain of social life; he who identified elements that allegedly made such organizations indispensable and inescapable in modern societies; above all he who sought to identify the distinctiveness of bureaucracies, as institutional bearers and paradigm exhibitors of the "rationality" uniquely characteristic of modernity. He was not the first, particularly in Germany, to emphasize these elements of organizational structure; plenty of nineteenth-century administrative theorists had done so. But he may well have been the first, and was certainly the most influential, to argue for the world-historical significance of these structures.

Weber's overarching concern was to understand what was, and what contributed to, the distinctiveness of the modern West. He considered its forms of "rationality," prominent among them those embodied in modern forms of administrative organizations, central to that distinctiveness. Rationalization took many forms, but common to them all were

a) the "disenchantment" (*Entzauberung*, more closely, demagification) of the world, which involved the separation of the sacred and the profane and the advance of the profane;
b) an increasingly "calculating" attitude to all things;
c) the relentless adjustment of means, in the light of such calculations, to the most efficient achievement of ends; and
d) an increasing *separation* of life spheres and, within spheres, of domains of specialization.

Critical among such separations was that between concerns relating to *ends* and those relating to the fashioning and employment of means. The advance of modernity involved an unprecedented rationalization of means, together with a draining in the sanctity of ends. Weber saw rationalization wherever he looked in the modern world: in its economic structures, its sciences, its architecture, its forms of political legitimacy, its law, its bureaucracies, even its music. In each of these domains, as in many others, rationalizing trends were developed to an extent unprecedented in the West and unparalleled anywhere else. Bureaucracy was both a prime example and a vehicle of these trends.

As he did with all the other forms of social action and power that interested him, Weber developed an "ideal type" of modern bureaucratic organization, a model of the institutional and operational logic associated with a particular type of administrative organization. Weber categorized and compared different forms in which power, administration, economy, and social action were institutionalized and exercised. Those forms were distilled by him into a limited range of abstracted types, which allowed for comparison and detection of systematic similarities and differences among different forms, over vast geographical space and swathes of time.

Of course, Weber stressed, such "ideal types" were nowhere found in unalloyed form. There will always be legacies of earlier forms, impurities, pathologies, corruptions, breakdowns, mixtures. But ideal types are not fantasies. They are disciplined "as if" thought experiments, intended to lay bare institutional logics immanent in real structures, forms, and practices, even if variably mixed and dominant there. Real-world organizations or economies or polities never operate exclusively according to any one such logic. There are typically competing logics at work, some inherited, some on the way in, some on the way out; and there are also other forces of context and circumstance that intervene. But the elements of a well-constructed ideal type are not haphazardly or randomly selected. Rather, as Selznick observed of later constructions of his own, such elements "are not unrelated to one another; on the contrary, there are determinate and systematic connections among them."[5] Identifying such elements and their connections allows one to stand above the unmanageable detail and complexity of the world and detect systematic pressures, tendencies, and trends, which a worm's eye view will miss.

To characterize the novelty and distinctiveness of modern administrative organizations, as they had developed out of absolutist states and had been adopted and adapted by capitalist enterprises, Weber drew his famous bureaucratic ideal type from Prussian administrative theory and European political history. How would an organization operate and look, if nothing else mattered in it but the logic of bureaucracy? Not just like any bureaucracy today but more like such a bureaucracy than like organizations where that logic is absent or the logic of another form of organization dominates. To the extent that an administrative organization is bureaucratic, rather than, say, patrimonial, particular things follow.

The bureaucratic type of organization is ordered by rules that apply generally and impersonally; business is discharged, both in state and capitalist bureaucracies "according to *calculable rules* and 'without regard to persons'";[6] indeed, "bureaucracy develops the more perfectly, the more it is 'dehumanized,' the more completely it succeeds in eliminating from official business love, hatred, and all purely personal, irrational, and emotional elements which escape calculation."[7]

Distinctive of the modern bureaucrat's way of working are separations between the official role and other engagements that, in other times and other ways of ordering affairs, were not sharply distinguished, if at all. These include demands of family, caste, friendships; particularistic engagements of all sorts. These are to be treated as "private" not "public" or "official" concerns; parts of life out of work, not at it. And in bureaucracies that distinction—between what pertains to the official role and what should have no role there—is crucial. Official is separate from private in every domain: workplace, monies, equipment, loyalties. Someone's private, personal concerns might well be of great concern to that person, but they should not influence what he or she does as a bureaucrat. Admission to work in a modern bureaucracy is based on impersonal criteria, formally defined. Professional obligations *at* work, too, are based not on loyalty to particular persons in or above the bureaucracy but rather to the official roles they occupy and to the organization's "*impersonal* and *functional* purposes."[8] The individual bureaucrat "cannot squirm out of the apparatus into which he has been harnessed. . . . In the great majority of cases he is only a powerless cog in a ceaselessly moving mechanism which prescribes to him an essentially fixed route of march."[9]

According to Weber, there is a fundamental difference in the role and responsibilities of leaders and bureaucrats. The leader *of* a bureaucracy does *not* occupy a bureaucratic role—for the leader is concerned with goals; the bureaucrat with means. Leaders look outward, to what they might or should do in the world; they make policy. Bureaucrats assist leaders in doing so; they administer those policies. These are separate domains. The leader leads but does not administer; the bureaucrat administers and is quite unsuited to lead. Administration is no small concern, and contrary to common stereotypes "independent decision-making and imaginative organizational capabilities in matters of detail are usually also demanded of the bureaucrat, and very often expected even in large matters."[10] Nevertheless, there is a categorical distinction between the work of the leader and that of the bureaucrat. Indeed, in Weber's terms there is something oxymoronic about Selznick's title, "leadership *in* administration." Leadership *of* administration, *with*, even *through*; but not *in*; for the leader should ideally stay out of administration, just as, conversely, administrators should be kept away from leadership.

Ideally indeed the distinction between leadership and administration should apply not only to jobs but to the people who fill them. For it is a matter not just of job descriptions but of "the ethos of *office*."[11] The bureaucrat is properly concerned only with implementing, *sine ira ac studio* (without anger or bias), ends arrived at by the leader. That is why Weber was opposed to bureaucrats becoming political leaders, as he feared had happened in post-Bismarck Germany. They were unsuited to the job of goal selection and policy making because their "ethos of office" required them faithfully and impersonally to implement decisions made by designated leaders. This rendered them radically ill equipped to make and take personal responsibility for decisions. Their role is paradigmatically instrumental; they are "cogs." They have a trained capacity for large-scale administration and for that very reason a trained incapacity for making policy. If they try, they will make a hash of it.[12]

Selznick: The Social Structure of Organizations

According to Weber, then, modern bureaucracies are distinguished from their forebears by the systematic combination of formality, impersonality, and rationality of their structures and processes. Selznick does not dispute this claim, and he explores its implications in *Law, Society, and Industrial Justice*, but the special concern of his early writings lies elsewhere. For what distinguishes bureaucrats from, say, patrimonial administrators is an uncertain and insufficient guide to how they actually work. You need to find the specific weight of these distinctive characteristics, as against others that might or might not be shared with different organizations. That might lead you to emphasize quite different elements of the same organization, elements that might otherwise be overlooked. A single-minded concern with what is distinctive might lead an analyst to ignore crucial aspects of the workings of bureaucracies, if only because they seem nothing new.

Given Weber's recognition that real types are never ideal, a sociologist who thought as Weber did might be led to investigate social pressures, informal groupings, intra- and interbureaucratic rivalries and so on, that impede the universal sway of bureaucratic rationality in the world.

Weber was aware of such things, and their existence is not inconsistent with what he argued. But in his sociological writings, though less in his essays on contemporary German politics, he said little about them. Selznick's emphasis on the social structure of large "formal" organizations, and the ever-presence of informal and personal pressures within them, went well beyond Weber's. His own contributions to organizational theory represent, most gently interpreted, a systematic supplement to Weber; more harshly, a substantial if implicit critique.

Selznick did not see informal groupings, attachments, rivalries, and so on, as a kind of residue of earlier times and forms yet to be purged from modern rationalistic organization but rather as an inevitable complement of such organizations. They are intrinsic, *part* of the (informal) operational logic of modern large-scale organizations, not an extraneous brake on them. Thus, to understand the characteristic workings of a bureaucracy the logics of such groupings, attachments, rivalries, and so on, need to be investigated in their own right. But that had rarely been done. Selznick was not alone in noticing this gap[13] and in seeking to remedy it, but his work was of special consequence.

Selznick knew that Weber was aware of such tendencies, but he also knew that they are not what Weber was concerned about theorizing because in his scholarly writings Weber was concerned with what *distinguishes* modern bureaucracies from alternatives, while Selznick is concerned with what is *characteristic* of them, whether or not it is unique. And the two interests can lead in quite different directions. Formality, impersonality, rationality might well distinguish modern bureaucracies from others. However, in accounting for what these bureaucracies are actually like, or why they do what they do, they might be less central. On the world-historical plane of comparisons where Weber put his ideal types to work, the *distinctive* is what is crucial. However, if one sought to explore the dynamics of particular organizations at particular times in a particular society, what is characteristic is key.

In his first published academic work, and his first piece on bureaucracy, Selznick captures well this distinction of purposes, of research programs, which many critics of Weber have ignored. Writing of Weber's account, "the outstanding work in the literature we have at present," Selznick observes:

> Weber's main interest was in the development of rational bureaucratic behaviour as a break from the ties of seignorial leadership set up under the feudal system. The development of centralized hierarchical administration did in fact

involve a tendency to vitiate that particular kind of personal influence. But what Weber seems to have only partly understood is that *the dynamics of the administrative apparatus itself* created new personal influences—those of the administrators themselves seeking their own ends and engaging, as newly powerful participants, in power relationships. . . . Although recognizing them, he seems to have neglected their theoretical importance.[14]

Selznick's approach is not "antiformalist," in the sense of denying the significance of formal rules in large organizations. Though his emphasis in these early writings was on informal structures and pressures, he stressed that "it does not follow, of course, that those patterns are uninfluenced by the character of the formal organization."[15] Indeed, in the work in which Selznick most systematically articulates his "institutionalism," he writes: "The technical organization, the rationally designed instrument, the legal system . . . is not the only source of order within the group or enterprise or society, but it can often be the most important."[16] As with so much else in his work, so here: To emphasize one aspect of reality is not automatically to deny significance to its apparent opposite. The task is to explore their interrelations and mutual implications. Nor, finally, was Selznick the first to notice the significance of informal patterns in formal organizations.[17] He did, however, offer one of the most perceptive and theoretically sophisticated examinations of them and of their far-going implications.

Selznick came early to this appreciation of the role and significance of informal structures and processes, in and around formal organizations. His master's thesis in 1942, and the revision published as "an approach to a theory of bureaucracy" in 1943, had emphasized that every organization generates an informal structure and particular ways of operating, as members are driven by their specific situations, problems, and needs, both operational and psychological, to make sense of what they do and work out ways of doing it. By these various processes the organization's official goals "are modified (abandoned, deflected, or elaborated)."[18] One result already noted in his political essays and *TVA* is that ultimate ideals are commonly squeezed out by more immediate goals in bureaucracies, "not because men are evil or unintelligent, but because the 'ultimate' formulations are not *helpful* in the constant effort to achieve that series of equilibria which represent behavioral solutions to the specific problems which day-to-day living poses." Some such ideals go under because they specify nothing concrete, but others suffer because though they do specify something to be done, they "require actions which conflict with what must be done in the daily business of running an organization. In that conflict the professed goals will tend to go down in defeat, usually through the process of being extensively ignored."[19]

One common consequence of these tendencies has already been mentioned: "the 'tragedy' of organization . . . the fact of organizational frustration as a persistent characteristic of the age of relative democracy . . . processes inherent in and internal to organization as such which tend to frustrate action towards professed goals."[20] Michels looms over this first statement of position, as such processes are said to "tend to concentrate the locus of power in the hands of the officials." However, the same processes can lead in other directions, too. This became plain when the general argument was extended in an article written at the same time as *TVA* and incorporated into that book.[21]

Modern organizations are "formal structures in the sense that they represent rationally ordered instruments for the achievement of stated goals." However, "non-rational dimensions of organizational behavior" can never be eliminated. For there is a "fundamental paradox" at the base of formal and rationalized organizations: These nonrational dimensions "remain at once indispensable to the continued existence of the system of coordination and at the same time the source of friction, dilemma, doubt, and ruin." They are indispensable, first because the formal system "is itself only an aspect of a concrete social structure made up of individuals who may interact as *wholes*, not simply in terms of their formal roles within the system" and second because system and structure "are alike subject to the pressure of an institutional environment to which some over-all adjustment must be made." Formal plans can never account for the whole of structure and environment, yet "at the same time, that which is not included in the abstract design . . . is vitally relevant to the maintenance and development of the formal system itself."

That people are not just roles but wholes complicates formal organization and control in many ways. While delegation assigns powers and functions to role-incumbents, these are assumed by persons with their own interests, priorities, needs, attachments, and goals. As a result, "individual personalities may offer resistance to the demands made upon them by the official conditions of delegation."[22] Nor is this an occasional or preventable matter. It is endemic. Indeed,

> In large organizations, deviations from the formal system tend to become institutionalized, so that "unwritten laws" and informal associations are established. Institutionalization removes such deviations from the realm of personality differences, transforming them into a persistent structural aspect

of formal organizations. These institutionalized rules and modes of informal cooperation are normally attempts by participants in the formal organization to control the group relations which form the environment of organizational decisions.

This being the case, two things follow. One is that, as Chester Barnard had insisted,[23] formal organizations are necessarily "cooperative systems" that depend on both control and consent; one cannot easily exert the former without marshalling the latter. Secondly, while formal rules are never irrelevant to an understanding of a large organization, they are equally never sufficient. Rather:

> A proper understanding of the organizational process must make it possible to interpret changes in the formal system . . . in their relation to the informal and unavowed ties of friendship, class loyalty, power cliques, or external commitment. That is what it means "to know the score."

One thing quickly evident to anyone who "knows the score" (or who had read *Enquiry* or *TVA*) is "the recalcitrance of the tools of action. We are inescapably committed to the mediation of human structures which are at once indispensable to our goals and at the same time stand between them and ourselves."[24] In Weber's language of cogs and machines, one might say there is a lot of grinding of gears—except that people are at the core of it all, indispensable to execute the will of leaders, but able, sometimes happy, to impede it too.

To cope with such potentially recalcitrant, but also indispensable, agents, organizations resort to "self-defensive mechanisms" of various sorts. As *TVA* demonstrated, co-optation is one, but not the only one, of these. Its significance is

> not simply that there is a change in or a broadening of leadership, and that this is an adaptive response, but also that *this change is consequential for the character and role of the organization*. . . . it is an adaptive response of a cooperative system to a stable need, generating transformations which reflect constraints enforced by the recalcitrant tools of action.[25]

These are general tendencies of organizational life. They do not supersede formal structure, do not render it irrelevant. But they complicate it, intervene in its operations. They are not merely inconvenient contingencies. To know what is actually going on in an organization, it will never be enough to read its "mission statements," full as they generally are of "unanalyzed abstractions,"[26] or to learn its formal structure. There is so much else in play, in varying ways, in different organizations and circumstances. To know how such pressures, tensions, and tendencies will work out, theory must be supplemented with close observation, particularly of the informal structures that develop and of the workings of the means chosen for declared ends, which they may well subvert.

But if these sorts of pressures to detach means from ends are ever-present in organizations, is it possible to counter them, to impose one's will on an organization? Well, apparently, yes: The Bolsheviks had understood the problem, and, though in aid of values Selznick opposed, had developed a complex and sophisticated organizational solution. Churches, armies, business organizations, all of which Selznick studied, also confronted these issues. How they did so could only be partially illuminated by Weber's insights because one needs to explore the complexity of *institutional character*, as he did not, and what is required to harness, direct, and redirect it.

ORGANIZATIONS AND INSTITUTIONS

I mentioned in Chapter Two that for Marx "class" is a concept with a social theory built into it, whereas "bureaucracy" never was. It begins to be for Trotsky, and it certainly is for Weber. By the time Selznick wrote *Leadership*, "institution" had come to be such a concept for him. Like the others a common enough word, it took on specific content and weight in this and subsequent work. Institutions have a host of features that his early writings had illuminated and that he now came to theorize.

Selznick frequently offered a capsule definition of institutionalization: "In what is perhaps its most significant meaning . . . to *infuse with value* beyond the technical requirements of the task at hand."[27] He later came to regret the single focus of that definition, for it seemed to suggest an overly psychologistic point, whereas there were many processes involved in institutionalization.[28] *The Moral Commonwealth* offers a larger conception: "Whether it is a group or a practice or both, a social form becomes institutionalized as, through growth and adaptation, it takes on a distinctive character or function, becomes a receptacle of vested interests, or is charged with meaning as a vehicle of personal satisfaction or aspiration."[29] Notwithstanding the amplification, Selznick never doubted that "infusing with value" captured the central, key, component of the process.

His writings explore two distinct but necessarily interrelated sorts of "infusion." One, the *process* of institutionalization, typically happens over time, intransitively as it were, undesigned by anyone in particular. It wells up from below in many organizations, as their members come to treat them as more than neutral instruments; develop group and institutional attachments, loyalties, and rivalries; adopt and promote institutional values; create and adapt to an "internal social world."[30] It also develops as a result of organizations' dealings with their external environment: "As a business, a college, or a government agency develops a distinctive clientele, the enterprise gains the stability that comes with a secure source of support, an easy channel of communication. At the same time, it loses flexibility. The process of institutionalization has set in."[31] In these and other often gradual, incremental and adaptive ways,

> group values are formed . . . together they define the commitments of the organization and give it a distinctive identity. In other words, to the extent that they are natural communities, organizations have a history; and this history is compounded of discernible and repetitive modes of responding to internal and external pressures. As these responses crystallize into definite patterns, a social structure emerges. The more fully developed its social structure, the more will the organization become valued for itself, not as a tool but as an institutional fulfillment of group identity and aspiration.
>
> Institutionalization is a *process*. It is something that happens to an organization over time, reflecting the organization's own distinctive history, the people who have been in it, the groups it embodies and the vested interests they have created, and the way it has adapted to its environment.[32]

As the leaders of the TVA showed by default, leaders ignore the incidents of such institutionalization at their peril.

Another way in which an institution might be infused with value, however, is transitive, active. Commonly it starts at the top. Here leaders seek to understand its values and character, to imbue it with values they consider appropriate (which means not merely valuable in general or in principle, but apt for *this* institution with its particular history, character and competences), or change the values with which it is infused. These are complex and difficult tasks, but they can be achieved, as the Bolsheviks, certain churches, armies, and business organizations, showed.

The two aspects of institutionalization are linked. Leaders must always be aware of the socially embedded, value-infused character of the materials with which they deal. A leader of an institution who treats it as a mere mechanical instrument will flounder, oblivious of sources of institutional recalcitrance, unable to summon potential sources of institutional energies. But someone who believes "I am their leader. I must follow them," has grasped only part of the truth of institutionalization.

Infusion with value can be a conscious, deliberate task of molding, fashioning; not just a spontaneous process of adaptation, fitting in. Not only can it be, but at crucial, character-forming, and transforming moments in an institution's development it must be. It is the leader's task to embody purpose in the life of the institution, and that will involve both fitting "the aims of the organization to the spontaneous interests of the group within it, and conversely to bind parochial group egotism to larger loyalties and aspirations."[33] Indeed where a leader is adept, the two senses of institutionalization merge, for "the leader is an agent of institutionalization, offering a guiding hand to a process that would otherwise occur more haphazardly, more readily subject to the accidents of circumstance and history."[34] Analytically, however, one can treat institutionalization as *process* apart from what might be called institutionalization as *project*, and in what follows I will.

Process

The process of institutionalization affects organizations in ways that an understanding focused on bureaucratic ideal types or managerial organization charts is destined to overlook. This is true for several reasons. The first is that the conceptual language we use, perhaps appropriate for some organizations, is inappropriate to the extent that they have become institutionalized. It is common to talk of organizations as tools, mechanisms, instruments, indeed even weapons. But though Selznick himself had written this way often enough—most notably, of course, in *The Organizational Weapon*—by the time of *Leadership in Administration* his language had changed. Some organizations, those that have undergone institutionalization, are described in a quite different style, full of organic metaphors, psychological parallels, humanistic and naturalistic terms, given as much or more to spontaneous growth and adaptation as to planned design and direction, bearers of histories as much as servers of purposes. Thus whereas an organization pure and simple is "a technical instrument for mobilizing human energies and directing them toward set aims . . . an *expendable tool,* a rational instrument engineered to do a job . . . [a]n 'institution' is more nearly a natural product of social needs and pressures—a responsive, adaptive organism."[35] The organic character of much of social life becomes an enduring theme of his work.

As with Weber the distinction is idealized, for the world is always full of combinations, "complex mixtures of both designed and responsive behavior,"[36] and "the existence of an institution is inescapably a relative matter and one of degree. Groups and practices are more or less institutionalized, that is, more or less expendable, more or less infused with value, more or less imprinted with a special character or competence, more or less tied to an effective social base, more or less preoccupied with maintaining themselves as 'going concerns.'"[37] Here too, however, we learn something when we find it is a closer approximation to one of the ideal types than to the other:

> . . . organizations are technical instruments, designed as means to definite goals. They are judged on engineering premises; they are expendable. Institutions . . . may be partly engineered, but they have also a "natural" dimension. They are products of interaction and adaptation; they become the receptacles of group idealism; they are less readily expendable.[38]

Organizations, then, become institutionalized when and to the extent that people cease to treat them as mere means but become attached in various ways to them or to parts of them or to conceptions of them, value them, connect their goals with them. Over time, such ways of relating to the institution really do seem to take on a life of their own and interact with the lives of those within them:

> The formal, technical system is therefore never more than a part of the living enterprise we deal with in action. The persons and groups who make it up are not content to be treated as manipulable or expendable. As human beings are not mere tools they have their own needs for self-protection and self-fulfillment—needs that may either sustain the formal system or undermine it. These human relations are a great reservoir of energy. They may be directed in constructive ways toward desired ends or they may become recalcitrant sources of frustration. One objective of sound management practice is to direct and control these internal social pressures.[39]

These human dimensions of institutions, then, offer both constraints and opportunities to institutional leaders—constraints because they render less malleable, tractable, replaceable, fungible, flexible, the institutional material with which a leader must work; opportunities because a successful leader can call on loyalties, felt imperatives, shared goals, unspoken but powerful traditions, sometimes even devotion from members of the institution. A successful leader must be aware of the constraints but at the same time capable of summoning the opportunities.

Administrative leaders often are aware of these things, without explicitly registering them. Administrative analysts, who are in the explicitness business, often ignore them. Institutional analysts take them seriously.

Selznick's version of institutional analysis is characteristically *humanist*, a term to which we will return in later chapters, because it seeks to theorize the implications of a familiar fact: Organizations are collections, "natural communities,"[40] of persons. And it is sociological because it observes that these persons are not random collections of atoms, but societies: organized, with patterned relationships, envies, rivalries, ambitions, goals and attachments, and with pasts that influence their present. So:

> When we say that the Standard Oil company or the Department of Agriculture is to be studied as an institution, we usually mean that we are going to pay some attention to its history and to the way it has been influenced by the social environment . . . Thus, the phrase "as a social institution" suggests an emphasis on problems and experiences that are not adequately accounted for within the narrower framework of administrative analysis.[41]

An institution, then, is a social structure, one that has typically evolved over time. Thus, "to become the master of his organization, the leader must know how to deal with the social structure in all its dimensions."[42] Like traditions, one cannot simply decree institutions or even the process of institutionalization. They develop, in manners often unwilled by anyone, at least anyone in particular; and at times they fail to develop. However, one can seek to channel such development, redirect it, draw on it, and shape it to particular purposes. Concern with such things is the province of the institutional leader.

Project

It is common to view a leader's role in relation to the organization she or he heads as equipping it best to achieve organizational goals. Had Weber given any thought to what leaders might do within the administration rather than in the wider world, that, presumably, is how he would have seen it. It was also the way the school of "scientific management," one of Selznick's targets, did see it. Even today, a great deal of work in organization theory has to do with how to improve organizational efficiency. Certainly efficiency concerns are important; in many "routine" aspects of administration they are central. And there are many such aspects. For such jobs, and organizations typically have many of them, management is required, but *leadership* is relatively "dispensable."

However, there is another set of concerns that are more distinctively those of a leader than improving its capacity to achieve routine, preset tasks. That is to confront "the question: What shall we *do?* What shall we *be?*"[43] That is not a routine matter of getting particular jobs done faster or at less cost than otherwise or working out "the detailed applications of established canons."[44] Rather, it is a matter of making *critical* decisions that have deeper, more pervasive consequences for the nature of the institution. Such decisions distinctively require leaders

> *to choose key values and to create a social structure that embodies them.* The task of building values into social structure is not necessarily consistent, especially in early stages, with rules of administration based on economic premises. Only after key choices have been made and related policies firmly established can criteria of efficient administration play a significant role. Even then, the smooth-running machine must accept disturbance when critical problems of adaptation and change arise.[45]

Organizations differ in the extent to which institutionalized self-understandings are important to them; they are less so the more precise their goals and technical their operations.[46] And lower levels of an institution are often primarily and rightly concerned with considerations of efficiency; "the logic of efficiency loses force, however, as we approach the top of the pyramid. Problems at this level are more resistant to the ordinary approach of management experts."[47] Moreover, the leader *must* connect both means and ends and be concerned with them both. This is a lesson from Dewey, not Weber.

In the absence of effective leadership, and by contrast with many routine operations of organizations that can run themselves, it is possible for an institution to wither, lose its way, decline, while its organizational base grows, perhaps even thrives. Inadequate institutional leaders often confuse the two processes, with sad results. Thus,

> The default of leadership shows itself in an acute form when *organizational* achievement or survival is confounded with *institutional* success. To be sure, no institutional leader can avoid concern for the minimum conditions of continued organizational existence. But he fails if he permits sheer organizational achievement, in resources, stability, or reputation, to become the criterion of his success. A university led by administrators without a clear sense of values to be achieved may fail dismally while steadily growing larger and more secure.[48]

Within an institution, when members of an institution cease to recognize "the business we are really in," they might at the same time manage to do more and worse. Deinstitutionalization may well be occurring.

TASKS OF LEADERSHIP

Cultivation of Institutional Character

As in our personal lives, many activities and decisions in an institution have, we might say, no ontological significance. We can change them, even self-consciously commit to changing them, and still stay the same. Selznick calls this "static adaptation." The lives of institutions, as of persons, are full of such changes that might affect the ways we behave but that don't do anything special to what we *are*. However, some sorts of experiences or decisions go deeper. These include and can effect "character-defining commitments." When actively pursued, they aim at "dynamic adaptations," "the reconstruction of need, the change in posture and strategy, the commitment to new types of satisfaction"[49] whether among persons or institutions. The student of institutions is particularly interested in dynamic decision making, and the specific type of task with which institutional leaders are charged is the taking of such decisions. They occur "in the shadowy area where administration and policy meet";[50] for these decisions bear on the *character* of the organization, a concept that, as we have seen, has a deep and enduring significance in Selznick's thought.

Just as psychoanalysts speak of a person's character and identity, so Selznick understands organizations to have characters and identities. The model of human psychology is apt, not because Selznick considers institutions to be humans writ large, or simply a collection of people, but because "it is the *logic*, the *type* of analysis which is pertinent."[51] This is a view he was to express throughout his writings.

The process that makes an institution of an organization goes directly to its character. It "produces a distinct identity for the organization. Where institutionalization is well advanced, distinctive outlooks, habits, and other commitments are unified, coloring all aspects of organizational life and lending it a *social integration* that goes well beyond formal coordination and command."[52] It is common these days to speak of the "culture" of an institution, but for Selznick, though character includes culture, it is not reducible to it. He made the point only much later, in *The Moral Commonwealth*, but it is a good point:

> As applied to institutions, "character" is a broader idea than "culture." Culture is the symbolic expression of shared perception, valuation, and belief. Therefore the idea of "organizational culture" properly emphasizes the creation of common understandings regarding purpose and policy. The character of an

organization includes its culture, but something more as well. . . . The character of a company or a trade union owes much to the structure of the industry, the skills of employees or members, the alliances that can be fashioned, and many other practical limits and opportunities. Attitudes and beliefs account for only part of an organization's distinctive character.[53]

An expression of the distinctive character of an institution is its *"distinctive competence or inadequacy."* Indeed, these three concepts are interdefined. They:

all refer to the same basic process—the transformation of an engineered, technical arrangement of building blocks into a social organism. This transition goes on unconsciously and inevitably wherever leeway for evolution and adaptation is allowed by the system of technical controls; and at least some such leeway exists in all but the most narrowly circumscribed organizations. Leadership has the job of guiding the transition from organization to institution so that the ultimate result effectively embodies desired aims and standards.[54]

What is distinctive of institutional *analysis*, then, is that it "asks the question: What is the bearing of an existing or proposed procedure on the distinctive role and character of the enterprise?"[55] The specific task of the institutional *leader* is to make the critical decisions that affect that distinctive character.

Recognizing, defining, fostering, nurturing, taking account of institutional history, identity, and character, knowing "the business we are in"; these are all among the essential tasks of leadership. And this is so even when—perhaps especially when—the aim is to change institutional character; "a wise leader faces up to the character of his organization, although he may do so only as a prelude to designing a strategy that will alter it."[56] Whether maintaining or changing, a leader *"is primarily an expert in the promotion and protection of values."*[57] He must "define the mission of the enterprise,"[58] a matter of some complexity given the tendency of institutions to define themselves for themselves, if allowed to drift. And definition is not enough. We have already seen that generalized statements of purpose, "unanalyzed abstractions," are unlikely to be of much effect. They must be *infused* into the activities, values, self-understanding of an institution and its members.

It is not common to discuss the TVA and the Communist Party in the same breath, and

The TVA and Boshevik experiences are of course widely different. Yet in each there is an emergent institutional pattern that decisively affects the competence of an organization to frame and execute desired policies. Commitments to ways of acting and responding are built into the organization. When integrated, these commitments define the "character" of the organization.[59]

The TVA had institutionalized certain commitments and constituencies that in turn molded what the institution would do and how. They also blocked it from doing other things in other ways. Much of this was inadvertent but consequential for the character and identity of the institution. The Bolsheviks, on the other hand, knew well that their party was "not like other parties," and that was no accident. In their mission to transform recruits into deployable agents, a lot of character-defining activity needed to be done. And much of what Selznick describes is how that was achieved, how one party among many in the socialist movement systematically differentiated its product, transformed its party structure, including "the attitudes and actions of the membership," recruited selectively, educated intensively, in general *molded* the character of members of the party to which they belonged, the "combat party," a party of a new kind. Thus, his study of Bolshevik organizational strategy was at base an "investigation of organizational character-formation. . . . Special measures must be taken to 'Bolshevize' the organization, that is, to see that its own commitments—to structure, personnel and doctrine—are so firmly set as to be virtually irreversible."[60]

Means and Ends

Selznick, as we saw in Chapter Two and will recall frequently, shared Dewey's distrust of "pernicious dualisms," central among them that between means and ends. The latter manifests itself in a range of defects of leadership. One of these is a "characteristic threat to the integration of purpose and commitment—hence to the adequate definition of institutional mission . . . an excessive or premature technological orientation. This posture is marked by a concentration on ways and means."[61] Such "retreat to technology" often takes the form of treating ends as given, quite independent from the organizational means used to achieve them. This flies against Selznick's deep conviction that ends and means, policy and administration, are inextricably intertwined as soon as institutionalization transforms an organization from a simple instrument to a "living organism," where goals affect means and means are rarely neutral in their impact on ends.

More generally, the retreat to technology offends the most deeply un-Weberian lesson he had learned from Dewey and the other philosophical pragmatists, about the continuity between means and ends. This issue is a deep and recurring theme in his work. Dewey frequently attacked philosophers for slighting means and focusing only on ends. Selznick criticized managers for doing the reverse. Withdrawal from reasoned consideration of ends "endangers the central task of goal-setting, particularly when there is need to accommodate a technical 'logic' to political conditions and aims."[62] And even when goals are settled, "the necessary means may have still to be created. Creating the means is, furthermore, not a narrow technical matter; it involves molding the social character of the organization. Leadership goes beyond efficiency (1) when it sets the basic mission of the organization and (2) when it creates a social organism capable of fulfilling that mission."[63]

Goals are not self-sufficient; means are not merely technical measures to reach them. On the contrary, some of our most exalted ideals, such as "education, science, creativity, or freedom," depend on "congenial though often mundane administrative arrangements." Conversely, "more restricted values, such as the maintenance of a particular industrial competence" also "involve ideals of excellence, ideals that must be built into the social structure of the enterprise and become part of its basic character. In either case, a too ready acceptance of neutral techniques of efficiency, whatever their other merits, will contribute little to this institutional development and may even retard it."[64]

So the continuity of means and ends has real practical significance, but the point is theoretical, too, for the focus on technology and efficiency "finds comfort in a positivist theory of administration" that rests on and deploys "a radical separation of fact and value"[65] to enable it to evade responsibility for discussion of goals. Even if values are *ultimately* unjustifiable by reason, "this cannot justify the judgment in a particular case that the anticipated irreducible element has actually been reached."[66] As his normative confidence increased in later writings, "the anticipated irreducible element" tended to recede from view.

Institutional Development

Two knacks crucial for institutional leaders seeking to "infuse value" into an institution are a sense of timing and a sense of proportion. These are themes that Selznick first raises as specific competences of institutional leaders, but they come to play a significant role in his thought about social development more generally. The general point is that, again like persons, institutions evolve, indeed exhibit recurrent patterns and stages of evolution. The particular implication is simple but of broad application: What is appropriate for an institution (or person) at a certain stage of growth might be quite inappropriate at another, and so there is "a need to place the interpretation of organizational behavior in historical perspective. Apparently similar events or practices should not be compared directly, but only as their relation to the organization's stage of development is determined."[67]

At a certain stage of development, particular sorts of tasks might need to be accomplished. These will often differ from what is needed earlier or later. If the tasks necessary at earlier stages were successfully accomplished, an insightful leader will turn to other, different goals that might well need to be dealt with in different ways, perhaps even by a new leader and new personnel, people with skills apt at one stage but not another.

Thus, a key step in institutional development has to do with forging and maintaining institutional identity and integrity. These are key elements of institutionalization, for unless identity is clear, secure, and understood, "what business we are really in" is always going to be ambiguous. But if it is crucial that identity be secure, and though it needs to be guarded against risk, its security is not always equally threatened; the risks it faces are not always the same or equally great. A sensible leader will recognize that:

> Although every effective policy requires sustaining social conditions, the urgency of this need varies greatly. It is most important when aims are not well defined, when external direction is not easily imposed or easily maintained, when fluid situations require constant adaptation, and when goals or values are vulnerable to corruption. This open-endedness . . . generates the key problems of institutional leadership. Among these is the defense of institutional integrity—the persistence of an organization's distinctive values, competence, and role.[68]

The key question is how *precarious* an institution's values are. Values insecure at some stage might be quite safe at another. It is a mistake to ignore this in recommending how an institution should respond, even to similar sources of threat to the same values. Where values are precarious, organizational activity of a particular kind might be necessary to cement them. If that has been successfully achieved, however, the focus can more safely shift to other problems and other ways of responding to them. This gives particular salience to recognition of circumstances where values are vulnerable and others when they are in good shape, and then to fashioning responses, *different* responses, to protect them in the former circumstance and build on their strength in the latter. Perhaps the price of liberty is not eternal vigilance, then, or at least not vigilance of the same intensity focused on the same threats, limited to the same range of responses. *Responsiveness* to the particular problems an organization faces at a particular stage in its development is a nuanced and variable affair.

Selznick discusses several examples of the evolution of strategies, in keeping with the evolution of the institutions to which they are applied. One is drawn from earlier work. Thus, one important strategy for developing integrity where it is weak involves strengthening the *autonomy* of the nascent institution and particularly of its elites, who bear key responsibilities for institutionalizing its particular culture and values. Here, too, these need to be developed when they are undeveloped, their autonomy nurtured when it is precarious. But if the institution is successful, the priority of nurturing such autonomy will wane. Thus Selznick discusses the Comintern's move from early isolation to later common front policies. The first task was to develop the communist combat party's "autonomy as an elite, isolating itself from the pressures of the political arena *until it was ready to resist those pressures.* . . . the Bolsheviks wished to maintain an institution embodying a precarious value: a party competent to deploy members as deployable agents. A period of organizational isolation, fostered by ultra-left propaganda, helped to contribute the sustaining social conditions."[69] That done, strategy changed:

> After 1935, organizational isolation was definitively—and permanently—rejected. Open Communist propaganda was increasingly retired to the background, and the party turned to slogans of "unity," "peace," and similar generalities that might offer access to wider sections of the population. . . . In effect the conclusion was drawn that the day for worrying about the Communist integrity of the parties was past; the basic weapon had been forged; the time for wielding it effectively had arrived.[70]

The point can be generalized: "It follows from our general theory that isolation is necessary during periods of incubation and maturation, but may be modified when this character-forming task has been accomplished. Moreover, the more readily subject to outside pressure a given value is, the more necessary is this isolation."[71] As we will see in later chapters, these simple developmental insights have significant implications for, among other things, that "master ideal" of a legal order, the rule of law.

Finally, there are the tasks set for a leader once an organization becomes an institution. Most briefly put, those tasks require "institutional responsibility," and that, as readers of *Enquiry* might already have learned, "can be summarized under two headings: the avoidance of opportunism and the avoidance of utopianism."[72] The opportunist pursues short-term advantages with inadequate concern for "how change affects personal or institutional identity." The utopian "hopes to avoid hard choices by a flight to abstractions" or hopes "the solution of technical problems will solve institutional problems." Successful institutional leadership

> steers a course between utopianism and opportunism. Its responsibility consists in . . . adapting aspiration to the character of the organization, bearing in mind that what the organization has been will affect what it can be and do; and in transcending bare organizational survival by seeing that specialized decisions do not weaken or confuse the distinctive identity of the enterprise.[73]

The Statesman

It is possible to read *Leadership in Administration* as a primer for managers: Be aware of this, do that, avoid the other. It has often been read that way among business enthusiasts, among them the eponymous founder of Ralph Lauren Sport Corporation.[74] However, large claims recur in this small book for the essentially *political* character of leadership and for the leader as in truth a statesman. Thus, Selznick explains that leadership in administrative organizations,

> like the larger study of government and society, requires our profoundest intellectual concern. We shall not find any simple prescriptions for sound organizational leadership; nor will it be purchased with a bag of tricks and gadgets. It requires nothing less than the proper ordering of human affairs, including the establishment of social order, the determination of public interest, and the defense of critical values. Thus conceived, our inquiry has ancient roots. The main problems and issues have been known for a long time, although they need to be restated for the purposes of administrative theory.[75]

Selznick argues for a continuity between administrative leadership and what might be called high politics on two separate grounds. The first has to do with continuities between the institutions more normally called political and those of business and other realms of life. The second concerns the character of the tasks involved.

At the first level, Selznick is aware that most people who have sought to understand leadership "have centered their attention on *political* statesmen, leaders of whole communities who sit in the high places where great issues are joined and settled."[76] He applauds such a focus but believes it must be complemented because:

Ours is a pluralist society made up of many large, influential, relatively autonomous groups. . . . [commanding] . . . large resources; their leaders are inevitably responsible for the material and psychological well-being of numerous constituents; and they have become increasingly *public* in nature, attached to such
interests and dealing with such problems as affect the welfare of the entire
community. In our society the need for statesmanship is widely diffused and
beset by special problems. An understanding of leadership in both public and
private organizations must have a high place on the agenda of social inquiry.[77]

Moreover, quite apart from *where* they do it, *what* leaders have to do in
large-scale institutions inevitably has a political character. This might involve struggles for power, but that is not of the essence. Rather, what connects the leader of an organization and a political leader in the more common understanding of the term is

the quality of statesmanship which deals with current issues, not for themselves alone but according to their long-run implications for the role and
meaning of the group. . . . it is the function of the leader-statesman—whether
of a nation or a private association—to define the ends of group existence, to
design an enterprise distinctively adapted to these ends, and to see that that
design becomes a living reality. These tasks are not routine.[78]

Because leaders in many sorts of organizations are involved in such areas
of decision, at least from time to time, "creative men are needed—more in
some circumstances than in others—who know how to transform a neutral
body of men into a committed polity.[79] These men are called leaders; their
profession is politics."[80]

IDEALS IN THE WORLD

I began this chapter with Hugh Heclo, and I will end with him. He writes:

Look not only into the book but behind the book to the questions that lie
behind the questions, and you begin to see the crucial thing about *Leadership
in Administration*. "To infuse with value beyond the technical requirements of
the task at hand"—So ran the book's famous definition of institutionalizing
what is otherwise merely an organization. With these words Selznick was in
fact also describing his own intellectual enterprise. Obligated simply by "the
technical requirements of the task at hand," the social scientist in him needed
to do only what so many academics did do and would continue doing: reveal
the follies of public and private bureaucracies, produce career-serving academic
tracts, set a school of disciples to work on your theories, and the like. Instead,
Selznick was trying to infuse value, a sense of larger purpose, into thinking

about organizations and their leadership. He was in fact offering an exercise in moral instruction, a case of statesmanship in the social sciences.[81]

These are large claims, even if Heclo also and rightly observes that "a casual reading can easily miss the overall point of what is going on in *Leadership in Administration* because Selznick moralizes *sotto voce*."[82] Both the main claim and the observation are important, and we will return to them. There is one intriguing thing that they miss, however.

It is, without doubt, a distinctive feature of this work that, in ways likely to surprise many of the managers who read it for practical advice on how to succeed, one is constantly reminded that larger issues are in play. In discussing the leader's role as goal setter, for example, Selznick observes that he or she "must confront all of the classic questions that have plagued the study of human aspiration. When is an aim, such as 'happiness,' specific enough to be meaningful? What is the right role of reason, and of opportunism, in the choice of ends? How may immediate practical goals be joined to ultimate values?"[83]

What are these large questions doing here? The answer in Selznick's case is not far to seek. For his project here, indeed his life's work, is driven by a higher-order, more philosophically driven pragmatism than he finds common in America, though it is a specifically American philosophical tradition. In decrying the shortsightedness of American administrative pragmatism, one tied to short-term efficiencies and profits, Selznick seeks to ground in administrative realities:

> the lessons of that peculiarly American philosophy, the pragmatism of William James and John Dewey . . . In that perspective, practical judgment must always be tied to the here-and-now; it must be rooted in genuine problems; it must be tested by experienced pain and satisfaction. But that is not the end of wisdom. In the philosophy of pragmatism all policy-making, indeed all of life, should reflect informed awareness of what is worth having, doing, and being. Pragmatism is not a flight from principle. It is an argument for discovering principles and for making them relevant to everyday life.[84]

Yet, this said, and allowing for the unusually value-packed language of this product of "value-free" sociology of the 1950s, in a book destined to be most feted in schools of management, there are strong self-imposed limits on Selznick's engagement with values here. At least explicitly, there is nothing said here about what values should be preferred. They should be "long-term" rather than short, "discovered" and made "relevant to everyday life," "infused" into organizations, but what in particular might they be? Selznick was not inclined, at this stage in his thought, to answer this, not small, question.

Perhaps this self-limitation stemmed simply from the fact that Selznick remained a card-carrying social scientist, committed, as most were at the time (and many still are), to social science as a value-free zone. Perhaps, too, it was a limitation shared with or derived from the pragmatism that so informed his thought; for, as he wrote in 1976:

> Pragmatism is process-centered and it rightly perceives that the moral character of a person or an institution resides in means used more than in goals sought. But character is not all. It is an irony of modern thought that the most articulate philosophy of instrumentalism should turn out to focus [more] on integrity than on achievement, more on character defining choice than on substantive outcomes. . . . Whatever the great merits of this position, it is not a prescription for leadership. [85]

And, whatever the great merits of the position, when and since he began to write about law, Selznick sought to transcend it.

CHAPTER FIVE

Pathos and Politics

Selznick's writings on organizations and institutions attracted a lot of attention, much of it conventional academic commentary and critique of narrow compass. However, two critics—Alvin Gouldner and Sheldon Wolin—whether they (or Selznick himself) knew it or not, engaged with enduring aspects of his thought and ways of thought. For this reason they remain interesting. Gouldner attacked what he took to be the unjustifiedly pessimistic character of Selznick's work; Wolin what he saw as its systematic decentering and miscasting of the character of politics. Each believed these defects were exemplary, symptomatic of pervasive errors in contemporary thought, of which Selznick was a negative paradigm. I begin with Gouldner.

PATHOS

In 1955, Alvin Gouldner, also a City College graduate (though among the enemies in Alcove 2) and one of Merton's doctoral students,[1] published an important and influential critique of a number of then-influential studies of bureaucracy.[2] Borrowing a phrase from Arthur Lovejoy, he claimed to identify a particular "metaphysical pathos" underlying those works. According to Lovejoy, what we notice in poetry we often overlook in prose: The writings of thinkers, and not only those of artists, commonly embody or evoke a mood, tone, sentiment, or emotional coloring, whether or not the writer intends it or the audience is aware of it. Its effects are typically more subliminal and unarticulated than explicit, and readers are commonly "susceptible to" it, Lovejoy suggested, quite apart from whatever evidence or argument a writer might use to support it.

Gouldner detects a bleak defeatist pathos permeating these writings, "which insinuates, in the very midst of new discoveries, that all is lost. For the metaphysical pathos of much of the modern theory of group organization is that of pessimism and fatalism."[3] Indeed, "Instead of telling men how bureaucracy might be mitigated, they insist that it is inevitable . . . Instead of assuming responsibilities as realistic clinicians, striving to further democratic potentialities wherever they can, many social scientists have become morticians, all too eager to bury men's hopes."[4]

Some of those he criticized were influenced by Weber; others even more darkly, by Michels: Selznick on TVA was his exhibit of the latter. Gouldner portrayed him as a card-carrying Michelsian, convinced, way beyond anything that argument or evidence could support, that "the iron law of oligarchy" will defeat any democratic attempts to deny or harness it. The pathos engendered by his work was more despairing and defeatist, "even more morosely pessimistic,"[5] than that of others.

Of *TVA's* analysis of structural constraints that make democracy hard to institutionalize without loss, Gouldner writes:

> For some reason Selznick has chosen—and this was not forced upon him by the data—to focus on the things which harry and impede democratic aspirations, rather than on those which strengthen and energize it [sic] . . .
>
> Are there no constraints which *force* men to adhere valorously to their democratic beliefs, which *compel* them to be intelligent rather than blind, which leave them *no choice* but to be men of good will rather than predators? The neglect of these possibilities suggests the presence of a distorting pathos.
>
> It is the pathos of pessimism, rather than the compulsions of rigorous analysis, that lead to the assumption that organizational constraints have stacked the deck against democracy.[6]

Readers of Selznick's later works, from *Leadership in Administration* onward, might well believe this message has gone to the wrong address. Already in that work, the aim was to show, in Heclo's words, how one might "think through the problem of maintaining ideals amid grubby organizational realities." As we shall see, by *Law, Society, and Industrial Justice*, Selznick was seeking to identify, and optimistic that he could find, incipient sources for the rule of law within complex organizations that had long done without it. And the "pathos" of *The Moral Commonwealth* is scarcely pessimistic or even agnostic about the enterprise of "strengthening and energizing" the values that, he argued, enabled individuals, institutions, and communities to flourish. If anything, that work is awash with pathos of quite the opposite sort. Gouldner's criticisms here could easily be taken as manifestos of any one of these works. Perhaps, then, Gouldner's accusations miss their target, or there was a profound shift in the mood of Selznick's writings, swinging from a pessimistic youth that issued in his *Enquiry* articles, *TVA*, and *The Organizational Weapon* to the opposite pole of a determined (if sometimes teeth-gritting) optimism. Actually there is a bit of both.

Gouldner's accusations were not baseless. *TVA* is not a book full of promise, so to speak. It speaks of pathologies more than of cures. *The Organizational Weapon* is all about success in achieving values, certainly, but they are values that Selznick deplores. And the chapter on institutional vulnerabilities, with its bleak assessment of mass society and its corrosive pressures on culture-bearing elites, is no bundle of joys. Without doubt, the tone of Selznick's writings, and the balance between light and shade, is darker in the early writings than later on. The points he considers it most important to stress—about the dangers that lie between proclamation of ideals and their effective pursuit—are different, too. There is a toughness, a flintiness in his prose, which softens as he develops.

Of course, this might well be more a circumstantial matter than one of general intellectual principle. There were reasons for negative assessment of Trotskyist idealism and that professed by the leaders of the TVA; in other writings of that period of war and then Cold War, reasons for buoyant optimism were not obvious on many fronts, and this was all the more the case for an ex-minority socialist fed up with the lack of realism of his comrades. Anyone thinking realistically at that time about "the conditions and processes that frustrate ideals or, instead, give them life and hope" might make a good case for finding more of the former than the latter.

Whatever the reasons for the contrast of mood, however, there is a more complex theoretical message available, even in his earliest, most tough-minded writings, than Gouldner intimates. Even those writings never promoted blanket pessimism about the possibility of breathing "life and hope" into ideals. He had arguments against such pessimism from very early on, and he maintained them all his life. They are the same arguments, even if the prominence and perhaps their rhetorical weight shifts. The evidence comes from two ever-present tendencies of his work: on the one hand, his Niebuhrian insistence on the indispensability of "moral realism," even in the most light and airy of his works; and on the other hand, his Deweyite commitment to the pursuit of ideals, maintained even in his bleakest writings. What is striking is his determination to maintain the insights of both Dewey and Niebuhr, rather than allow one to extinguish the other.

Certainly, from the beginning Selznick was impressed by the "recalcitrance" of tools, the "tyranny" of means, and the sources of institutional goal displacement. Indeed, as he had long learned from Niebuhr, not only are our tools recalcitrant; so too are we ourselves. This conviction runs through his youthful pieces in *Enquiry* when he sought to teach organizational realism to his Trotskyist and ex-Trotskyist colleagues, and through *TVA*, which spelled out some of the ways in which organizational imperatives and pathologies asserted themselves. It is reiterated in all his later works, and nowhere more so than in his last major book, *The Moral Commonwealth*. This un-Deweyite realism leads to Selznick's respect for Hobbes and other threat experts, whom we ignore at our peril.

But Selznick does not want to stop where Hobbes stops. Though he stresses the presence and resilience of evil and the need for strenuous efforts to contain it, he holds out for more. "Damage control"[7] is a great, but not the supreme or only, good. Indeed, though recognizing danger might be the beginning of wisdom, it is only half—over time less than half—of the story.

And this, pace Gouldner, was evident from very early on. Recall Selznick's repeated warnings against "looking at the devil with fascinated eyes," and denials that the "general tendency" Michels had identified was an iron law. It was, rather, merely "the way organizations will develop under present conditions, if they are permitted to take the line of least resistance";[8] it merely "set a problem." It did not eliminate the possibility of a solution.[9]

Selznick's repeated insistence on the complexity of relations between threat and promise has both theoretical and practical implications. Theoretically, it is crucial to insist on the difference between acknowledging that dangers to what we value are common, even systemic, and presuming that they are omnipotent. Neither pessimism nor optimism has any general theoretical claim to wisdom in the understanding of social affairs, notwithstanding that sometimes one, sometimes the other, will prove better grounded and more accurate.

Practically, we should recall, Selznick warns that, unless we are prepared to live with the psychic, intellectual, and sometimes moral complexity involved in giving both threat and promise their due, "we become easy victims of careless optimism or enervating pessimism."[10] Moreover, there is a more particular Deweyite lesson to be learned, and one that has animated almost everything he has written. It has to do with the limitations of ungrounded philosophy or unworldly idealism more generally. Recall Selznick's argument (in explicit response to Gouldner's critique), that:

> Sociological realism, thus pitilessly applied to moral abstractions, can be an exercise in skepticism and an apology for passively accepting things as they are. But it is also a way of taking ideals seriously. If ideals *are* to be taken seriously, there must be genuine concern for their embodiment in action, and especially in the routines of institutional life.[11]

Nevertheless, Gouldner was onto something: an internal dialogue, and at times a real tension, that pervade Selznick's work. Niebuhr had the best lines at that time; but over the years Dewey reasserted himself; never completely, and never without Niebuhrian qualifications and challenges, but considerably and perhaps as much for programmatic as for analytic reasons. It is at times not clear whether optimism flows from the analysis or drives it. In any event, the balance of Selznick's energies shifted from stressing the difficulties of attaining ideals to seeking ways of vindicating them.

POLITICS

In 1960, Sheldon Wolin published *Politics and Vision*,[12] a suggestive, sweeping, and occasionally swingeing interpretation of the history of Western political thought. According to Wolin, for over two and half millennia political philosophers had shared an understanding of what was truly political and what was not. Boundaries shifted, and even more so particular institutions. However, notwithstanding the many parallels and similarities that might be plausibly found or loosely alleged between the true domains and institutions of politics and those of other spheres, it was understood that politics had its own special place and concerns. It was "uniquely concerned with what is 'common' to the whole community."[13]

From the late eighteenth century, however, things changed. The distinctiveness of the political was obscured. Whereas Hobbes, for example, saw political sovereignty as the necessary frame without which there could be no civil society, Durkheim and the sociological tradition more generally put *society* first and reduced everything, politics included, to second-order organs serving its "needs." For sociologists, "society" was primary and the polity a distant second. And in roughly the same period, liberal political economy spawned another self-generating domain, the "economy," also to overshadow the polity. This combination of beliefs in self-sustaining domains of society and economy, according to Wolin, spelled curtains for claims to independence and indeed distinctive importance, of the polity.

There were some among these thinkers, such as the technocratic pre-socialists, Saint-Simon and the utopian socialists, who interpreted this dethronement of the political as signaling a coming "nonpolitical condition," one form of which was "the attempt to substitute administration for politics as the central method for handling social problems."[14] More pervasively modern, however, has been the decline, less of the specifically *political* than of the *specifically* political. The claim has become less that politics can or should be eliminated than that it can be found elsewhere: in organizations, churches, families, schools; virtually anywhere, it would seem, but its traditional home.

Organizations were particularly important because they were rightly seen in the nineteenth century as the coming thing, as much by conservatives who saw organization as the antidote to the dissolutions of modernity as to Lenin who saw it as the vehicle for revolution. And, only an apparent paradox, enthusiasm for organization was joined by a parallel and overlapping current: lament for vanishing community. Conservatives like Burke lamented the fissiparous anticommunitarian tendencies of modernity; so, too, did revolutionaries like Marx. Burke wanted to resist them; Marx to transcend and overcome them. According to Wolin, these two themes came to be joined in a somewhat counterintuitive mix:

> The idea of community and the idea of organization did not develop as two separate and parallel strands during the nineteenth and twentieth centuries. What is interesting, and at times poignant, is the way that they converge. The nostalgia for the vanished warmth of the simple community and the obsession with the possibilities of large-scale organization are frequently piled on top of each another. As the century wore on and men were sobered by the impracticality of recapturing the shared warmth of a close communion, they stubbornly refused to surrender the hope of community. Instead, they insisted on imputing its values to the stark and forbidding structures of giant organizations.[15]

According to Wolin, Selznick is a modern emanation and the prime exemplar of these tendencies. He expresses "the modern writer's continuing search for a synthesis of power and community similar to the one achieved by the mediaeval church";[16] for him and many modern thinkers like him, "the mission of organization is to supply not only goods and services, but fellowship as well."[17]

But, of course, the modern organization's rationalized self-image, its impersonal rules and bloodless efficiencies, don't at face value lend themselves to communitarian interpretation. So modern organization theorists try "to engraft elements of community onto the main stem of organization, hoping thereby to lessen the contrast between the two."[18] This is no easy matter in modern mass societies, which have eroded so many bases of community, so the task of communitarian organization theorists is "to discover communal values in the large corporation and administrative organization. . . . The major theorist of this development is Philip Selznick."[19]

To this ambition Wolin attributes Selznick's discovery of the significance of informal structures, personal connections in modern organizations, emphasis on the

> organic aspects of an organization [and employment of] the pure language of Burke: spontaneity, natural processes, adaptive organisms, and non-rational behavior. But it must be remembered that Selznick is describing not a rural and pre-industrial society, a world of squires, manor houses, and faithful retainers, but the world of General Motors, the Pentagon, and the large public university.[20]

In these conditions, spontaneity must be contrived; *manipulated* is Wolin's term of choice. And thus the key role of leaders, elites, arch-manipulators-become-"statesmen," is to rescue from the swamp of mass society islands of socially integrated, loyal members of institutions—quasi-citizens indeed, though no longer of an overarching polity but of the particular organizations in which they work and to which, in a deep sense, they might be made to belong. Politics shrinks in turn from the polity to the internal life of these organizations, the "politicalness" of which, as Wolin interprets Selznick, stems directly from their size and their power.

On Wolin's reading of Selznick, something desperately needed to be done about mass society, "where men are isolated and their lives depersonalized and bleak,"[21] because "history has not only been unkind, it has been positively malicious. Instead of the highly self-conscious proletariat, the proud bearers of man's historical destiny, history has given us the vulgar mass; instead of Adonis, Quasimodo."[22] To replace Quasimodo with Adonis, we need elites who understand the possibilities of organization. Lenin was one; Selznick another. Indeed, Selznick did to Lenin what Marx did to Hegel: "that is, turned him upside down. The new formula is not pure Leninism, but Leninism clothed in the language of Burke."[23] In the guise of conserving group loyalties, spontaneities, and commitments, organizational elites are advised how to manipulate those under their control. Selznick's real strategy, notwithstanding all these "hurrah words" that "might appear to be either a bit of careless usage or a deceptive strategy . . . is also squarely in the manipulative tradition. Selznick's notions of 'commitment,' 'loyalty,' and 'rational, free-willed consent' have as much of choice and spontaneity about them as Lenin's theory of 'democratic centralism' has of democracy."[24]

Thus politics undergoes "sublimation" by being shrunk and removed to "forms of association which earlier thought had believed to be non-political."[25] Rather than a groupwide polity, ruled by statesmen who engage in the peculiar and indispensable craft of politics, "the contemporary vision of the social universe is one where political society, in its general sense, has disappeared. Selznick offers us a society dotted by large bureaucracies, each an autarchic polity with no connections between them, only an arena of diplomacy and negotiation for the new organizational statesmen."[26] But this won't work:

> The divorce between what is political and what is general has repeatedly led recent writers into paths of futility. . . . they have tried to pose political problems in what are essentially non-political settings; the result has been a series of dead-ends. . . . When used in a political sense, citizenship and loyalty have meaning only in reference to a general order.[27]

Selznick replied to this critique of contemporary follies, and choice of him as their exemplar, in a collection edited by Amitai Etzioni.[28] Selznick acknowledges the "wide-ranging and perceptive" character of Wolin's study and notes the latter's lament over "the eclipse of political consciousness and the waning of distinctively political values," the apparent diversion of politics from the whole to its parts, "the fragmentation of political man, and the moral impotence that goes with it." He notes, too, Wolin's charge that all this "finds stimulus and support in contemporary social theory":

> The sociological perspective, he argues, is especially resolute in its rejection of political reality. When the political process is "group process," when political participation is molded and directed toward parochial interests, then politics properly understood becomes unreal, epiphenomenal. And when the sociologist claims to analyze the political *dimension* of group life, he but salts an open wound.[29]

In all, Selznick agrees that Wolin is "right to insist that apparently technical and specialized theories are not so innocent after all. . . . I agree that the social scientist should acknowledge responsibility for the larger implications of what he has to say."[30]

But what are those implications? On the one hand, Selznick readily admits that there is an "antipolitical strand in sociology," in the sense that sociology "is antiformalist in spirit, critical of received categories, always inclined to blur institutional boundaries," and to situate erstwhile insulated categories "in society." It also tends to concentrate on "the concrete, problem-solving actor responding to his immediate circumstances . . . His relation to larger, more distant, more impersonal settings is viewed as less compelling."[31] Indeed this is no concession; these are among the specific qualities for which sociological insight is to be valued. Nor, Selznick insists, do these tendencies amount to a slighting of the political or its importance.

Selznick also claims that his view is frequently the opposite of that attributed to him. Rather than insist that politics is nothing more than administration, he wants to claim that certain aspects and kinds (only *certain* aspects and kinds) of what is often seen as merely technical administration are nothing less than political. To note that is not to degrade the importance of politics but to affirm it. It is not to relocate politics from the state to the organization but to show that politics, "a realm where the ends of group existence are defined,"[32] exists in the life of *some* organizations at *some* junctures: more organizations and junctures than you might think, but *not* every organization, not every juncture. Pure organizations have little political in them; institutions have more. Managerial decisions are frequently technical and routine; the mistake is to believe that management is leadership. And it is not, as Wolin alleges, the size or power of organizations that makes them political. Rather it is the degree of *"openness* of the system, the leeway it allows for the play of interests, the opportunity it affords for meaningful participation by at least some significant number of members and subgroups. The internal nature of the group, not its external power, is the main criterion."[33] Thus, and for certain responsibilities and decisions in certain, particularly institutionalized, organizations, a "political orientation" is illuminating, and the lack of it blinding.

Nor is the political role of an institutional leader all about "social integration"; it has rather to do with the "achievement of a *distinctive competence*." True, it involves winning consent, as does every form of political leadership, but

> to call any process of winning consent within specialized associations "manipulation" simply begs the question. Our problem is to distinguish the genuine from the sham. While it is proper to call attention to administrative pretense, co-optation, and the rest (that is another theme in *TVA and the Grass*

Roots), it seems wrong, both scientifically and morally, to settle the issue by definition.[34]

Nor (as anyone who waited for *Law, Society, and Industrial Justice* would soon learn) is there much in common between Selznick's hope to find and develop the rule of law in organizations and Lenin's determination to use and subordinate *everyone* to the Party's domination, discipline, and subordination. Lenin was not big on the rule of law.

In a sense, Selznick inverts and returns Wolin's complaint, without quite denying its force. There *is* a danger in sociologizing the politics out of the polity, in reducing comprehensive concerns to nothing more than those to be found in the most mundane and local areas of everyday life. On the other hand, political concerns are not solely the preserve of those we call politicians. Given the increasing, at times overwhelming, role of organizations in modern societies, denying that they might have analogous concerns, practices, and pathologies is to blind us to precisely those elements of our institutional worlds that go beyond our everyday, commonly technicized understandings of the processes increasingly dominant in our lives. It is also to deny the benefits of "funded experience" from one sphere to any other. The irony of that, Selznick argues, is "that we ignore the political dimension of organization life only at the peril of sharing responsibility for just that reduction of politics to administration that Wolin himself regrets."[35]

These are fair points, fairly made. However, as Selznick admits in his response, there *are* differences between the political in the state and in other institutions, and they matter, but he has a lot more to say about similarities than differences. What the differences are and how much they matter we will have to go elsewhere to find. They are not really on Selznick's agenda then or at any other time. Nor, in any but his earliest political essays, is close attention to the state. We learn much more about the statesmanlike qualities of organizational leaders, nonstate "statesmanship" as it were, than we do about the statesmanship of statesmen themselves.

Whether something is lost by this definitional expansiveness and displacement is a serious question of legal, political, and ultimately social theory. After all, there is an important and often distinguished tradition, from Hobbes onward, for which politics is not merely to be found in a central place, occupied with comprehensive concerns, but is *architectonic*. Society, or at least a society of peace and civility, is impossible without it. Selznick is well aware that states and their political arrangements are important, but he never engages with the tradition that considers them fundamental. In his reply to Wolin, he simply misses this point. For all his real and sustained interest in and understanding of politics, his social theory is often strangely apolitical. It is *society* that, for him, is at the center, where and for which significant action seems to start and in relation to which all else is to be understood (as we will see, this is true of his approach to law as well). Such "society centeredness" doesn't distinguish him from a host of other sociologists, for whom also society is primary and everything else second,[36] but it is a significant opportunity missed, particularly by a thinker who has thought seriously about politics.

Also, and in retrospect intriguingly, there is another omission from Selznick's reply. While he mentions "community" once, just to deny that he thinks it apolitical, he has nothing to say about the deeply communitarian character of his own work, which he noted explicitly over twenty years later but which began very much earlier. It was well captured, even if perhaps exaggerated, by Wolin almost a decade earlier while Selznick had nothing explicitly to say about it. Whether it deserves accusation or applause can be debated. It is, however, a deep commitment, at once intellectual and moral.

Sometimes perceptive misunderstandings can be more insightful than shallow accuracy. Gouldner was blind to the complexity of Selznick's realistic idealism, but he spotted its bias in the early writings and protested against it. Selznick never thought he was influenced by Gouldner's critique, but the trajectory of his thought for the rest of his life was precisely the one Gouldner recommended. Selznick's answers to Wolin are effective, but he never explains just why his sociological tendency drew him away from high politics in his academic work, nor did he appear conscious of how strong was the appeal of community to him, long before he learned it was possible to be a "communitarian." His most comprehensive treatment of these themes occurs in his later writings, as does the prescience of these critical observers. In the meantime, however, these lines are explored and new trajectories develop on new terrain: that of law.

PART III

Law

CHAPTER SIX

Jurisprudential Sociology

In 1952 Selznick was invited to join the Sociology Department at UC Berkeley. By the time he reached Berkeley, he was a recognized figure in sociology generally and in organization theory more specifically and had begun (with Leonard Broom) to prepare an introductory sociology text that became the leading such work in the United States for many years.

Soon after he arrived, he began to take an interest in sociology of law, a marginal subject among American sociologists, though not among their European forebears: most famously and best known to Selznick, Emile Durkheim, and Max Weber, but also Eugen Ehrlich, Leon Petrażycki, and Georges Gurvitch. In the early 1950s Selznick started auditing courses at Boalt Hall Law School. In 1956–1957 he spent a year as law and behavioral sciences senior fellow at the University of Chicago Law School, where some of the first large-scale empirical work on law was being undertaken. He started reading intensively on law and legal philosophy: coming back, among other things, to Morris Cohen's essays that connected law with philosophy, and his own work with that of a teacher for whom he had the highest regard. He also began his first major law-related project—on employee–employer relations and due process—that was to culminate in *Law, Society, and Industrial Justice*. The rest of his life was shaped by his legal interests.

Though continuities are plain between his interests in institutions and his new focus on law, Selznick did not later have a clear recollection of what prompted the move. He did recall that he was becoming restless about a career in organizational theory. He was concerned that this "would have a narrowing effect, would divorce [him] from the things I had loved so much when I was young: philosophical concerns, history of ideas, broad issues."[1] He also recalled that getting into law was very different from his passage to the TVA:

> I didn't feel "ha, I know what's going on there." With *TVA* that was easy really. But the transition to law had so many implications to it. In some way I knew about some of the jurisprudential theories, but it struck me as a very appealing thing to think about for someone who definitely did not want to be committed to organizational studies, could have done more studies, or gone on the organizational guru circuit, but my instincts told me this was the wrong thing to do. So I spent some time trying to learn what I could, get some background. And then perhaps it was post hoc that I traced this connection between organization theory and sociology of law, but I don't think it was only post hoc. I think at some level of my thinking I was aware of this legal dimension. I was certainly aware of this authority dimension.[2]

It may not have been a coincidence that Chester Barnard, whose *The Functions of the Executive* was a key influence on Selznick's early organization theory, had expressed his debt in the preface of that book to a "chance reading of Ehrlich's *Fundamental Principles of the Sociology of Law*."[3] Barnard particularly commended that book's emphasis on the *social* rather than doctrinal and formal roots of legal orders, which countered what he took to be the prevailing "legalism that prevents the acceptance of essential facts of social organizations."[4] Barnard clearly discerned a kinship and overlap between his understanding of organizations and Ehrlich's of law. When Selznick came to write about law, he discerned a similar relationship. He refers to Ehrlich in his first article on sociology of law, returns to him frequently in later writings, and shares his conviction throughout that "the center of gravity of legal development lies not in legislation, nor in juristic science, nor in judicial decision, but in society itself."[5]

Other continuities are also plain. In his first piece on sociology of law, Selznick explains that, among a number of reasons for "the present outcropping of interest in law on the part of sociologists,"

> Interest in law has also been encouraged by new work in the sociology of administration. These studies have restated some older problems regarding the interplay of formal systems of social control and the spontaneous behavior of men and groups. Some of us who have worked in that field have discovered that in studying formal organizations we were also studying legal systems. It is clear that what we were learning about the functions of formal rules, the interdependence of authority and consent, and similar matters were not really new from the larger perspective of legal sociology. It is also painfully evident that some sociologists are prone to repeat mistakes of the past by overempha-

sizing the informal and spontaneous and deprecating the significance and the peculiar problems of a legal order.[6]

In any event, whatever the specific conjunctures of Selznick's move, and though he had not thought much about law before, there is something natural about it. For law is, of course, a major social institution conceived, administered, applied, and enforced by huge organizations and on them. It is replete with tensions between formal requirements and informal practices; typically highly *institutionalized* in Selznick's specific sense, from head to toe bound up with values and ideals, its participants self-consciously and systematically aware of its history, or at least of its presently normative tradition. In every society law raises the issues with which Selznick's life has been concerned, for it is intertwined, inescapably and with broad reach, with purpose, authority, responsiveness, values, and ideals. That is true of its subjects, its consequences, its implications, and, perhaps more explicitly in the United States than in many Western countries, its discourse, and the nature of the arguments that figure in its doctrine.

SOCIOLOGY OF LAW

In 1957, Selznick presented this first piece on law at the meeting of the American Sociological Association, and it later appeared in the volume edited by Merton. Like several pieces commissioned from him over the next dozen years, it was a survey of the field of sociology of law.[7] Like them, too, it was only partly concerned to map what people in the area were doing, for all these articles were also programmatic renditions of what the enterprise was and might be, viewed from a particular and distinctive conception of the field and what it required.

According to Selznick, the sociology of law "may be regarded as an attempt to marshal what we know about the natural elements of social life and to bring that knowledge to bear on a consciously sustained enterprise, governed by special objectives and ideals."[8] There is, in this characterization, one unstressed word and one distinctive phrase that carry special freight.

The word is *natural*. After all, Thomas Hobbes did not consider much about *social* life, properly so called, to be natural. Man-in-nature was antisocial. Without the rule of an artificial creation—an all-powerful sovereign, a supreme law-maker—there could only be a "state of nature" that was a state of war "of all against all." Again, sociologists are often prone to stress "culture" over "nature." But Selznick follows John Dewey in this as in so much else, in regarding society (and culture)[9] as natural responses to natural human predicaments. Because the predicaments vary, so do societies, but they don't vary so much that they have nothing in common, and a lot that they have in common has a natural source. Society is a natural, if naturally variable, response to the character and coincidence of human nature, needs, strivings, plurality, and particular circumstances. So too, many of the standard social activities, obviously parenthood, but also socialization, culture, and, as we shall see, values too, are naturally recurring practices. For Aristotle, humans are by nature political, by which he also meant social, creatures. For Selznick, like Aristotle, that is a truth pregnant with both empirical *and* normative consequence.

The phrase worth a second look is the characterization of law as "a consciously sustained enterprise, governed by special objectives and ideals." This echoes the Harvard lawyer and theorist, Lon Fuller's, insistence that law should be understood as an *enterprise*, that is to say a purposeful activity with immanent goals and values, rather than "a piece of inert matter."[10] Purposes are at its heart, and like the goals of values of any practical enterprise, these can be varyingly achieved. Selznick commended this view for two reasons. First, because it

> calls attention to the fact that the legal order is more than a set of principles and norms. It is a *kind of activity* carried on by living men in living institutions, subject to all the external pressures and constraints, and all the inner sources of recalcitrance, that frustrate ideal ends. Second, to present law as a way of accomplishing something is to stress the *variable* nature of that achievement. Legality is not something given by definition. It is not its own warrant. Rather, a developed legal order is the product of continuing effort and posits values that are always incompletely fulfilled. In this perspective we can speak of more or less legality.[11]

As will become clear, not every sociologist would be happy to accept this characterization either of law or of what its study should pay attention to.[12] Yet the sociological provenance of these articles is plain.

Thus there is the insistence that law exists *within* society, not just beside it—so much so that Selznick came to endorse Fuller's criticism of the logo shared by the Law and Society Movement, as it came to be called, and his own "law *and* society" center, on the grounds that law is a *part* of social life, not merely a partner of it; so, "law *in* society," not "law and . . ."[13] One particular elaboration of that orientation, which became central to *Law, Society, and Industrial Justice*, was the search for "major legal trends, particularly those which reflect broader social changes and which may point to emergent or incipient law."[14] It is not just law's context that is social; so too is law itself; "Therefore the personal and social characteristics of lawyers, judges, police, and administrators must be studied, as well as the social dynamics of the organizations in which they work."[15]

This links, too, with the *antiformalism* characteristic of sociology that Selznick endorses, though in a characteristically qualified way. The objection is to formal*ism* not to formality per se; thus, his last sentence at note 6, above. Similar themes occur in his sketch of the "aspirations and perspectives" of the Jurisprudence and Social Policy program, written some twenty years later. Those later comments deserve to be quoted at length because they best bring together what he had come to believe about "forms in action" in the context of both institutions generally and legal institutions more specifically:

> In social inquiry, the perspective of action strikes an antiformalist note. Formal roles and formal categories are abridgments of reality. "Action" points to the concreteness of experience. The acting person pursues goals, interprets meanings, responds to opportunities, and confronts difficulties. He tends to spill over the boundaries of defined roles. His life is dominated by immediate concerns. Even if he prefers to "follow the rules," that aspiration is only one element in the situation, to be weighed against others. A similar logic applies to the acting group as it resolves inner tensions and copes with a problematic environment. . . .
>
> It does not follow, however, that we must embrace a radical antiformalism. In its critique of legal abstraction, antiformalism has encouraged skepticism and even derogation of rules and purposive arrangements. This was paralleled in social science when students of organization, having discovered "informal" structure in so-called formal (usually bureaucratic) associations, tended for a while to deny the importance of formal systems of authority and communication. Now we understand that the distinction between formal and informal is only a starting point for social analysis. The operating organization is made up of *both* formal and informal relations. It is the interplay of the two that counts. The same caution applies to Pound's distinction between "law in books" and "law in action."[16]

The sober complexity of these observations characteristically exhibits, as does Selznick's work generally, that "tolerance for ambiguity" that he later commended, his resistance to dramatically posed but often unnecessary choices, his alertness to the common possibility that tensions between structures and forces might exist and endure, without definitive resolution one way or another, and yet without our having to place all our bets on one or the other. The *déformation professionelle* of lawyers is to overemphasize formality, that of sociologists to exaggerate what bypasses and undermines forms. These tendencies can mislead, but they are not necessarily inspired by foolishness. We need to heed their insights while avoiding their excesses.

A third characteristic of sociology of law is "to blur the distinction between state law and other forms of social control. . . . State law is only a part, and not necessarily the most important part, of the sociolegal order."[17] This, with Selznick's explicit endorsement of Eugen Ehrlich's focus on the "inner order of associations," becomes a central motif of *Law, Society, and Industrial Justice*.

The fourth and normative element of the sociological orientation to law

> reflects the strongly instrumentalist orientation of sociological jurisprudence. Instrumentalism is the enemy of legal isolation, for it demands that received law be justified by its responsiveness to social needs, claims, and interests. Furthermore, the demand that law yield to social purpose quickly turns attention to the role of social knowledge in law. For if laws are instruments, they are open to interpretation and revision in the light of changing circumstances. This gives the social scientist a legitimate place in the legal dialogue.[18]

Selznick's stress on the instrumental nature of law and of sociological jurisprudence was no surprise, given his pragmatist convictions. What precisely the social scientist might have to say in the "legal dialogue," however, was yet to be specified. It became the preoccupation of the rest of Selznick's life.

While some of the foregoing is quite singular, Selznick had not strained the boundaries of what mainstream sociologists would recognize as their domain. However, he went on in his first article to hint at a larger, philosophical, ambition for legal sociology, that he shared with few mainstream American sociologists, but was convinced could not be avoided either by him or by them. Hitherto, he observed, sociological investigations of law could be pursued without much concern for "ultimate problems of definition and of philosophical perspective." However, he ultimately argued that sociolology of the purposive enterprise that is law could not avoid becoming entangled with philosophical, jurisprudental questions of the most basic kind, about those purposes, about law's authority, its legitimacy, the role of reason in law, and about the character of the phenomenon and concept of law itself.

This was more than a general argument in favor of meshing disciplinary perspectives, of crossing boundaries, though that was an argument

Selznick was happy to make, for Selznick went on to venture some substantive conclusions, as yet incompletely worked out, about what might
emerge from such a meshing of sociology and legal philosophy. These were
conclusions of a sort uncommon among sociologists or, for that matter,
lawyers and philosophers.

As readers of his earlier work would have known, if law is institutionalized, as in all thriving legal orders it is, it will tend to be "imbued with
value." Sociologists of law, then, need to concern themselves with the values with which legal institutions are imbued. The central legal value is
what he then called legality. A key concern of legal sociology, then, is an
exploration of "the meaning of legality itself." At this early stage, he used
"legality" and "the rule of law" as interchangeable terms. Later he came to
prefer to speak of "the rule of law" because "legality" can also be parsed
without normative entanglements, and he was interested in those entanglements.[19] Even then, however, he insisted that law is not just something
that exists or doesn't. It comes in various qualitative states, some closer to
its animating ideals and some further from them.

In a singular combination of Aquinas and Dewey, Selznick concluded
this first essay with the claim that there are "foundations in reason for
choosing among human norms those that are to be given the sanction of
law," a statement with which philosophers, at least those of a naturalist
orientation, might agree. But, one might ask, and several sociologists have:
What has this to do with sociology? Selznick's answer is tantalizing both
for its brevity and its unfamiliarity. Sociology properly understood gives
us grounds for understanding why we do what we do and, more contro-
versially, what is good for us. Applied to law, it can aid us in choosing
between legal norms. Acceptance of that proposition:

> will bring us, I cannot doubt, to an acceptance of some version of a doctrine of
> natural law, although it may not, and perhaps should not, be called that, given
> its historical associations. A modern naturalist perspective may be preferable . . .
> But whatever the philosophical auspices, the search for principles of criticism
> based on social naturalism must go on. . . . The natural order, as it concerns
> man, is compact of potentiality and vulnerability, and it is our long-run task to
> see how these characteristics of man work themselves out in the structure and
> dynamics of social institutions.[20]

This deliberate mingling of factual and normative, scientific and philosophical, aspirations and judgments was not commonly found among
mainstream sociologists in the 1950s, nor is it today. When it was, when it is,
it was and is commonly rebuked, at least by many who consider themselves

social scientists, notwithstanding its Deweyite, and thus science-friendly, lineage. Selznick's conclusion intrigued John Noonan, then editor of the *Natural Law Forum*,[21] the leading American journal of natural law philosophy. Noonan challenged Selznick to expand on his compressed recommendation.[22] The result, "Sociology and Natural Law,"[23] became the clearest and most ambitious statement of his intriguing claim that sociologists and natural lawyers shared the same jurisprudential concerns and territory—to the likely surprise and discomfort of both.

SOCIOLOGY AND NATURAL LAW

In the late 1950s and early 60s, natural law was a subject of a good deal of discussion and controversy in jurisprudence. There was the celebrated debate between the Oxford legal philosopher and positivist H. L. A. Hart and the Harvard jurist and idiosyncratic natural lawyer Lon Fuller. Hart's Harvard lecture appeared in the *Harvard Law Review* in 1958 with a long reply by Fuller.[24] The articles themselves were much discussed, and each culminated in a book elaborating, developing, and defending the positions their authors had launched in the debate. Hart's *The Concept of Law*,[25] in particular, had a profound influence on the development of Anglo-American legal philosophy, perhaps deeper than any other work of legal philosophy in the twentieth century. Fuller's *The Morality of Law* also had a significant, if smaller, influence and following. A related debate occurred between Fuller and Ernest Nagel in the *Journal of Philosophy* in 1956.[26] So even if (outside, perhaps, the *Natural Law Forum*), natural law was not regarded as the winning side in Anglo-American jurisprudence, it was at least treated as a significant protagonist; but not so in sociology. And that is part of what is striking in Selznick's advocacy of natural law *from the perspective* of sociology.

"Sociology and Natural Law" signals many of the central themes to which Selznick's writings return throughout his life and some of which were already hinted at in earlier work. It is revealing of Selznick's deepest, if still developing, intellectual commitments. Selznick proposes a non-metaphysical interpretation of natural law that has, he insists, profound affinities with the sociological enterprise, notwithstanding the lack of appetite shown by participants in either for the other.

In a later review of Lon Fuller's *Anatomy of Law*, he came to call this approach "legal naturalism,"[27] to lessen secular allergies to it and to underline its lineage in the pragmatist account of ideals grounded in nature, that he accepts. Fuller's naturalism, Selznick argued, was revealed both in its "problem-solving orientation" and recognition of "the continuity of legal and nonlegal phenomena." These elements, of course, are redolent of Dewey, and explicitly so. They are key to his version of natural law. It is worth quoting his later account because it illuminates the perspective he had begun to explore a decade earlier:

> Legal naturalism finds its sturdiest philosophical support in John Dewey's pragmatism. Dewey espoused a problem-centered naturalism . . . Inquiry flourishes when it is rooted in genuinely problematic situations and is not deflected or made sterile by imposed analytic schemes. Second, the organic world exhibits its "nature" in the course of responsive, tension-reducing, problem-solving adaptation . . .
>
> A striking feature of Dewey's naturalism, and one that sets him off from positivism, is his normative approach to human and social experience. Dewey saw valuation as a natural process, a phase of man's quest for need-satisfaction; and he saw *what* is valued as warranted by its contribution to that satisfaction. It may have arbitrary elements, and must be refined by the exercise of conscious intelligence, but it is founded in man's conative and cognitive nature.
>
> Applied to jurisprudence, pragmatic naturalism validates and encourages the study of legal ideals, not as imposed by an external ethic but as emergent from the requirements and the dynamics of a type of social ordering. To what extent such ideals do arise in legal experience, and what their fate may be, is always problematic, never to be taken for granted. The study of pervasive problems is one way of bringing such issues to the forefront of jurisprudential thought. At the same time, the theoretical questions are tied closely to empirical investigation of what happens to the system at the most practical levels of organization and decisionmaking.[28]

Selznick pursued this sociological and jurisprudential program for some forty years.

Of sociologists' lack of appetite, indeed distaste, Selznick was well aware. Among them, he wrote, "the reputation of natural law is not high. The phrase conjures up a world of absolutisms, of theological fiat, of fuzzy, unoperational, 'mystical' ideas, of thinking uninformed by history and by the variety of human situations." This was unfortunate, Selznick suggested:

> because sociology should have a ready affinity for the philosophy of natural law. Both are anti-formalist in spirit. Each looks beyond what is given and immediate to what is latent and inchoate; each is committed to the study of "nature" as yielding something more permanent and more universal than the transitory judgments of the hour or the epoch.[29]

Selznick's conception of natural law has no supramundane component, however redolent the concept is of the language (and his thought of some concerns) of theologians. Instead, its naturalism purports to be "in all respects consistent with the spirit and logic of scientific inquiry. I offer only the caveat that it is John Dewey's philosophical pragmatism, and not a narrower positivism, which frames my view of naturalism."[30] His advocacy of sociological natural law or naturalistic sociology of law goes well beyond pointing to similarities or overlaps in their character or themes. The claim is that sociology and natural law complement and need each other, as does jurisprudence need, and contribute to, them both.

Facts and Values

One reason why natural lawyers and social scientists tended to keep a wary distance from each other, Selznick believed, was the latter's reluctance to engage with values. Technically ever more adept, able to operationalize and measure the most complicated social variables, sociologists exhibited (as many still exhibit) "a strong feeling against speculative inquiry and especially against moral philosophy. At least, these ancient preoccupations are thought to have no place in modern sociology, whatever other value they might have as literature."[31] In particular, it was believed such inquiries habitually did, and social sciences never should, mix questions of fact and value. Quite apart from his attention to the traditions of natural law, Selznick was long disposed to question this attempted segregation.

The article begins by seeking to soften up sociological opposition, by rendering problematic the distinction, or at least the dichotomous implications drawn from the distinction. It is common in Selznick's work to find positions criticized, strongly but gently, for taking laudable motives to unfortunate extremes. Thus it is with the distinction between facts and values. Selznick sees both the scientific and pedagogic impulses that drive social scientists to distinguish between "what the world is really like from what they would like it to be."[32] In commonsense terms, the distinction matters and must be observed. As he put the point some thirty years later:

> From this distinction between *kinds of statements* it does not follow that fact and value, as *aspects of existence*, belong to wholly separate realms. It is one thing to derive sentences from other sentences as a matter of strict logic. It is something else to "derive" norms from facts, if by that we mean basing normative judgments on relevant empirical conditions.[33]

What disturbs Selznick is social scientists' consignment of facts and values to different and unbridgeable ontological and epistemological realms and their demand that one choose to investigate the former at the expense of the latter. This, he believes, represents an overreaching that was philosophically untenable, as he had been persuaded by Dewey,[34] and sociologically misleading, as he himself sought to demonstrate.

Selznick's major argument is that adherence to such an austere value-free scientism in effect incapacitates social scientists from dealing adequately with a crucially important feature of the social world: that it is full of what he calls "normative systems." These are social practices, arrangements, institutions—among them many of the most important in our lives—that generate, call on, are informed by, and need to be understood in relation to, values. Social science needs to understand such systems, but this cannot be done without reckoning with how central values are to them. This is one reason he soon came to call his conception of what should animate social science, normative theory.[35] There are plenty of social phenomena, such as "friendship, scholarship, statesmanship, love, fatherhood, citizenship, consensus, reason, public opinion, culture (in its common-sense and value-laden meaning), democracy"[36] and law, "whose very nature encompasses the realization of values."[37] These and many other social practices and relationships embody and generate ideals to be attained and *pre*scriptions and *pro*scriptions about how they are to be sought. These in turn are not unrelated, happenstance injunctions. Rather, they form normative systems "in a special and 'strong' sense of that term . . . It is impossible to understand any of these phenomena without also understanding what ideal states are to be approximated. In addition we must understand what forces are produced within the system, and what pressures exerted on it which inhibit or facilitate fulfilling the ideal."[38] Just as, in his earlier work, institutions were taken to differ from organizations by being, inter alia, "infused with value," so, more generally now, "[a] normative system is a living reality, a cluster of problem-solving individuals and groups, and its elements are subject to change as new circumstances and new opportunities alter the relation between the system and its master ideal."[39]

To reduce love, say, or families or parenthood or democracy to some cut-back behavioral or abstemiously value-free account is to misdescribe them, not because there are no false loves, dysfunctional families, bad fathers, rudimentary or failed democracies, but because even to say this is to presuppose a sense of higher achievement in which love is requited and enriching; families don't destroy their members but nourish, socialize, and develop them; democracies do actually give voice to the demos; and so on. Each of these phenomena has "a natural potential for 'envaluation' [that] is not an abstract possibility but an empirical likelihood founded in conditions that are routinely generated by the experience or relationship."[40] Each is "readily transferred into a relationship guided by ideals."[41] So, too, is the case with law.

These ideals, in turn, are not merely the idle (or ideal) impositions of analysts, but rather, in line with what he had learned from Dewey's humanist naturalism, a product of humans' problem-solving encounters in the world. Human beings are part of that world, they are *in* nature, and human values are a natural product of that encounter.

Values generate and are generated by the "internal dynamics" of developing institutions, practices, relationships. And so, to understand important social practices and the rigors and disciplines to which they are subject, one must understand the ideals—whether latent or patent—that inform them, the challenges these ideals face, the means appropriate to realizing them, and the degree to which they have been achieved.

However, as anyone familiar with Selznick's earlier writings (or Dewey's) would appreciate, acknowledgment of general ideals is not enough. One does not understand a complex institutionalized practice, such as democracy, simply by examining the democratic ideal. Rather, one has to understand the ways of the world, the obstacles they generate, and the opportunities, too; "Only thus can we know what specific norms are required to fulfill the ideal."[42]

And it is not enough to have some understanding of what people generally are like or how they behave because different normative systems generate different social and normative imperatives. What is going on in a particular system, what are its manifest values, what are the values latent in its structure, practices, informal networks, and so on: These will all vary among types of systems and among different examples of the types. That is why sociology is a house with many mansions. Selznick's early works investigated such things in organizations. But similar observation and investigation are necessary wherever we encounter normative systems, for understanding their "master ideals" is not a merely philosophical task, nor is it an abstract one. It is a task for social science, attentive to specificity and variation.

Indeed, Selznick argued thirty years later that "the main issues in political science, sociology, economics, anthropology, and social psychology are defined by the values at stake in social experience. . . . The closer we come . . . to what is central in the discipline, the more important is evaluation."[43] And yet sociologists commonly approach the task apprehensively if at all. Most deny that it is any part of their job:

> there is an odd reluctance on the part of social scientists to deal with normative systems. The disposition is to reduce such phenomena to arrangements that can be studied without assessment by the investigator, even when that assessment would entail nothing more than applying a culturally defined standard as to how far an implicit ideal has been realized. Thus, in the name of objectivity and rigor, the idea of friendship is left largely unanalyzed, and sociometric studies of reciprocal choice or differential association become the major line of inquiry. These measures, of course, say little about the quality of the relationship, not so much because they are incapable of doing so as because the studies do not begin with the normative perspective that would be appropriate . . . Again, social scientists have been much happier with the word "culture" since they have been able to strip it of normative significance and to bar the view that the idea of culture has something to do with excellence.[44]

Selznick thinks this coyness is misguided. It also misrepresents what is actually available within social science itself. One example:

> There is not much of a theory of friendship, or of love, in social science, but we do have the concept of the "primary relation," of which love and friendship are characteristic illustrations. What is a primary relation? It is a social bond marked by the free and spontaneous interaction of whole persons, as distinguished from the constrained and guarded arms-length contact of individuals who commit only a part of themselves to the social situation. In the primary relation, there is deep and extensive communication; individuals enter this experience as a way of directly attaining personal security and well-being, not as a means to other ends. This rough and elliptical statement is very close to what most sociologists would accept. Yet clearly it states an ideal only incompletely realized in the actual experience of living persons.[45]

Social scientists tend to strip down concepts such as "friendship" or "democracy" to their observable and measurable elements. In doing so, they miss a great deal that matters in every friendship and democracy. And so, though social scientists are happy to build models, even to consider "ideal" and "pure" types, "when the realization of values is involved, social scientists seem to lose their zest for model-building."[46] Or, as Selznick put it in an unpublished speech, "to put it bluntly, our keenest minds in the social sciences didn't know what to do with an ideal except handle it gingerly and view it with alarm."[47]

In "Sociology and Natural Law," some ambiguity, perhaps uneasiness, remains about the role the investigator's *own* values might play, and we will return to this issue in Chapter Nine. Selznick sought to reveal how much awareness of values might enter social science without engagement of the observer's values at all; without what his colleagues might regard as pollutants of scientific purity. Thus, unwillingness to deal directly with matters of value is often defended on the basis of a commitment to objectivity. But Selznick insists that an observer does not have to identify with the values at play in a particular normative system, not even value them; "Whatever the assessment, it is always *from the standpoint of the normative system being studied*. The student of a normative system need not have any personal commitment to the desirability of that system." "The study of normative systems is one way of bridging the gap between fact and value. At the same time, the objectivity and detachment of the investigator can remain unsullied. The great gain is that we can more readily perceive latent values in the world of fact."[48] Or, as he wrote some years later, in his manifesto of the JSP Program, "Our normative models should be founded in inquiry regarding what people actually experience as deprivation and how institutions function in fact. They are also subject to correction as new conclusions are warranted regarding the desired, the desirable, and the possible. . . . Normative theory in social science is not the pursuit of one's 'own thing.' It is the study of values in the world and the conditions under which they are fulfilled or frustrated."[49]

Because values stem from the character, vulnerabilities and natural propensities generated within social arrangements, then, to speak of the well-being or flourishing of a practice is not just arbitrarily to commend it on the basis of judgments brought to it from outside but to engage in immanent diagnostic critique. The attitude might well be one of clinical detachment, like that of a dispassionate or disinterested or even misanthropic physician diagnosing a condition of ill health in a patient, even an obnoxious patient, in terms of a conception of the constituents of good health scientifically derived.

Consider the sociology of the family. A "good" father is not simply a father judged to have done well according to some external standard that observers bring to bear (though he might be that too). He is a person who has met immanent naturally and socially generated values implicit, if often latent, in his role. Such values will vary considerably with time, place, circumstance, and culture, and it is a task for normative theory, through investigation and theorization, to attend to the variations and seek to explain them. But, whatever the variations and however well or ill met, there will be demands. And one neglected part of the sociologist's calling is to investigate what they might be *and* to what extent they are fulfilled.

For fathers, to stay with them, are not just biological sires. They are key and specific parts of that singularly important normative system, the family. If they behave cruelly, irresponsibly, carelessly, unaffectionately, over affectionately, and so on, as many do, families will suffer. For families to endure and then do well, certain values are appropriate and need nurturing. A normative theorist will seek to establish what these values are, even in the face of particular families who lack them, in whole or in part. Indeed, the fate of families who lack them well might contribute to the theory of what they need. Notwithstanding the numerous inter- and intracultural variations among "family values," these are never matters of normative indifference within any culture. Normative theorists will take both this universal fact and its variable incarnations equally seriously.

Again, socialization is an activity found in every society. Some people are chronically undersocialized or ill socialized. What makes for good socialization? What values are involved? What is at stake? These are questions of normative social theory. They cannot be answered in the abstract, so sociological and historical investigations are necessary. They cannot be answered just by looking, so our understanding of the character of values needs to be refined by philosophy, including moral philosophy. One can argue and provide evidence for why certain values need to be tended to if a system is to survive, even more to flourish. One might often get things wrong, and answers might well vary between different contexts, including cultural contexts, and be controversial; but that, Selznick insists, doesn't mean anything goes.

The enterprise of law, too, has standards, including standards of excellence, internal to the practice itself. Central, though not exhaustive, among them—as with all practices and structures that exhibit the "strain to envaluation" characteristic of normative systems—are normative requirements. That is a truth in teachings of natural law.

The point is neither that any particular normative system will necessarily evince its latent standards nor that anything anyone values necessarily *has* value for humans. Many things people value are pernicious, and it is again a job for normative theory in its critical and diagnostic moments to say why. Rather, Selznick insists, in general and in principle the generation of values is something human beings do and must do to deal with problems they face. It is not an accident that they do so. How well they do is not predetermined and can be assessed.

In such roles, systems and practices, values are "latent" in even poor examples of the species. They are responses within particular sorts of enterprise to real and recurrent needs, satisfactions and dissatisfactions, demands and criticisms made by participants, and new possibilities, as these develop over time. This produces a "strain" toward more elaborated developments of the ideals. That strain is often weakly felt and successfully resisted, just as it can be encouraged and supported. Nothing much happens *necessarily* in social life. And values do not come from nowhere. To understand them requires understanding of social facts, the normative pressures to "envaluation" that they generate, what spawns their satisfaction, what thwarts it, and what might be done to aid the former and diminish the latter. To discern such things involves discovery and interpretation, not invention and imposition. There is, then, no warrant to expunge values from the concerns of science, still less to ignore the ways in which facts and values commingle in the world. It is the sociological connections, continuities, and interdependencies, among what that other "moral scientist" Durkheim sometimes called "social facts" and sometimes "moral facts,"[50] that Selznick wants us to recall.

Qualitative States

Values latent in a practice might be undeveloped, inadequately nurtured, overwhelmed from inside or out, deformed. Ideals are, after all, hard to realize, even partially. Even where there is a will to achieve them, it might be diverted by "the tyranny of means" or run into sand because of the "impotence of ends." In any event, practices often exist in "rudimentary states," where, whatever values are latent, they are not much in evidence. Still, normative theory will not ignore such states. It must be alive both to what is required for friendship, scholarship, and so on to be plausibly said to *exist*, and also to the *kinds* of friendship, and so on, that there are. Our analytical equipment and social understanding must be adequate to encompass both "rudimentary" and "elaborated" states.

Chary of evaluation as they were, sociologists typically set their sights too low. There is, Selznick writes, "a strong and understandable tendency to identify what is required for the maintenance of a system with what is required for the *bare survival* of a group or individual," even though "in fact, however, systems may decay despite the continuity of individual or group life."[51] This is a point he had already stressed in his theory of institutional leadership, but it applies more broadly. Survival is good in itself and a precondition for other goods. However, sociologists need to attend to what is required for a system to thrive, not merely to survive. Doing so, attending to differences among qualitative states, is not an abstract idealistic concern, to be probed solely by the analytical tools of philosophers or indulged in by sermonizers and moralizers. It is an attempt to bring social science to bear on a fact of common knowledge:

> To be sure, *some* systems are indispensable if life is to exist at all; but other systems are required if a certain *kind* of life is to survive. And it is fair to say that in social science the most important analyses have to do not with the bare continuity of life but with certain kinds and levels of organization.[52]

Over the years Selznick came to advocate a variety of juxtaposed contrasts for social analysis. One is between definition and concept, elsewhere definition and theory; another, different but related, distinguishes conditions of survival from those of flourishing. Social science, he came to insist, "is best served when definitions are 'weak' and concepts are 'strong'"[53] That is to say, one should begin with definitions capacious enough to include all plausible members of a category, be it a family, culture, democracy, legal order, or whatever. But what is useful as a starting point is insufficient for a developed concept: "A strong concept is more demanding in that, for example, it may identify attributes that are latent as well as manifest, or offer a model of what the phenomenon is like in a fully developed (or deteriorated) state."[54] *Theories*, as distinct from definitions, cannot settle for rudimentary states. They need to be sensitive to the variety of *qualitative* states in which phenomena can exist and help us discern the character and conditions of "elaborated" ones. They must also be capable of adequately rendering the "potential for 'envaluation'" inherent in important social practices. And they should explore what are the kinds of envaluation to which law as a particular form of institutionalized practice is prone; for law is one of the central, most elaborated, and thoroughly institutionalized normative systems we have, and so, "sociological inquiry has ample warrant for the study of law as a normative order. And this is the first, indispensable step toward a rapprochement between sociology and natural law."[55]

Law as a Normative System

Among the reasons Fuller's definition of law, as the enterprise of subjecting human conduct to the governance of rules, so appealed to Selznick was that it reveals an attractively sociological sensibility. It specifies the enterprise involved, frees it from necessary attachment to the state, and leads to a search for what values are *internal* to an enterprise of this specific sort:

> for to him the ideals of legality are rooted in the requirements of a type of order. They are not imposed from the outside to meet standards derived from alien premises. Thus Fuller is aware of the fundamental distinction between conventional moralism on the one hand and, on the other, sociological sensitivity to latent values in personality and group life.[56]

Another implication Selznick draws from Fuller's approach is that law is a normative system, that is, an institutionalized social practice with certain values specifically appropriate to it and at least latent within it. Though they use a different terminology, this is in effect what natural lawyers believe, and they are right to do so. A theoretical understanding of law, particularly one that seeks to link its sociological and philosophical dimensions, will have to accommodate its intimate strain to value.

But what value? The "master ideal" of law, as we have seen, is what Selznick called "legality," or, as he came to prefer, "the rule of law." In expounding this ideal, he commonly recurs to two themes that he believes mutually imply each other. One has to do with reason, the other with arbitrariness. Thus, legality is "the governance of official power by rational principles of civic order,"[57] and its aim is *progressively to reduce the degree of arbitrariness in the positive law.*"[58]

Legality, then, is not merely an "external" criterion for appraisal of law, applied by observers outside the system. Nor is it external in a second sense, having to do with how well a law achieved some extralegally given objective. Rather, it is a value apt to be generated (in conducive conditions) by the nature and character of legal institutions as well as of the expectations they generate. It is law's peculiar excellence, and it remains that even when, as often happens, it is violated. It belongs, in other terms, to what Fuller called law's "internal or implicit morality, a morality defined by distinctive ideals and purposes."[59] Selznick didn't draw the comparison, but it is there to be drawn, between Fuller's "internal morality of law" and Selznick's own concern for a very long time, with the "specific competence" of particular institutions. Selznick's concept applies more broadly than Fuller's, but the logic is the same.

The rule of law then is a master ideal of the enterprise of law itself, manifest when we are lucky, merely latent when we are not, and achieved to greater or lesser extent by different legal orders in different times and circumstances. It is a complex ideal, embracing, as it does, "standards for assessing and criticizing decisions that purport to be legal, whether made by a legislature or a court, whether elaborating a rule or applying it to specific cases;"[60] "Legality imposes an objective environment of constraint, of tests to be met, of standards to be observed, and, not less important, of ideals to be fulfilled."[61]

States of Law

The understanding that law is a normative system is relevant not only to the concerns of sociologists. It is equally important for lawyers and philosophers. "Legality" or "the rule of law," is a rubric for a cluster of values that derive from, are latent in, the experience of attempting to regulate life through law and that, when realized, constitute the specific excellences of that enterprise. This internal dimension must be acknowledged in any fully specified theoretical account of law. As a "master ideal" it is never fully attained, of course, but it embodies values peculiarly related to and generated by the difficulties, vulnerabilities, hopes, and potentials involved in the practice of subjecting human conduct to the governance of rules.

Another way of putting the point is to say that it is specifically concerned with the *legal* qualities of law. That phrase is not the tautology it might appear but a reflection on the fact that laws and legal systems can vary in the degree to which they approach the ideal of the rule of law. This, then, is why "legality is a variable achievement. . . . We can unblushingly speak of more or less legality, meaning nothing more obscure than that some systems of rules, and some modes of decision, are less arbitrary than others. A major topic in legal sociology is the study of empirical conditions that reduce or exacerbate the arbitrary element in making or applying rules."[62] That legality can vary is a fact readily accommodated by normative sociology, used as it is to distinguishing between qualitative states of affairs.

Of course, it is common to recognize qualitative distinctions by distinguishing concept and qualifier, the former dealing with what is internal to the phenomenon and the latter appraising it on the basis of some external criterion: for example, law and good law, "the law that is" and "the law that ought to be." In relation to latent values, however, Selznick considers this way of talking inadequate. The connection between law and good law is variable, but it is not merely contingent, accidental. What one seeks are *immanent, internal* qualities of legal orders, not merely to attach a label of approval or disapproval, according to one's own lights.

Laws can be bad *as laws*, then, notwithstanding that their purposes may be exemplary; and, conversely, laws of impeccable legality might be turned to evil ends (though there are reasons to doubt that this is always as easy to do as it is to say).[63] On the basis of its internal morality, one can criticize a law as *inferior* to other laws, not merely or necessarily because it is law that does bad, but because it is bad law, that is, law that is more arbitrary than other laws, and so lives up less successfully than it should to the master ideal of legality.

One domain of law where the ideal of legality is particularly pertinent, but applying it is particularly complicated, is that exemplary display of reason-in-law, judicial reasoning. It is long (and in the United States already was long in 1961) since anyone really believed that legality required or could require mere "application" of existing law. For many reasons explored by legal philosophers among others, what Oliver Wendell Holmes derided as "mechanical jurisprudence" is no longer even thought to be a live option, however nostalgic some lawyers and conservative politicians might be for it, or however live the controversies are about what can and should be done in its absence. But if judges are free to be, still more compelled to be, creative in some sense or measure, what is to distinguish their acts from the freewheeling political and moral choices of lawmakers, or any of us, for that matter? And if the answer is nothing, or nothing much, why do they wield the authority that they do? What is *legal* about it? Of course, whatever process leads to it, it is legally obligatory, but that merely speaks to its consequences, not to its character and provenance.

This has been one of the central areas of debate in modern jurisprudence. Selznick moved into it a few years before Ronald Dworkin came to occupy it but with arguments that are strikingly like several of those with which Dworkin came to dominate Anglo-American jurisprudence. According to Selznick, the crucial problem is "to justify *as legal* the exercise of judicial creativity. That there is and must be creativity . . . is no longer seriously disputed. The question remains, however, whether there is something beyond the bare authority of the court, or reliance on a vague 'sense of justice,' to support the idea that judge-made policy has the stamp of legality."[64] But what else is there, what *could* there be?

Selznick follows Roscoe Pound in stressing that judicial reasoning does not merely amount to the identification and application of rules, but neither is the law necessarily spent, when lawyers' reasonings go beyond rule identification and application, for the law is not necessarily exhausted even when its formal rules are unclear, ambiguous, contradictory, or vague, in relation to particular circumstances and problems. Like Dworkin after him, Selznick recognized a particular jurisprudential significance of this:

> even a cursory look at the law will remind us that a great deal more is included than rules. Legal ideas, variously and unclearly labeled "concepts," "doctrines," and "principles," have a vital place in authoritative decision. . . . many familiar concepts . . . purport to grasp some truth and provide a foundation for the elaboration of specific rules. In addition, of course, there are even more general ideas or principles . . . It would be pointless to speak of these as merely a "source" of law; they are too closely woven into the fabric of legal thought and have too direct a role in decision-making.[65]

The law, then, includes a variety of layers. Judges can make better or worse use of this rich store of *legal* guidance, a source which, because it includes softer-edged, more open-textured value-laden contents than rules and often blurs distinctions between legality and justice more broadly conceived. Where they or legislators make worse use of them, or no use of them; when they defy or corrupt them, or merely ignore them—then they might well produce perfectly valid positive law, but what they produce "is not the whole of law, and it may be bad law."[66]

There are other internal understandings of sources of weakness and strength, inferiority and superiority, among legal judgments, which together add up to show that "if all laws are authoritative, some are more authoritative than others" because with them "an essential foundation is laid for a viable theory of justice."[67] On that foundation, one can better appreciate what is right and what wrong in the common assertion that judges appeal from "the law that is to the law that ought to be," as Selznick cites his teacher Morris Cohen's parsing of the truth in natural law, or "the law that they think ought to be," which is common folk positivism and realism. Cohen, Selznick observes,

> was almost right in arguing that we must be able to appeal from that law that is to the law that ought to be, from positive law to principles of justice. But he did not quite see that at least some principles of justice are ingredients of the ideal of legality and are therefore part of "the law that is." In many cases, we appeal from specific rules or concepts in the law to other concepts and to more general principles that are also part of the law. . . . Both belong to a normative system whose "existence" embraces principles of criticism and potentialities for evolution.[68]

Natural Law

And so say natural lawyers, whose "chief tenet is that arbitrary will is not legally final. . . . an appeal to principles of legality and justice is always available. This appeal assumes that every legal order, to the extent that it is one, has an implicit constitution."[69] Natural lawyers seek to identify that constitution. And it is here that their enterprise and that of social scientists do, or could and should, connect. Embodying a long tradition of thought about social values, natural law at its best has sought to establish generalizations based in nature about what is good for persons, what in law might help achieve it, and how. That is just what normative social theory does, or should do. So they are in the same business, whether or not they would all accept the same generalizations. Where their enterprises converge is in a quest *not* for God's supramundane dictates—Selznick lacks "God hunger"—but for sound and warranted proposals for human well-being. As he wrote much later,

> Natural law is not a quest for absolutes, nor is it the positive law of God's commandments. Natural law invokes the ultimate sovereignty of social knowledge, that is, principles derived from human experience regarding power and its dangers; egoism and its limits; the functional necessities in social life; what we may aspire to, what we fear or rely on in our quest for safety and contentment.[70]

It is difficult to exaggerate the importance, and centrality throughout Selznick's writings on law (and most other things), of this combination of normative and scientific commitments. While some readers of the *Natural Law Forum* might have hoped Selznick's ruminations might lead to God, and others might have feared the same, their proximate and deep source was clearly John Dewey. As Selznick reflected over a decade later:

> My own views on natural law owe most to Dewey's pragmatism. Dewey rejected the separation of fact and value as he did many of the other great and ultimately sterile dichotomies in philosophical thought. He believed in a thoroughgoing naturalism. In jurisprudence, what I have called *legal naturalism* looks to a social science of legal ordering. All aspects of law as a human enterprise—the aspirations associated with it no less than the discontinuities and the failures—are viewed as part of problem-solving experience, rooted in the continuities of personal and institutional life. Legal naturalism differs from much in the traditional philosophy of natural law but it shares a fundamental impulse: let us try to discover how far legal rules and legal judgment can be founded in reason, that is, in warranted assertions about man and society.[71]

Pursuit of natural law generates normative social theory to the extent it develops testable claims based on evidence and argument about human goods, to be established, corroborated, refined, or refuted, in the normal scientific way by the normal scientific standards. It is thus that one generates a "science of justice":

Natural law *presumes inquiry*. . . . *Legal norms are "natural law" to the extent that they are* based upon scientific generalizations, *grounded in* warranted assertions about men, about groups, about the effects of law itself.[72]

Social scientists already, and with a clean conscience, engage in research aimed to improve our knowledge of how law and life interact, and on the basis of that knowledge many suggest ways to improve the operations of law itself. Selznick commends such activity and recommends more:

> To put the matter this way may seem all too innocent. Among those who seek to improve legal doctrine and the administration of justice, few people would question the importance of having more knowledge about how people behave in legal settings. Studies of deterrence and criminal law, of jury behavior, of arbitration, and of legally relevant changes in industrial organization, would all be welcome. In principle, however, there is no reason why the most general concepts of law—equality, reasonableness, fairness, and the like—should not be as subject to criticism, on the basis of scientific investigation, as are narrower legal concerns. When that occurs all innocence is lost and the quest for law is uneasily resumed.[73]

So, sociology normatively conceived pushes in the direction of natural law, which in turn, properly conceived, depends on investigations apt "to discover how the system can be brought closer to its own inherent ideals."[74]

What will come out of these investigations is in principle open, fallible, and revisable as, on Dewey's pragmatist account, are all our judgments. For natural law depends on scientific investigation, and scientific conclusions are continuously open to revision and correction. Moreover, there is a second sense in which natural law can never be etched in stone. It *presumes* changing norms, for

> its basic commitment is to a governing ideal, not to a specific set of injunctions. The ideal is to be realized in history and not outside of it. But history makes its own demands. Even when we know the meaning of legality we must still work out the relation between general principles and the changing structure of society. New circumstances do not necessarily alter principles, but they may and do require that new rules of law be formulated and old ones changed.
>
> In a system governed by a master ideal, many specific norms, for a time part of that system, may be expendable. The test is whether they contribute to the realization of the ideal.[75]

What emerges is a complex commitment, not at first sight easily recognized as their own by either sociologists or natural lawyers, but dependent on both. It could be presented in dilute form as merely a critique of excessive positivism in social science, but its grounds are deeper than that: a quest for normatively unembarrassed social science combined with a philosophically informed appreciation of human values, firmly grounded in the ways of the world. Thus a distinctive ambition for sociology of law has crystallized:

> The major problem of legal sociology remains the integration of jurisprudence and social research. Unless jurisprudential issues of the nature and functions of law, the relation of law and morals, the foundations of legality and fairness, and the role of social knowledge in law are addressed by modern investigators, the sociology of law can have only a peripheral intellectual importance.[76]

CHAPTER SEVEN

The Rule of Law: Expansion

Selznick wrote "Sociology and Natural Law" in 1960 while he was a fellow of the Center for Advanced Study in the Behavioral Sciences at Stanford. That decade, and the next two, were significant for two other reasons as well. One was that, for the United States generally and for Berkeley in particular, the 1960s did not merely mark a period of time. It witnessed, and Selznick was influenced by, significant social movements. The other was that, starting that year and culminating at the end of the subsequent decade, Selznick came to institutionalize his approach to law and social science.

THE 1960S

From early in the 1960s, the United States generally and Berkeley quite specifically were in the midst of turmoils that could not but affect the thinking of people involved, particularly if their concerns had to do with leadership, authority, morality, and law. That was certainly true of Selznick. The churnings of those years had specific effects on his thought.

The first significant event that forced a taking of sides in heated debate, and had long-lived effects on many of the participants, occurred at the end of 1964. Students at many universities in the United States were already becoming politicized by the civil rights movement of the late 1950s and early 1960s. They were to be dramatically radicalized by the Vietnam War, the draft, and the antiwar movement of the late 1960s and early 1970s. In between, there was a major crisis at Berkeley, paralleled in many universities throughout the world, which could be variously interpreted: as students valiantly fighting for important values against an intransigent and bone-headed university administration, or tactically manoeuvring for larger political game while repeatedly and deliberately wrong-footing that administration, at the expense of the distinctive values of an academic community. Selznick began with the first view. Later he came to believe the movement had changed, and he lost sympathy with it. But it had lasting effects on his thought.

In 1964, for reasons that remain obscure, the university decided to enforce a distinction in existing regulations between public "speech," which would be allowed, and "advocacy and organization," which would not. This was the occasion, or to the students' critics the pretext, for confrontation between students and the administration. The confrontations were dramatic and, on rare occasions at that early stage, violent.

Everyone appears to have agreed that the administration handled and in ensuing negotiations continued to handle the confrontation with consummate lack of skill. The question soon arose as to what might be done to defuse an inflammatory situation. A large majority of faculty, in which Selznick was prominent, condemned the administration's behavior and distinctions. It rejected university restriction of content of speech or advocacy, allowing only "reasonable" regulations as to "the time, place, and manner of conducting political activity on campus."

Selznick was chair of the Sociology Department during these events (from 1963–1967). In 1965 Nathan Glazer, his associate from Trotskyist days, member of the department, and later coeditor of Irving Kristol's *The Public Interest*, published a piece in *Commentary* that was highly critical of the students and derivatively of the faculty who supported them. Selznick replied (and Glazer responded to Selznick). Where Glazer saw a ham-fisted administration defending important values against unprincipled and uncouth attack by students who were traducing them, Selznick saw something very different: a failure of academic leadership by those running the university, a denial of basic academic values, and a fight for just such values by students rightfully enraged. Glazer's article asked, "What happened at Berkeley?" Selznick replied:

> Something basically good has happened here. If we still have something to teach our students about the relation of means to ends (and I believe we have), it is also true that they have had much to teach us. Their mode of instruction has been passionate and in part irresponsible, but it has not been such as to justify a shrinking back in horror. Much of what the students did was clearly

necessary if we were to be made to *really listen*. I think they accomplished that. And considerably more.[1]

The university, Selznick insisted, is an institution of a particular character. To lead it well, one must seek to understand that character, what would serve to reinforce it, what values were in keeping with, and inconsistent with, it. Instead, as he appraised the view of the president, Clark Kerr, who had sought him for Berkeley and with whom he had been on good terms:

> the university is an organization like other large-scale organizations in our society. Individual freedom and institutional well-being are best served if there are limited commitments on both sides. He lacked a vital theory of the university community and of the conditions under which its greatest potentialities might be realized.[2]

But shouldn't the students have obeyed the rules? Selznick concedes that they crossed several lines they should not have, but he insists that what might rightly be required of them and how one might rightly act in relation to them were intimately related. In making the point, he elaborates on what he took to be some of the key elements of legality:

> Glazer tellingly documents the administration's rigid and inept handling of the dispute. But he does not grasp the significance of the fact that arbitrary administrative action lay at the base of the controversy, and was fuel to its flames at every step . . .
>
> The obligation to obey the law is among the more subtle and variable of human commitments. In assessing that obligation, we take account of the nature of the setting, the character of the rules and of their enforcement, and the legitimate interests of the offender. . . . While we cannot do without it altogether, a very strong emphasis on administrative authority is out of place in higher education. Here, if anywhere, the spirit of consultation should prevail. So too, arbitrary rule-making or administration saps its own authority and provides the offender with a defense. And if the offense carries forward a legitimate purpose, such as freedom of expression, or self-defense, it has some chance of vindication . . .
>
> Legality is a two-way street. He who insists on obedience to rules should be ready to justify the rules themselves. At Berkeley the administration adopted a posture of intransigence and as much as said that it would yield only to pressure. There was little concept of true consultation with students on matters affecting their interests. In this setting, a loss of confidence and respect was inevitable. To many of the students, it seemed to justify direct action.[3]

Glazer did not believe that freedom of speech was truly at issue at all, or that it was what motivated the students. He saw their complaints as diversionary tactics, of a kind of which "one of the most brilliant analyses . . . is, of course, to be found in Professor Selznick's *The Organizational Weapon*."[4] Other admirers of that book wondered what had come of Selznick's analysis of the vulnerability of institutions of mass modern societies to subversion by determined foes who preyed on uncomprehending elites. Selznick did not admit the analogies. He believed that, in the first stages of the Berkeley events, the students were sincere and their case just, and that, by contrast, the leaders of the university sought, both wrongly in principle and ineffectively, to rule the university by fiat. He made this point several times on important occasions. While not a public being, what he did, particularly given his prominence generally and within the university, had public significance.

Later, as students became increasingly radicalized, trashing chancellor's offices and seeking to use the university for larger "revolutionary" aims, Selznick had had enough. In the first stage, he believed the students' protests were consistent with, indeed in furtherance of, values intrinsic to the university. In the later years, particularly by the 1970s, he came to believe they were using the university as a platform and instrument to pursue other goals, to be seen only as a venue for conduct of revolutionary activity, without any interest in the welfare of the university at all and at its expense. When he came to believe this, he "got off the train," though less noticeably than he had got on it.[5]

His first trajectory, favoring the students, parted him from some of his oldest colleagues, among them two—Glazer and Lipset—who subsequently left the Berkeley department, and from his oldest and perhaps best friends—Irving Kristol and Gertrude Himmelfarb. Already after the first of the Berkeley events, Glazer wrote that "afterward men who had been friends for years but had taken opposite sides approached each other with hesitation, and felt it necessary to reaffirm their friendship, so deeply had their emotions become involved."[6] In 2002, after a lot of time had passed, Selznick made a similar point: "Taking the position I took then was a kind of watershed, I think, that divided me from my more conservative friends. For them that was really the critical thing. What you thought about what was going on in the campuses at Berkeley, Columbia, and so on. That made all the difference for how you were conceived."[7] His old colleagues, such as Glazer, Lipset, and Kristol, wondered why he had ever got on the train; a younger friend, Kornhauser, broke with him for alighting, in what Selznick later recalled as a "searing experience." By then, however, he had travelled some distance.

These events played significantly into strands already present in Selznick's thought, in his radical past, his pragmatist leanings and his organizational theories, and they accentuated some of them. In subsequent books and in interviews, Selznick several times returned to these themes:

> The student movement made us much more aware of the practical importance of arguments that tied authority and consent. You can go back to [Chester] Barnard's book of the '30s, that it doesn't make sense to issue orders that won't be obeyed. The '60s gave a much stronger spin to all of that, and to the importance of criticism. For example in the reply to Glazer, for example, [I wrote that] "legality is a two-way street." I probably wouldn't have said that earlier. I wouldn't have been as aware of the ways that authority can be eroded by the way it's used.[8]
>
> It underlined the importance of thinking about the critique of rules and the authority of rules by considering the reasons behind the rules and very strongly influenced the notions I had about authority. I say "influenced." I think it more underlined and strengthened views I'd already had. I had written about it, and quoted Merriam—"the poverty of power"—many years earlier. I was always interested in that, in Barnard's notions of the interplay of authority and consent, but I think the experience of the '60s and especially what happened in the universities gave a much stronger impulse to think about and deal in some positive way with the limits of obedience to law and the ways authority depends upon proper conduct. You couldn't just have authority based on something that was received. Someone puts a mantle on you, and you speak with authority. In a sense this was nothing new, I had long before thought about the relations of authority and consent and authority and competence . . . But I think this torrent of events very much nourished and informed and gave a lot of resilience and strength to these ideas. I think that was the origins of thinking about responsive law and responsive government, and, what people saw as somewhat strange, seeing responsiveness as having dual concern to maintain the integrity of the institution at the same time as it tries to deal with successfully with new interests, voices and circumstances.[9]

The first extended working out of these continuities and changes of views occurred in *Law, Society, and Industrial Justice*. Much of the work on it was done by Selznick and other members of his Center for the Study of Law and Society (CSLS), which began operations in 1961.

THE CENTER FOR THE STUDY OF LAW AND SOCIETY

By the mid-1950s a number of foundations were beginning to take an interest in law and social science. In 1960, Selznick negotiated a grant from the Russell Sage Foundation to establish the country's first law and society center at Berkeley. The Meyer Research Institute also gave a grant for the Berkeley center. Several others followed.

The CSLS was established in July 1961, with Selznick as chair and his former student from UCLA, Sheldon Messinger, as vice chair. The center's brief, as stated in its first annual report, was "to help develop a program of research into the nature of the law and its social, political, and economic settings."[10] It began modestly as an "organized research unit" (ORU) of the university, a kind of hub for people on the campus with interests in matters to do with law and society, to meet, discuss projects, run seminars, host visitors, advise students from various faculties. It drew faculty and students from many departments, as well as a growing number of international visitors. Some faculty, such as Caleb Foote from the Law School, made their homes there from the start, though their appointments were elsewhere; others dropped in. Selznick made his office there until he became chair of sociology in 1963, when he moved between offices. An increasing number of scholars from an array of faculties (including the usual suspects—law, sociology, political science, philosophy, anthropology, rhetoric, and social work—but also some less usual, among them Assyriology and mathematics) appear in its reports as staff, associates, graduate associates, visitors from around the country and increasingly from abroad; the publication list swelled, and the CSLS was well and truly established. It also came to occupy a lot of Selznick's thought and time.

From the start, the center had a more pronounced and explicit theoretical and normative focus than other groups working in the field. As Messinger later recalled, "The jurisprudential focus was there from the start. The other arm was that legal writing lacked an empirical base and one of the things that the center could help do was provide an empirical base."[11] The general perspectives that frame its first report embody characteristic themes of Selznick's investigations of law thereafter, as does one of its first projects on "private government," "an area where an ever more central preoccupation of the social sciences, the study of complex organizations, bears closely on legal theory." This ultimately issued in *Law, Society, and Industrial Justice.* An underlying center concern was with "the social foundations of legality," or the rule of law, and potential tensions between that "practical ideal" that "rests in part on pessimistic premises regarding the nature of man and society," on the one hand, and "law as creative governance," capable of providing "substantive solutions for new and continuing problems," on the other. As it became established, the range of projects the center supported steadily grew, and the publications that stemmed from work associated with it became substantial. One such publication was the product of Selznick's long-term investigations of industrial and labor relations, *Law, Society, and Industrial Justice.*

LAW, SOCIETY, AND INDUSTRIAL JUSTICE

In his *Encyclopedia of Social Sciences* entry on sociology of law, Selznick argued that, given its centrality among legal values, the rule of law "must be a chief preoccupation of legal sociology,"[12] and he pointed to a good deal of research that spoke to that theme. Though they might have spoken *to* it, however, in the sense of bearing on it, most sociologists did not speak *of* the rule of law or analyze it particularly closely.[13] It is not obvious why, because if the rule of law, understood as at least in crucial part a brake on arbitrary exercise of power, matters legally and politically, it certainly matters socially. Arbitrary exercise of power is a common cause of social disorientation and in the worst cases catastrophe, and it is a proper matter of social concern what might be done to prevent or lessen it, as it is to understand its social preconditions.

But there are many things that conspire against close sociological exploration of the rule of law. Prominent among them are purists' fears of disciplinary contamination. The rule of law is *so* associated with law, politics, and the state, that sociologists have tended to keep their distance from this hallowed legal ideal—too normative, too legal, too political, too formal, too disconnected from life; and how is it to be measured? That neglect is matched by legal and political theorists' immaculate conceptions, untainted as they have remained by social theory or empirical social research. This mutual ignorance is unfortunate, for some of the central questions about the rule of law are sociological ones.[14]

Several such questions are posed in *Law, Society, and Industrial Justice.* Although this book has to do with a very specific subject—the chances of bringing restraint on arbitrary power into large modern organizations—in fact it is an exemplary demonstration of what is involved in, and how one might think about, bringing to bear important legal values on significant contemporary and emergent social realities.

The book was the culmination of work begun in the 1950s while Selznick was still much involved in organization theory and beginning to think about law. It was published in 1969, by which time law had long been his central concern and reflection on recent events had led to some novel inflexions in his thought. It draws on, deepens, and extends many of Selznick's earlier ideas, fuses them with novel interests and engagements, and focuses them in a quite specific context. It also combines sociological analysis of law-affected behavior with sophisticated doctrinal understanding of large bodies of law. The result is a book about industrial relations that, as is typical of Selznick's thought, has more than its ostensible target in mind.

The central questions with which the book is concerned are whether the rule of law might be extended to relations between employers and employees, and, if so, whether it should be. His answers, put briefly, are "yes" and "yes." He also has something to say about how this might come about. That may be all a reader in a hurry wants to hear. But it isn't as simple as that—for, as Selznick makes clear in the book's first two paragraphs, there are larger issues in play:

> This is a study of industrial organization, viewed in the light of moral and legal evolution. "Moral evolution" is a somewhat unfashionable phrase, but it can usefully denote the progressive clarification of human ideals, and the enlargement of institutional competence to serve them. Our concern is with a special ideal—the rule of law—and its extension to the conditions of employment in modern industry.
>
> The larger context of our inquiry is the embodiment of ideals in institutions, the infusion of group life with the aspirations and constraints of a moral order. We take it for granted that this achievement, where it occurs, is partial and incomplete; that it is often born of confusion and sustained in struggle. We assume that to study the institutional embodiment of values we must look closely at the values themselves, at the characteristic ways they are elaborated and extended, and at the social circumstances that invite or resist them.[15]

There are many familiar themes here. From Selznick's first writings, we have a focus on the inner life of organizations and the significance of "the embodiment of ideals in institutions," "the infusion of group life with . . . aspirations and constraints," the "enlargement of institutional competence." From his essays on law we have "a special ideal—the rule of law," and the claim that it is immanent, at least latent, in "the enterprise of subjecting persons to the governance of rules." We know, too, that an analyst must "look closely at the values themselves, at the characteristic ways they are elaborated and extended," and "at the social circumstances that invite or resist them." But how does all this come together in the particular context of management–labor relations?

Why all this heavy metal, in what can be read, plausibly and at one level, as a work of advocacy with a simple message: Organizations should respond better to, better protect, and better fulfill, the interests of labor? But why should they? Why now? Can they? Are they likely to? How might they? How deep will any recommended or legislated ideal penetrate? What sources of resistance can be expected? What are the chances that it will last as a governing ideal? What sorts of slippage might we expect between ideal and real?

Imagine someone, say a politician or administrator or lawyer, asked to consider extending the rule of law to industry. What might that involve? Perhaps the extension of appropriate legislation—clearly drafted, publicly promulgated, stable—to factories? Perhaps, more adventurously, justiciable legal rights for workers in industry? None of these would be implausible renditions of the claim, and all would easily find sources in writings on legality.

Selznick, however, had spent almost thirty years pondering the recalcitrance of people, practices, and institutions, the precariousness of the finest ideals, the complexity and delicacy of attempts at institutional transformation, the ease with which fine motives are refracted in unexpected directions. At the same time, at least since *Leadership in Administration* it had become clear to him that, while wisdom might begin in recognition of obstacles, neither it nor virtue end there. A normative theorist will seek out latent values in social arrangements that might, in the right conditions, develop and even be helped to develop. The time of such values might have come, or be coming. Then again, the times might not be ripe, circumstances might be unfavorable, opportunities of development minimal or less. How can one tell?

In *Law, Society, and Industrial Justice* Selznick examines particular legal and social developments in a way that seeks to inform a concern for consequence with sociological and philosophical understanding, sociology and philosophy with each other's understandings, law with them both, and all of the above with jurisprudential reflection; in fewer words, jurisprudence and social policy. Though he had not yet coined the phrase, the concept was clearly in hand.

Law and Association

The problem the book addresses, put bluntly, is what law might offer to improve one pervasive consequence of relatively recent social transformations: "the condition of Administered Man."[16] Most people in modern Western societies spend much of their time dealing with large governmental and nongovernmental bureaucratic organizations; huge numbers spend their working lives within them. As these organizations and their significance have grown, so too has the importance of relationships within them, prominent among them power relationships and "new modes of belonging and dependency."[17] The importance of "freedom *of* association" has long been recognized in Western law; concern for "freedom *in* associations" is more recent. Yet the large modern organization has become "*a generic phenomenon*, a locus of authority, commitment, dependency and power. It is the reality of this nexus . . . that poses problems of freedom and civic participation."[18] Life in organizations generates relationships within which most of us are enmeshed for our whole working lives and by which we are, in one way or another, affected for all our lives. Such forms of association are not intermittent or self-chosen, as they once might have been, but systematic, enduring, unavoidable. That leads to strains and opportunities. We discuss some strains in this section; opportunities in the rest of this chapter.

Given that so much of a person's life is spent in and depends on supposedly "private" organizations, Selznick argued, "The loss of a job, or the right to pursue a profession, or the opportunity to continue one's education, may be far more hurtful than a term in jail. When these deprivations are inflicted arbitrarily and there is no recourse, a gap in the legal order exists."[19] One reason for such gaps is that the law regulating modern nongovernmental organizations—primarily the law of corporations, contract, and property—was increasingly ill suited to transformations in the "condition of Administered Man." Thus traditional concepts of the corporation, focusing on consequences of formal legal status, have difficulty dealing with the social realities of *institutionalization* in modern organizations. That institutionalization often occurs in large and enduring organizations, whether formally recognized as corporations or not, and it "sets problems for the legal system."[20] Where an organization becomes institutionalized, as we saw in Selznick's organizational writings, it "takes on a distinctive character, competence, or function, and becomes charged with meaning as a vehicle of group identity or a receptacle of vested interests."[21] This, in turn, has law-related significance of various sorts. There is a demand "for legal cognition of the nature of the institution," where that nature is not merely a result of legal definition but "is known by its mission and competence, its commitment and capacity to perform a social function." That in turn is tied up with "the social structure of the agency—the roles and relationships, the norms and values, that comprise an operating social system. Types of institutions have characteristic structural attributes and requirements, and the law of associations is continually pressed to develop ideas that fit these realities."[22] Finally, there is a

> strain toward public accountability . . . What may have begun as a purely private effort to mobilize resources for particular ends becomes in time a captive of the broader interests that have become implicated in its existence. Sociologically, if not legally, there is a movement from private to public responsibility whenever leadership loses full freedom to manipulate resources and becomes accountable to the interests of others and to the enterprise itself as a continuing system.[23]

Selznick is well aware that any such trends do and must encounter resistance; indeed, "a great deal of managerial effort is devoted to blocking and overcoming the drift toward institutionalization, with its attendant broadening of responsibility and dilution of power. But the more enduring the organization, and the larger the scale and scope of its activities, the more likely is it that the strain toward public accountability will be manifest."[24]

Selznick approaches the two other key relevant areas of state law—contract and property—with similar sociological and diagnostic attention. Classical voluntaristic, individualistic contract law expressed a social imaginary inhabited by roughly equal, independent right-and-duty bearing individuals, engaging with each other at arm's length, in specific, self-chosen transactions, bounded and limited in scope by the participants' choices. Participants pursue their individual projects, cooperating when they choose to; outsiders to contractual bargains are truly, or at least in the contractual imagination, outside. But the modern bureaucratized, *institutionalized* world puts all these assumptions in question, for classical contract law is unable "to grasp the reality of association."[25] And so:

> To the extent that continuity and concerted effort are prized, each element of the contract model is subject to attrition and distortion. The movement is from limited to diffuse commitment, from reciprocity to interdependence, from mutuality to unilateral obligation, from equality to subordination, from privity to openness, from self-regulation to external constraint.[26]

Property law, too, "has hindered the development of a theory adequate to deal with the internal ordering and external effects of modern economic organization."[27] It is alert to possession, domination, and subordination; deaf to association, stewardship, and authority. It has difficulties with collective ownership, for that "invites scrutiny of the inner order of the enterprise, especially the way power over persons is generated and used," as it does with concentrations of wealth and power in large and complex organizations "that are immortal and know no boundaries."[28] All these accumulated changes "create a demand for restraint and accountability, for countervailing institutions, and for a conception of the organization that yields a theory of authority."[29] That theory is required,

> not only by the fact of subordination, but by the socialization of ownership and the concentration of power. All of these developments have undermined the social acceptance of unfettered domination. In one form or another, the principle of stewardship, of fiduciary responsibility, is being reasserted. . . . This requires that external control be geared to the reconstruction of the association's inner order, especially the way authority is generated, sustained, and renegotiated.[30]

Together, corporation, contract, property all "fail to grasp the reality of association,"[31] and in so failing they fail, too, to ground authority. Authority in institutions will wane unless reinscribed in altered terms that do justice to the social realities of the modern work- and life-space. The search for those terms, Selznick suggests, might be cast as a

> quest for the corporate conscience: its origins, its locale, its sustaining forces, its legal implications, its troubles and limits. . . . What is at stake is the capacity of the institution to do justice. That competence is located in the attributes of a social system, conceived as an arena within which authority is exercised and rights are asserted. To grasp the nature of that system, and to draw the legal conclusions, is the major task of a law of associations.[32]

Law in Society

As we have seen, among the reasons Selznick found Lon Fuller's capsule definition of law—the enterprise of subjecting human conduct to the governance of rules—"remarkably congenial to the sociological perspective" was that it did not limit the subject of inquiry to the state. Instead, Fuller recognized that law was "endemic in all institutions that rely for social control on formal authority and rule-making. That legal experience occurs in the 'private' associations of religious, educational, or industrial life is a postulate of legal sociology, a precondition of much significant inquiry."[33] It has not been everyone's view of where law might be sought or found.

In common language, among lawyers, and in legal philosophy, the association of law with the state commonly goes without saying. However, within sociology of law, there is a broad stream with many tributaries that suggests that law is all around us.[34] Selznick had already referred, in "Sociology and Natural Law," to the sociological truism that "education, politics, religion, and other social activities are found outside of the specialized institutions established to deal with them. Sociology has located these phenomena 'in society,' that is, in more informal and spontaneous groupings and processes."[35] Continuing with the view that so disconcerted Wolin, he believed the same was true of law. Conceiving of law as a particular *kind* of practice or enterprise, Selznick was more concerned with exploring the character, imperatives, purposes, and requirements of that kind of enterprise than with identifying it with one highly visible source.

So, formal provenance is not definitive; law can develop in many sorts of nonofficial locations. Selznick was aware of at least some of the Central European authors who were struck by the extent to which "customary," "folk," or "indigenous" normative orderings seemed to have more salience in people's lives than the often distant and locally suspect dictates of the rulers of the empires they inhabited.[36] Indeed, at the end of his first chapter, he endorses Ehrlich's dictum that "the center of gravity of legal development lies not in legislation, nor in juristic science, nor in judicial decision, but in society itself."[37] What might this mean?

Eugen Ehrlich himself, one of the earliest and most intriguing contributors to sociological jurisprudence and the sociology of law, had in mind at least two things. The first is that the sources of the law by which we live, "living law" as he called it, are not found primarily where it has become conventional to locate them—official legal structures—but in the normative arrangements that govern everyday social life. That can just sound like a sociological platitude, often of little weight because so unspecific, but in Ehrlich's work it amounted to considerably more because the "society" to which he referred is not some opaque black box in which everything happens but a web of the "associations" in which we participate, the "inner orders" of which are *normative* for us. A sociology of law has to attend to those inner orders, rather than merely to the pronouncements of jurists or even, as Pound famously (mis-)interpreted Ehrlich, to the (official) "law in action." For that is really just the "law-in-books-in-action," that is, what happens to the law-in-books when manifested (or not) in the actual operations of legal officials in the world. But Ehrlich had something different in mind.[38] "Living law" was not in the first instance official state law even "in action," though it influenced it and in turn was affected by it.

Selznick cites Ehrlich with approval in several writings, but he did not later think he had been actually *influenced* by what he had read, as distinct from agreeing with it.[39] There were, in any event, other sources of the points Selznick makes, and those points flow naturally from his earlier organizational writings. Nevertheless in *Law, Society, and Industrial Justice*, of all his writings on law, Selznick shares a number of themes with Ehrlich. First, the insistence that law is "generic," "found in many settings; it is not uniquely associated with the state."[40] A key task for sociology of law is to attend to the law of such settings in those settings. Selznick accepts this, though he does not follow Ehrlich in according *priority* to the nonofficial. His ambition is, rather, to *extend* our understanding of law to encompass both official and nonofficial settings, indeed "all institutions *that rely for social control on formal authority and rule-making*."[41] As so often when confronted with dichotomies, Selznick's tendency is to be suspicious of the choices they demand. Law often can be found outside the state, but it can be found inside it, too. To rule either out or establish a priori some universal order of priorities is to blind oneself to complexities and to sources of useful guidance wherever they can be found. Thus, "the concept of law should be available for study of any setting in which human conduct is subject to explicit rule-making; and when we deny the place of law in specialized institutions *we withhold from the private setting the funded experience of the political community in matters of governance*."[42] For a follower of Dewey, of course, "funded experience" was no small thing.

A second theme is the importance of attending to the "inner order of associations," a phrase that Selznick adopts and parses as "the natural settings and adaptive outcomes of group life."[43] Selznick was familiar with the "inner order" of large-scale organizations, with their particular and complex hierarchies, internal orderings, modes of institutionalization, and the attendant centrality of association and membership in the lives of their members. These set the particular normative frameworks, the "living law" in accordance with which we conduct many of the most important interactions of our lives.

Thirdly, even within official domains, law should not be conceived narrowly but "extends to administration as well as adjudication,"[44] "applies to public participation as well as to the conduct of officials,"[45] and so reaches all sorts of activities subject to "formal authority and rule-making."[46]

Finally, stressing, as Ehrlich had, that law might grow up gradually out of people's associations rather than descend from peremptory official imposition, Selznick suggested sociologists must be alert to the possibility of finding within associations what he called "incipient," "inchoate," "emergent" forms of law, generated in response to internal pressures, dynamics, and demands.

Sources of the rule of law will not always be found full blown and ready to go, nor where lawyers are accustomed to look, Selznick noted. On the contrary, sociologists, used to ferreting around in "the problem-solving practices and spontaneous orderings of business or family life," should be alert for patterns of "incipient law . . . [i]mplicit in the way in which public sentiment develops or in any increasingly stabilized pattern of organization; . . . a compelling claim of right or a practice so viable and so important to a functioning institution as to make legal recognition in due course highly probable."[47] Among these he mentions "some of the private arrangements worked out in collective bargaining agreements, especially seniority rights and protection against arbitrary dismissal." These figured centrally in his exploration of *Law, Society, and Industrial Justice*, for:

> A focus on incipient law bridges the concepts of law and social order without confounding the two; it assumes that law does indeed have its distinctive nature, however much it may rely on social support or be responsible to social change. On the other hand, some law is seen as *latent* in the evolving social and economic order. For example . . . the growing importance of large-scale organizations carries with it the likelihood that new claims of right will emerge, based upon a new perception of organizational membership as a protectable status.[48]

Selznick is looking for latent, liminal signs of legal growth and development out of the pressures and changes that occur in social life. Incipient law is one such sign. As it develops, *if* it develops, it can generate in turn "inchoate" law, that is,

> unordered and unsystematic, often based on *ad hoc* but convergent pronouncements. Instead of a clearly enunciated authoritative principle, there may be many diverse evidences, coming from a variety of official voices, that new claims are being recognized, new powers or expectations affirmed. Thus inchoate law is something more than incipient law. The latter is mainly an attribute of social practice and belief; the former is an attribute of law itself.[49]

Incipient, emergent, inchoate, these legal seeds are potential starting points and stages in legal evolution, of a sort that might both develop legal characteristics within the social settings from which they derive and then infiltrate official state law itself. And influence can run the other way too. Both these unofficial and official developments are important, *legally* important, within a suitably expansive concept of law.

Selznick also believed that incipient law might, as Ehrlich thought it did and needed to, come to influence and be absorbed into the official legal order. Rather than always start with official legal institutions and end up with individual recipients of legal directives, law spurred by sociological realities within human associations will often come to be taken up by official legal organs; "Incipient law is emergent *positive* law, responsive to, and made possible by, particular social circumstances."[50]

This is a theme consistent with some of the most enlightening of studies by "legal pluralists," that demonstrate, as one of the best of them, Marc Galanter, has put it, that justice typically occurs "in many rooms," not all of them visited by mainstream legal scholars. The implications of that are not small. As Galanter observes,

> The mainstream of legal scholarship has tended to look out from within the official legal order, abetting the pretensions of the official law to stand in a relationship of hierarchic control to other normative orderings in society. Social research on law has been characterized by a repeated rediscovery of the other hemisphere of the legal world. This has entailed recurrent rediscovery that law in modern society is plural rather than monolithic, that it is private as well as public in character and that the national (public, official) legal system is often a secondary rather than a primary locus of regulation.[51]

On the other hand, Selznick insists that not every sort of normative regularity or social control should count as law. What matters is whether *authority* is engaged, and what type of authority it is. Selznick always resisted the identification of law with coercion, not because the association never occurred but because a deeper connection existed between law and authority, understood as "a rightful claim to deference or obedience. . . . a *kind* of power—the power to win assent, deference, obedience—but its distinctive basis is a recognized claim of right."[52]

Though law is "generic," then, in that it is not solely associated with "public" legal institutions, it is not so capacious a category that it threatens to envelop the whole of life, or even whatever is considered obligatory, wherever it occurs. That would be to distinguish "law properly so called" from nothing much, which was a sociological (and anthropological) temptation to definitional laxity and emptiness that Selznick did not favor.[53] For to say law is in society is not the same as saying it is no different from anything else in society. He is concerned that we acknowledge its distinctive, authoritative, features, at the same time and as much as we understand its inextricable connections with the society it inhabits.

The Rule of Law

What, then, does it mean to extend the rule of law so conceived? Law, we learned, is a normative system with immanent sources of "envaluation," normative pressures provoked and stimulated by the nature of the practices themselves, expectations generated within them, and by them, and of them. The relevant value, or cluster of values, is the rule of law, abridged by Selznick as the "progressive" reduction of arbitrariness in law and its administration. So, "to infuse" the "mode of governance [of an organization] with the aspirations and constraints of a legal order"[54] is to extend the rule of law to and within it, where that means "to build it firmly into the life of society, to make the master ideal of legality a true governor of official conduct."[55] The argument of the book, then, is that the "condition of Administered Man" can be improved by an infusion of legality and a consequent reduction in arbitrary exercise of power, and that his circumstances include forces that strain in that direction. Only investigation and theorization can disclose, however, how strong at any time are these strains to the rule of law, how strong are forces that pull in other directions and what are the relative weights of force and counterforce. Outcomes are rarely predetermined.

The concept of arbitrariness is not a simple one, and in our interviews Selznick agreed that he had never tied it down conceptually. Like most who write about it, he associates arbitrariness with traits such as capriciousness, wilfulness, and, most of all, with the absence of reasoned justification. The role of reason as a governor of action varies, and so then does the extent to which action is arbitrary. The task of partisans of the rule of law wherever it occurs, and the task of those who seek to better "Administered Man's" condition, is to seek "progressively" to make it less so.

The rule of law can be approached "progressively," in at least two senses. Understood sociologically, as we have seen, legality is a matter of degree, more or less, rather than all or nothing. Presumptively, more is better than less. Secondly, it can be understood in a minimalist or more expansive way. As we have seen, this distinction, and this *type* of distinction, between baselines and aspirations, is a key structural feature of Selznick's thought, as it was of Fuller's, and it recurs in a variety of contexts.

We need to be able to think of law, as of any normative system, in a way that is alert both to its minimum conditions and what it is capable of, and understand both levels as aspects of an adequately elaborated theory of law and the rule of law. Usually, however, people tend only to either one or the other. Thus Selznick distinguishes between one way of thinking of law, Hobbes's way, as a "functional necessity," without which we suffer, while another, say his own, also "invest[s] it with hope and promise." He observes:

When law is conceived as a functional necessity, the focus tends to be on order and control. Law is summoned by elementary urgencies: keep the peace, settle disputes, suppress deviance. Authority pays its way, and redeems its coercive sins, if it can establish tranquillity, facilitate cooperative action, and uphold the mores, whatever they may be. This might be called the *minimalist* view of what law is and does. For it, "justice" is not a compelling symbol and at an extreme may even be scorned as the refuge of hopelessly muddled men.[56]

By contrast, a "normative concept of law, or any similar phenomenon, seeks to expand attention from necessity to fulfillment. Instead of concentrating on the minimum functions of law, or on the minimum conditions that signify its emergence, the emphasis shifts to law's civilizing potential."[57] A properly wide-angle concept will not reject the former sort, but it will not rest with it. Instead it will accommodate "a theoretical warrant for treating at least a *strain* toward legal development as objectively grounded."[58] While it "begins as a principle of constraint . . . it promises more than a way of moderating the uses of power."[59] It must not slight the former, and importantly so, because "the assumption is that no man, no group of men, is to be trusted with unlimited power." On the other hand, it should stretch to the latter too, for:

> The "progressive reduction of arbitrariness" knows no near stopping-place. The closer we look at that process, the more we realize that it calls for an affirmative view of what it means to participate in a legal order, whether as citizen, judge, or executive.[60]

Legal Evolution

There is no doubt that Selznick favored extension of rule of law values in the industrial domain. But he did not believe or suggest that they would be extended, simply because that would be a nice idea. The argument that they might be so developed is based on quite other, sociological, premises. In this argument is a strong suggestion of movement and direction over time. This is not inadvertent. He believed as a matter of general theory and specific observation that forces were at work that pressed—not in any sense inexorably, but really, "objectively"—in the direction of legal transformations in the industrial field. The job of institutional assessment was to discern their weight, direction, and prospects.

It was, of course, possible that these prospects would turn out to be nil. Societies are littered with legislative dead letters and proposals for legal reform that seemed good ideas at the time because someone thought them smart in principle and/or because they thought they suited the times. How to tell, and what to do? Here social theory meets legal and political theory.

Even though, as we have seen, Selznick had enumerated vulnerabilities to which members of organizations were exposed, and holes in legal protection of them, it was not from these difficulties by themselves that he thought change would be generated. He might have cited, and would certainly endorse, Max Weber's incisive observation from another context, that the existence of a need does not necessarily generate a solution; needs can go unmet for eons if solutions are not thought up, and there is nothing automatic about that.[61]

Again, Selznick had long assimilated from Chester Barnard notions of the interplay of authority and consent. His experience of the university turmoil of the 1960s highlighted the need for law to be *responsive* to social realities and demands, both because that would be a good way to behave and because commands are impotent if people ignore them. Indeed the (complex and uncertain) virtues of responsive institutions became a central question of his next book, *Law and Society in Transition*.

As we have seen, Fuller said one should speak of "law *in* society," and Selznick was struck by the point. As he said in an interview with me:

> Those are just phrases, but if you think about it you are led to concerns with the ways law is embedded in social life, arises directly from social life, speaks to the needs of social life, looks to creation of authority and law, which is not over and above society but that is in conversation with society, always resulting in some kind of negotiated order, some way of adapting law to new understandings as well as new circumstances. I'm not sure that Lon Fuller understood that that deeply, but intuitively I think that's what he was after, and it reflects a lot of what goes on in the Law and Society movement. They haven't articulated it very well. Studies of law in action bring law down to the ways people perceive it and respond to it and are governed in very direct ways, or fail to be governed by it. One integrates.[62]

Selznick had long been persuaded that there are evolutionary logics at work in the careers of institutions (as of persons and societies). *Law, Society, and Industrial Justice* itself represents, within Selznick's own thought, an evolutionary development and working out of that point of view. Trends, moments, opportunities, possibilities, develop in societies. One can seek to understand, at times exploit and sometimes further and fashion, such developments. Where they are favorable,

> The rise of new centers of potential oppression may be less important than (1) the changing aspirations of the community and (2) the opportunity to do

something about them. Subordinate and dependent men have always been treated badly by their masters. The contemporary situation is different in this, that new expectations are penetrating areas hitherto closed to scrutiny or immune to challenge; and modern organizational settings make possible new ways of asserting claims and institutionalizing victories.[63]

As we have seen, Selznick had also long insisted that "master ideals" were often latent in even rudimentary forms of normative systems, and that one important job of normative social theory is to identify such ideals and their propensity to develop. It is not far from Aristotle's concept of a telos to Selznick's understanding of latent values, and Selznick was conscious of the affinity. That identification would not be a mere moralistic projection by an external observer but would rather announce as potential what truly *is* potential even if unrealized, the tree in the acorn, even if the acorn never grows an inch. One cannot assume that such latent dispositions will be there to find—a stone may just be a stone—but one cannot reject the possibility merely because they are not readily apparent, nor discount a disposition merely because it has not become manifest.

Selznick's conception of moral and legal evolution has both a negative and a positive implication. The negative point emphasizes that ideals cannot be successfully grafted onto institutions simply because *we* would like it. All his institutional investigations told against that, and it goes very deep in his thought. As we have seen, even earlier, as a young socialist, he inveighed against idealists who ignored the recalcitrance of the social stuff out of which, and the historical conditions within which, they planned to shape a radiant future.

But Selznick's evolutionism has a positive aspect, too. While "progress" is never inevitable, it is also not simply random, accidental. For the logic of institutional development often produces the *strain* he has often written about, to realize immanent values. Such logic is never inexorable; it competes with other forces, values, tendencies; it will often be defeated. There are no guarantees of success, either metaphysical or empirical. And yet, such a logic can be discerned in many contexts and theoretically explained. And, then, it might be nurtured. We have seen examples of this in earlier chapters. There is nothing inevitable about an acorn becoming an oak tree, still less a thriving one, but there is a disposition that in appropriate conditions might flourish. And a poppy seed needn't try. Horticulturalists identify such conditions and seek to furnish them or at least support and nurture them. Less expertly, perhaps, and often with more fervent hope than deep understanding, so too do many parents. Failure is not unknown in either endeavor; nor, however, is success.

Normative systems develop in part as a result of internal tensions, the resolution of which provides pressures apt to propel the system to higher stages. Moreover, when certain things occur, whether as a result of conflict or other sources of development, others can be contemplated, people do contemplate them, and often something can be done about them. Sometimes that is a matter of new possibilities, as is common in the evolution of technological systems, but also in human and other ways of maturing. Sometimes, and also common in institutional development, new dissatisfactions arise at particular stages of development in the light of possibilities revealed that were earlier unconceived, indeed inconceivable. Participants angry that previously unheard-of values are ignored or traduced make new demands and criticisms and generate new systemic tensions. Maturity may not occur, dissatisfactions may simply be ignored or suppressed, but a new disposition is available that was not there before. It creates a strain to and in congenial circumstances can lead to novelty.

In the specific case of law, a key source of development is the need for *legitimacy*. As Selznick well knows, there is nothing unimaginable about governance predominantly based on force. However, as Weber emphasized, it tends to be unstable: *Macht* (power) is harder to depend on than *Herrschaft* (authority). Law does better when it is accompanied by, and contributes to, more willing acceptance than flows from mere submission to force. Legitimacy can be claimed on all sorts of grounds, only some of them connected with legality. Yet,

> legitimacy carries the lively seed of legality, implanted by the principle that reasons must be given to defend official acts. For reasons invite evaluation, and evaluation requires the development of objective standards. At the same time, implicit in the fundamental norm that reasons should be given is the conclusion that where reasons are defective, authority is to that extent weakened and even destroyed.[64]

Selznick emphasizes that nothing inevitably propels a legitimate order to the rule of law. Notwithstanding the sources of itchiness immanent in the very idea of legitimation, not every sort of legitimacy is as itchy as every other; "If power is justified on the basis of hereditary succession, for example, it is difficult to find the leverage for calling officials to account."[65] Normative social theory does not pretend that tradition leads necessarily to the rule of law, just as Weber did not think it necessary that "patrimonial administration" led to bureaucracy. However, there was what might be called a social logic of values at work in both cases, and in particular circumstances that is how things worked out. Again, there are plenty of legal orders where rule of law values are scarcely recognized, plenty where they are outweighed by competing values. The claim is just that there are immanent tendencies in the "enterprise of subjecting human conduct to the governance of rules" that, given congenial conditions, will incline toward the values of legality and that a legal order is more successfully developed to the extent that those values are manifest in its operations.

A major job for normative sociology of law is to understand what those conditions of legality are. What are "the social bases of the rule of law"? What *qualities* do social phenomena such as, for example, consensus, public opinion, obedience, reasoning, discretion, restraint and self-restraint, have to manifest to sustain the rule of law and what, in turn, might sustain those qualities? In particular, and in keeping with the central motifs of Selznick's work, one can say of any of these phenomena what he says of one of them—self-restraint:

> Historically, self-restraint has been supported by public consensus on the nature and limits of authority, professionalization of lawyers and other officials, and the evolution of clearly defined roles, such as that of the judge. But there is considerable variation in that achievement, and under modern conditions there is a need for more attention to the *organizational* sources of self-restraint as distinguished from mechanisms of socialization. Ethical conduct is mainly found in settings that nourish and sustain it, that is, where such conduct makes sense for the official in the light of the realistic problems he faces. To design such settings is properly the chief aim of the architect of legal institutions.[66]

Attributes of existing practices, then, as well as expectations and frustrations engendered by them, produce that "strain" toward more elaborated developments of the ideals, of which Selznick had earlier written. But why imagine it to be a strain to improvement? After all, Selznick does not speak merely of change but of "moral and legal evolution." And that is clearly conceived to be movement in a positive direction, "the progressive clarification of human ideals, and the enlargement of institutional competence to serve them." Why believe that the "strain" will be in that direction? Is this just a piece of progressivist faith; eschatology-lite for secularists and skeptics? Selznick resists this interpretation, though, as I will argue in Chapter Nine, not with complete success. Instead he draws on theories of personality development, social development, and institutional development, not to anthropomorphize societies or institutions but to point to the developmental logic that he believes is common to change in them all.

He refers to Durkheim's theory of social development, Piaget's and Mead's of individual moral development, Weber's of the development of society and institutions, Mary Parker Follett's and Chester Barnard's of developments within organizations. In each he discerns a story of moral development "understood as a natural process, a kind of maturation."[67] Each in their own context and way postulated development, whether over the life course of individuals or over generations in societies and institutions, toward a "morality of cooperation . . . a morality of rational rules, interdependent activities, and autonomous individuals."[68] Even Weber, so notoriously ambivalent about the "rationalization" he saw sweeping the world (as indeed is Selznick himself) and so determined to keep evaluations and science apart, "nevertheless . . . did trace a pattern of change in which a received morality of constraint—traditional norms and forms of authority—was replaced by a new morality founded in the requirements of rational action. A basic feature of that morality was the reduction of arbitrariness in official conduct."[69] A morality of cooperation emphasizes personal autonomy and competence; norms rooted in experience (rather than, say, deference to authority figures or traditions); dialogue and problem solving, rather than demands for conformity. The *strain*, in other words, is toward "an ethos of problem-solving . . . [and] . . . strongly opposed to a morality of constraint, which imposes solutions and limits alternatives."[70]

That ethos and that evolved morality, Selznick believes, fit closely with the rule of law insofar as each "abhors arbitrary judgment and constraint, presses for justifications, invokes the authority of agreed-upon purpose, and values the competent participant."[71] These features of morality and legality add up to a constellation that, Selznick claims, is not merely what he values (though pretty clearly he does value it), but rests "on a natural foundation and has objective worth. It may lose out in competition with other values, or be blocked by the absence of congenial conditions, but the legal ethic finds its warrant in the contribution it can make to human growth and self-realization."[72] A disposition in this direction is likely "where rational forms of social organization prevail," and these forms themselves militate against arbitrariness. Directed movement occurs because "when the ethic of cooperation makes sense historically as the preferred way of organizing human relations, a dynamic toward legality is created. For this reason, we see legalization as a peculiarly salient issue for the modern special-purpose organization."[73]

Of course, law cannot be fully purposive because of the weight of precedent at its heart. There are reasons why law moves slowly and seeks not to squander its past. Yet, as we have already seen in Chapter Six, legal orders draw on principles, concepts, and doctrines that generate ways of elaborating specific rules that can differ in the light of particular and changing facts, and yet still reflect their origins. In this process, "the achievement of legality is seen as the refinement of basic principles, their application in depth, and their extension to new social settings. As this evolution takes place, however, *the line between the legal and the political is blurred*."[74] Where this happens, where legitimacy, legality, and political justification start to merge, "the polity becomes the touchstone, not the legal order treated as a realm apart."[75]

Notwithstanding these fairly abstract and apparently idealistic formulations, Selznick has concrete social processes in mind. He takes an example from the modern university. He had some glimmering of the idea in his earliest academic writings, but it was obviously freshened and made more salient by the "Berkeley events," of which he had been an engaged witness.[76] Demands are increasingly made for legalization and restriction of the arbitrary power of university officials. Where this is successful, the rules are formalized to specify rights and obligations, reduce administrative discretion, and spell out the rules of the game; "Having made what they conceive to be a transition to rule-governed administration, the university officials congratulate themselves—and await obedience."[77] But that is not how things turn out:

> Unfortunately for the administrators' peace of mind, the quest for law generates new aspirations and more comprehensive goals. Once the rules become problematic, authority is in disarray. There is a demand that the rules be legitimate, not only in emanating from establishing authority, but also in the manner of their formulation, in the way they are applied, and in their fidelity to agreed-upon institutional purposes. The idea spreads that the obligation to obey has some relation to the quality of the rules and the integrity of their administration. A critical spirit emerges which insists that decisions be justified and that channels be available for effective review and the hearing of grievances When discipline is imposed, it is demanded that due process be protected. . . .
>
> As awareness expands and the dialogue is pressed, issues of academic "law and order" merge into larger questions of governance. Attention turns to the distinctive nature of the academic polity . . . law is the servant of polity not its master. It follows that legal procedures and rules are not self-justifying, even if they are offered as extrapolations from the ideal of legality. The contribu-

tions they make, and the costs they exact, must be assessed in the light of substantive ends.[78]

There is no direct train that takes you from latent to manifest, no guarantees, no certainties. There are just dispositions and circumstances. Whether the dispositions have formed, how far they have emerged, whether they are being deflected or redirected; these are questions to be answered in part empirically, by evidence of "incipient" and "inchoate" signs in the development of the persons, institutions, or societies under scrutiny. One looks for signs of emergence, and then one asks questions directed by theory:

> First, the social viability of the practice is in question—its functional significance for group life and especially for new institutional forms—must be considered. Second, the contemporary evolution of relevant legal principles must be assessed to see whether the new norm can be absorbed within the received but changing legal tradition. Thus incipient law is not based on abstract postulates; nor does it reflect the moral preferences of the observer. Incipient law is emergent *positive* law, responsive to, and made possible by, particular social circumstances.[79]

Incipient Law

Much of the book is therefore a search for "incipient," "emerging," even if yet "inchoate" signs of legality in the life and law of modern industrial organizations. Selznick finds many, particularly in transformations in organizational management, the impact of collective bargaining on the organization, expectations of employees, and in the relationship of public policy to once "private" institutions.

He draws on Weber's theory of bureaucratization, and more broadly rationalization, to characterize the social and organizational transformations from social orderings dominated by "kinship, fealty, and contract" to ones where "the principle of *rational coordination* dominates the scene."[80] He notes that Weber (but he could be speaking of himself) "was not imposing a 'rational model' on human affairs. To him the coming of rationality was a historical process—always problematic, always dependent on congenial circumstances, always bearing with it unintended effects."[81] He is aware of Weber's complex and ambivalent appraisals of rationality, and of the latter's many-layered consequences. Nevertheless, Selznick agreed with Weber that bureaucratic forms of organization contain seeds of legality. Whether the seeds will grow cannot be determined with certainty, but bureaucracy contains them in a way that other forms of organization did not:

> If bureaucracy obeys an inner impulse to create a legal-rational order, it does not follow, of course, that the impulse is always manifest in reality. The idea of bureaucracy is dispositional. It identifies a phenomenon that has significant latent potentialities. Just how much of this potentiality will be fulfilled depends on environing circumstances. In a heavily status-oriented community, or in a society where any official job is a high prize, an emerging bureaucracy will have mixed features, to say the least. In a totalitarian setting, where bureaucratic organization is supervised, stretched, and pummelled by political agencies, the rational-legal potentialities will be frustrated. On the other hand, if the theory is correct, we should expect the latent disposition to make itself felt as these constraints are attenuated or removed.[82]

Though Selznick had never slighted this aspect of bureaucratization before, he had certainly not given it the emphasis he came to here. On the contrary, he had generally emphasized pressures in contrary directions. However, he now emphasizes "one striking feature of the bureaucratic model, with its stress on objectivity and impersonality. *In theory, bureaucratic administration is the antithesis of arbitrary rule.* Bureaucracy formalizes every facet of decision-making and in doing so sets an ideal of limited discretion."[83] This is central to Weber's account of bureaucratic authority as "legal-rational," a feature of modern bureaucracies, whether or not they are offices of state; "the 'legality' of bureaucratic authority does not necessarily derive from the public status of the agency or enterprise . . . *The source of these attributes is internal; the dynamic they create calls forth the ideals of legality.*"[84]

Selznick sees similar developments, "a strain toward internal legality,"[85] with the decline of family-based firms in American industry:

> Pre-bureaucratic management was typically one-man rule . . . The pre-bureaucratic business leader was impatient with formal rules and procedures. He liked to keep his accounts in his hat and to run the organization from day to day without clear-cut policies . . . The bureaucratic way is directly contrary.[86]

This should systematically push toward managerial self-restraint. So too the "flowering of 'personnel policy' and a concomitant elaboration of rules and procedures . . . [that] limit the arbitrary exercise of managerial prerogative"[87] spread of seniority as a criterion of decision, formalization of disciplinary procedures. Selznick acknowledges that bureaucratic enterprise is "not mainly in the business of dispensing fairness" but rather of ensuring enterprise success, and that "bureaucratic authority is not easily checked and challenged from below."[88] Bureaucratization is therefore no sufficient condition for the rule of law, still less for democracy. On the other hand, for all their differences in form and purpose, Weber was right to see that both bureaucracy and modern law were part of the same larger historical story and had affinities that did not exist between legality and, say, charismatic or traditional ways of running organizations. Bureaucratization

> cannot be *relied on* to sustain legality. Our argument is not that bureaucracy itself produces a high form of legal order. It is rather that the strain toward legality, being "natural" to bureaucracy contributes to an evolution that requires impetus, and gathers support, from other sources.[89]

Pressures for development do not stop. Postbureaucratic tendencies are generated that seek to temper bureaucratic rigidities with flexibility, though they rarely erase what went before; "bureaucracy will not be completely eliminated. It will leave an indelible mark on the post-bureaucratic age. That mark will be a principle of self-restraint, especially in the use of human resources."[90]

A second, more recent development bearing inadequately recognized "'legal' potential,"[91] is the school of "human relations" in management theory, which has brought a "new image" of the worker, and "new ideas that are reconstructing the premises of management."[92] These have been salutary, in particular because they have yielded "enlarged awareness of human motivation and response. Employee, patient, client, inmate, soldier, student—each is seen as a whole person in inevitable (though highly visible) conflict with the requirements of administrative discipline. This awareness brings with it a change in the foundations of authority."[93] The weakness of "human relations" is its lack of "a political perspective,"[94] a perspective that Selznick seeks to supply.

Human relations writers are interested in lubricating industrial relations to make them smoother and more productive. What they lack is "a proper appreciation of power, and of appropriate responses to it."[95] They are concerned with how people *feel*, more than what structural and other conditions need to be satisfied for members actually to *be* "competent participants in a civic order."[96] In words that foreshadow Philip Pettit's republican critique of liberalism,[97] Selznick observes:

> One might treat a slave humanely, with due regard to good "human relations." His personal and emotional needs would be considered, if only as a price to be paid for reliable service. But this would still leave the slave as a dependent "unperson," incapable of asserting his own will save privately and by indirection. The political perspective asks that this basic dependency and incompetence be transformed; it blends into a legal perspective as the transition is made to orderly process for the invocation of rights and the redress of grievances.[98]

That, in turn, won't happen without "latent power,"[99] which requires organizational support and forms of participation that are "public and legitimate."[100] It is one thing to connect workers to each other and to the organization; but it is another, and false to a political perspective on their membership, to submerge the former in the latter. The watchword is accommodation, not absorption, and certainly not extinction.

According to Selznick, this is not just preaching but diagnosis and prognosis. He finds contract law pressed by the changes in the social and organizational environment. It is subject to transformative pressures in industrial settings, with the development of new forms of labor law, including collective bargaining. That in turn generates rule making for the continuing administration of the agreement and so

> "creates" a system of government . . . by helping to reconstruct the managerial process. Management becomes more conscious of rules, more conscious of rights, *and more capable of building that consciousness into the routines of institutional life*. The administration of "things" becomes the governance of men as this reconstruction proceeds.[101]

Other straws in the wind abound. Grievance arbitration "and the legal evolution to which it has contributed, lend much support to the governmental analogy. For in this institution we see a response to the need for lawfulness in the day-to-day administration of the large enterprise."[102] Creative arbitration, many of the principles of which Selznick seeks to review, "adapts generic legal experience to the industrial setting."[103] All of this contributes to a development from the "master's" prerogative to something far more directed and constrained.[104]

Selznick draws on other pieces of evidence as well, to show the existence of a *"receptive institutional setting* within which further legal change may take place."[105] It is not certain, but neither is it merely wishful thinking. It is a story of immanence and incipience, and that is a powerful, though not insuperable, combination:

> To say that a corporate conscience exists is not to say that we can rely on it. In questions of power and justice, we do not rely upon the individual consciences either. Our legal and political system necessarily postulates the existence of evil, especially the danger that some merely human form, believing itself free of error, will attempt to match its claimed perfection with unlimited power. Because of that risk, we cannot rely upon good will, personal or institutional.
>
> We should distinguish, however, what we can rely upon from what we can aspire to. The ethic of rational coordination provides the foundation for new expectations, new claims of right, new legal controls. The existence of internal order within the enterprise validates external control and, at the same time,

makes it feasible. It is just because fairness is already institutionalized to a large extent in the private sphere that an appeal to the larger political community, to the legal order, is warranted. The firmer the sense of legitimate expectation, the more likely it is that there will be an appeal beyond the immediate setting. Moreover, if a quasi-legal system of fair dealing already exists, there is some assurance that the routine case will be handled satisfactorily. Therefore, enforcement of exceptional claims for redress of grievances becomes feasible.

. . . we now have the possibility, a product of modern history, of extending the ideals of due process to private associations. This might always have been a worthy objective, but the development of an inner order within the modern enterprise brings that objective into close accord with what historical reality makes possible.[106]

Polity

In the last chapter of the book, Selznick sketches what he calls "the emergent law," whose substance is a "law of governance." And this connects to an old theme in his work, at least since *Leadership* . . . : Just as law does not stop with the state, nor does politics, nor indeed is it inappropriate to conceive of a nonstate *polity*. In relation to that, however, the state polity and its laws have a crucial role, partly as exemplar and partly as instrument.

The state serves a role, *not* as the sole locus of legality but rather as a source and inspiration for building the rule of law "into the life of society," infusing governance "with the aspirations and constraints of a legal order." But what is governance, and where is it to be found? Here there are continuities with the understanding of politics in *Leadership* . . . , and broad analogies with Selznick's approach to law: Seek out function, don't obsess about location. This is peculiarly important in contemporary circumstances for, as he wrote in one of his last published articles:

> Although the United States has done pretty well in restraining public government by the rule of law, we have had much less success in doing the same for private government. . . . The leaders of these [large, complex] organizations . . . have great power over the lives of employees, the security of investments, the safety of products, and much else that goes on in the life of a large enterprise. The leaders are governors because they have responsibility for the enterprise as a unified whole, a living reality. They make rules by which ordinary people must live, and they make decisions that affect the public interest and safety, environmental protection, and fairness in the hiring and promotion of employees. If the leaders neglect or abuse those interests, we can say that the power thus exercised is arbitrary and oppressive. These practices cry out for control by the rule of law. This cannot happen unless our understanding of the rule of

law extends to private as well as public government. Taking this step has been a major challenge for American jurisprudence.[107]

Selznick sees a number of sources of convergence between what are conventionally understood as "public" and "private" domains.[108] Central among these is the decline of the persuasiveness and symbolic power of "sovereignty" as distinguishing public institutions. In parallel, the enormous growth of large-scale institutions in "private" spheres has eroded the distinctive state orientation of public law. Similarities come to blur differences, both in the sense that "governmental" powers can be found, and that "nongovernmental" activities occur, in both state and nonstate organizations. Governance is not simply a product of what we call "government": State-relatedness is neither necessary nor sufficient for it. Not everything governments do involves "the distinctive functions of a sovereign";[109] not everything private organizations are involved in should be understood as private. To the extent that nonstate institutions themselves "become to some degree political communities" and affect participation in the larger polity, issues of governance are potentially engaged within them; "This raises the question whether we have a theory of public law adjudication adequate to deal with the group structure of modern society."[110]

Just as with law one needs to steer between too narrow a focus on the state and too broad a reach to every form of social control, so the concepts of public law, Selznick argues, should be applied "wherever the social function of governing is performed, wherever some men rule and others are ruled."[111] That relationship is not confined to state–citizen relations but neither does it extend to every relationship, not even every relationship where there are asymmetries of power. It occurs where there is *"a special form of human association"* different from kin relations yet equally not the same as pure contractual association. It shares features of both: With contract it involves "objective and impersonal standards, determined by the requirements of that system," with kinship (and citizenship) membership as a source of social identity. Here the logic of institutionalization returns and generates a demand for recognition of *status*:

> Participation thickens, it takes on a new dimension, as people in organizations strive for personal satisfactions and for protection against threats to their personal security.
>
> This quest for personal meaning and security encourages a process by which minimal affiliation ripens into membership. As this occurs, we see a movement from contract to status. What matters is who you are, what position you occupy, what role you play, rather than what voluntary agreements you

may have entered. Nor is this only a product of personal psychology. Other forces, at least equally important, are also at work. Wherever there is an effort to create and sustain a going concern—based on continuing relationships rather than discrete transactions—a drift to status may be expected.[112]

With this development of status in organizations, it will be both appropriate and likely to be demanded that rights of employees be made more secure; "With the emergence of status we may expect a claim of right."[113] This bears analogies to the right of *citizenship*, which is "a special kind of group membership. It is known by the public rights accruing to the individual who occupies that status . . . minimally, the right to a civic identity and to civic participation."[114] Contexts where it makes sense to speak of citizenship occur in both state and nonstate settings, then, where membership of the association is a source of social identity and a basis for social demands.

In response to such developments, positive law can contribute, at the same time, to legality and to governance. Such a contribution can be made by the public law of due process, the principles of which Selznick explores and explicates and takes to represent "a *common law of governance*"[115] whereby "the rule of law [may be extended] to areas hitherto controlled only by concepts of private law."[116] These principles are *sources* for detailed application and development; they are not recipes. Different settings will generate different principles and procedures, sometimes markedly so, but Selznick does view these as variations on a theme, and that theme is restraint of arbitrary exercise of power.

Of course, as critics have observed, Selznick commends and recommends these developments; so can one dismiss this whole enterprise as a wish list with sociological trimmings? Not quite. One might argue, as I will in Chapter Nine, that Selznick's hopes have infiltrated what he claims to follow from analysis. But that requires *argument*, based on theory or evidence, not mere inference from Selznick's normative commitments. True, he does not try to hide what he hopes for, and that goes way beyond due process minimally understood. As the sense of connection deepens and broadens, he writes, so too will grow demands of a political character, demands for recognition of members as persons, for protection from arbitrary power; "the transition from an administered machine—in which human beings are deployed as fully manipulable resources—to a system of governance will have begun."[117] And there is more in store. For not only might we expect (or at least have reason to hope for) a richer legality within organizations, but it is possible that further evolution might bring in train something more than legality: "In the end, the quest for justice may be indistinguishable from the quest for civic competence and personal autonomy."[118]

On the other hand, you can't always get what you want. In the particular case, Selznick is skeptical that all that he would wish to come to pass is likely to; "We can speak with far greater assurance about the social foundations for limiting arbitrary power than for sustaining democratic decision-making. By the same token, it is easier to see a basis for managerial self-restraint than for affirmative social responsibility."[119]

More generally, and crucially, none of this can simply be imposed by some enthusiastic Selznickian legislator. What is required, to repeat, is a *"receptive institutional setting,"* without which legislators are just whistling in the wind. And if they wish to learn when and where their performances might be heard and heeded, they must be prepared to understand the specific settings in which they hope to intervene. And that must involve concrete institutional *assessment*, not merely an assumption or some abstract theorization:

> We cannot argue from an abstract ideal to an institutional prescription. The whole point is that the conditions for governance must be found in the life of the institution itself. On that basis, the law of governance may be invoked. Without that basis the law is irrelevant, its application self-defeating.[120]

This is, after all, merely to apply to the particular case the general point about legislation and nonstate law, which underlies this work of depth, complexity, and broad implication:

> If social evolution has taken place, it does not follow that legal change is not needed or expected. On the contrary, the legal order is pressed to put into practice ideals that have always had an abstract validity but which may not, in the past, have reflected the institutional competence of the society. Law works best when appropriate social foundations exist, but those foundations do not obviate the need for legal support and direction, to confirm rights and to extend them.[121]

Lauren Edelman and Marc Suchman have observed that "reexamined and refracted through the lens of subsequent work in both organizations theory and socio-legal studies, the central themes of Selznick's book pervade the literature on law and organizations even today."[122] Still, there is room for debate about many things in this work. There is the very enterprise of mixing analysis and evaluation, which is at the heart of Selznick's "humanist science" and anathema to positivist social scientists. There is the theory of institutional evolution that Selznick has elaborated in several of his works and that has aroused the ire of many empirically minded critics.[123] There is its particular assessment of the character and development of American industrial law.[124] There are matters of methodology, with some, particularly empirically driven researchers, preferring Ehrlich's "bottom-up" derivation of values, beginning with what people think about the law rather than with Selznick's allegedly "top-down" normative theorizing about legality and its incipient sources.[125]

There are also normative questions: Is what Selznick clearly favors an example of, perhaps a contributor to, that "creeping legalism" that Lon Fuller so opposed? Donald Black predicted that Fuller might think so,[126] and, for once, perhaps just once, he was cleverer than he knew. In correspondence between Fuller and Selznick, that is exactly (though without that phrase) what Fuller complained of.[127] And one might develop, inspired by Selznick's book, an analysis of the interaction of public and private that points to quite a different sort of outcome than the colonization of private by public that he hopes for and in part expects. Thus, Lauren Edelman sees organizations setting up internal grievance procedures to deal with allegations of discrimination, which they don't do very well, but then courts defer to these internal practices and take their existence without more, as satisfying the requirements of antidiscrimination legislation. As a result, Edelman argues, this practice of "legal endogeneity" "allows patterns of injustice that become institutionalized in the organizational realm to be incorporated into—and legitimated by—public legal rules and norms."[128] This might well be interpreted as an example of negative institutionalization of the sort that Selznick wrote illuminatingly about in *TVA*.

Apart from issues of empirical detail, there are important matters of theoretical principle here to which I will return to in Chapter Nine. The primary concerns of this book and this chapter lie, however, less with the specific bearing of *Law, Society, and Industrial Justice* on the American legal and social development that it treats, to which I am an outsider, than with the place of its deeper themes in the character and development of Selznick's thought, in particular the combination of intellectual continuity with transformation of focus that this book represents. I conclude with one observation.

I have no idea how many people who read *Law, Society, and Industrial Justice* had also read *Leadership in Administration*. Like so many of Selznick's writings, they seem to speak of different subjects to different audiences. The continuities, however, are strong. They are strong in substance—large organizations, institutionalization, moral evolution, the generic quality of politics and governance—and they are strong, too, in ambition. In both books, Selznick was pondering the play of values in the world, how they develop and how they might be encouraged to develop. He was also, less explicitly in the earlier than the later book, exploring a way of talking about such matters. And, as Heclo wrote of *Leadership*, Selznick also in both books "was in fact offering an exercise in moral instruction, a case of statesmanship in the social sciences."[129] But, as well as continuity, there was also development, again of both subject and sensibility. The later book is less top-down than the former, less concerned with the problems of leaders than with those of the led. And of course law, which doesn't appear in the former, is central to the later book, not as a vehicle for leaderly ambitions but as a servant of social purposes. Both aspects of this development become increasingly central in subsequent work.

CHAPTER EIGHT

The Rule of Law: Transformation

JURISPRUDENCE AND SOCIAL POLICY

Though the official mission of Selznick's Center for the Study of Law and Society was research, students from various faculties, with an interest in law and society, fetched up there increasingly and worked with center faculty. According to Messinger, over time "one of the things that kept happening is that students kept coming asking for reading lists, 'don't you guys offer classes?'"[1] By 1971–1972 the center had come to offer its own program for the study of law and society, an MA degree in "Law and Society," for law students who wanted to add it to their JD and to doctoral students in the social sciences as a field of specialization in their doctoral programs. That program ended at the end of the 1975–1976 academic year with the expiration of funding from the National Institute of Mental Health.

By then it was coming not to matter, however, because a new and unprecedented graduate program was under consideration. In 1974, the university endorsed the proposal developed by a committee Selznick chaired, to make over a dozen dedicated new hirings in Boalt Hall Law School to staff a program and offer a PhD in Jurisprudence and Social Policy. The new offering was covered with Selznick's fingerprints. It was to link social sciences with jurisprudence, that is, the philosophical (and in his rendition other humanistic, particularly historical) ways of thinking about law. And such thinking was to be linked to exploration of policy consequences. This, he believed, held the promise to "broaden the mission of the School of Law . . . [and] break down the insularity of the legal community."[2] It also promised to enrich and expand both law and the social sciences themselves. Selznick's committee explained that the JSP

> should not be thought of as a venture in law and social science. Legal ideas and institutions are deeply implicated in philosophical traditions and they are decisively conditioned by historical contexts. The new department should encourage humanist as well as social science perspectives. It should contribute to a reunion of legal, political, social and moral philosophy; it should bring new vitality to legal and social history.[3]

Though he met some opposition, from some such as the anthropologist Laura Nader to housing the program in the Law School, from others, such as Jerome Skolnick, to connecting it explicitly with jurisprudence, it was fundamental to Selznick to insist on both, and the link to jurisprudence became distinctive of the "Berkeley approach." This has been a central part of its charm to some, and it has alienated others, particularly more scientistic social scientists, ever since.

In 1977, Selznick became professor of law and sociology, and in 1978 the JSP program began admitting students. Its staff quickly came to include leading figures in a range of fields that study law, among them criminology, history, economics, sociology, political science, and philosophy. *Law and Society in Transition: Toward Responsive Law*, coauthored with his colleague and former student, Philippe Nonet, which appeared in the same year, in many ways might be taken to represent a manifesto for the JSP approach and in particular its commitment to ground legal philosophy in history and the social sciences, illuminate social science with philosophical attention to fundamental concepts, and focus them all on questions of policy relevance. As we should expect, its domain extends far, but its particular focus is the rule of law.

THE RULE OF LAW

Many thinkers have combined a high regard for the rule of law with a negative view of it. This is only an apparent, verbal, paradox, for it is common to understand the rule of law as good less for what it creates than for what it might prevent. On this understanding, its point is to *block* the possibility of unruly power, to curb, restrain, and channel power's exercise. This is not a new view. Thus the historian John Philip Reid emphasizes, of the English legal tradition imported to the United States, "from time immemorial the legal heritage of Europe beyond the pale of Roman law had been law as restraint, not law as command."[4] He quotes Bracton's revealing metaphor from the thirteenth century, of law as "the bridle of power," by which a just king, as distinct from a "tyrant," must "temper his power."[5] The characteristics most associated with law changed over the centuries, particularly moving from custom to legislation,[6] and with those changes went different conceptions of what the law needed to be like to do its proper work. However, the identification of the rule of law's purpose with constraint endured. And it still does. Where the rule of law is commended, it is typically for what it rules out rather than what it rules in; what it restrains and prevents, rather than what it generates or encourages to flourish.[7]

Selznick understands the appeal of this negative conception, and he has often emphasized its importance. Thus, he agrees with those who see the rule of law as a precious protection against abuse of power. The primary way to take these matters seriously, he has often written, is to realize that "in the end only power can check power—and the opportunity to do so must be a secure resource in every moral community."[8] This is one reason why forms, procedures, and structures are important: They help institutionalize restraint on power. Principles of governance and the rule of law constitute "the most important way repressive authority can be countered,"[9] and thus institutional *autonomy* has a special significance as "the chief bulwark of the rule of law."[10] His early treatments of the rule of law stressed this "negative" purpose. As he put it in the first annual report of the Law and Society Center at Berkeley in 1962:

> The rule of law is a practical ideal, which is to say, it rests in part on pessimistic premises regarding the nature of man and society. . . . this view does not require the belief that any man, given the chance, would misuse power; rather, the premise is that there is a sufficient risk of such misuse to forbid *reliance upon* the idealism and good will of men in authority. . . . The essential point remains . . . that the rule of law is a system of restraint. It presumes that an impersonal guardianship is vital to a free society.[11]

On the other hand, the promise of law, Selznick insisted already then, is not exhausted by this negative, constraining conception. Already in that same report, he enunciated a second "main theme" in the study of law and society: "law as creative governance," and he explained that while

> building the "legal state" is surely of great moment, . . . it is far from the exclusive concern of the legal craftsman. Not less important is to help provide, through law, "creative governance" or substantive solutions for new and continuing problems. The resources of law are not unlimited, but they are being

pressed into service on many fronts. As new problems of order arise, legal institutions are being increasingly relied upon to do the work of social control. New values and sensibilities are demanding more affirmative responses from courts, legislatures, correctional institutions, and administrative agencies. This does more than increase the burden of work; it asks for a redefinition of roles and missions.

As legal institutions become less passive, as they become more fully committed to the accomplishment of particular ends, such as the rehabilitation of offenders or the maintenance of industrial competition, the tension between legality and creativity is made more acute. This tension sets a general problem. It defines an area within which much research needs to be done.[12]

Moreover, as we saw in the last chapter, Selznick argued for an understanding of the rule of law that combines "necessity" with "fulfillment," "hope and promise." What this might mean, what it might involve, whether and how the different functions might be combined, what form it might take in contemporary circumstances, and what it might reveal about the nature and variety of legal forms, are subjects of *Law and Society in Transition: Toward Responsive Law*, coauthored with his colleague and former student, Philippe Nonet.

LAW AND SOCIETY IN TRANSITION

Though *Law and Society in Transition* is small, its ambitions are not. Most generally, they are to contribute to "a reintegration of legal, political, and social theory."[13] Central to this large enterprise is "to recast jurisprudential issues in a social-science perspective."[14] There are theoretical reasons to do this, and practical ones too.

Theoretically, it is crucial "to grasp the significance of *variation*."[15] Philosophical accounts of the concept of law tend not to do this. Staples of legal philosophy are built around universal answers to single questions: What *is* law? What *is* the relationship between law and morality, between law and coercion, law and politics, law and reason? And so on. Typically such questions are posed as though a single universal answer is appropriate to each of them: For John Austin, law is the command of a sovereign, while for H. L. A. Hart it is a system of two types of rules. For natural lawyers there is a necessary connection between law and morals, for legal positivists, not.

Selznick believes, by contrast, and thinks it a natural and fundamental sociological insight, that law and the relationships between it and other phenomena, like all social phenomena, vary in characteristics, presence, and salience. Moreover, these variations are not merely random or contingent but systematic and susceptible of explanation. Thus one turns to "a social science strategy [that] can more readily and explicitly recognise the plurality of legal experience."[16]

Not only do philosophy and sociology need connection; as pragmatists had long taught, theory and practical consequences also will benefit from alignment with each other. Connecting theory and practice was of course Selznick's long-standing aim and was concurrently becoming institutionalized in the JSP. That aim and that program both rested on the belief that "jurisprudence gains focus and depth when it self-consciously considers the implications it has for action and institutional design. Philosophical analysis, in turn, helps ensure that basic issues of policy are closely examined, not buried under unscrutinized assumptions and perspectives."[17]

More concretely still, the book is an attempt to respond to challenges to the legitimacy of law that had emerged in America, and elsewhere in the developed world, most dramatically in the 1960s. From these tumults of criticism, questioning, response, and defense, emerged "a continuing tension between two approaches to law, freedom, and social control." One was a "*low-risk* view of law and order" that is alive to the fragility of social orders, the centrality of law within them, the precariousness of "systems of authority and civil obligation." It insists on obedience to law by citizens, strict observance of it by officials, and a strict separation among the institutions, values, and justifications that go into the making and evaluating of laws, on the one hand, and those appropriate to the interpretation, administration, and application of them, on the other. Contesting this view is a "*high-risk* view of law and order," that "emphasizes the potential resilience and openness of institutions . . . is more careless of authority, more accepting of challenge and disarray," values law "as a resource for criticism and an instrument for change . . . open to reconstruction in the light of how those who are governed perceive their rights and reassess their moral commitments. . . . The line between law and politics is blurred, at least where advocacy and legal judgment speak to issues of controverted public policy."[18] Nonet and Selznick sought to explain, appraise, and respond to the tension between these two views, within a frame in which sensitivity could be shown to, and sense might be made of, their sources of appeal, strengths, weaknesses, costs and benefits, and the realities from which they grew.

The argument is developed with the aid of a generalized typology, of remarkable sweep. It is intended to illuminate "different modalities of legal experience"[19] by focusing on the characteristic "postures" of legal orders. Nonet and Selznick specify no geographical or historical restrictions, though it seems that in this work, unlike in Selznick's previous book and not obviously in keeping with his pluralist sympathies, they have only state law in mind and American state law first of all. They do not deal with "stateless" societies, their focus is firmly on the work of official agencies, and it is clear that American contemporary developments motivate this work throughout. However, Selznick certainly believed they were illuminating larger trends.

Like many such typologies, including their ur-models in the work of Max Weber, the types constructed were supposed to distill, from the mass of particularity and contingency that makes every example of a category unique, underlying social and institutional logics that allow one to categorize them as examples of a particular type or kind. These, and their institutional implications, were to be laid bare and rationally reconstructed in models sufficiently abstract to rise above the buzz of the everyday but concrete enough to capture and represent in relief, as it were, major underlying features, tendencies, and connections. By exhibiting such logics, these types could serve both to distinguish among fundamental, molding, forces that accounted for differences *between* legal orders and also to illuminate particular tendencies and domains *within* particular legal orders, where different logics were more or less in play.

Though the scope of such constructions is commonly broad, it is also true that the concerns that drive them have typically been as much local and contemporary. Weber's were to illuminate the distinctive features of modernity, among them modern law. In the process, and as a measure of his genius, he managed to illuminate many other things as well. Roughly contemporaneous with Nonet and Selznick, and responding to the same legal developments, including "legalization," "delegalization," and what Europeans call "materialization" of law, other writers also developed typologies of legal orders, some of great similarity to theirs.[20] These too were general in their proclaimed application but primarily motivated to illuminate contemporary shifts in legal form, ideology, purpose, and effect.

It is also true, and it is the case here, that many who construct typologies are as concerned about illuminating *development* to (and sometimes from) the present, as they are about cataloging differences. It should be no surprise that Selznick is among them.

Law and Its Types

Proceeding from Selznick's postulate that definitions should be capacious and weak, "generic and protean,"[21] while theories are strong, Nonet and he adopt H. L. A. Hart's concept of law, as a combination of two sorts of rules: primary rules that specify what people are permitted to do and prohibited from doing, with secondary rules, rules about rules, that regulate how laws are to be recognized, changed, and adjudicated. This provides their conceptual entry into the field, the "minimal elements of a legal order." Law properly so-called occurs where a normative system incorporates both sorts of rules in systematic interconnection.

Whereas analytical jurists have devoted a vast literature to Hart's concept of law, Nonet and Selznick use it only to identify the boundaries of their concerns—"not all social control is legal: Law is selective in its recognition of social norms."[22] Indeed, there is not a lot going on at this preliminary, boundary-staking stage, and one might argue with what does go on. Hart himself resisted the call for a definition of law and denied he had produced one,[23] and there are many reasons to doubt that Hart's concept is an adequate basis for sociological understandings of law.[24] But it makes little difference to this book, seeming to act as a placeholder rather than something to be pondered. All the real work is on what sorts of things we are liable to find within those boundaries, how those things vary, and how they develop. And this is what social science, they believe, has to offer jurisprudence.

They are unsatisfied by the generalities of legal philosophy, both because so much that is important is unilluminated by them and because the significance of many of the staple components of jurisprudential accounts of law varies in differently configured legal orders. Moreover, this variance is not a matter of accident or coincidence, nor is it without consequence for what jurists claim as essential to law and the concept of law.[25]

The typology they propose distinguishes among three ideal types of law: repressive, autonomous, and responsive. These each have characteristic elements in systematic internal interconnection, and they differ in determinate ways from each other. They can be combined in particular legal orders, but their logics are different, and their morphology follows their logic. Moreover, the history and development of "law" is not a continuous deployment and redeployment of a single phenomenon, but the *transformation* of the character and conformation of legal orders, in response to different pressures, aims, and ecological conditions.

Legal orders whose primary aim is repression, for example, will tend to embody—not simply serve—views of the nature and proper relationships between ruler and ruled, and among the ruled themselves, different from those intended to set out clear and reliable rules of the game for the benefit of those who play it. Moreover, not only are the ends very different, but the character of the legal means will also differ systematically. For particular forms of law and institutional configurations—whether they are public and clear or secret or opaque, for one example, or stress crime control more or less than they allow for due process,[26] for another—are more congenial to some purposes than to others. Laws intended to achieve centrally determined repressive or bureaucratic or transformative objectives will follow systematically different logics and embody systematically different characteristics from each other, and even more from laws intended to aid individuals to choose, plan, cooperate, and stay out of jail. The nature, identities, rights, and obligations of principals and agents will be differently understood and located, the degrees of official discretion allowed, publicity and accountability required, flexibility thought warranted, formality insisted on: All will be affected by assumed, often unarticulated but presupposed, aims of the law.

Of course, no politico-legal order has just one aim. All are mixed, and the balance among different aims differs among orders, within them, and over time. So too with the particular institutional vehicles developed to achieve them and that come to embody them. Often the real task is to discern how to manage tensions that occur when the implications of different logics push in different, often inconsistent, directions. However, at different times, under different pressures, particular logics are likely to dominate, to challenge and be challenged, to wax and to wane, as characteristic and pervasively evident "postures" adopted by particular legal orders. Thus Nonet and Selznick develop their typology on the assumption that:

> the elements of one type may be more or less salient, strongly institutionalized or only incipient, in the foreground of awareness or only dimly perceived. Thus although a legal order will exhibit elements of all types, its basic *posture* may nevertheless approximate one type more closely than the others.[27]

In this book Selznick refines the developmental arguments of *Law, Society, and Industrial Justice.* Here, as in the earlier work, indeed in all Selznick's work, the emphasis is on *internal* evolutionary dynamics rather than on external pressures or predicted real-world outcomes. Here as elsewhere that is not because external pressures are denied or even because the internal ones are considered more decisive for what happens in the world. Rather, the strategy is to explore, at an abstract level, characteristic *dispositions* to change, leaving it to particular empirical examination to reveal the extent to which these dispositions prevail or are strengthened, weakened, defeated, by external configurations.

This is the approach Selznick had adopted at least since his first encounter with Michels, but perhaps because his work is so rarely considered as a whole, critics too easily pass over its rationale:

> We want to argue that repressive, autonomous, and responsive law are not only distinct types of law but, in some sense, stages of evolution in the relation of law to the political and social order. . . . The underlying quest is for theories that can account for unplanned and recurrent transformations whose sources and direction are built into the structure of a phenomenon, for example, the movement from sect to church, the "iron law of oligarchy," the attenuation of culture, the stages of growth to psychological maturity in Freudian theory, and the transformation of the morality of constraint into a morality of co-operation in child development. These theories do not necessarily deal with the transformation of whole societies or even of whole institutional systems. Whatever their scope, the main point is that a determinate disposition to change is traced such that systematic forces set in motion at one stage are said to produce characteristic outcomes at another. Thus, every developmental model postulates an "inner dynamic."[28]

There is no suggestion that this dynamic will bear all before it or necessarily be reflected in actual historical developments. Rather, what is proposed "is a theory of institutional change and response whose intellectual function is to identify *potentials for change* in a specified range of situations."[29]

The theory involves not just change but, as we saw with *Law, Society, and Industrial Justice, evolutionary* development. Some stages have priority over others, not always in time or importance but as stages in successful development. There are basic problems that must be solved by a legal order before more complicated questions are asked of law or at least before law can successfully answer them, before more complex legal responses to social problems can be devised, and before social institutions are robust and sophisticated enough to deliver them. One such is the maintenance of social order. Then another is the curbing of arbitrary power. A third is contributing in competent ways to the solution of complex social problems—and so, repressive, autonomous, and responsive law. Selznick insists that solutions to such problems are not random but cumulative. A legal order that cannot keep the peace cannot do much for the resolution of complex problems of social ordering and justice. Sometimes first things really must come first. Until they do, second and third things will be difficult to contemplate, let alone achieve. If they do, however, there might well be more ground, foundation for further and different initiatives to be asked of the legal order.

The point has been made succinctly by Stephen Holmes: "The Hobbesian problem has to be solved before the Lockean solution looks attractive."[30] That does not make an effective legal order *more* important than a fair or just one, but rather a condition for the latter. Later stages depend on the achievement of earlier ones, for without them the later ones will not be able to emerge or, if they do, to thrive. But when a condition of effectiveness is secure, it might become possible, and pressure might develop, to contemplate law of sorts unavailable and perhaps unimaginable under earlier stages. Thus law might require crude imposition of power and move through constrained application of autonomously generated rules toward more complex and interrelated possibilities that call for refined, nuanced, flexible, variable, and *competent* responses to problems. It might then become possible to "establish new competencies while resolving the persisting and more basic urgencies of earlier states."[31]

The developmental theory is not conceived as prophecy, even prediction, however, because so many other factors, within and without the law, may overwhelm internal dispositions. It also in no simple way amounts to advocacy because a development good for some values might be bad for others; one that is more *competent*, say, might also be more vulnerable to dangers or threats that occur, or a promised good might come at too high a risk of vulnerability to bads that it brings in its train or is not well suited to dispel.

In constructing their typology of law, the chief variables Nonet and Selznick consider are "the role of coercion in law; the interplay of law and politics; the relation of law to the state and to the moral order; the place of rules, discretion, and purpose in legal decisions; civic participation; legitimacy; and the conditions of obedience. Each of these variables differs significantly as the context is changed."[32] Moreover, variations are neither random nor unconnected. On the contrary,

> there are determinate and systematic connections among them . . . Of course such connections are contingent and probabilistic. To the extent they occur, however, the legal order comes to form a "system," with a constellation of attributes that has internal coherence. Different systems, in that sense, represent distinctive mixes of the basic law-related variables.[33]

Nonet and Selznick's focus is on three such animating values with systemic significance. I will take them, as they do, in turn.

Repressive Law

In many political orders, law has been conceived of and wielded primarily as an instrument for repression or at least top-down direction of subjects, and often nothing much more. Indeed the word *subject* is ambiguous in regard to those governed by these laws. The ruled are subjected *to* the law and in that sense are more subjects than citizens. On the other hand, they do not relate to the law as active subjects, as a subject does to a verb, for example. They are better seen as the objects of power and the institutions through which it is exercised, including law. Its grammatical subjects are the rulers, who use laws, among other instruments, for their own purposes. Indeed law has often been a very useful vehicle (and at times equally useful camouflage) for the exercise of legally unrestrained power.[34]

Nonet and Selznick start, for in a real sense they believe that (state) law starts, with such law, which, for obvious reasons, they label "repressive." Here law is one instrument (often among several) for imposition of power. The center has to *establish* itself, and doing that, if necessary over others' interests or opposition, is the overriding aim of law rather than, say, regulating, restraining, and channelling acts of power; informing citizens of the circumstances in which coercion might be invoked; facilitating their choices; or helping them resolve some of their difficulties. In this constellation, coercion comes to the fore and into its own.

This has large institutional implications. There will be little or no distance between law and political power, no or stunted forms of autonomy, such as those Roberto Unger identified (in contrast to what he called "bureaucratic law") with the modern legal order: substantive, institutional, methodological, and occupational.[35] Instead, law and political power come from the same source, point in the same direction, serve the same purposes. There is no conception that they may conflict, let alone that one might or should be an institutionalized restraint on the other. Instead, "the courts and legal officials are the king's ministers. They are perceived (and perceive themselves) as pliable instruments of the government in power. Legal institutions serve the state; they are not a counterfoil within it. The idea of sovereignty pervades legal imagery."[36] The model is top down, where the top is little restrained, official discretion widespread, and the further down you go the fewer the opportunities to constrain, question, criticize, those above. The language of rights will not be much developed and seldom heard, for the point of law is not to secure citizens' rights but to attain rulers' objectives. Rules will exist, but because their point is to attain ruling purposes rather than "cue in" and guide the self-chosen activities of citizens, the extent to which they are public, clear, non-contradictory, stable, and so on, depends on the contingent purposes of the ruler not the interests or needs of subjects.

Apart from discussing the contours of this type of law in some detail, Nonet and Selznick also suggest why it occurs, how it develops, and why it generates tendencies, not always but not without explicable cause, to transcend it. First of all, why is law so often so repressive? A short answer might be: Why not? When there is room for those with power to act repressively, they are sooner or later likely to. If you want to avoid it, something must be done and someone (other than those in charge) must be in a position to do it. That is consistent with Selznick's repeated insistence that "only power can tame power" and consistent in spirit, too, with his common warnings, particularly in his earlier writings, of the need to take into account tendencies, such as to oligarchy, that will develop unless they are blocked. And, in this book, Nonet and Selznick do not reject this view; indeed they emphasize that their "strategy throughout is to emphasize that repression is 'natural.'"

Why so? "A common source of repression is the poverty of resources available to governing elites. For this reason repression is a highly probable accompaniment of the formation and maintenance of political order, and can occur unwittingly in the pursuit of benign intentions."[37] They develop the historical-sociological implications of this claim thus:

> Nation building is ultimately a transformation of loyalties and consciousness, but in its beginnings it is the work of emerging elites who have little to draw on beyond force and fraud. Later, as national institutions take shape, the state can move forward to provide services and win allegiance. A prior necessity is the establishment of the "king's peace," together with the "political expropriation" of potential challengers.[38]

This suggests an apparent paradox. Repressive legal orders, which seem so strong, are in some fundamental ways weaker than more moderate alternatives,[39] for where law is and is obviously merely the servant of power, and official discretion is "rampant," law has difficulty even in distinguishing itself from power, let alone legitimating either itself or power.[40]

This might often not matter, "but when consent is problematic and accountability is more vigorously demanded, a regime that indulges the manipulation of law will fail to preserve an aura of legality."[41] What, then, might make consent problematic? Here the examination of internal strains, vulnerabilities, weaknesses, and also potential sources of incipient trans-formations, occurs. The repressive state "borrows power from the strong," "institutionalizes disprivilege . . . [and] dependency," and organizes "social defence against 'dangerous classes.'" It is allied with the strong because it is weak. That makes its law in growing part their law, but that in turn af-fects the character of that law. It has a public law branch, "operated by spe-cialized state agencies, attuned to the demands of political and administra-tive expediency; its business is control; its ethos is prescriptive and heavily penal." But it also has a law for the privileged, "which is rights-centered, facilitative, and largely 'private'":

> The law of the privileged protects property and upholds autonomous social arrangements, for instance, for devising estates, contracting, and associating. It is relatively insulated from political intrusion, administered by independent courts, fashioned by precedent more than by legislation. Here the state is con-fined to a passive role; it is an arbiter of private disputes and a keeper of rules it did not make.[42]

And here is the ultimate paradox:

> Thus the dynamics by which the legal order upholds social subordination are paradoxically a chief source of evolution away from repressive law and toward legal institutions that can remove themselves from, and tame, the power of the state. They lay the foundation of a "rule of law" capable of holding govern-ment accountable. In other words, dual law builds into the very structure of repressive law a mechanism of transition to autonomous law.[43]

Autonomous law

Thus we move toward autonomous law, which in *Law and Society in Transition* is identified with the rule of law. The identification of the rule of law with a particular configuration of institutions rather than a large, and variously implementable, "practical ideal"[44] is, I will later argue, in-consistent with much else in Selznick's work, both as it appears earlier in "Sociology and Natural Law,"[45] and later in *The Moral Commonwealth*.[46] It also seems to me an unfortunate, limiting choice too often made, to tie an enduring and significant ideal to a particular institutional implementation of it.[47]

In this book, however, Selznick is unequivocal: "The rule of law is better understood as a distinctive institutional system than as an abstract ideal. The chief characteristic of this system is the formation of specialized, relatively autonomous legal institutions that claim a qualified supremacy within defined spheres of competence."[48] The special claim of autonomous law is that it "becomes a resource for *taming* power. . . . a legal and political aspiration, the creation of 'a government of laws and not of men.'"[49] As it developed, at least in the modern West, it emphasized and came to institutionalize a series of linked values: separation of law and politics; a stress on the centrality of rules as the basis for legal decision; on "regularity and fairness, not substantive justice, . . . [as] . . . the first ends and main competence of the legal order";[50] and insistence on "strict obedience to the rules of positive law."[51] The analytical presupposition of this position is legal positivism, with its stress on the possibility and desirability of distinguishing, at least analytically, among positive law, morality, and politics. The moral posture is what has more recently been called *ethical* positivism, which is a view of what those involved with law *should* do in relation to it—keep law and extralegal values separate.[52] Whatever the law *is*, the ethical positivist argues, a legal order does better when legal issues, interpretations, institutions, and decisions are treated as distinct from ethical, political, and other normative matters. Though *ethical positivism* is a new term, coined by Tom Campbell in recent years, it is an old belief and one that, in this work, Nonet and Selznick associate strongly with partisans of autonomous law and its associated "rule of law."[53]

Legal officials, we learn, are attached to legal autonomy because their legitimacy depends on it. Just as "the chief source of transition from repressive to autonomous law is the quest for legitimacy, . . . [so in turn] . . . each major attribute of autonomous law can be understood as a strategy of legitimation."[54] Every regime seeks legitimacy, but how much it gets and how deep it needs to go are highly variable. The former point is obvious—some regimes are more, some less, legitimate. But some regimes demand more detailed, specific, legitimacy than others; "the basic transition is from a blanket certification of the *source* of power to a sustained justification of its *use*."[55] When that happens,

> it is helpful if the interpreter of those principles is removed from the day-to-day work of government and if his voice is heard to speak in a distinctive idiom. . . . he who exercises the power to legitimate has his own problems of legitimacy. If he can convince the world, and himself, that his judgments are untainted by compromising associations and that his authority derives from a peculiar

competence, his problems of legitimation are eased. To assert and protect that competence, he must register a claim to institutional autonomy. Therein lies the foundation of what we have come to know as the separation of judicial from legislative and executive powers. The social process of differentiation, which brings into play new groups and vested interests, completes the job of forming the institutional system we call autonomous law.[56]

Thus law is separated from politics, only partially and conditionally in any event; a "bargain" whereby judges gain "independence" so long as they do not mess with politics. There is restraint of power here, but it is on terms, and it deals with only an aspect of political decision: "To be effective in moderating the exercise of power, autonomous law must reaffirm its commitment to the policies it receives. It tames repression, but its capacity to do so is closely dependent on a prudent self-limitation."[57] Thus too, limitation on judicial discretion, and stress on fidelity to rules. In all,

> As legal agencies, doctrines, and techniques become stabilized and self-conscious, they form a differentiated institutional sphere. To guard their chief social function—legitimation—and their hard-won authority—the law-men adopt a self-protective, self-limiting, and conservative stance.[58]

Two sorts of questions might be raised here. One has to do with the sociological explanation of why legal, particularly judicial, partisans of this posture are attached to the autonomy of law; the other with an evaluation of its real and proclaimed implications and consequences, among them normative consequences. As to the former, Nonet and Selznick's answer is rather brisk, and one might ask for more. They are aware of Weber's and Unger's (derivative from Weber) historical explanations of the development of autonomous law in the West. They point readers to these sources,[59] and their own account of the strains that are likely to be felt and to develop within repressive law reflects them. However, given Weber's complex account of the coincidence of otherwise very different sorts of interests in demanding autonomous and fixed law (those of "officials, bourgeois business interests . . . monarchical interests in fiscal and administrative ends . . . politically dominated strata,"[60] for example) because they share an interest in the *predictability* of legal rules, it is hard to see why Nonet and Selznick focus virtually exclusively on the quest for legitimacy. It may be true that the reason judges insisted on legal autonomy is as part of a legitimation strategy. It may also be true that they believe what they say, and that is why they say it. Sometimes a cigar is just a cigar. And there might be a complex mix of motivations as well. Many people have called for autonomous and predictable legal treatment, for many reasons, most specifically and understandably because they feared arbitrariness in the exercise of power. Why is the only one examined here the shoring-up of legitimacy?

And whatever the answer to that, another question remains: Is what they say true? Is the autonomy of law necessary to restrain power and to generate legal predictability? Is it effective? And does a lessening of institutional autonomy lessen the capacity of legal institutions to serve these ends? The response of Nonet and Selznick to these questions is altogether more ambivalent than their somewhat monocausal explanation of why legal officials answer them as they do. It is not too much to say that they agonize over them, throughout the book and arguably much later as well. This is not surprising, given how often Selznick had insisted that reduction of arbitrariness in the exercise of power was at the heart of the latent ideal of legal orders and that only power can tame power. We will return to these agonies in the next section.

For the moment my focus is on sources of strain within autonomous law. We have already learned that things don't fail just because we don't like them, and they are not in the script of history just because we do. What, then, might generate change? Here again, identification of immanent strains and claims is important. As in *Law, Society, and Industrial Justice*, and as in Selznick's discussion of the pressures toward autonomy that build under repressive law, there are pressures here, too. One comes from felt tensions between formal and substantive justice:

> formal justice is consistent with serving existing patterns of privilege and power. The sense of fairness is affronted when a system that prides itself on the full and impartial hearing is unable to vindicate important claims of substantive justice. The justice of autonomous law is experienced as sham and arbitrary when it frustrates the very expectations of fairness it has encouraged. In time, the tension between procedural and substantive justice generates forces that push the legal order beyond the limits of autonomous law.[61]

A sense of institutionalized injustice is only one, extreme, source of erosion of autonomist verities, however. A larger source of transformation lies not in the pathologies of the system but in its deepest character, indeed in its signal virtues:

> The very effort to develop a legal order sets in motion forces that undermine the rule-of-law model . . .
>
> The main competence of autonomous law is its capacity to restrain the authority of rulers and limit the obligations of citizens. An unanticipated result, however, is to encourage a posture of criticism that contributes to the erosion of the rule of law. This is not an ideological stance, for the rule-of-law

model is more likely to celebrate submission to authority than criticism of it. But the practical operation of the system presses in another direction. As the institutions and procedures of autonomous law develop, criticism of authority becomes the daily occupation of law-men. . . . This commitment puts the courts in the business of defining opportunities for the assertion of claims. Thus advocacy comes to rival adjudication as the paradigm of legal action. The outcome, however unintended, is a rights-centered jurisprudence.

Advocacy . . . encourages self-assertion and a searching criticism of received authority. The long-term effect is to build into the legal order a dynamic of change, and to generate expectations that law respond flexibly to new problems and demands. A revision emerges, and the possibility is sensed, of a responsive legal order, more open to social influence and more effective in dealing with social problems.[62]

Responsive Law

A developed casuistry, increasing social complexity, and increasingly rapid change push toward "the *generalization* of law's objectives . . . the emphasis shifts to more general ends that contain the premises of policy and tell 'the business we are really in.' So a distinctive feature of responsive law is the search for *implicit values* in rules and policies."[63] These values are drawn on to generate new rules, in a process of appeal to "principle and purpose," the significance of which was already argued by Selznick in "Sociology and Natural Law."

Drawing on their familiarity with organizations, Nonet and Selznick stress that such generalization of purpose is not unique to modern law or indeed to law. It is a familiar source of flexibility and development in organizations of all sorts, an antidote to the goal displacement that is one of their notorious pathologies.[64] Moreover, the search for underlying values is an essential part of the activity of interpretation of and within an interpretive practice of any complexity.

That being the case, responsive law is not conceived as in *contradiction* to autonomous law, as arguably the latter is to repressive law. Rather, it is claimed to be its enrichment, though one in considerable tension with what it purportedly enriches. Thus, "the more sophisticated autonomous law becomes, the more it must look to purpose in the elaboration of rules. Responsive law builds on that experience. Indeed, there is no radical break because artificial reason contains the seed of its own mitigation."[65]

Purpose, then, is increasingly, and with increasing explicitness, called in aid by law. Instead of rules acting as exclusive and exhaustive reasons for decision, they are treated as guides to purposes, the terms of which may not be explicit. They are also grounds of criticism, as rules and decisions come to be evaluated according to underlying purposes, rather than literalistic fidelity to prior rules. A consequence of that increasing resort to argument to and from principle and policy rather than invocation of authority, is

> the enhancement of rationality in legal reasoning. . . . A sign of the change is the waning of "artificial reason." Legal sophistication fosters a gradual elimination of arcane language, fictional classification, and tortured analogies. Freed from formalism and ritual, legal inquiry can be more systematic and more empirical.[66]

Again, transformation is not simply a response to outside pressure but is generated by the casuistic process of autonomous law applied to particular circumstances. Distinctions are made, authorities weighed, values balanced, judgments affected by specific circumstances thrown up by individual cases. All this *internally generated* refinement generates the (often internally suspect) result that "in a developed system the logic of legal judgment becomes closely congruent with the logic of moral and practical judgment."[67]

With the erosion of the strength of authority and fiat comes a concomitant blurring of the lines between legal logic and the logic of the wider world. That in turn opens the legal process to more voices because the lawyer's voice has lost its unique authoritativeness. Whereas the autonomous legal order, like the bureaucracy that Weber saw as associated with it, concentrates authority and voice, responsive law, like postbureaucratic forms of organization, seeks to expand "participatory decision making as a source of knowledge, a vehicle of communication, and a foundation for consent."[68] So the legal order is opened up to social advocacy, rules of legal standing are relaxed, and other ways develop in which "groups and organizations may participate in the determination of public policy. It is less exclusively perceived as a way of vindicating individual claims based on recognized rules."[69]

This puts real strains on the institutions of an autonomous legal order. Legal criticism grows, felt obligation lessens, institutions are open to more voices speaking discordant languages and demanding results that can be justified on grounds of substance, not merely formal pedigree. Yet the techniques and institutions of autonomous law were not set up for all this, however much they might have spawned it. On the contrary:

> the paradigmatic function of the legal order is adjudication rather than policy making or administration. Policy issues arise in adjudication, but only inciden-

tally, more out of logical necessity than out of direct responsibility. Autonomous law is court-centered, and its constitutional arrangements ensure that the courts remain "the least dangerous branch," the branch least competent to assemble and deploy resources, institute systematic changes in policy and practice, or address the problems involved in getting things done. The court's commitment is to hearing claims; its expertise lies in procedural fairness; its contribution is to restrain authority and vindicate individual rights. In none of these ways can law address the problem of making purpose effective in guiding institutions.[70]

Institutions and practices of these sorts might be capable of generating the *criticism* of decisions considered to deny embodied or valued purposes; they are less equipped affirmatively to generate, or help attain, such purposes. For them to do that, a lot has to change. To the extent that it does, law will lose its innocence, certainly its purity. Distinctions between legal institutions and those of administration and politics will remain, but they will increasingly be blurred. Legal institutions will need to be more apprised of social facts and consequences than autonomous institutions have traditionally needed to be, and they will be assessed more in terms of their contributions to substantive results than of their fidelity to legal authority. Moreover, the facts that need to be taken into account will increasingly be "legislative rather than adjudicative facts . . . *systematic* effects of alternative policies, rather than . . . particular outcomes,"[71] and the results that come to matter will be systemic results more than those unique to particular individual litigants. And, where results are concerned, so a premium will come to be placed on institutional *competence* as assessed in the wider world and by its citizens.

What does competence mean in this context? In their discussion, Nonet and Selznick emphasize two aspects, which they do not clearly distinguish. Gunther Teubner, much influenced (though diverging from) Selznick, has sought to do so.[72] I follow his distinction between "substantive" and "reflexive" elements of responsive law. In the former sense already discussed, competence refers to the rendering of substantively satisfactory (rather than merely formally authorized) outcomes. This was the hope, after all, of the legal realists and of sociological jurists such as Roscoe Pound. Selznick acknowledges his debt to them as, of course, to John Dewey, apostle of "problem solving" and critic of slavish devotion to authority. Rather than an abandonment of the values of the rule of law, they see it as a deeper vindication of them, in line with Selznick's familiar distinction between negative and affirmative realizations of an ideal. And so they claim:

> The ideal of legality needs to be conceived more generally and to be cured of formalism. In a purposive system legality is the progressive reduction of arbitrariness in positive law and its administration. To press for a maximum feasible reduction of arbitrariness is to demand a system of law that is capable of reaching beyond formal regularity and procedural fairness to substantive justice. That achievement, in turn, requires institutions that are competent as well as legitimate.[73]

Another sense of crafting "institutions that are competent" echoes Selznick's own past work on administrative leadership as "the institutional embodiment of purpose."[74] Teubner calls this "reflexive law." As Nonet and Selznick explain the role that law can play in this "widely coveted but not easily attained" objective, it involves "the absorption of law into the larger realm of administration. The lawyerly art becomes the art of giving affirmative authority to purpose, that is, of ensuring that purpose is taken seriously in the workings and deliberations of legal-governmental institutions."[75] Reflexive law doesn't look directly to delivering outcomes; rather it frames and shapes social processes in what are taken to be salutary ways.

Teubner disagrees with Nonet's and Selznick's stress on substantive law. Following his teacher, Niklas Luhmann, he argues that this legal "opening" to the world is doomed. It is unable to cope with the increase of social complexity in the increasingly differentiated and self-generated spheres of modern societies. Reflexive law, he argues by contrast, is ready to adapt to them. Some of Teubner's examples are neatly summarized by Vincent-Jones:

> Labor law shapes collective bargaining by providing a general framework for negotiation and by expanding the "competencies" of workers. Consumer law fosters organizations for the representation of consumers and the articulation of their "voice" and interests. The law of private organizations "constitutionalizes" participatory governance structures for corporations. Contract law helps redress inequalities in bargaining power through doctrinally established obligations on parties to behave fairly and to act in good faith. And many public tasks are delegated by legislation to private or semi-private bodies exercising accountability established by the state.[76]

According to Nonet and Selznick, both substantive and reflexive law require "a new kind of lawyerly expertise . . . in the articulation of *principles of institutional design and institutional diagnosis.*" There would be a "blending" of law and politics, in that legal agencies would be involved in fashioning institutional processes to achieve political outcomes, but the distinction between them would not die. It would still be the preserve of government as a political actor to choose ends, and decide what to spend on them, "but government must then proceed as a *legal* actor, to establish the agencies and mechanisms by which public ends will be furthered."[77] Law would be integrated into the processes of what the realists called "law-government," and what were understood to be the tasks of law would be transformed. Arbitrariness would still be the enemy, but what it meant and how law was to combat it would be reconceived. In the new (not yet achieved, and perhaps not to be achieved) dispensation:

> law is a problem-solving, facilitative enterprise that can bring to bear a variety of powers and mobilize an array of intellectual and organizational resources. . . . Any theory that makes problem solving a central function of law readily appreciates that the barriers by which institutions are separated, "spheres of competence" defined, and bureaucratic turfs enclosed hinder the deployment of resources necessary for effective action. This is why a responsive legal order must postulate that "the danger of tyranny or injustice lurks in unchecked power, not in blended power."[78] In other words, and more generally, the risks of arbitrariness in the exercise of power should be controlled in ways that facilitate, rather than hinder, the enlargement of institutional competence. For in proportion as the law assumes ever wider responsibilities incompetence becomes an ever more lively source of arbitrary power.[79]

Not only would law and politics be blurred; so too would public and private. In what John Braithwaite and Christine Parker call "meta-regulation," an important aspect of responsive legal development is the design of institutional forms for private self-regulation of large organizations, and intra-organizational forms of regulation.[80]

By now we have moved a long way from a negatively conceived rule of law. Opposition to arbitrariness remains, certainly, but it has been reconceived, and its institutional embodiments and indeed its meaning are considerably, some would say unrecognizably, unsustainably, transformed. What should we make of this?

Legal Responsiveness and its Critics

One answer is to deny that the changes Nonet and Selznick point to are occurring or are matters of any great moment. Ideal typologies accentuate differences because that is their job,[81] but law is never monolithic, either in purpose or form, and tendencies ebb and flow. So what reason is there to believe that its complexity or development can usefully be rendered in any lockstep progression of single and contrasting types?

Close-grained empirical researchers, suspicious in principle of such large and sweeping generalizations and amalgamations, are drawn to this argument. Thus Malcolm Feeley complains that Nonet and Selznick:

> may only have identified different elements of *all* legal systems, distinct features that must coexist in perpetual tension. Law is much too complex and multi-faceted an institution to have a single or even dominant goal or style; it encompasses a bewildering array of goals and orientations all of which can exist simultaneously in any legal system. At different periods, one or another of these characteristics may be more *salient* in the public's eye than the others, but temporary saliency is different from distinct stages.[82]

That is a powerful caution, though voiced with such generality it does make it hard ever to contemplate doing what Weber did so often and so well, and Nonet and Selznick attempt here: seek a theoretically and empirically informed level of abstraction that allows one to plot significant, categorical, shifts in institutional character. Capitalism *was* different from feudalism, even though there was always a lot going on that could be attributed to either or neither and that overlapped them both. The same is true with bureaucratic and patrimonial administration. While history, as Nonet and Selznick recognize, follows no predetermined script, it is also not simply "one damn thing after another." Writing off *in principle* any attempt to decipher some of its patterns is probably less likely to succeed than exploring and, if apt, exposing, any particular attempt. On the other hand, anyone seeking to *defend* the particulars of Nonet and Selznick's account would need to provide much more detail than the impressionistic sweeps that characterize this book. I don't know that this has been done by anyone; certainly not by Nonet and Selznick.

Still, there have been many observers who have discerned similar patterns in the development of contemporary law.[83] Many of them have gone on to argue that the rise of responsive law in Western legal orders represents a *crisis* in contemporary law. There was a rush of such talk in the 1970s and 1980s, then, with neoliberalism, a lull. However, with the publication of Brian Tamanaha's *Law as a Means to an End: Threat to the Rule of Law*, which develops such arguments at length, and with the newly reactivated postfinancial crisis state, such preoccupations seem likely to recur.

The worries appear to have been of four sorts. First, one objection to the rise of responsive law mixes an external and political dimension, with an internal legal one. It has to do with the purposes of the wielders of legal instruments, rather than with the character of these instruments themselves. Thus, libertarians and so-called neoliberals in theory (Nozick) and in power (Thatcher, Reagan) objected on political or economic or philosophical grounds to what they took to be the hyperactivity of the modern state. The *goals* of responsive law were what they objected to, quite apart from the character of the means. Responsiveness is commonly demanded by people who want the state to do more. Neoliberals have argued that it has only a few, though important, things to do: primarily keep the peace and frame and facilitate individual coordination and choice. Meddling attempts to use law to "respond" to social problems are seen as inadequate solutions often to non- or insoluble problems, which in turn create their own problems, among them for the rule of law.

Friedrich von Hayek had great influence here. He took the modern welfare state's "instrumentalization" of law, purportedly in the interests of social justice, to be the pursuit of a mirage, because social justice was a nonsense concept, and to threaten the end of the rule of law because of the style of law that it generated. For him the notion that law must flexibly "respond" to social needs—other than basic ones for a clear framework of general rules for individuals to guide their actions and interactions—emanates from a flawed social theory and presages a damaged polity. It pretends to a knowledge that no individuals but only markets, which aggregate more knowledge than anyone separately has, can possess. And those markets depend on clear, stable, general rules of the game, interpreted and enforced by independent arbiters, not on open-ended policy directives, increasingly vague and unspecific in their terms, and implemented by centrally determined goal-directed bureaucrats.[84] Bad goals in turn generate bad means, laws that don't guide, frameworks that keep being adjusted, prescriptions too vague and malleable to be followed, but altogether labile in the hands of their wielders.

Secondly, even those who do not share Hayek's political or economic analysis have expressed similar sorts of views about the consequences of legal responsiveness for the form and character of the law itself and thus for the rule of law. Many such writings appeared around the time of *Law and Society in Transition*. Thus, Roberto Mangabeira Unger saw a flat contradiction between the rule of law and the forms of law generated by the welfare state. For him, welfare state efforts to render law "purposive" and responsive engender "policy-oriented discourse" that "forces one to make explicit choices among values," the "pursuit of procedural or substantive justice [that] requires rules be interpreted in terms of ideals that define the conception of justice," an "escalating use of open-ended standards and a swing toward purposive legal reasoning and procedural or substantive approaches to justice." Together these trends "repeatedly undermine the relative generality and the autonomy that distinguish the [autonomous] legal order from other kinds of law, and in the course of so doing they help discredit the political ideals represented by the rule of law."[85] Eugene Kamenka and Alice Erh Soon Tay offered a similar diagnosis to Unger's, but their evaluation was closer to Hayek's. The development of "bureaucratic-administrative" regulation that subordinates legal clarity and generality to goal-delivery, and *gemeinschaftlich* demands for legal responsiveness to community needs threaten the *Gesellschaft*, the individualist liberal-capitalist state, and its law; so much so, they claimed, that there existed "a crisis in the *form* of law, the result of its inability, on its existing form and principles, to accommodate the new content and role being demanded of it."[86] Lest such anxieties all seem a thing of the past, Brian Tamanaha's recent work suggests that they have not died.

Thirdly, and in a long tradition that seeks institutional ways of guarding the guardians, many who are suspicious of responsive law see it as just a modish label for a long-familiar tendency to weaken legal restraints on those who exercise power. However fancy the language and noble the ostensible motives, releasing officials from the constraints of "black letter law" will erode the restraining and guiding functions they consider precious in legal autonomy and the rule of law. In contrast to the "legal instrumentalism" of despots, they insist on the importance of clear legal restraints and hear with nervous skepticism demands for more substantive, still less reflexive, contributions from law. They fear that law will become indistinguishable from, or the servant of, politics.

There are, after all, considerable liberal and democratic reasons to insist that law be or strive as much as possible to be a "law of rules,"[87] where rules are understood to act as "exclusionary reasons";[88] that is, reasons that exclude recourse to extra-rule considerations that might in other practical settings be considered relevant, whether these be considerations of politics, morals, consequences, or whatever. That, on the autonomist view, is what is meant by *applying* the law that you have, rather than speculating about why you have it or making a new law different from the one in front of you. On this view, for a rule to have the signal attribute of "ruleness" and to do the jobs the rule of law requires of it, it must, to the extent possible, be treated as an unambiguous, mandatory, and exclusionary rule to be preferred to nonrule considerations; not a mere rule of thumb, simply to be taken into account along with them, or an emanation of some more important principle or policy yet to be deciphered. Otherwise there is nothing to set against the whim of the "interpreter" of law, no way to guard the guardians. Set the distinctiveness of law aside, adopt an "instrumentalist," "responsive," jurisprudence, and, as Nonet and Selznick interpret the critics of responsiveness to say:

> officials and citizens can more readily do as they please . . . law loses its capacity to restrain officials and command obedience . . . Unchecked discretion is alien to legal ordering, not only because it may free "nine old men" to enact their preferences into law but, more important, because legal institutions are made overly vulnerable to the pressures of the political environment. A too open legal order loses the ability to moderate the role of power in society; it regresses to repression.[89]

Finally, and poignantly, there is a characterization of modern trends that doesn't bother with their instrumental weaknesses as much as lament them at what might be called an ontological level. One such view is that of Philippe Nonet. Not too long after the publication of *Law and Society in Transition*, Nonet came to break with many of his earlier beliefs, among them those he shared with Selznick,[90] the enterprise of social science, and, in relation to law, all conceptions that sully law with other disciplines ("law and . . .") both at the level of legal scholarship and at that of the practical workings of law. Increasingly influenced by Nietzsche and then by Heidegger, he came to reject most that was distinctive of modernity, including any attempt to reduce law's autonomy and increase its "responsiveness." Such moves, he became convinced (where earlier he had with Selznick tentatively outlined a possibility among several), were aspects of what Nietzsche had understood as the "nihilism" of modernity. It signalled the "death of law." He did not doubt that law had developed in the directions sketched in *Law and Society in Transition*, but he came to despise—not too strong a word—everything these developments represented:

> "The last bastion has fallen." The walls of the city have at last been overrun. The walls of the city were its shelter: they kept out of the city what did not belong in it. With its walls overrun, with its walls no longer serving as walls, wall-less, the city has lost its power to exclude and expel what does not belong. It has dissolved into what had surrounded it . . .
>
> The last bastion fell to treason. Some lawyers, well intentioned, indeed like most traitors overflowing with good intentions, let the engineers in. The story of that high treason . . . may be told with that of the word "policy." . . . Soon, all rules were gone, and policies moved in their stead, raising "policy questions," requiring "policy analysis," and calling for "techniques" of social engineering.[91]

There is more where that came from. It is hard to think how one might argue with it, either for or against; the volume's too high. However, the anxieties are recognizable and their sources far from trivial. It is clear, however, that Selznick's taste for nuance, balance, and tempered reflection has not rubbed off or, perhaps, has been rubbed off.

Whatever the ultimate evaluation of these developments, common to all these diagnoses and others is a tone of crisis. That is a tone that is recognized but not echoed in *Law and Society in Transition* and Selznick's other writings on these themes. How so?

Tolerating Ambiguity

As the quotations from Selznick in the first part of this chapter make clear, he believes both that restraint against arbitrary power is crucially important and that it depends on institutional autonomy. Perhaps for rhetorical purposes, that point is rather soft pedalled, though not denied, in *Law and Society in Transition*. However, more commonly, as he emphasizes in *The Moral Commonwealth*, he agrees, indeed insists, that institutional autonomy is "the chief bulwark of the rule of law. Judging, lawyering, fact-finding, rule-making: all require insulation from pressures that would corrupt them."[92]

If this is so, however, why not stop right there? It is not that in *Law and Society in Transition* he was unaware, forgetful, or scornful of these anxieties. On the contrary, its pages are full of them. Thus Nonet and Selznick note that "autonomous law recoils from the unsettling effect of purposive thinking" and comment that there is "much warrant for such caution and restraint . . . How far the authority of purpose can replace the authority of rules is open to serious question."[93] Again, while it is less easy to displace goals by concentrating on "technicalities" when purposes are generalized, and that is a good thing, every reader of *TVA* (or indeed *Enquiry*) will remember that "to generalize responsibilities is to run the risk of diluting them. General ends tend to be impotent, that is, so abstract and vague that they offer neither guidance in decision nor clear standards of evaluation."[94] There is a danger, as factual inquiry becomes more accepted and more wide ranging, that it will come to approximate "a more sophisticated pragmatism, in the spirit of John Dewey." That sounds good, but "in that perspective values are always multiple, interdependent, and potentially conflicting. Therefore a pragmatic approach runs the risk of aggravating the elusiveness of purpose and of degenerating into an ad hoc, unguided 'balancing' of competing goals and interests."[95]

As responsive law develops its new modes and forms, civic participation is encouraged, and that, we have seen, is a good thing, too, at least in parts. On the other hand, "civic participation can undermine as well as support institutional efficacy," for as *TVA* and *Enquiry* taught, "sustained participation depends on the work of committed elites. As a result there is always a risk that more articulate constituencies will drown out weaker, less visible, or more passive publics."[96] This and other aspects of widened participation have the paradoxical effect of making

> the definition and protection of the public interest precarious and problematic. As institutions are opened to their constituencies, they become (1) more vulnerable to the imbalances of power in society and (2) more readily focused on a narrow range of special concerns. They become, in effect, less accountable to the larger polity, more tenuously informed by its problems and aspirations.[97]

Finally, this proliferation of significant actors, and the "administrative explosion of modern times,"[98] have a paradoxical and similarly double-edged effect "reflecting many of the aspirations and problems of a purposive and responsive law." On the one hand, their very profusion signals a "withering away of the state," in Engels's phrase (here wrongly attributed to Lenin) and interpreted to suggest not "the end of all government . . . [but] a transformation of government away from monolithic and repressive forms of the state."[99] On the other hand, the weakening of monolithic sovereignty raises "the specter of a multitude of narrow-ended, self-regulating institutions, working at cross-purposes and bound to special interests; of a system impervious to direction and leadership; incapable of setting priorities; of a fragmented and impotent polity in which the very idea of public interest is emptied of meaning."[100]

In all, what makes this discussion of responsive law so tantalizing and full of tensions is that, for all its promise, Nonet and Selznick emphasize repeatedly that:

> The quest for purpose is a risky venture for legal institutions. In the large business enterprise the heritage of the past is readily perceived as a hindrance to rationality. In principle, the organization is free to demystify its rules and alter its procedures. But some institutions, notably religious and legal, have depended heavily on ritual and precedent to sustain identity or uphold legitimacy. For them the road to responsiveness is necessarily perilous; it cannot be contemplated with easy optimism. The differences between autonomous and responsive law follow in part from contrasting assessments of that risk. Autonomous

law adopts a "low-risk" perspective. . . . In calling for a more purposive and open
legal order, the advocates of responsive law opt for a "high-risk" alternative.[101]

How is it possible to hold all these balls in the air at once? How to regard
the rule of law as the master ideal of legal orders, yet be critical of autonomous law in which it is embodied, at the same time be sharply aware of the
vulnerabilities of the alternative you pose to it, and yet have more than a
bit of warmth for that alternative? How to speak at the same time of the
virtues of both autonomous and responsive law and of the vices of both of
them? Why is Selznick so concerned to say all these things? Is he trapped
in some sort of vicious circle, where whatever he says in praise of the rule
of law is vitiated by his criticisms of it, while the strength of his criticisms
makes it hard to understand his attachment? Or is he an exponent only
on some days, or in some writings, and a critic on other days and in other
writings? Or is he simply incoherent?

To answer such questions, we need to attend to some pervasive features
of Selznick's thought and ways of thought, many of which come together
in this short work. I have in mind characteristics as much of his moral and
intellectual sensibility as of his arguments. They require, but they also go
some way to explain, his tolerance for ambiguity.

Framing so much of Selznick's discussion, and itself an example of such
tolerance, is his determination to connect realism and idealism, in both directions. One thing wisdom teaches about the realization of values, he often seems to be saying, is that it is hard, at times very hard, often will work
against natural tendencies in the world, and is bound to be incomplete.
Another is that one should never stop trying. This sour-sweet combination
is a crucial element of Selznick's intellectual and moral character, and it is
on show in *Law and Society in Transition.*

This determination to be a realistic idealist and an idealistic realist generates many of the "on the one hand"/"on the other hand" agonizing of
the book, but also some of its levelheadedness. Some who seek to rebut
criticisms of legal autonomy, among them the supposedly critical, evade
the problem by rejecting the distinction between law and politics as sham
all the way down. Selznick, however, does not think the distinction, or
many other aspects of "autonomous law," are shams, and yet he is prepared
to question single-minded devotion to them and to propose alternatives.

The world is full of tensions: some productive, some that we can and
should alleviate, some that we might simply have to live with. And often
we do so successfully enough. Part of his pragmatist heritage is to deny
that analytic contrasts are necessarily real-world contradictions. It is one

thing to aspire to responsiveness and even to consider it morally a higher achievement than autonomy. It is another to deny autonomy its place or, with spurious drama, claim that they cannot be combined. This is precisely the sort of context where attention to variation is key, and where "more precision is required as to *what kind of* autonomy and *how much* is required or desirable."[102]

It should be recognized that Selznick is not coming for the first time to the sort of tensions between autonomy and openness that he discerns in the controversies over legal forms. None of these tensions is unprecedented either in other times or in other institutions. After all, one recurrent theme in Selznick's investigations over a long time had been the tension in the life of institutions, and indeed in the moral life, between the need to secure a distinct identity and to be responsive to the demands of the world outside. In *TVA*, we witnessed an organization so conscious of the latter need that, in considerable measure, it lost control of its own direction. *The Organizational Weapon* analyzes the Communist Party's organizational challenge of dealing with the "inherent tension" between developing a distinctive competence in turning recruits into "deployable personnel," on the one hand, and then successfully "deploying" them into the wider society, on the other. That requires communication and maintenance, often in extraordinarily difficult circumstances, of the distinctive character of the Party but with an aim ultimately to be competent to act decisively in a society full of competitors, temptations, and threats; hence the need to guard against both "excessive isolation on the one hand and liquidation on the other."[103]

Again, in addressing issues of policy Selznick emphasizes that there will commonly be tensions between what is appropriate to have and to do, to ensure basic security, and what is apt for flourishing. Avoiding evils, for example, comes at a potential price in terms of the good one can do, just as a single-minded pursuit of improvement might erode or destroy important sources of security. Not every measure apt to reduce our fears is equally apt to help us attain our hopes. The "integrity" of an institution is often bought at a price in terms of its "responsiveness," and the reverse is equally true.

Selznick finds that pattern in many institutions. Law is just one of them. So, while he agrees that "there is indeed a tension between openness and fidelity to law, and that tension poses the central problem of legal development. . . . The dilemma is not unique to law: All institutions experience a conflict between integrity and openness." Excess on one side breeds "formalism and retreatism, rendering institutions rigid, incapable of coping with new contingencies." The virtues of openness, flexibility, and adaptability, on the other hand, can degenerate "readily into opportunism, that is, unguided adaptation to events and pressures."[104]

Responsive law is to be built on an autonomous legal order; it is not intended to undermine it. Thus, "there is or should be a dual focus on *baselines* and *flourishings*. We hold fast to the vital minimum even as we reach for the more subtle, more elaborated, more problematic ideal."[105] But, still, how can one accommodate both if, as Selznick admits and indeed emphasizes, they pull in different directions?

One bridge between the negative and a more affirmative conception of legality Selznick sees within the law itself, in the form of principles and a legal culture that authorizes interpretation in terms of purpose. Selznick repeatedly stresses that these more open-ended embodiments of value are *parts of the law* and therefore routinely accessible to common or garden-variety legal interpreters. On the other hand, like Dworkin, Selznick believes that principles point beyond the law positivistically conceived and are apt to blur lines between law and other norms. They are *"points of transition from law to justice"*[106] that allow interpreters—indeed require them—to look to the *purpose* and the *spirit*, rather than rest merely with the letter, of the law.

But not even this quasi-Dworkinian version of an expanded kit of legal tools can encompass Selznick's ambitions, for his "higher instrumentalism" would often seem to reposition the center of law from adjudication to regulation. How would this "higher instrumentalism" be consistent with what there is to value in the traditional understandings of the rule of law, which many take to be its noninstrumental and independent self-sufficiency? Here Selznick's theory of *development* serves its turn.

Differences among institutional values might be constant, but the strategy is often serial: First strengthen the institution, then open it to the world. Institutional integrity is not a freely gotten good, the presence of which can simply be assumed. On the other hand, once it is achieved, it can be built on, including doing things that might be destructive at earlier stages.

The evolutionary dimension is crucial here. Selznick's legal developmentalism is subject to all the antinecessitarian cautions we have discussed, and it is understood, both sociologically and morally, more in the Hegelian sense of *Aufhebung* (roughly, changing while preserving, transcending) rather than annihilation, so that the achievements of earlier stages both are in fact, and ought to be, maintained in the later ones. But it *is* development, not a simultaneous array of zero-sum choices. Thus, in a passage that compresses many aspects of Selznick's character into a single space, we learn:

> Our thesis is that responsive law brings larger institutional competencies to the quest for justice. This evaluation, however, does not entail an unambiguous prescription or counsel. In our view responsive law is a precarious ideal whose achievement *and desirability* are historically contingent and depend especially on the urgencies to be met and the resources that can be tapped. Where maintaining order or taming repression require all available energies, a call for responsive law can only be a harmful distraction from more basic urgencies.[107]

Or, as he puts it elsewhere, "if an institution is too weak (or too inept) to defend its integrity, we should call it opportunistic rather than responsive."[108] This recalls the argument in *Leadership in Administration* that "isolation is necessary during periods of incubation and maturation, but may be modified when this character-forming task has been accomplished."[109]

So it might be argued, where a legal order is secure and rights guaranteed by "autonomous law" well anchored, it should be better able to satisfy demands generated, among other things, by the weaknesses and pathologies of the law itself. Normative theorists can make plausible claims about the effects of laws in the world only if they are prepared to take circumstances and variations in institutional strength, support, and resilience into account. It is important to distinguish sensible caution from paranoia. Many opponents of legal instrumentalism compare relatively autonomous "noninstrumental" legal orders with repressive and arbitrary ones, and they prefer the former—and rightly so. But these are not the only alternatives because legal orders differ greatly in the extent to which the values and practices of the rule of law are strongly embedded within them or, alternatively, highly precarious.

To expand a little on Selznick's argument: In strong legal orders, such as those of Western liberal democracies, for example, there are large cadres of people trained within strong legal traditions, disciplined by strong legal institutions, working in strong legal professions, socialized to strong legal values. Western legal orders are bearers of value, meaning, and tradition laid down and transmitted over centuries, not merely tools for getting jobs done. Prominent among the values deeply entrenched in these legal orders over centuries are rule-of-law values, and these values have exhibited considerable resilience and capacity to resist attempts to erode them. Not every legal order is so strong. That suggests that not every legal order is equally at risk from limited incursions on its "ruliness": Some will be much threatened, others less so.

Selznick insists on this point, in arguing for consideration of a legal order more responsive to changing needs, particular circumstances, principles of justice embedded in legal traditions, and considerations of justice more broadly. Responsive law, in Selznick's theory, is not a horse for all courses, not equally salutary in every time and every place. But just as it would be sinister (or frivolous) to demean the values and institutions committed to restraining power, conversely:

> the very stability of the rule of law, where that has been achieved, makes possible a still broader vision and a higher aspiration. Without disparaging (to say nothing of trashing) our legal heritage, we may well ask whether it fully meets the community's needs . . . So long as the system is basically secure, it is reasonable to accept some institutional risks in the interests of social justice.[110]

In place of the zero-sum confrontation of so much crisis talk, Selznick agrees with the concerns of those realists who stress restraint on power and see the rule of law as essentially and preciously negative: a protection against arbitrariness. On the other hand, the promise of law and of the rule of law need not be exhausted by this negative, constraining conception. And this is not merely realistic, but it is an important point to recall when we are considering ideals.

If there is so much to be said for autonomous law, however, why would anyone want to endanger it? Here the last general characteristic of Selznick's thought to be mentioned in this chapter is important. Like Max Weber and Isaiah Berlin, though with less of a taste for demonic and tragic confrontations than either, Selznick repeatedly stresses that what we value often comes at a price. The negative conception of the rule of law stresses fidelity to existing law, which often will involve bracketing of particulars, concrete circumstances, and social realities but which will maintain the integrity of the legal order and may well serve the clarity, stability, and predictability of the law. The affirmative conception stresses openness to just these specificities, which will often involve deviation from strict precedent or authority. If "legality," which he applauds, can degenerate into "legalism," which he condemns, so, too, "openness," he recognizes, easily falls into "opportunism." And quite apart from tensions with traditional conceptions of the rule of law, "the desirability of greater responsiveness may depend on how far a society or an institution should go in sacrificing other values, such as the achievement of high culture, to the quest for justice."[111] Still, and as seasoned Selznickologists would again expect, "we should keep that risk in mind, but we should not allow it to frustrate inquiry, or to sound retreat to a rule-of-law model that has its own great failings and limits."[112]

Like so many goods that Selznick considered through his long life, those of autonomy typically come at a price, for that conception has its own potential vices and pathologies. It can successfully thwart not merely bads but goods as well. In particular, just as bureaucratic insulation from purpose, responsibility, responsiveness, and substantive outcomes is generated by considerations, many of which are worthy in themselves, so too with autonomous law. That price is often discounted or ignored by those who exact it, because "a morality of means comes to encompass the whole of legality and justice. Substantive justice is derivative, a hoped-for by-product of impeccable method."[113] Such tendencies are common among the bureaucrats he understood so well. They are not obviously less common, and for similar bureaucratically virtuous evasion of ends, among servants of autonomous law. But the method might thwart the result. Again, like so many other goods he has considered, a negative, strict, conception of legality is a good in its place, but not when it takes up all the space. When that happens, we have degenerated into legalism and a real virtue turns, as it so easily will, into a regularly associated vice.

So, legality might degenerate into legalism, means triumph over ends (as, uncorrected, they always tend to do); rules over "purposes, needs, and consequences";[114] formal over substantive justice; institutional integrity over openness to social reality; abstract propositions over concrete problems; fidelity over competence. There are virtues in each of the elements of these couplings, but legalism systematically prefers the system-maintaining virtues, as Selznick sees it, to the problem-solving ones. He understands the concern, but his own bias lies in the other direction.[115] Thus:

> In contemporary discussions of the rule of law we find much that goes beyond the negative virtue of restraining official misconduct. . . . This thicker, more positive vision speaks to more than abuse of power. It responds to values that can be *realized*, not merely protected within a legal process. These include respect for the dignity, integrity, and moral equality of persons and groups. Thus understood, the rule of law enlarges horizons even as it conveys a message of restraint.[116]

In this understanding, arbitrariness, and its antidote the rule of law, both take on a larger meaning, attached to values to be vindicated, rather than simply to a set of institutions and practices imagined to serve them. Arbitrariness is not found merely when a strict rule is overstepped but equally when law is "inflexible, insensitive, or justified *only* by history or prec-edent,"[117] as works by Selznick's colleague, Robert Kagan among oth-ers,[118] make plain. To counteract the arbitrariness fostered by "going by the book," space needs to be made for an expanded understanding of the rule of law, more open ended and open to the world.

Responsive law might never be realized. If it is, it might well come at a high cost in terms of existing values and new ones. Even if the cost is toler-able, things will be left undone. All of these are good reasons for care, but none of them for abandoning hope or effort. Hope of what? Effort in aid of what? Such questions draw us deep into some of the largest questions of social philosophy. And so they drew Selznick, and will shortly draw us, into *The Moral Commonwealth*.

CHAPTER NINE

Values, Conflict, Development

VALUES

Science or Jurisprudence?

The unifying thread of Selznick's various investigations of law as of life, concern with values, in turn came to be central to what came to be known as the "Berkeley approach" to law. This was fostered in the Law and Society Center and the JSP and exemplified in the works we have reviewed. A corollary, as Philippe Nonet articulated it in 1976, was that "just as other branches of sociology need to be informed by the normative thought on which they comment *so sociology of law must be jurisprudentially informed*" . . . "*The sociology of law must integrate jurisprudence.*"[1]

This, of course, is Selznick's teaching, part of his larger conviction that normative, descriptive, and explanatory questions and approaches to understanding depend on each other and require integration. As he was well aware, not everyone agrees. Most sociologists and jurisprudes give each other a wide berth, often combining a confident ignorance of, with a touch of disdain for, whatever it is the other does. Typically such disciplinary parochialism goes without saying, but occasionally it is articulated. An extended review of *Law, Society, and Industrial Justice*, by the spirited advocate of sociology as "pure science," Donald Black, was one such occasion, and Selznick responded to it. Black represented a pole as distant as is available from Selznick, on the proper relationship between what has been described as "the scientific, the descriptive, and the legal-normative elements in sociolegal research."[2] So there is something emblematic in the encounter.

The review is at the same time a scrupulous account of the themes and ambitions of that book and a dismissal of it and them as having anything to do with sociology *pur sang*. For a key element of that purity, Black insists, is its disengagement from any consideration or invocation of values.[3]

At the start of his review Black identifies a looming conflict between two schools of thought in the sociology of law:

> The first is pragmatic and sometimes normative; the second strives for detachment and neutrality. The first moves freely between fact and value, seeing a rigid separation as undesirable if not impossible; the second clings to this separation and shows no sign of weakening. The first finds the second naïve, but is in turn criticized as confused. Call the first a natural-law approach, the second a positivist approach.[4]

Black identifies Selznick as the leading exponent of the first approach; he himself represents the second. He acknowledges *Law, Society, and Industrial Justice* (hereafter *LSIJ*) as "undoubtedly the most erudite and imaginative example of the natural-law approach to appear"[5] and praises it as "a very fine, even extraordinary piece of legal scholarship. It displays much craftsmanship, depth of learning, and creativity. It is elegant in style and graceful in presentation."[6] That's the good news; the bad follows: Selznick is an "advocate" and *a fortiori* no scientist. He seeks latent ideals in the law, something science can't do; "Science is unable to divine what is just from the law's own point of view, since this is a moral and political question . . . Selznick attempted to make a kind of value-free value judgment. He attempted the impossible."[7] And thus, "every legal sociologist should read it *[LSIJ]* knowing exactly what it is—a good example of what the sociology of law is not."[8]

Black insists that only "pure sociology" is true sociology, and he polices its boundaries with uncomplicated confidence and zeal.[9] Above all, what threatens to pollute scientific endeavor, and any manifestation of which sociology must *shun*, is values. Pure sociology cannot study them, evaluate them, or express them. To do any such thing is to leave science for the unscientific arts of jurisprudence, or advocacy, or policy. In particular, a sociologist has no business seeking to "compare legal reality to an ideal with no empirical referent, such as 'the rule of law' or 'due process,' [lest she or he] may inadvertently implant his personal ideals as the society's legal ideals. At this point social science ceases and advocacy begins."[10]

Selznick pretends to be practicing sociology of law, according to Black, but he cannot be doing so. His normative engagements, his engagement with legal doctrine, his concentration on values, mean he was doing something totally different: sociological jurisprudence, not sociology of law:

> To say this about a book by Philip Selznick seems almost outrageous, and it must seem ungrateful as well. But at the beginning I gave warning of my positivist commitment.[11]

For positive sociology, by contrast,

> Law can be seen as a thing like any other in the empirical world. . . . from a sociological standpoint, law consists in observable acts, not in rules . . . From a sociological point of view, law is not what lawyers regard as binding or obligatory precepts, but rather, for example, the observable dispositions of judges, policemen, prosecutors, or administrative officials.[12]

Selznick responded to Black's review with arguments whose ingredients long preceded this debate; he had been fighting this fight for some long time. On the fact/value distinction, he repeats and somewhat tightens points he had made in "Sociology and Natural Law." Yes, of course we must

> distinguish what the world is like from what we would like it to be. . . . It does not follow, however, that fact and value, as phenomena, belong to such different realms that a wall of separation should be raised between them. Facts have consequences for values, and sociological study of the fate of values must bring the two realms together. Furthermore, the factual order is often instinct with value, that is, it establishes conditions out of which, with some probability, and in the ordinary course of human experience, opportunities and expectations arise.[13]

He returns to the examples of primary relations and socialization, which he had discussed in his earlier article:

> It is difficult to analyze these contexts of human commitment, and retain fidelity to the subject matter, without considering latent values and without diagnosing the troubles that stem from their incomplete realization. The primary-relations model is not a sociologist's dream. It is a way of summarizing the dynamic, value-relevant properties of a certain mode of human relatedness. And these properties are value-relevant not in the sense that they speak to the sociologist's preferences but rather because they matter to the participants themselves. Much the same may be said of socialization, at least when that is seen from the standpoint of the individual. . . . it would be a strange sociology that failed to recognize in that process a poignant interplay of constraint and striving, fact and value.[14]

His reply to the other distinction that matters so much to Black, between legal sociology and sociological jurisprudence, is typical of his impatience with self-appointed border guards of science. He doesn't mind if his book is called sociological jurisprudence, as Black insists, but what is the force of the label? Is it that no one who does it should seek to do sociology too, inform the insights of one with those of the other? Why? Is it that the taint of bias is unavoidable? But why should that be, and because we all have biases, how could we ever avoid the problem? By denying or submerging them? Or perhaps by watching out for them and seeking to guard against their consequences? It is true that he would prefer some outcomes of the processes he studies to others, though (as he made plain in the book under review) there are some outcomes he would prefer that he considers un-likely for sociological reasons. Of course, there is a danger that he might read his preferences into his analysis. He doesn't believe he has, but there are ways of checking. Certainly, he mixes sociology with jurisprudence and with other normative disciplines as well, but why not? "It seems late in the day, after so much waywardness and so much sterility, to insist upon a full divorce of the theoretical and the practical. In social science, as elsewhere, we place our bets on the enterprise of self-correction, not on a claim to complete objectivity."[15]

Pragmatism

The debate between those who demand that the human sciences can and should emulate the methods of the natural sciences and those who believe they demand their own rationales and criteria, appropriate to the peculiar meaning-and-value-filled character of their subject matter, is a long one. This is not the place to rehearse the large arguments that under-lie this particular debate, and I am not philosopher enough to guide them confidently to a safe harbor. However, it is at least worth stressing that the possibility, still less desirability, of "pure science" is not something that goes without saying, not within philosophy generally[16] and certainly not for anyone as steeped in classical pragmatism as Selznick was.

Black states his case with exemplary boldness, and perhaps less exem-plary dogmatism. Yet there is considerable philosophical debate about the relationships between facts and values and the "objectivity" or "subjectiv-ity" of moral judgments, debate that Black simply ignores. He knows it's all subjective; he certainly doesn't seem to think it's just his opinion. In the years since he wrote, normative theorizing has become more respectable, and over the years Black's work itself has changed course considerably, if not always explicitly.[17] It remains true that, apart from his explicit admirers,[18] there are many other social scientists who share his distaste for mixing analytical and normative concerns, who "to put it bluntly, . . . didn't know what to do with an ideal except handle it gingerly and view it with alarm,"[19] and who have a highly scientistic and exclusive view of what it is academically legitimate for them to do. Are they right to do so? More particularly, was Selznick right to do otherwise? This raises philosophical and sociological, as well as practical issues.

Recall where Selznick was coming from in this debate. In the first passage I previously quoted, Black describes the "school of thought" to which Selznick belongs as "pragmatic," but the word appears in lowercase and without inflection, and it is unclear whether Black has the philosophical movement in mind at all. He seems just to be saying "interested in consequences." For Selznick the word is more specific and weightier.

It is standard pragmatist teaching, after all, that the distinction between fact and value is one of the most pernicious of the dualisms that we construct and that obscure the continuities of the world. This is not a mere assertion or confusion, but an argument, or series of arguments, that the great pragmatists, central among them Dewey, developed. Their objection is not to a distinction, useful for some purposes, but to the suggestion of an ontological and logical gap that cannot be spanned without peril. More recent pragmatist philosophers, among them Hilary Putnam and Cheryl Misak, have returned to these themes and developed them. Just as Selznick reminds us of normative systems and their inextricable tendencies to "envaluation," for example, so Putnam stresses that much in the world is pervaded by "the entanglement of fact and value."[20] So many of our standard-issue concepts are interlarded with descriptive and evaluative components that resist separation:

> We classify people as cruel or compassionate, socially skilled or inept, connoisseurs or tyros, and sometimes with a high degree of intersubjective agreement; yet there is no reason at all to think that these classifications could be reduced to some fixed physicalistic vocabulary. Moreover, some of these classifications are classifications of phenomena whose very existence is partly brought about and sustained *by* the classifications.[21]

Think of gender as distinct from (though not necessarily opposed to) sex.

There is, he insists, no escaping it. Our investigations of matters of fact presuppose values, among them those of relevance, coherence, simplicity, but also of the point of the exercise. These are not always moral values, but in terms of the fact/value distinction what applies to one sort of value applies to the others. If then values are to be excluded from science, so must the conduct of science itself, which presupposes values. But no "pure scientist" says that—or could. Our values in turn grow out of real, "factual" problems we seek to resolve.

Pragmatists also deny Max Weber's influential claim that while our means can be rationally evaluated (how well or ill do they generate our ends?), our ends are beyond rational scrutiny or control. For Dewey, as we saw in Chapter Two, ends and means interact; they are the same sorts of things, often indeed the same things, as means are ends until achieved, then in turn become means to some further end, and so on. Whether they were good ends to pursue depends, and can be rationally assessed to depend, in part on the extent to which they resolved the problem that generated them as ends, and in part on whether seeking them makes sense in terms of what is required to achieve them; "Ends are neither laid up in a Platonic heaven nor the mere whims of individuals; they are, rather, ends-in-view, they guide conduct; in that capacity they are themselves means to solving a problem and as such rationality is competent to pronounce judgment upon them."[22] The gulf that Black envisages between "science" and "advocacy" is bridged on both sides: science depends on values; otherwise one would not know what to look for or how to look for it. And advocacy ignorant of facts is baseless.

But are our ethical views irreducibly "subjective," as postmodern common sense and positivist philosophy both take for granted? According to the famous popularizer of pragmatism, Richard Rorty, perhaps they are. Selznick and Dewey and Putnam are, however, made of sterner stuff. Selznick rejects Rorty's denial of the possibility and therefore the point of "getting things right,"[23] as a fundamental distortion of pragmatism. Dewey, he insisted, was "very much in the business of getting things right."[24] True, they cannot ground "objectivity" simply by direct appeal to correspondence with "facts of the matter" in the world, known to exist independently of our own inquiries. On this, positivists and pragmatists agree. But then, objectivist pragmatists continue, neither can our knowledge of facts themselves be so established. Both gain their "objectivity" from the fallible but grounded character of "a well-pursued inquiry."[25] As Misak puts it:

> Pragmatism . . . abandons the kind of metaphysics which is currently in so much disrepute—it abandons concepts which pretend to transcend experience. Truth and objectivity are matters of what is best for the community of inquirers to believe, "best" here amounting to that which best fits with the evidence and argument.[26]

Moral reasoning reaches toward objectivity when:

> the practice of moral deliberation is responsive to experience, reason, argument, and thought experiments where we, for instance, put ourselves in another's shoes. Such responsiveness is part of what it is to make a moral decision and part of what it is to try to live a moral life. . . . an objective area of inquiry must be such that its beliefs are sensitive to something that can speak for or against them.[27]

We have no ground for saying we have reached indubitable certainties in matters of morals, of right and wrong, justice and injustice, but neither do we in matters of fact. However, we have very good reasons for distinguishing between rational and irrational beliefs in both domains.

The ontological and logical bases of "pure" value-free science, then, are not self-evidently secure. I don't risk putting it more strongly because neither is the objectivity of morals. It remains a matter of philosophical contention. That being the case, one might reflect on how much that matters in social life is left out by the self-denying ordinances of those who would have the human sciences emulate particle physics. A parallel point was made by Arthur Stinchcombe, a onetime student of Selznick's, discussing Black's *The Behavior of Law*. He found its lean esthetic attractive. Nevertheless:

> I see no particular purpose in crippling oneself by choosing a sociologistic style that ignores the intentions of people. Strip the intellectual structure to the minimum needful, yes, but intentions and judgments are the core of the matter . . . Forcing the sociology of law into that hypothetico-deductive mold, as Black does, seems to me to ignore most of what is interesting for the sake of what little fits the mold.[28]

That is a question of *what* one should study. *How* one should study is another question that, as we shall see, Selznick does not always distinguish from the first. Still, in regard to either, it is clear, disciplinary chastity is not a form of abstinence that he recommends: Humanist science, and its offspring normative social theory, are for him not oxymorons but ambitions; much opposed, not much practised, hard to do, easy to get wrong, but pregnant with possibility.

The extent to which social scientists strain and pretend to avoid such entanglement changes with time and fashion, but, as a practical matter, it would be nice if there were more normative theory and humanist science about. They are useful antidotes to contemporary specialisms, with their often daunting combinations of sharp and narrow, recondite and arid.

They might help us too. What precisely is wrong with what Hirschman imagined might become possible "down the road"?:

> a kind of social science that would be very different from the one most of us have been practicing: a moral-social science where moral considerations are not repressed or kept apart but are systematically commingled with analytic argument without guilt feelings over lack of integration; where the transition from preaching to proving and back again is performed frequently and with ease; and where moral considerations need no longer be smuggled in surreptitiously nor expressed unconsciously but are displayed openly and disarmingly. Such would be, in part, my dream for a "social science for our grandchildren."[29]

By coincidence, I am writing this paragraph having just finished reading *The Idea of Justice*,[30] by the economist/philosopher, Amartya Sen. I am happy that he was never dissuaded from his ecumenical ventures (or shunned from the discipline of economics) by purist devotees of either economic "science" or philosophy, of whom there have been many. For as Sen writes elsewhere, "the case for bringing economics closer to ethics does not rest on this being an easy thing to do. The case lies, instead, on the rewards of the exercise. I have argued that the rewards can be expected to be rather large."[31]

Varieties of "Value-Centeredness"

That said, there are hazards in such an enterprise, not always avoided in Selznick's discussion. One concerns a blurring of different forms of "value-centered" inquiry. Within Selznick's works, there are at least four ways in which values figure, not always at the same time, and not always explicitly. Selznick does not do enough to separate these stages, either logically or chronologically, though each of them makes different epistemological and normative demands.

The first three of these are unambiguously to be found in his writings, at least from "Sociology and Natural Law" in 1961. The first is his Dewey-inspired claim that people have values and ideals that are important to them and their lives together, as natural results of their strivings and problem-solving activities. The second is that some of our most important engagements, practices, and institutions form normative systems with a "tendency to envaluation." Third, we move to "clinical" assessment, something Selznick also advocated from the start. His argument was that such evaluation too need not be from the evaluator's own perspective but from that of the system itself. That is to say, in the light of study of normative systems, we can offer quasi-technical assessments of whether they are doing well or are in bad shape, in terms of values latent within them, and those necessary to sustain them and enable them to flourish—as things of *their* sort, not necessarily our sort. We may have no commitment to these practices and systems, Selznick claims; we may loathe them, but we can still evaluate clinically, diagnostically, "the state of the system" and its conditions of existence and flourishing. Thus, as we saw, though *Leadership in Administration* is very affirmative (by contrast with *TVA*) about what a leader should do to infuse an institution with value, there's nothing there about what the values should be. Hitler actually fits the bill quite nicely (not a manager, but a value-infuser; a clear sense of mission, well run through the organization, and so on). And while Selznick doesn't mention Hitler in this regard, he does credit communists with understanding what leadership is about.

Finally, there are moral judgments one is prepared to make, in the first person, of states of the world. This is uncontroversially, even tautologically, a reflection of one's own views, though it may well be grounded on evidence and argument, assessment of the nature and character of social processes, and argument about what is good for them and why. And, as we have seen, there are strong arguments within the pragmatist tradition that this can be understood as objectively warranted judgment as well.

Selznick adopted stages 1 and 2 early in his thought, then moved to 3 and finally to 4. There are differences that he does little to spell out, however, between the concerns and the assumptions that underlie each of them. The first two can be uncontroversially accepted by any positivist social scientist who appreciates that to understand meaningful social behavior one must understand the "internal point of view" of participants.[32] The latter pair are more contentious, even though the enterprise can be defended, even commended, as we have seen. Particularly in his later writings, Selznick moves rather swiftly between them all, however, as though the recognition that people have values is not different from saying that certain things are good for them. Or, to put it another way, it was at times unclear whether he saw any distance between a theory about the normative aspects of social life and a normative theory of that life.

This can leave puzzled those who might accept stages 1 and/or 2, while being more skeptical about the warrant for stage 3 and even more so 4. Trained as Selznick was in the conventions of midcentury social "science," it took him some time explicitly to reach, or acknowledge reaching, these later stages too. His movement is reflected in his increased tendency to adopt normatively loaded words for concepts he initially characterized in sparer terms: Dangers of co-optation moved to be among the "perils of responsiveness"; legality became the rule of law; each move propelled by his determination to use concepts that plainly signal the entanglement of fact and value. The last move, from stage 3 to 4, from purportedly "clinical assessment" to advocacy of a systematic moral vision, was the longest in coming, though elements of the latter were long implicit in his writings. But at least by *Law and Society in Transition*, he's well into stages 3 and 4, and it would be implausible to see *The Moral Commonwealth* as mere diagnosis by a disinterested clinician.

The common lesson for sociology of the first two claims is that values are important features of the social world, which any social science needs to take into account. If we ignore them, we are ignoring key components of our subject matter, quite apart from the moral importance, importance to us as humans and not just specialist investigators, of the fate of values in human affairs. In neither case, however, need the analyst be committed to the values analyzed, though identifying values generated within normative systems will quickly take us beyond surveys of their members. All the more is this the case with "clinical" assessment and of course social philosophy. As one goes through the numbers, however, positivist hackles must rise.

One question about stages 3 and 4 is Black's: How "technical" can "clinical assessment" ever be? How independent of the analyst's own values? What warrant, other than one's own opinion, does one have for one's claims? That engages the controversy about facts and values that I have already rehearsed and to which pragmatists have a serious response. I won't pursue the point further. However, as soon as one moves from what the people in a particular system happen to value, to make claims about what is valuable for the system itself, one makes assumptions about the nature of a social "system," what is good for it, what bad, and so on. And then, even if one believes the objectivist pragmatist account of ethical judgment, another problem arises, and that is a factual one. On what basis can one assume that a social "system" has connected and coherent goods, when it is made up of people whose interests often do not cohere at all? In other terms, what about conflict?

CONFLICT

It is not only with values that it is important to distinguish what one finds in the world from what one brings to it. Sometimes one's claims depend on assumptions of entangled fact, value, and theory that are neither self-evidently warranted by the facts nor obviously valuable for all nor impervious to theoretical criticism either. This has often happened to sociologists who fail to take conflicts sufficiently seriously. For conflicts are often very serious.

Of course, Selznick is well aware of conflict; indeed, it is a key to his developmental analyses. His is not a consensual world but one driven, in Hegelian fashion, by conflicts that lead to resolutions on higher planes. Indeed, his account of institutional development is an aspect of what he liked to call "dynamic functionalism," associating it with Marx (and Hegel) and Freud, rather than with the anthropologically based static functionalism that was once prevalent. As he recalled in discussion with Roger Cotterrell:

> I tended to associate functionalism, when that was a serious topic, with Marx and Freud and not with the anthropological functionalists . . . And that made a big difference, because if you think about Marx and Freud, of course, there's a lot of functional analysis; there's a lot of identification of systems; but the notion—I called it dynamic functionalism, because it has to do with the ways in which—you're identifying a system by appreciating its contradictions. The contradictions produce a dynamism that results in a reconstruction of the system. And that's very different. So to me, the idea of opposing functionalism and conflict theory didn't make sense.[33]

This is a very particular way of taking account of conflict, however. It is to see it as a (positive) ingredient in the development of a system, the needs of which it purportedly, and presumably often despite appearances or peoples' own views, serves. But what if conflicts are more dramatic than that, or simply over incompatible, zero-sum, and indissolubly distinct, interests? One might think of the former Yugoslavia, for example, or maybe contemporary Afghanistan; but one does not need to go that far, for the problems conflicts present to an analysis that theorizes in terms of whole systems, and philosophizes, as we will see, in terms of communities, are not always far from home.

Selznick consistently echoed Dewey's alertness to continuities, suspicion of dichotomies, commitment to seeking resolution differences, and Morris Cohen's principle of polarity, which "stresses the interplay of contrasting ideas and standpoints, and the importance to good sense of showing how they involve each other."[34] These injunctions are often salutary, revealing possibilities of connection and resolution that might otherwise remain invisible. However, they also can be pressed too far. Selznick's tendency is often a sober antidote to flaccid relativism or factitious melodrama, but what if there is just real drama, even tragedy, involved? The problem here is not Rorty's—that there are no "truths" to be had—but that as a matter of fact some true values or what is truly valuable for some might be purchased only at the price of other values, or what is truly "disvaluable" for others.

In another context, James Rule has observed a "curious adaptation of medical and quasi-medical language to politics,"[35] curious because medicine has a "clearer view of its ultimate ends than does the study of 'social problems.'"[36] Though Rule does not speak of him, Selznick often used that language. However, as Rule points out:

> "social problems"—social conditions people might regard as ripe for improvement—actually represent clashes of value or interest. That is, they represent situations where one group or one set of interests stands to lose by others' gain.[37]

Rule takes the point to vindicate Weber's dichotomy between fact and value. Even if one chooses not to follow him that far, the existence of potentially irreconcilable or at least competing interests is an empirical question, a matter of fact about interests and values: Are they truly, as a matter of fact, irreconcilable? It is also a practical question: How are these differences to be resolved? Neither question will readily succumb to holistic analyses of systems and their needs, even where these are conceived of as dynamic. To this extent, organic analogies such as those Selznick often favors might mislead. They suggest an overarching unity, where it may simply not exist. Social conflicts may lead to nothing else than more social conflict, or nothing good, and those in conflict might just continue to compete, though often (and predictably) some will win and identify their interests with those of the "system" more frequently and successfully, simply because they are stronger.

DEVELOPMENT

Finally, and perhaps implicit in what went before, there is an abiding danger, which Selznick acknowledged but did not always avoid, of eliding what one finds in the world with what one hopes to find there, or at least of paying more attention to the latter and perhaps importing for it a greater prominence than is warranted. This is particularly evident in his discussions of social and institutional "development" connected with law.

Selznick makes a compelling case for seeing tensions, conflicts, dissatisfactions, opportunities as linked in dynamic interaction to generate change: new demands, new possibilities, institutional transfigurations. But why concentrate so disproportionately, as he did in his legal writings, on immanent tendencies to "maturation" rather than, say, degeneration, on virtuous circles rather than vicious ones?

Selznick is of course scrupulous in denying determinism, acknowledging contingency, external and not merely immanent influences and so on, but why then are the immanent tendencies that are given the central parts, those that seem to drive the story unless waylaid (a possibility always allowed for, never explored), the positive ones? The key immanent tendencies seem always to be pointing forward, notwithstanding that Selznick's sophisticated realism always recognizes that obstacles might get in the way. Where in his reflections on legal development, however, do we find investigation of intrinsic and immanent dynamics that lead in unsalutary directions, not as contingent deviations but as settled tendencies? That could be a way of expressing Lauren Edelman's interpretation of endogenous tendencies in large organizations, referred to in Chapter Seven of this volume, that generate the institutionalization of injustice in complex organizations. But *Law, Society, and Industrial Justice* and *Law and Society in Transition*, for all their openness to complexity and contingency, have nothing to say about *immanent* negative tendencies. It is as if, in his legal writings, Selznick had so internalized Gouldner's scolding of *TVA*, asking why he did not explore immanent positive developmental tendencies, that he spent the rest of his life responding to the jibe. I don't believe that was the case, but one might be forgiven for thinking it.

One reason for this concentration on immanent tendencies to progress, I suspect, is Selznick's attraction to analogies between institutional and individual development. However, it is one thing to note that many natural organisms, among them humans, have immanent dynamic tendencies, given appropriate conditions, to go through stages of maturation. It is another to claim that socially constructed institutions follow the same "moral logic." The link flows more from analogical association than demonstration, if only because socially constructed institutions, such as universities or post offices, do not obviously obey the same natural developmental imperatives as biological organisms.[38] At least one would like to see the argument. And yet, although the developmental stories of the last two chapters depend in significant part on such association, only the analogy, not the argument, is made.

Another reason Selznick accentuates positive possibilities is that he is looking for them. When I asked whether he thought "history was on our side," he denied it. Indeed, he worried that many of the master trends of modernity are not. Still, he went on:

> I don't think we need that to express our moral aspirations, but we do need some confidence that the values we are talking about are rooted in experience and supported by experience. This doesn't mean that that support will necessarily win out in the end, but that it is something upon which we can build and do something about evils in the world.[39]

Increasingly and with increasing self-consciousness and explicitness, he sought not merely to conduct social analysis but to articulate a social vision anchored in real, available, demonstrable, trends, whose victory was rarely inevitable but perhaps, with help, possible. In doing that, he exhibited an admirable degree of what Gramsci called "optimism of the will," which may be a necessary accompaniment of social visionaries and may even be a noble accompaniment to pessimism of the intellect. But sometimes such optimism can tend to color both what one seeks and what one finds. Perhaps that is how it came to be that, in Selznick's published accounts, the past and projected future of legal development in the West, or at least of the United States, reads as though it has been building up over centuries to culminate in precisely the moral recommendations of John Dewey. Unlike Black, I don't believe this follows inevitably from Selznick's enterprise of attending both to facts and values, and neither do I think moral celibacy is a necessary or advisable antidote. But there are risks.

There are also benefits, however. Even were learned wisdom about some of the goods of life and what might succor them not to be acceptable as "science," it would still be a good thing to have. We don't suffer from a surfeit. Selznick's later writings, to which we now turn, display some.

PART IV

Social Philosophy

CHAPTER TEN

Morality and Modernity

All Selznick's work, we have seen, has to do with the sources and fates of values in the world. It is one thing, however, to write about many particular subjects with a common or linked set of general concerns in mind and another, to address those underlying concerns directly and in the round. That is the ambition, the large ambition, of Selznick's most wide-ranging book, *The Moral Commonwealth*. It is, fittingly, a large and ambitious work. His last two slighter works—*The Communitarian Persuasion* and *A Humanist Science*—distill and develop elements, one substantive (communitarianism), the other methodological (humanist science), in a more programmatic, less academic manner. However, *The Moral Commonwealth* is the mother lode. It is the primary subject of this chapter and the next.

The Moral Commonwealth is social philosophy (or philosophical sociology) on a grand scale. It is deeply considered, richly textured, and driven by a relentless, at times remorseless, insistence on the complexity of the human condition and styles of thought adequate to comprehend it. From this insistence stem the dominant tones of the book: its recognition that moral quandaries, choices, and dilemmas are inescapable, but also its resistance to melodramatic exaggerations of them, of the predicaments that generate them or that they generate; its attention to the range of values in play in difficult decisions and circumstances, to their variety, and to ways in which circumstances alter cases; its alertness to nuance, ambiguity, and distinctions of degree; its insistence on the importance of variation and context.

The argument develops by way of critical discussions of the thought of philosophers ancient and modern, psychologists, social theorists, jurists, religious thinkers. The book is full of cameo distillations of complex ideas, valuable in their own right. However, though one learns a lot about a lot from this book, yet Selznick's own concerns and ideas connect and direct its many subjects, themes, and layers and draw them into a finely articulated structure of argument.

David Lieberman has spoken to me of the architectural quality of Selznick's writing, and the metaphor is particularly apt of this complex and tightly planned construction. At the same time, to strain the metaphor somewhat, it is a sustained exercise in bridge building. It spans, joins, and builds on many fields in positive and normative psychology and sociology, political and moral philosophy, law, legal and social theory, and much else. At times, indeed, the book's range and density can threaten to distract a reader from the tightness of its design. One reads about so many thinkers and thoughts that it can be hard to keep track of the intricate pattern that they are enlisted to form. Anyone so distracted might heed Wittgenstein's suggestion as to how philosophers should greet each other. He said they should say, "Take your time."[1]

Apart from what Selznick makes of the thoughts of others, there is a second general characteristic of the work that displays his distinctive cast of mind, his intellectual character, not merely what has nourished it. That is the extent to which ideas of his own, earlier crafted to illuminate specific subjects and in answer to particular questions, are adapted, refined, and brought to bear on the more encompassing range of problems tackled in this, not final but in many ways culminating, work. This is not so much a matter of having a bunch of useful thoughts on hand for redeployment than of developing a systematic approach that his particular studies had presaged. The book attempts to integrate his thoughts on many subjects over many years into a systematic whole and to vindicate by example his plea for a humanist science that brings together social explanation and moral evaluation.

MODERNITY

This book deals with many particular issues, but there is one overarching concern: sources of "moral well-being" in modern times. Modernity, as the specific context and subtext of modern moral concerns, is the subject of the first part of the book. Each of the three "moral actors" Selznick is concerned with—persons, institutions, and communities—occupies a successive part of the rest of it. All are considered in the context of, for each has to contend with, the pressures and the promises of modernity.

"Modernity," of course, is a substantive, not merely a temporal concept. "Modern" is not just "recent," even though historically speaking it is pretty recent. So is sociology, and the connection is not coincidental. As Charles Taylor has observed:

> From the beginning, the number one problem of modern social science has been modernity itself: that historically unprecedented amalgam of new practices and institutional forms (science, technology, industrial production, urbanization), of new ways of living (individualism, secularization, instrumental rationality); and of new forms of malaise (alienation, meaninglessness, a sense of impending social dissolution).[2]

Modernity has generated specific structures and processes that form the inescapable context of contemporary moral thought and action. These set a pervasive source of challenge and risk, but also of possibility, for moral well-being. We inhabit modernity and are shaped by it. Indeed, modernity inhabits us. It has formed not merely our context but our nature. For better or worse, on Selznick's view for better *and* worse, that is highly problematic from a moral point of view. With its "steady weakening of traditional social bonds and the concomitant creation of new unities based on more rational, more impersonal, more fragmented forms of thought and action,"[3] modernity has, as all the great social theorists recognized, transformed the world.

It has generated, or been borne along by, four "master trends"—"separation of spheres" of life; secularization and with it the "waning of sacredness"; weakening of social ties; and the growth of rational coordination, primarily on the models of contract and bureaucracy. The combination has profoundly and pervasively transformed social structures and relations, institutions and persons, ways of life and modes of thought.

Each of these trends is "uneven and incomplete"; each—particularly secularization—"generates resistance and backlash"; each "has produced many sources of moral disarray"; each, however, has been associated with "major advances in moral sensibility." The challenge is to be alert to the moral strains of modernity while remaining alive to what it makes possible and might promise:

> Criticism of modernity need not look backward to a mythic past, need not ignore the miseries and brutalities that so often characterized earlier ages. Contemporary anxieties arise in part from raised expectations and from vulnerabilities born of success . . . More is asked of us, and we ask more of

ourselves. The peril, therefore, need not be understood as a sign of pervasive decay. It may also be understood as a price paid for certain kinds of moral development.[4]

I have referred often to Selznick's tolerance for ambiguity. Modernity requires a lot of it, but it can be in short supply. Perhaps because it is so overwhelming, many thinkers have become impaled on one or the other horn of the dilemmas it presents us with, what it destroys or what it creates; less common is appraisal that seeks to gain its complex measure, without smoothing away its internal jarrings, ambivalences, and complexities or squeezing them into some uniform, homogenized texture and shape, whether emancipatory blessing or technologically driven prison.

Selznick's appraisal is characteristically nuanced. Each of the master trends he identifies can be "a tonic to the moral order." Each has been a "powerful engine for the release of energies, the achievement of excellence, and the protection of rights."[5] These benefits are great, but they are "purchased at the price of cultural attenuation." That is a high price, for:

> The fundamental truth is that modernity weakens culture and fragments experience. The gains of modernity are won, not easily and smoothly, but at significant cost to the harmony and stability of human experience. For most of human history, a received culture—embodied in expressive symbolism, sustained by integrative institutions—has been the main resource for moral confidence, steadiness, and discrimination. A genuine culture is not a collection of abstract principles or precepts. It is a web of person-centered meanings whose coherence makes possible a world taken for granted, whose directives trump desire and chasten inclination. To say with Nietzsche that God is dead is to mourn in metaphor the atrophy of culture.[6]

Yet, if the price is high, it is one we cannot avoid. We cannot re-create tight, tradition-soaked, stable, and small communities any more, even if we wanted to; and a little reflection should persuade most of us that we wouldn't want to. We gain treasures from modernity, both literal and metaphorical, but not without loss or cost. Our challenge is to recognize and secure those treasures while recognizing what they have cost, what might have been lost, what might need to be generated or regenerated to replace them. We might need to contemplate the *design* of alternatives to what was once undesigned, to reduce the price of being what we are where we are, where many of us want to be and do well from being, which is anyway a place we cannot leave, and yet which is host to discomforts as well as comforts all its own—and our own.

Selznick surveys various movements in thought that are products of and responses to modernity, including rationalism, romanticism, modernism, postmodernism. As usual, he finds insights and oversights, perceptiveness and exaggeration, in them all. One source of exaggeration came in the late eighteenth and early nineteenth centuries, with the first excited recognition of the changes modernity was wreaking. In their first flush of amazement at these momentous transformations, their partisans (and some of their shriller opponents) too easily and eagerly forgot the perennial existence of constraints, many of them *natural* constraints, on what we could and should do and not do. Instead, they became intoxicated by the apparent malleability of the world and of what had long been taken to be binding, natural, not ours lightly to make or break. That includes ourselves.

In recent years, by contrast, postmodernists have enjoyed deflating modernist hubris, replacing enthusiasm with skepticism, irony, unmasking, and often distaste. Selznick thinks some such deflation is due, but characteristically he worries that postmodern tendencies to deconstruct the pretensions of modernity "often lead to grossly exaggerated claims, with little attention to variability and context. Every disunity is a radical disunity; every evidence of superficiality and incoherence is accepted; every evidence to the contrary is ignored or discounted."[7] He decries such overblown diagnoses and critiques, partly on empirical grounds—they often flatten to one overwhelming and discordant tone the polyphonies of modernity. One senses also that his displeasure is not a matter just of disagreement but also of intellectual taste and sensibility. Shrill reductionism goes against his grain, both as thinker and moralist.

The writings of Michel Foucault are a good example. Selznick respects their brilliance and insight, draws from them, but ultimately finds them irritating. All is reduced to domination; all power. Selznick prefers diagnoses and critiques, however harsh, to be strenuously faithful to the complexities, variations, tensions, mixtures the world displays. He prefers, too, analyses that allow us to recognize in a complex achievement what is valuable as well as what it cost, sometimes what is valuable precisely *because of* what it cost; what is glorious where it is, what tawdry, and those many places where the glorious and the tawdry rub shoulders, as so often they do.

His own guide in thought is, as we might expect, Dewey's pragmatism, more specifically "pragmatic naturalism," that combines a (modernist) "spirit of liberation and reconstruction" with acknowledgment that "all is constrained by the continuities of the natural world and the human . . . This steadying framework presumes there is, in some significant sense, a message to be derived from nature."[8] According to this tradition, "authentic human ideals have material foundations. They are rooted in existential needs and strivings. When a proposed ideal denies these roots it is to that extent a source of moral confusion and psychic malaise."[9]

If values are thus grounded in nature and fact, so too must be thinking about them. One thing to know, that pragmatists knew and sociology teaches, but not everyone takes to heart, is that

> Human beings are products of interaction; they are embedded in social contexts. This is a truism, but one that must be taken seriously. It is a challenge to recognize how much we depend on shared experience, including nurture, communication, stimulation, and support . . . The chief objects of moral concern are situated beings, not abstract individuals.[10]

In other words, "the idea that humans are social animals—not as insects are social but in and through self-awareness and symbolic communication—speaks to the ontology of human nature. It purports to identify what it means to be human and thereby to grasp the distinctive quality of human life."[11]

None of this stress on the intrinsic and inexorable sociality of humans is new to readers of Selznick; nor is his allied reflection that, if so much depends on social connections, then the *quality* of those connections will matter. Among the things for which they matter, Selznick is particularly concerned with an attribute of character prefigured in his early writings but given an added normative gloss here: competence, in this context *moral* competence. Modernity at the same time expands and tests that competence in distinctive ways. In particular, it profoundly affects its social sources.

MORALITY

Sources is an important word here because it reminds us of a distinctive feature of Selznick's thought, brought to bear on moral matters in *The Moral Commonwealth*. That is his lifelong concern with what makes for a successful actor, not merely what qualifies as a successful act. Earlier[12] I quoted Sheldon Messinger's observation that central to *The Organizational*

Weapon was "a directive . . . to make the leap from consideration of what one must do to achieve a given goal, to what one must do to construct and preserve means of action appropriate to a given goal." That is an important distinction to keep in mind when reading *The Moral Commonwealth* as well. Most evidently, of course, whether you act morally depends on the choices you make and what you do. But, in a deeper sense, the choices you are likely to make depend on what sort of actor you are and on the ways you are disposed to behave. A psychopath might happen to treat children with consummate kindness, but there are reasons why psychopaths are not likely to be exemplary moral actors. And while anyone might act morally from time to time, it is Selznick's social scientific—humanist scientific—ambition, to disclose what sort of actor is well *disposed to* act morally on a more than random basis.

That will not guarantee moral action, of course. We are easily misled; other forces within and without might overwhelm our good intentions; we might be sucked in by hostile circumstances; moral choice is often difficult, sometime tragic, and yet it often cannot be avoided. Nor can temptation or base inclination. But dispositions suited to good behavior are good dispositions to have. Selznick seeks to discern the sources of such dispositions, ways of nurturing and securing them, and circumstances in which they might prevail. His particular focus is on social sources, broadly conceived.

Moral well-being, Selznick argues, is not mere happiness, utility, satisfaction of preferences, or even warmheartedness and benevolence. It entails "enhancement of fellowship and fellowship requires a dual concern for the interests of others and for one's own integrity."[13] That concern in turn is not primordial. It requires "a kind of will, commitment, and *competence*. 'Moral competence' is the capacity to be an effective moral actor. This requires reflection as well as feeling, responsibility as well as love. It demands an ability to distinguish 'the enjoyed and the enjoyable, the desired and the desirable, the satis*fying* and the satis*factory*.'[14] Moral competence is a variable attribute of persons, institutions, and communities."[15] These variations have sources, some internal to the actor, many external, some taught, some absorbed, some imposed. Selznick's task is to uncover and unravel some of these sources.

Of course, competence is an old term of art in Selznick's thought, used to characterize qualities exhibited in different forms and degrees by institutions from the Communist Party to the Catholic Church, which commonly institutionalize specific and distinctive competences. "Moral competence" is an application of that term to the specific context of moral action. Some actors are more morally competent than others.

We learned already from *Leadership in Administration* that an institution's "specific competence" is not merely a matter of what it *does* on particular occasions but of what it *is*, a question of institutional character. Similarly, to be reliable, moral competence needs foundations in character, and it has effects on character, as well. In this respect, the "moral worth of an act or rule" is assessed

> by considering its consequences for character. This is a guide to making rules and to applying them as well. The question is: What kind of person, institution, or community will result from following a particular course of conduct or from adopting a given rule or policy? This focuses attention on the *internal relevance* of what we do.[16]

This was a theme of Selznick's work, of course, well before he started to think about law. It was central to his theories of organizational leadership.

We learned, too, from Selznick's early writings that central to the sustained competence and character of an institution is its *integrity*, so much so that a key task of administrative leadership is "the defense of institutional integrity—the persistence of an organization's distinctive values, competence, and role."[17] So, too, is the case with morality. The teachings are old:

> In an important sense, the perspective just outlined is very traditional. It makes the central problem of ethics the salvation of souls . . . Soul is the moral unity and competence of a person, institution, or community. It is that elusive, fragile, but nonetheless real and valued phenomenon we call integrity. To be in peril of one's soul is to place integrity at risk; to save one's soul is to establish or mend one's moral character.[18]

The continuities between Selznick's organizational theory and his moral theory are patent, and they go deep. From the beginning, he had been convinced that the actors he studied, primarily bureaucratic and legal institutions, had a need to establish and sustain competence, character, and integrity. Otherwise, while they might survive, they were unlikely to do well or do good. Universities, for example, might grind out students and suck in funds, but if they manifest no understanding of the specific sorts of institutions they are, the nature of their institutional character, their specific competences and potential excellences, the values and goals that should animate them, what it might mean for them to flourish as institutions of that sort and not some quite different sort, they will not do well.

Nor will they, however pious their talk and their "mission statements," if their processes militate against achievement of those values and purposes. They might grow, they might even grow rich, but they will still fail to fulfill the ideals appropriate to them, as the TVA in part did fail. Competence, character, and integrity are key to acting well, whether one is a person or an institution; so Selznick had long believed. It is the argument of *The Moral Commonwealth* that particular kinds of character, competence, and integrity are also key to achieving moral well-being.

PERSONS

Among "moral actors," persons come first: They "have moral and ontological *primacy*. They are ultimate objects of moral concern, whereas institutions must be judged by the contributions they make to personal and social well-being. Institutions may be highly prized, but they are always more or less utilitarian, more or less expendable."[19] However, though "collectivities are ultimately instrumental," that "does not mean they have no moral worth or cannot be moral actors."[20] Moreover, the features of each *as* moral actors bear important similarities and connections, he believes. Each is subject, so Selznick argues as we saw him arguing before, to the same "moral logic, . . . because the concept of moral actor is more general than that of person. The logic of moral action governs all moral actors, collectivities and persons alike."[21] Their fates are closely intertwined as well; while the well-being of each kind of moral actor has internal sources, each also depends on contributions from the others. More generally, Selznick's "premise is that social contexts can be regenerative: appropriate environments bring forth and sustain 'the better angels of our nature.'"[22]

"Our Nature"

One common casualty of modern sophistication in general, and of the modern social sciences in particular, is confidence that there is anything sensible to say in general terms about "our nature," still less about its "better angels." The former, so it is often thought, is infinitely variable; the latter infinitely arguable. Modernity has been thought to underwrite both propositions; it certainly seems to have led to them, though in its first universalistic and optimistic flush it did not start with them. And sociologists, creatures as much as analysts of modernity, have been among the most prominent sources of skepticism. As one might expect from a partisan of "humanist science" and as was already evident in "Sociology and Natural Law," however, Selznick does not share that common skepticism about our ability either to speak sensibly of our nature or to explore what might be good or bad for it.

Of course, the value of any conception of human nature will depend on its plausibility in the light of evidence, but the aim is to produce normative theory, Selznick argues, not a photograph. Thus the concept of humanity:

> is both descriptive and normative: descriptive in that it is based on what we know of human capacities and inclinations; normative in that it stands for certain ideal states (or the striving for them) which are moral, spiritual, and aesthetic. When we speak of avoiding "dehumanization" or of exemplifying "the human spirit," we have in mind better ways of being human.[23]

Selznick seeks, as he argues Hobbes, Rousseau, Marx, Freud, Dewey, and many others did before him, "a conception of humanity that could be made the basis for social prescription, especially the design of institutions. . . . salient attributes, including *reliable* motives and *critical* vulnerabilities."[24] The point of the theory is "to discover what personal well-being consists of, what it depends on, and what undermines it. . . . We cannot do without a theory of what should be prized by human beings if they are to survive and flourish and if they are to attain moral well-being."[25] There are truths to be discerned here, both general and local. As he put it once, "The point is that human group life generates satisfactions and expectations. Some of these satisfactions and some of these expectations are generic—they are ingredients of a common humanity."[26]

These are controversial claims. For Selznick, however, they are fundamental. One source of controversy has been the highly particularistic findings of generations of social anthropologists, findings to which he paid considerable attention, especially in his thoughts about the significance of culture,[27] of community and of particularity in the making of moral well-being. However, the abiding message he took from the social anthropology he read first as an undergraduate was that underlying the many, great, and significant differences among societies and cultures, there was a "psychic unity of mankind . . . a phrase not known now but it was then. They had wanted people to appreciate particularity and also recognize that humanity was one."[28]

That doubled appreciation of the claims of universality and particularity is central to Selznick's own conception of human nature and indeed more generally to his thought as a whole. It is engaged in what he calls "the paradox of humanism." For humanism, driven precisely by its commitment to understand humanity in its complexity and variety, to make the human person its subject, is a particularizing tradition: It is on the side of particular empathic understanding over the search for general laws, historicism over universalism, concreteness before abstraction, "thick description" over the development of abstract laws, the *Geisteswissenschaften* over the *Naturwissenschaften*. Moreover, so too are its subjects.

For the vast majority of us, particularity is our lived and, in the most salient aspects, our preferred condition. It is because we are the sorts of creatures we are that particularity and locality matter in the ways they do. That human nature and predicaments are typically encountered in contexts larded with particularity is not a denial of common humanity but a feature of it, not a contradiction but an implication. So we can speak sensibly of human nature. But that implies that not everything that matters to us can be captured by that inclusive but undiscriminating idiom. So we should pay as much attention to what evades it as what it includes. This has both descriptive and normative elements.

Descriptively, the elementary truism of social theory is that humans are born, live, and die as *particular* persons, not abstract categories; found not in societies-in-general but in particular societies, that change and vary almost without end. That, after all, is one reason why sociology has so often led in antiuniversalist directions. And Selznick is a sociologist. He agrees with G. H. Mead, another pragmatist who greatly influenced him, that "'the self is essentially a social structure, and it arises in social experience' . . . In the beginning is society, not the individual."[29] Moreover, "Man works upon his environment, both the physical and the social, to fashion a setting to which he can relate, and which can be related to him, as a person. This . . . is the culture-creating act."[30] And, we needn't be told, cultures encode particular histories, myths, moral norms, and taboos, and they differ.

Nor are these particularizing cultural features of human existence accidental or unfortunate. Even as modernity has a tendency to erode them, humanist sociology quickly understands them to be fundamental and in principle beneficial:

> It is an elementary lesson of social science that the human animal, if it is to grow and flourish, needs a framework of social support that must include moral guidance, symbolic expression, and a secure way of life. Hence we may say that, in principle, culture is a good thing.[31]

And here again an apparent paradox: Not only do human beings in general depend on societies and cultures that are particular, but it is their very particularity that they commonly find valuable in them:

> human nature is not only *compatible* with diversity, it is a *spur* to difference and distinctiveness.[32]
>
> The idea of humanity necessarily speaks to what human beings have in common. But what they have in common *includes the particularity of cultural experience* . . .
>
> People live and thrive in concrete settings. Abstract regularities and abstract principles are only pale reflections of human ingenuity, only weak indicators of the texture of social life. It is in the concreteness of social participation, especially moral, aesthetic and religious experience, that much of what we call distinctively human emerges.[33]

Many moderns perhaps most, many postmodernists perhaps all, who have gone this far find it no distance to sign on to Ortega y Gasset's slogan, *"Man, in a word, has no nature; what he has is . . . history."*[34] Notwithstanding their political distance from him, it is difficult to see how Clifford Geertz or Richard Rorty could dissent from de Maistre's mordant observation that:

> In the course of my life, I have seen Frenchmen, Italians, Russians. . . . I know, too, thanks to Montesquieu, that one can be a Persian. But as for man, I declare that I have never met him in my life; if he exists, he is unknown to me.[35]

Yet Selznick doesn't agree. He sees in such claims, as he frequently does, a good point stretched too far. The trouble with cultural relativism "as is so often the case . . . comes from overreaching and not from egregious error."[36] The human being is not unknown to humanist social theory, and though none of us can see her outlines too distinctly or in close detail, it is crucial not to forget her.

There is biology, which "provides the materials to which society must fashion a response, and that response is not wholly free."[37] There is also psychology:

> The sociological perspective is a denial of *pre-formed* personality, but it is far from a denial of persistent human attributes. To say that humans are social animals is to characterize them in decisive ways. Above all, it is to say that they depend on others for psychological sustenance, including the very constitution of the self, and that this dependency is the source of typical strengths, failings, and strivings.[38]

Nor is it just biology and psychology. Selznick might differ over details from Martha Nussbaum's Aristotelean enterprise of discerning basic human capabilities, but I imagine he would find that enterprise congenial, important, and feasible. Like his own, Nussbaum's is a normative/empirical project that seeks the conditions of human survival and well-being. Like his, it is based on a "postulate of humanity," grounded not in metaphysics but in what we can know of human nature by examination, here and now and there and then, with our conclusions subject to refinement in the light of new evidence and further reflection, including normative reflection.[39] Selznick would not demur from Nussbaum's conviction that:

> the deepest examination of human history and human cognition *from within* still reveals a more or less determinate account of the human being, one that divides its essential from its accidental properties . . . Separating these two groups of properties requires an evaluative inquiry: for we must ask, which things are so important that we will not count a life as a human life without them?[40]

In terms familiar from earlier work, Selznick argues that a sociologically grounded moralist must start with

> the identification of reliable incentives and recurrent vulnerabilities. This leads readily to what we may call *baseline* morality—the idea that moral requirements should be closely tied to urgent problems . . . A baseline morality is often the most we can aspire to; and it is always a precondition for further development.
>
> Nevertheless, we need not be content with limited aspirations. Once a baseline morality is secure, we can respond to opportunities for extending responsibility and enriching fellowship. The conditions of *survival* are easier to meet than those of *flourishing*, which are more complex and more fragile. It does not follow, however, that we should fail to treasure what is precarious or cease to strive for what is nobly conceived.[41]

Beginning with baselines, one might start with certain basic vulnerabilities, drives, and needs that all humans share. Notwithstanding the condescension of anthropologists such as Geertz toward the "bloodless universals"[42] seized on by partisans of a common humanity, not all universals are bloodless. As Shakespeare reminds us through the words of his character Shylock, one universal is that we bleed, and that can be extended metaphorically, as he extended it,[43] quite far, if some of our most urgent and universally shared vulnerabilities are to be considered. We are weak reeds and, what's more, weak in many of the same ways, vulnerable to many of the same hurts.

There is more to say (and Shylock said some of that too). One is that, apart from physically injuring them, people and institutions can systematically *humiliate* persons, and that such denial of respect can be a terrible thing for human beings to experience. As many have observed, it is commonly facilitated by a denial of their humanity.[44]

Apart from vulnerabilities, there are capacities: for enjoyment, growth, fulfillment, self-realization, and so on, whose forms will differ widely, but which humans, not perhaps necessarily but nevertheless as a natural matter and commonly, share.

Apart from our nature, there are also our circumstances. One is the "requirements of group life."[45] Another is that possibilities are not endless. We are all constrained by what Goldenweiser calls the "principle of limited possibilities."[46] Alternatives are many, but there are reasons why not just *anything* can happen. And so, that there should be overlap among the normative repertoires of human societies, the "moral universals" of which the anthropologists Selznick read in his youth spoke, should not be a surprise.[47]

On Selznick's view as on Nussbaum's, then, if our natures include common vulnerabilities and capabilities, our predicaments are not all completely random, threats to us not always unique, our means and resources not infinite, we do well to think about how to protect against those vulnerabilities, deal effectively with recurrent predicaments and threats, as well as secure conditions for our capabilities, among them the "better angels of our nature," to flourish. Some general lessons emerge.

"Better Angels"

Of one thing we can be sure: Our better angels are unlikely to spread their wings without help. There are conditions of moral well-being, many of them found in the contexts in which we live: Desperate extremes of poverty, hardship, and oppression, for example, are rarely (though perhaps occasionally) good for us in any sense, material or moral, and we need not resort to such extremes to make the point. Moreover, there are conditions of well-being internal to actors themselves—though they in turn will be influenced by external circumstances. One central such condition is moral competence. We are not born morally competent, yet many of us become so, more or less, not overnight but over time. How? And why doesn't everyone?

Readers of Selznick's earlier works will not be surprised to encounter the notion of *development* here:

> In the study of human nature, as it bears on morality, a key idea is development. The argument is that individuals are disposed to change—and under

congenial conditions are likely to change—in directions that enhance moral outcomes. The challenge is to show that moral competence is an objective condition and not an instance of reading into "nature" our own preferences or fears.[48]

The starting point, here as elsewhere in Selznick's work, is Aristotle. Selznick seeks to make plausible to moderns the notion of a telos, as point and criterion of a well-lived life. The details of Aristotle's conception of *eudaimonia* are less important than the general notion that *"ideal states may have natural foundations"*[49] and its particular application that *"there are ends proper to man's nature."*[50] What such states might be is not a matter of blind assumption but of investigation, he believes; proper subjects for a humanist science.

Such beliefs are relatively, though not completely, uncontroversial of physical health. Selznick believes they are also true of psychic health and with that of moral health, too, because "psychological truth shades into moral truth as it attends to the integrity and well-being of the self. Psychological theories of responsible choice, healthy relatedness, self-reliance, and self-esteem, for example, broadly overlap the concerns and conclusions of moral inquiry."[51]

Of course, whoever proposes a telos for anything needs to bring thought to bear on the subject, but it is not only thought, and there *is* a subject:

> What makes it a *telos* is the fact that it builds on the strivings and capacities of ordinary people living ordinary lives; on the experienced difference between being foolish or wise, shortsighted or prudent, self-destructive or constructive in the management of one's life.[52]

A telos is not necessarily a particular outcome or end state; it may be a process or a way of being in the world. Progress toward it might involve conflict, indeed is likely to do so because conflict is, as we have seen, often a spur to progress. And, as always in his writings, Selznick stresses that no necessity is involved, no inexorable stages of progression. There is disposition, and there is direction, but both can be thwarted, derailed, rerouted, routed. Nevertheless, "the psychological *telos* is not mysterious or ineffable. Like biological health, it is a potential state of well-being wherein needs are reduced and satisfactions are enhanced, a state toward which impulses are directed and in light of which they are transformed."[53] And finally, expanding on a point he had stressed about responsive law in *Law and Society in Transition,* although *enhancement of competence and sensibility* is central to moral development, we need not suppose that this outcome, or any other developmental outcome, is necessarily the most stable, the best adapted, the most efficient, or the most likely to survive. On the contrary, the emergent condition may be quite precarious. . . . Complex ideals or states of well-being often depend on fragile networks of supporting circumstance.[54]

As he did in *Law, Society, and Industrial Justice*, and in part relying on similar sources of inspiration, among them Mead and Piaget, but also Freud, Kohlberg, and Gilligan, Selznick examines the logic of, and internal pressures toward, moral development. What are the internal sources that drive people, not merely to age, which there is no happy way to avoid, but to develop, in particular to become more morally competent? He is not interested in backing one or another particular postulated set of stages of development—Freud's, Piaget's, Kohlberg's, Gilligan's—nor any specific outcome. Rather, he is interested in discovering evidence of *dispositions* that, if successfully nurtured and established and not derailed, lead in the direction of moral competence.

As he interprets the famous differences between the accounts of moral development given by these thinkers, they are explorations of internal psychological dispositions to moral development. They are not, or if they are they should be criticized for, foisting "an external ethic" on their subjects. Rather they are debating the natural foundations of moral ideals:

A moral ideal or achievement has a natural foundation if it is *latent* in human experience and is *viable* in the light of that experience. A latent ideal builds on dispositions and strivings that arise in the course of growth and interaction. . . . An ideal is viable if it is more than an abstract possibility or potential. It is not necessarily likely to be actualized and certainly it is not inevitable. But it must be a live option, sustained and encouraged by dependable needs, wants, and energies; and it must hold promise of contributing to personal well-being.[55]

As this passage indicates and as in all his accounts of developmental dispositions, no victory can be promised. On the contrary,

Contingency and probability prevail. To be sure, we look to an "inner dynamic." A need, conflict, or other disposition sets problems for a system and presses it in directions that may strengthen one or more of its capacities . . . No inner dynamic is inexorable. Every impulse depends for fulfillment on congenial conditions. These are not always forthcoming, if only because countervailing conditions are always at work.[56]

And, again as always, it is not merely countervailing external conditions. Threats to moral competence come not merely, perhaps not even mainly, from without, though there are plenty of them out there; many of their sources are within. There are "malignant hearts" such as Eichmann's; there are "vulnerable wills," like those of the conformists observed in the Milgram experiments and the like. And there is evil. As we have seen, on Selznick's view, pragmatists had difficulty accommodating the presence of evil in the world. Especially, they and other American optimists found it particularly hard to come to terms with the fact that the worst evils are not always foisted on us from outside. Rather, in the perspective of the moral realism that Selznick commends:

> evil is a sickness of the soul. In its most serious forms it is a pathology brought on by forces at work *within* the human psyche and *within* groups and communities. The most important evils are those we generate ourselves, from ourselves, rather than those imposed upon us by external conditions. This is a lesson liberals and radicals have been slow to learn and loath to accept.[57]

With that in our nature and as our predicament, it is not surprising to learn that "in the design of human institutions Hobbes must be taken seriously. He showed what in human nature we must guard against."[58] Like Hobbes and Freud and Niebuhr, but unlike Dewey, Selznick demands acknowledgment of "the darker side of human life . . . the demonic and destructive aspects of personality and society."[59] Like Hobbes, he warns us to attend to our defenses, whatever our hopes might be.

These concerns, which underpin Selznick's lifelong insistence on balancing idealism and realism, are as manifest in the programmatic *Moral Commonwealth* of 1992, as they were in his earliest, allegedly "pessimistic" writings. The tone and balance change, but the argument remains. Though *The Moral Commonwealth* is anything but a pessimistic tract, Selznick is as conscious as any macho realist of the dirt and toughness of the world and the specific form this takes in the *modern* world. Thus, echoing the argument of his first wife, Gertrude Jaeger, in 1944,[60] the one criticism Selznick voices of Dewey and pragmatism has to do with their failure

> to meet the challenge of modernity, which requires a robust understanding of evil, especially evil encouraged by the sovereignty of will. . . . Human frailty and recalcitrance; the persistence of domination; genuinely tragic choices; the collusion of good and evil: these are theoretical orphans. They are by no means wholly overlooked, but they have no secure place in the pragmatist interpretation of moral experience. The need to modify pragmatism in this respect informs our discussion at a number of points in subsequent chapters.[61]

That need is reflected in the "moral realism" that Selznick insists must always balance any form of idealism. It presumes a tough-minded conception of evil. It is not enough to recognize that corruption and oppression are pervasive. Nor is it enough to think of specific evils as problems to be solved or as obstacles to be overcome. Rather, the perspective of moral realism treats some transgressions as dynamic and inescapable. They can be depended on to arise, in one form or another, despite our best efforts to put them down.[62]

Just at this point, however, where "realists" might be prepared to embrace him, Selznick characteristically complicates matters. In the only world we know, realism has a lot of material to work with, much of it far more evident than what might support our ideals. But to settle for realist ambitions is to sell our possibilities short, and wrongly so. We need to pursue ways that we can avoid evil without hamstringing our efforts to do good and, conversely, do good without threatening our defenses. We should avoid both locking ourselves in a world so tightly secure that not even dreams can get in and leaving things so loose that our dreams threaten to become nightmares. Or, in Selznick's own words:

> I have sought to make clear that moral *development* finds an inescapable, unwelcome, but challenging counterpoint in moral *regression*. Both belong to human nature, the one as a genuine possibility, the other as a limiting reality. Unless we take both into account, recognizing how they involve each other, we become easy victims of careless optimism or enervating pessimism.[63]

Given our internal sources of "frailty and recalcitrance" and our dispositions' dependence on congenial conditions for development, Selznick insists the lesson is clear, as, ever since he encountered Michels, he knew it was clear: There is *work to be done* for moral development to succeed.

In societies, the major systemic agency of this work is found in processes of socialization, which are essential to "the first stage of moral development . . . the formation of a self capable of making rational choices, exercising self-restraint, and participating in social life."[64] Socialization occurs in every society, though in ways, and with consequences, of enormous variety and ranges of success. There is nothing automatic or automatically successful about the process, however essential it may be. Rather, drawing in this regard on the realism of Freud and not the sunnier optimism of the pragmatists, Selznick believes that:

> social life is no tranquil haven of nurture and support. Social experience is *necessary* to psychic well-being but does not *guarantee* it. On the contrary, the minimally or perversely socialized person may be wounded and brutalized, spiritually impoverished, socially incompetent. These findings remind us that socialization is a precarious venture, and a healing art.[65]

And it is not all socialization. Persons are not simply malleable matter, waiting to be shaped. Their formation as persons is not automatic or instantaneous. Socialization can be morally ambiguous, its effectiveness dependent on all sorts of social, institutional, parental elements that might not be there or might not be in good order. It is also not all we need if we are to avoid becoming social puppets, for our *selves* have internal and relational sources of strength and weakness, too. It is, however, essential. Without it Tarzan might perhaps survive, but he would have difficulties as soon as he met Jane. He would have many other difficulties and probably cause some, as well. For he would be without many things on which successful and moral social interaction depend, central among them a well-formed social conscience. The development of conscience, its socially learned content, and its emotional underpinnings are, therefore, central subjects for a science of moral development.

A Moral Self

A moral person, then, is an achievement, both psychological and social. Such a person has attained a "responsible self" capable of being "genuinely other-regarding and, at the same time, genuinely self-preserving."[66] Persons are not, cannot be, self-constituting monads. Rather we are all "implicated selves,"[67] "whose obligations are neither wholly voluntary nor wholly imposed."[68] And to be an effective moral actor, the self must not only be implicated but also, in a complex sense of the term, "responsible." Like the responsive institutions of which he had written, an implicated self in good shape is not *submerged* in the interests of others but must be capable and available to act with responsibility for self and responsiveness to others at once and as well. And so, while self-regard is not to be reduced to base selfishness, it must be seen to include self-preservation as the basis for sustainable regard for others. Indeed there are crucial self-regarding virtues, the most important of which "help form a mature, well-tempered, and effective personality."[69]

As Hobbes recognized, in the first instance responsibility runs to oneself, and Hobbes's narrow conception of that responsibility therefore deserves due regard. Hobbes is our most perceptive "baseline" man, and, when all else is unwell, the baseline might be very base indeed. However, even at the level of responsibility to self, one must look beyond Hobbes:

> Beyond lies the prospect of a moral experience enriched by more sensitive ways of thinking, feeling, and relating. To the extent this is achieved, survival in the

narrow sense recedes as an operative goal; its meaning is enlarged to include more stringent criteria of moral well-being. Among these is a different understanding of what self-preservation entails.[70]

In that larger understanding, *integrity* is a central component of the moral actor. This is not reducible to consistency, for one can be consistent without integrity and some forms of inconsistency will not violate integrity. What is required is "honesty and coherence . . . *both wholeness and soundness*,"[71] manifested not by the abstract individuals of modern ideologies— "This abstraction is one of the more barren and dehumanizing legacies of modern rationalism"[72]—but by *persons*, with particular names, characters, histories, values, integrity, and significant relationships with significant others.

Personal integrity, however, is not easily come by. Early modernity was challenged by a "strong sense of self and a weakened culture."[73] Late modernity spawns a modified pathology, well captured by Erving Goffman: "the insubstantial self in an insubstantial world, a world that is, nevertheless, opaque and oppressive."[74] Strong moral actors, in the context of modernity, need to combine the openness and competence that modernity liberates, "thickened" and made "more determinate" by a combination of "integrity and personhood."[75] As Australians like to say, this is a big ask, and not one we are likely to answer with the same success in every age or circumstance, and certainly not on our own. We must connect.

Self and Society

Central among the kinds of attachment that affect the development of moral persons are those of *core* participation. These are found in healthy primary groups but not limited to them. Paradigm examples are families, friends, associates—including organizational and work associates—with whom one shares or develops many connections, not just one; interacts as a whole person not merely incumbent of a role; communicates openly and trustingly; accepts obligations that are not narrowly defined and restricted; shares "a sense of belonging together and sharing a common identity."[76] In his earliest work, Selznick had emphasized the significance of such attachments, and he had always considered such "core" "organic ties to persons, history, deeds, and nature"[77] key both as sources of moral character and reliable moral motivation and as foci of moral action itself. Thus secured, a person can soar to heights and over distances, some of them necessary for the more sublime moral achievements. However, moral achievement of any sort is at risk without organic, or quasi-organic, particular ties to people, milieux, sources of loyalty, that can satisfy our "need for a stabilizing center in human life."[78] That need is less easy to satisfy, Selznick believes, in the circumstances of modernity.

Societies differ. One way in which they do, potent in its consequences, is in the degree to which they have come in modern times to be "mass societies," a development that had long troubled him. Discussions of "mass society" had been current before and after the Second World War, partly to explain social vulnerability to mass mobilization, partly in a broader attempt to capture some of the distinctive pressures of modernity. Selznick was influenced by those discussions and influenced some of them.[79]

According to Selznick, "mass" is itself a qualitative phenomenon. A mass society is not merely or even necessarily a large one. Rather, a society becomes a "mass" to the extent that formerly potent sources of social cohesion, patterned differentiation, and cultural transmission have atrophied, been diluted and/or thinned, and replaced by agglomerations in which cultural attachments are weakened, social differentiations have melted, culture-bearing elites have lost authority, social participation is highly fragmented, individuals have lost the belief "that they are living in a world of valued modes of life, all ultimately integrated by a sense of kinship."[80]

Of the "mass" corrosions of society that concern Selznick, that of culture is crucial, for:

> Humanist and anthropologist alike must see in mass society the principle of anti-culture. Of the lessons of our age not least important is the truth that society can persist despite the attenuation of cultural meaning, the emptying out of symbols, the transformation of institutions into organizations. It is possible to see much that is benign in mass society and to prefer the present, with all its shortcomings, over a past that had its own great limitations. However we decide on that score, we must still confront the evidence that what anthropologists think of as a 'valued way of life' has a hard time surviving in the world described by theorists of mass society.[81]

Even in his darkest reflections, Selznick always treated "massification" as a matter of degree, a general tendency or trend, not an iron law. He never thought mass society had conquered all, and explicit references to it occur only from time to time. Nevertheless, he was long concerned about massifying tendencies and their impact on social relations and the psychic and moral competence of moral actors. When he returns to the issue in his later writings, he is concerned with finding ways to identify, restore, replenish, and generate, sometimes anew, sources of moral well-being.

Every society has core relationships, families, friends, long-term associates. However, modern mass societies proliferate another sort of "segmental" social interaction, as found in single-interest business transactions and much public interaction, at least in one-off encounters. In his early writings on mass society, Selznick tended to contrast core and segmental attachments more starkly than later. By *The Moral Commonwealth*, he took pains to emphasize that segmental participation serves many good purposes, some of them moral. It extends our reach and range of potential cooperation and fellow feeling, for example, opens us to connections and inspirations beyond our tribes, allows us to conceive of a common humanity, to which we belong and owe obligations and with which we share rights. These are all precious, recent, and often precarious achievements. However, societies where core participation is under strain and segmental participation is pervasive have a problem, and it is partly a moral problem. Mass society threatens the health and primacy of core participation and breaks many encounters with others into segmented, single-interest, instrumental ones. Though these can be important sources of liberation from the oppressive weight of kings and cousins,[82] the pervasiveness and corrosiveness of modern segmental participation can present a major problem from the moral point of view.

Though core participation might be a prima facie good, however, no particular example of it can be assumed, without more, to be good. It often can hem us in, at the expense of more far-reaching and universalistic moral responses. Indeed, many forms of core participation do just that. On the other hand, core participation in good shape gives us a strong and secure platform on which to stand, a strong sense of who we are and who else is with us. A source of moral strength, then, is not the *absence* of segmental connections but the building of them by persons with robust and healthy core attachments: "The sociological lesson is not that the clock must be turned back. It is, rather, that we must now more frequently acquire by sensitive design what once could be taken for granted."[83]

One centrally important vehicle of such design; a potential thickener, focus, anchor, and spreader of links among individuals; and a source of attachment and identity, is institutionalization.

INSTITUTIONS

The large organization, readers of Selznick need not be told, is a centrally important part of the modern social order and modern social life. Societies are not just made up of the individuals within them; modern societies least of all. Large special-purpose organizations, of the sort that he had spent much of his life studying, proliferate. And many of the most significant, as he had often shown, are not merely impersonal instruments of individual purposes. They are enmeshed with our ambitions, needs, vulnerabilities, loyalties, and relationships, as well as our goals, values, ideals, and capacities to achieve any of these.

What socialization is to persons, institutionalization is to organizations: "One lends shape to individuals; the other forms groups and practices."[84] Both are fundamental to forming a specific identity, character, competence, and connections. Michels went too far, we recall, in saying that "Who says organization, says oligarchy"; but Selznick is happy to parody him to make a point: *"Who says organization, says obligation."*[85]

To the extent that institutionalization is "thickened" by informal structures to which individuals and groups bring their "personalities, values, and interests . . . a unity of persons rather than technicians is formed. *New energies are generated*, which may or may not be constructive from the point of view of the organization."[86] To the extent that institutionalization occurs, it overlays and complicates any notion of an organization as a fixed, determining, closed, and formal structure. It pushes the organization toward openness to, and in many ways binds it to, interests, information, and influences both within and without the formal organizational chart.

For these reasons, Selznick argues, institutionalization is a kind of way station between individual and community. This is seen both *within*— "The culture is sustained by a sense of community, that is, in the context of organization, by person-centered sharing in a common enterprise"[87]— and in relation to the larger society—"the institutionalized organization is a locus of value and a center of power. The surrounding community has a stake in its existence and in the proper conduct of its affairs. . . . For an open system with permeable boundaries, no transaction with the environment is more important than negotiating its place in the moral order, that is, dealing with demands that it be responsible and responsive."[88]

In such transactions, an institution is sensibly understood as a "moral actor," not itself a person but also not reducible to the individual persons who comprise it; variably open to, affected by, and with consequences for, communities within and without. This is not a metaphysical claim, but a sociological one. It is not that there are institutional "beings" other than individual persons, making their self-chosen ways in the world. On the contrary:

> In principle, we must be able to *locate* the collective phenomenon in what indi-
> viduals want, do, and perceive. It does not follow, however, that the behavior
> of individuals is self-defined or that organizational characteristics are noth-
> ing more than the characteristics of individuals. If social cohesion exists, there
> must be an objective correlate in individual feelings perceptions and conduct,
> but that does not change the collective nature of the phenomenon.[89]

Many moral consequences and dangers, of sorts with which Selznick had
long made us familiar, flow from the inescapable presence of organization
and organizations in modern societies. There is the "Michels effect," so
important to Selznick's own intellectual development and so "troublesome
to Marxists and to others who have hoped that humanist and democratic
ideals might be fulfilled without taking personal and institutional recalcitrance into account."[90] There are the ways in which within an institution,
individual "motives are structurally induced or frustrated,"[91] and in which
"organizations of many kinds are notoriously prone to turn moral persons
into immoral agents."[92] There are institutional racism and sexism, which:

> are products of history and culture, that is, of largely unconscious disposi-
> tions and preferences . . . [and] sustained by practical routines and vested inter-
> ests. . . . Because the practices and the discriminatory outcomes are systemic, a
> sociological diagnosis is needed—which is not a quest for something ineffable
> or disembodied. Institutional racism must be located in what individuals do
> and how they react. But to identify institutional bias does not require that we
> prove willful or purposive misconduct.[93]

There is goal displacement, "a product of . . . the tyranny of means,"[94] so
common in bureaucracies. And there are organizational incentives to both
opportunism and utopianism, the link between which is one of "the iro-
nies of moral sociology" and again would be familiar to readers of *Enquiry*
or *Leadership in Administration*:

> Wherever purpose is overgeneralized, endemic opportunism is likely to ap-
> pear. . . . When purposes are abstract, yet decisions must be made, more realis-
> tic but *uncontrolled* criteria will govern. Thus do the polarities of opportunism
> and utopianism meet and embrace.[95]

Yet while there are many perils associated with modern organizations, not
all is perilous. Bureaucracy is easily criticized, and Selznick had criticized it
in his time. Nevertheless, and typically in his writings, there is a balancing
story to be told. Thus:

> The pathologies of bureaucracy are, to a large extent, unwanted byproducts
> of its distinctive virtues. Upholding rules and protecting a special mission

or competence are virtues that encourage the characteristic drawbacks of bureaucracy: rules, policies, and precedents become sacrosanct; authority is husbanded, rather than risked and shared; official lines of communication are too easily defended; co-operation is sacrificed to organizational rivalry; routine is rewarded, initiative discouraged. Most important is a disposition to protect "the system," which thus comes to matter more than individual persons or even the organization's purposes or goals. A weakened sense of purpose helps produce complacent bureaucrats and unresponsive government.[96]

Such pathologies are among many reasons that Selznick favors "post-bureaucratic" tendencies to increase openness, flexibility, and responsiveness of bureaucracies in ways that parallel his advocacy of responsive law. However, a "postbureaucratic" order is not one that has left bureaucracy behind but rather one that seeks to ameliorate the excesses of bureaucratic tendencies and zeal—for bureaucratic virtues are real. The presidency of Richard Nixon was a negative reminder of the bureaucratic virtues of principles and process that are slighted when subverted in an onslaught "driven by political expediency and sustained by unprincipled loyalty."[97] More recent negative examples from the War on Terror are similarly instructive. Again, in many ways, "the bureaucratic principle limits efficiency and effectiveness. From the standpoint of purposive rationality the separation of powers is a burden and stumbling block. That was intentional"[98] as part of an institutional architecture designed not simply to maximize efficiency and effectiveness, but to restrain the capacity of power holders to abuse their power.

Here, as everywhere in Selznick, complexity is demanded of discussions that have often done without it. Thus, critics of domination in modern societies often seek to unmask the often subtle and complex connections between modern organizations and domination, a theme central to the writings of Michel Foucault, Jürgen Habermas, and others. Characteristically, Selznick gives due regard to the power of Foucault's writings and the "more responsible, if less arresting"[99] insights of Habermas. He shares with both of them concerns about "the human costs of technology, including, above all, technologies of social control."[100] While he has little critical (or, for that matter, enthusiastic) to say about Habermas, he is characteristically impatient with Foucault's "refusal to recognize *empirical variation* in the pervasiveness of domination. If all is subjugation, and if society is inherently coercive, it becomes impossible to make sense of relative freedom, authenticity, and individuality,"[101] the role of law in protecting citizens—which Habermas has increasingly recognized and emphasized—is neglected or derided, and Foucault is left unable to distinguish between "discipline that gives coherence to life and sustains autonomous projects from techniques of control that regiment, denude, and degrade."[102]

In this muddying of moral and categorical distinctions between *kinds and degrees* of domination, Foucault is not alone. It is, I suspect, part of the frisson generated by his dramatic writings and part, too, as Selznick claims, of the "ideological style" that Foucault shares with Marx and many other homogenizing critics of domination. While rightly protesting against any system "that reduces persons to abstractions or that denies the human need for respect, communication, and concern"[103] and illuminating oppression often disguised in palatable garb, exponents of this style tend to blur crucial differences among kinds of states of affairs. They may also, in focusing their attention on the interestingly insidious, weaken our apprehension of the merely gross and obvious:

> In our preoccupation with subtle forms of oppression and with high aspirations for fairness and well-being, we may forget that resistance to domination must begin with the obvious and the unsubtle. Arbitrary power is all too often blunt and crude; the pain it inflicts is readily apparent; there is no need for a guide to suffering, no need for consciousness-raising. Rather, we require elementary constraints on the abuse of power. When these are discounted—as "mere structures" or as "liberal legalism"—people are left unprotected where protection is most urgent. This posture often signals a failure to appreciate the gains other generations have won and that are now taken for granted. We may lose sight of the need to build on these foundations as we reach for more sensitive and demanding standards.[104]

Much of the rest of the book seeks ways of preserving and recognizing such precious foundations, without barring ascent to higher ambitions— for these are not the only tensions institutions face, nor are they independent of each other. They underlie and overlap with many others that will be familiar to readers of Selznick's earlier work.

One overarching tension was already explored in *Law, Society, and Industrial Justice*, between the imperatives and proper claims of management and those of governance. The former are crucial, of course, in any enterprise. Organizations have to achieve specific purposes, and managers seek to enable them to do so at less cost and with greater efficiency, effectiveness, and so on. But purely managerial concerns may be met with only instrumental concern for the welfare of the persons who work in the organization. Indeed, they might seem to, and might actually, conflict with such concerns. Governance, however, must address them. Principles and institutions of governance build these matters into the life of an institution, and so these considerations recur in Selznick's reflections on institutional morality.

Not everything that serves organizational purposes is morally valuable or indeed justifiable. Some managerial inclinations and temptations need to be tempered by moral considerations. And one source of moral constraints on what an organization might otherwise choose to do is the interests of its members. It is in their interests, for example, that there should exist institutionalized restraints on the capacity for repressive exercise of authority within an organization, and "the most important way repressive authority can be countered . . . is the appeal to principles of governance and the rule of law."[105]

This, of course, was the central argument of *Law, Society, and Industrial Justice*, and many themes of that work are developed here and integrated into Selznick's newly articulated "communitarian" commitments. An organization rightly committed to achieving particular purposes can and should also be charged with concern for communities within and without. The question arises, "How far the special-purpose organization, if it is to be a moral institution, must take the community as a model, and do so without undermining the organization's distinctive responsibilities."[106]

As Wolin might have predicted, Selznick argues that these intimations of community flow together with and from institutionalization. This is both because communal consciousness, and hence communal demands, are more likely to be generated in highly institutionalized organizations, and it is proper that such considerations should temper purely managerial ones in determining what happens there:

> The life of the organization generates groups of various kinds . . . constituencies. Negotiation and compromise, interest-balancing and dispute resolution are activities intrinsic to the institution . . . The members are not only members but persons as well; they have strong connections to families and other groups; they are embedded in the community as a whole. All these factors give a political cast to the operations of even a moderately complex special-purpose institution.[107]

Some organizations demand little of their members, and the reverse is also true. And so is the extent to which considerations of governance, that is ones that have "*the care* of a community or quasi-community"[108] at their core, will vary with the character of the organization. What matters is whether "the very purpose of the institution demands that management be tempered by governance."[109] Some institutions, such as schools, for example, whether they are formally private or public, need to marry effective management together with recognition of "the importance of schools for students as persons."[110] What one must bring to bear is not some formal, categorical bright line that divides public from private organizations but rather a "robust theory of the institution—of its mission, character, and distinctive methods."[111] Such a theory will also affect ways in which and the extent to which it is appropriate to empower members by forms of institutional participation, the central criterion of evaluation being "the creation of viable communities so far as may be possible within the framework of purposive institutions."[112] Where the interests of persons are centrally affected, "the claims of purpose and efficiency are strong, but they cannot justify practices that reduce human beings to 'means only.' Such practices make them victims of domination."[113]

The moral claims on institutions do not stop with their members, however. There is the character of what the institutions do, and there are the relationships they have with, and their effects on, the larger community of which they are parts. Each of these raises moral issues; each has been considered by Selznick in other contexts and with other immediate concerns in his earlier writings. As to character, the moral questions are, like those questions befitting leaders in *Leadership in Administration*, not merely technical, having to do with the relationship of means chosen to given ends, but rather equally about the institution's ends themselves. Leaders, it will be recalled, make strategic decisions; they are statesmen, concerned not just with means and the interrelationships between ends and means. Moral reasoning addresses the same span of concerns:

> Moral reason . . . makes goals problematic and broadens responsibility. It asks: Are the postulated ends worth pursuing, in the light of the means they seem to require? Are the institution's values, as presently formulated, worthy of realization? What costs are imposed on *other* ends and *other* values?[114]

To answer those classic pragmatist questions one must ask not merely what business we are in but also what business we should be in, what is in accord with our specific competence, what suits our institutional character, and what is required to act with integrity there.

"Integrity" was a concept already evident in Selznick's early works. It is, as we have seen, the central organizing virtue of individuals in this one. For both individuals and institutions, it is neither simply nor always the same as consistency. Rather: "The chief virtue of integrity is fidelity to self-defining principles. To strive for integrity is to ask: What is our direction? What are our unifying principles? And how do these square with the demands of morality?"[115] To answer these questions in the institutional context, we need to ask about the particular institution itself and what is required to further its core principles; to ask, in other words, what is required to display "fidelity to standards that define and uphold a special competence."[116] The competence in question will differ from institution to institution, and within even one institution there will be variation with time and circumstance. To delve into the "internal morality" of a particular institution is to probe central aspects of its character. To grasp the "spirit" of a practice, rather than rudimentary rules of satisfactory performance, requires an appreciation, of course often implicit and unstated, "of the whole matrix of values, purposes, and sensibilities that should inform a course of conduct."[117] A person or institution manifesting such an understanding, and acting in faith with it, manifests integrity. Where internal morality is strong, external regulation can be effected with a light hand; where it is not, intervention is more likely to be required.

Pursuit of integrity in and by institutions faces familiar tensions between autonomy and responsiveness. The first "safeguards values and competencies by entrusting them to their most committed agents and by insulating them from alien pressures and temptations"; the second "widens support for the institution and provides opportunities for growth and adaptation."[118] Each response has strong claims; each has characteristic ways of degenerating: legality to legalism, for example; responsiveness to opportunism, or to what Selznick had begun by calling co-optation and now revisits as one of the "perils of responsiveness."

Autonomy is especially important for the nurture, sustenance, and protection of institutional values where they are precarious and so, especially in formative stages: "Once the system or policy is secure, that need becomes less compelling. Then more precision is required as to *what kind of* autonomy and *how much* is required or desirable."[119] Selznick had developed these points already in the context of administrative leadership;[120] and he extended them to the possibilities of responsive law in *Law and Society in Transition*. He argues here that they are general institutional truths, parts of a larger truth, that had occupied him in *Law, Society, and Industrial Justice*, that requires practical concretization and implementation, and that has practical consequences:

> if moral competence is to be meaningful, it must be built into the social structure of the enterprise. Thus understood, the corporate conscience is not elusive or indescribable, nor is it mainly a psychological phenomenon. A corporate conscience consists of specific arrangements for making accountability an integral part of corporate decision-making.[121]

Perhaps in the 1990s this might all have sounded rather pious and "wet," to use Margaret Thatcher's evocative put-down of those who suggested that moral and social constraints on corporate behavior might be appropriate, even necessary. It sounds somewhat less moist as I write in the wake of the unprecedented financial and economic meltdown of 2008–2009—not only drier, but also more descriptively acute, as it meshes with an impressive body of empirical scholarship on the multiple interactions between state-and-corporation-engendered regulation and "meta-regulation" characteristic of the modern capitalist economy and world.[122]

Selznick's insistence on viewing the corporation "as a social institution" is not a rejection of capitalism. On the contrary, the corporation is "primarily an engine of capitalist economic activity," and as he adds characteristically in a footnote, "At issue is a *kind* of capitalism, not capitalism itself."[123] But for him, "The question is what perspective, what vision, is brought to bear on that activity." A neoliberal vision of directors' duties as running only to owners, that is these days shareholders, "obscures the realities of power, authority, and subordination. It dims the legal perception of how corporate, collective property is organized and what human values are at stake."[124] And when its corollary guilt-free focus on profit *maximization*, "without regard to source, becomes the operative goal" this both flies in the face of Selznick's general observation that maximization is generally inappropriate in a context where there are multiple values and goals in play, and, more specifically,

> detaches profit-making (or activities, such as buying and selling corporations) from substantive decisions. The provision of particular goods and services takes a back seat to financial manipulation. When this occurs, the mission of the enterprise is likely to be disoriented and subverted. Quality suffers, including the quality of transactions in banks and other financial institutions.[125]

COMMUNITY

The distaste for atomistic conceptions of social reality and moral obligation that underlies that last passage runs deep in this book. It is thus no exaggeration and not much of a compliment to be told, at the beginning of the book's final part, that "at many points in the preceding discussion an attentive reader will have readily discerned intimations of community. A communitarian perspective is, indeed, an irrepressible subtext of the argument thus far."[126] The sympathies implicit in Selznick's discussion of modernity, individuals, and institutions at many points become explicit when he comes to discuss community.

Though well over a century older, the term *communitarian* came into vogue in the years Selznick was writing *The Moral Commonwealth*, initially to describe a philosophical reaction to Rawls's *Theory of Justice*, which was published in 1971 and set the agenda for Anglo-American political philosophy for the next several decades. That great liberal work was alleged by its communitarian critics to depend on excessively atomistic, individualistic assumptions derived from classical liberalism.[127] From there, communitarian critiques of liberalism multiplied in the 1980s, some attacking what was alleged to be its inadequate account of the self, some accusing it of slighting the importance of traditional and communal attachments, the centrality of connection to a well-lived life, indeed to social life itself. Some communitarian critics accused liberalism of generating dysfunctional social, moral, and political consequences; others thought it reflected dysfunctional social developments; still others thought both processes were at work.[128]

It is not hard to see why communitarianism might have seemed so congenial to Selznick. The term might have been new to him in the 1980s, but one might say, indeed Sheldon Wolin *had* said, that he had been speaking communitarian prose for most of his life. He was communitarian avant la lettre.[129] Partly the affinity simply stemmed from the fact that he was a sociologist. After all, even when performed by philosophers, the communitarian critique of liberalism is a fundamentally *sociological* one, which seeks to ground moral and political philosophy in what are allegedly social necessities that liberals either erode or ignore. In conversation with Cotterrell, Selznick is enlightening about this. Charles Taylor's influential critique of atomism, Selznick reminds us, was "part of basic sociology for a couple of generations. The whole idea of a social self, the idea of human interdependence. The whole idea of a social self, the idea of human interdependence. Many of the themes that were associated with the development of communitarian ideas were, it seemed to me, wholly consistent with sociological reasoning. So that's really how it began." Of his own work, he recalled that from the start:

> When I look back on it, it seems to me I had been working on it [community] for a long time. I didn't give it, as a concept, very much thought. It was just some implicit ideas that I had, but I had never really addressed it that directly. . . . [However] on a sub-surface level, it was a very important idea for me because even back in the TVA study, when you talk about organizations

and their environments, that's another way of talking about organizations and the surrounding community.

I was quite interested in the impact of the TVA on local communities. I think that later on . . . without really realizing it, I think I had in my mind this transition that I later talked about, organization to institution to community, that in the formation of institutions, one of the major options available to people is the formation of community, and institutions are often made stronger if they have the sources of cohesion that we associate with community. . . .

When I was writing about institutionalization in organizations, I was kind of fascinated by this idea of transforming organizations into institutions, but latently, I think there was this idea of community, because you're creating a common culture, you're creating the nexus of interdependence among departments, you're using leadership to try to create shared understandings and common bonds and so on.

And also the idea of community is implicit also when you begin to enlarge the idea of institution. And so in *Industrial Justice* I was really talking about that, because I was saying, in effect, the enterprise has to be understood as including, as many people have said in recent years, a variety of stakeholders, and especially bringing in the employees, recognizing the employees as members. And so there was, again, some tacit understanding of community. . . .

Even this goes back to [Chester] Barnard, because Barnard wrote about—it interested me that some of his passages have always remained with me—about the problem of who was a member and what does it mean to be part of an enterprise. What about your customers? Aren't they part of your enterprise? . . . Things like that. So he was implicitly talking about the ways communities are formed.[130]

Moreover, many communitarian concerns have to do with the *quality* of common life and culture, concerns that pervade Selznick's lifework. Thus, on the one hand, there was his anxiety over the pathologies of mass society, an anxiety of long standing. On the other, there was his theorization of the significance of social attachments, even when unplanned and in unexpected places, of institutionalization, of integration, of the significance of core participation. These were all richly developed and well-formed concepts in his mind, not just words that flowed from his pen. And there are his convictions about the importance in social life of historicity, identity, mutuality, plurality, autonomy, participation, and integration, which, as it happens, are precisely the characteristics that, in *The Moral Commonwealth*, he takes to characterize community.[131] Communitarian themes then had been stirring in his thought for a very long time. They were named, and their implications for his liberal commitments thought through, from the 1980s onward.

Selznick recommends treating the concept of community as he treats most sociological concepts: with attention to variation and with an eye to conditions of both existence and flourishing. On the first point, though he draws on those staple ideal types that seek to capture the distinctiveness of modernity—*Gemeinschaft* versus *Gesellschaft*, status versus contract, mechanical versus organic solidarity—he adopts none of them in their dramatic dichotomizing forms. Rather, community is a variable, a matter of more or less. A group is a community "to the extent that it encompasses a broad range of activities and interests, and to the extent that participation implicates whole persons rather than segmental interests and activities."[132] Social relations are everywhere; communal ones are a particular species. They can be found in different degrees and in many different locales, but they are far from universal. They occur insofar as there exist *"the opportunity for, and the impulse toward, comprehensive interaction, commitment, and responsibility."*[133] Such opportunities flourish given congenial conditions and wilt when circumstances are unfavorable. It is part of Selznick's enterprise to explore some of the sources of, and the differences between, flourishing and wilting.

And just as a group can be more or less of a community, so too it can be a better or worse sort of community. The definition of community, like all Selznick's definitions, is intended to be capacious; the *theory*, on the other hand, is more demanding, and one of its demands is that:

> We should be able to distinguish the better from the worse, not only according to some neutral criterion, such as "degree of social cohesion," but in the light of the best understanding of what makes for moral well-being. At the same time, we should pay close attention to the relevant descriptive sociology, that is, of the actual experience of living in communities. If it is to be effective as a guide to criticism and reconstruction, a normative model must build on that experience.[134]

Modernity, with its massifying, relativizing, culture-attenuating tendencies, in many ways unleashes forces that threaten to erode both the degree and the quality of community in modern social life. There are reasons for this, among them good reasons, and that is not all that modernity brings. Good or bad, as we have seen, we can't wish modernity away or, for that matter, whistle community back. And there are many forms of community we should resolutely resist coming back.

Without any way back, and with no clean slate going forward, we need to think both about what sorts of community are available to us, what sorts are good for us, and how elements of them might be (re)generated or their virtues (re)captured. That need is itself a product of modernity, which puts many communal bonds under strain.

In a community in good shape, participants are members, and that matters to them, but they aren't mere parts. They have their own lives, tastes, preferences, associates, intimates. That should be true of the sub-unities of any larger communal unity, and it is true within those subunities as well. As Selznick had argued of organizations in *Law, Society, and Industrial Justice*, so here: Within communities, and all the way down, it is necessary "to protect freedom *in* associations as well as freedom *of* association":[135]

> A common life is not a *fused* life: in a fused life there would be no need for regulation or governance, no need to take account of individual differences, no need for adjustment, reciprocity, or cooperation. The tacit assumption here is that people and groups participate in any community, large or small, as individuated and self-regarding entities. They are independent as well as interdependent.[136]

Selznick's community, favored at the same time for sociological and moral reasons, is a "federative" one, a "unity of unities," which respects its members' liberal rights, immunities, and in general chosen *variety*, as it also connects them; "what we prize in community is not unity of any sort at any price, but unity that preserves the integrity of the parts."[137] As he already implied in 1951, though he was not then using the word, a community that is socially functional and morally desirable preserves "intricately related, institutionally bound groupings which form a healthy social organism."[138]

Such a community nurtures, supports, and affects the development of its members. It is not primarily a psychic thing, a matter of feelings, a sensed connectedness, of which many have spoken. Though participation in a community generates characteristic kinds of feelings:

> Something more is wanted than a "sense" of community. Communities are sustained by the realities of everyday life, including interdependence, reciprocity, and self-interest. If people do not need each other, if little is to be gained from participation and commitment, communities are not likely to emerge or endure.[139]

All this takes work. And it takes *institutional* settings and vehicles. Communities are structured, and these structures can be complex, particularly if the goal is a federated "unity of unities," central to the health, resilience, and flourishing of successful communities is the strength of institutions within them. These can focus the energies and command the loyalties of their members and act at the same time as unities within larger unities and as links between each other and a more encompassing whole. Both for their power to connect their members internally and to their environments, and as a shield and source of variation and distinctiveness, institutions are key. They are:

> the chief agencies and most reliable safeguards of community. Institutions embody values and enhance integration, but they do so in ways that resist homogeneity and sustain differentiation. Strong communities are *institution-centered.* . . .
>
> This perspective has special relevance for the place of community in modern mass society. We cannot be optimistic that community will flourish under conditions of high mobility and fragmented experience, where mutual commitments are weak, spans of attention are short, and gratifications are undeferred. These conditions undermine institutions. Their effects, however, can be resisted and contained. Even under conditions of mass society many institutions retain, and others develop, significant resources of continuity and strength. That is so because what they do has great practical worth, and because they become vested interests capable of generating loyalty and support. The contemplation of mass *populations* may drive us to despair. We may take some comfort from the relatively greater resilience of institutions.[140]

As always, Selznick emphasizes the variety of qualitatively different states of affairs, within any particular community and among them. Like many of the other normative systems that he has considered, among them culture, law, friendship, family, community is a "prima facie good thing." It warrants "a presumption of moral worth."[141] But a presumption is not an assumption. No particular instance of a prima facie good can itself be assumed to be good, and:

> The presumption is rebuttable on a showing that a given community is too narrow or attenuated to provide an effective framework for common life, or that it is too rigid and stultifying to serve the needs of personal and institutional development or too insular or self-destructive in its dealings with other communities, or that it is otherwise inadequate from the standpoint of critical morality. The same logic applies to our appreciation of family, friendship, law, and culture.[142]

Some communities are stultifying, pernicious, illiberal, a danger to their members and whoever has to deal with them, as are some families, friendships, laws, and cultures. Nevertheless, certain kinds of each of these are crucial to a well-ordered society. The question is: What kinds? More particularly, because we are speaking of modernity, what kind is appropriate to its distinctive and demanding conditions? Much of *The Moral Commonwealth* is devoted to making the case for *liberal* community. We now turn to that case.

CHAPTER ELEVEN

Communitarian Liberalism

What moral and political standards are appropriate to action and judgment in modern societies? For most of his adult life, Selznick's answers were drawn from the liberal tradition, though after his first revolutionary years he had an openness to conservatism that was not shared by all liberals; in the early 1960s an openness to the student movement that was not shared by many conservatives, including close friends; and for the whole of his life an ecumenical openness to intellectual nourishment broader than is usual in the modern academy. Writing *The Moral Commonwealth*, he came, without denying his fundamental liberal commitments, to supplement and qualify them with communitarian elements, explicitly and in an increasingly sustained way. He emerged a "communitarian liberal," one for whom the noun is still primary but the adjective a fundamentally important qualifier.[1]

Modern communitarianism, Selznick insists, must absorb the achievements of modernity and the values of liberalism, the latter a product and particular interpretation, in political practice and theory, of the former. It must because there is no realistic alternative to the former, and there is no morally acceptable alternative to the latter. Once he had shed his youthful revolutionary ideals, this was the position he always adhered to. However, as always, he believed in the importance of differences between kinds, species, qualitative states of affairs; the species of liberalism most apt for modern times, he came to believe, is communitarian. This move was true to his general perspectives and particular insights. However, it is also the case, as he says in *The Moral Commonwealth*, that "the multi-valued perspective outlined above demands a high tolerance for ambiguity. This has not been easy to come by."[2] Both sentences are true.

LIBERALISM OLD AND NEW

According to Selznick, two fundamental commitments distinguish liberal doctrine from others:

> (1) it seeks to free individuals, institutions, and practices from the restraints of custom, dogma, vested interest, and centralized authority; and (2) it holds that liberation must take place within a framework of orderly process, constitutional principle, and respect for social continuity.[3]

Selznick recognizes that there are many different forms and emphases within the liberal tradition, and in particular he notes the way that in America laissez-faire liberalism has become associated with conservatives, while the term *liberal*, drawing on late-nineteenth-century English tendencies (and, a foreigner might add, the absence of a politically competitive social democratic movement, that in much of the rest of the world fills this space) has come to denote "welfare liberalism." New and old are connected by a commitment to autonomy and rationality. The difference lies in how those concepts are interpreted. Early liberals sought to free individual actors from much, particularly state, action that might impinge on individuals' ability freely and rationally to determine their *own* course. Welfare liberals "have sought a richer meaning of autonomy and rationality." To them,

> mere freedom from restraint is not an acceptable criterion of liberation. In itself such freedom may deny to most people the social support they need for genuine autonomy when they face psychological or economic dependency, and it may leave them without effective protection from the powerful and the greedy. Similarly, genuine rationality cannot be realized if it is limited to individual action for individuated goals; rational cooperation for collective goals is necessary if the underlying value, reasoned pursuit of human well-being, is to be achieved. And justice is illusory if it overlooks social conditions, such as inequality, or the interplay of private and public power, that distort legal outcomes.[4]

Selznick has many sympathies with both old and new liberals, particularly the latter. But he believes that even they, though clearly moving in a communitarian direction, do not go far enough. That leaves them with a "troubled ethos,"[5] in a sort of intellectual halfway house: unsatisfied with unadulterated individualism, uncertain about the claims of community, unable to think their position through to the end or act on it to satisfying effect.

FALSE DICHOTOMIES

In one sense, it must be stressed, the opposition between liberalism and communitarianism is artificial, at least as these ideas have been developed by their recent Western partisans. None of the philosophical communitarians with whom Selznick made common cause advocates some *völkisch* unity of the nation, the pure, the chosen, the saved. None is interested to reject central liberal values, such as freedom of expression or association; just as few liberals are likely to deny the potential value, for an adequately nurtured and satisfying life, of families and other core social connections.

And yet not everything that can logically be accommodated within an intellectual tradition finds a comfortable home there. Over time, a kind of grain of acceptable ways of thought comes to be etched into such traditions, full of familiar emphases, leanings, commonplaces, prejudices. Participants commonly find it easier to go with the grain than against it. This can lead to ready acceptance of what slides most smoothly, rejection or neglect of what catches. Congenial lines of argument are pushed too far. Complicating considerations are often not recognized, when recognized little theorized, and when theorized often rejected, even when there might be space within the tradition—it might even be good for the tradition—to recognize, theorize, and accept them.

It is Selznick's constant ambition to accommodate such complexities— in general and in this case—and this both for temperamental reasons and as a product of intellectual conviction. After all, sharing Dewey's suspicion of "pernicious dualisms" and Morris Cohen's "principle of polarity," Selznick's preference is always to explore continuities, to expect and accept blurred boundaries rather than to police borders. Not every tension is a contradiction: Values that are in tension, even the very tension itself, can all be fruitful. There are many dilemmas where you want to hold on to both horns.[6] He finds good where many people see only bad—piety, say, or modernity; bad where others see only good—piety or modernity again. To paraphrase Yogi Berra: When Selznick sees a fork in the road, his tendency is to take it or at least to consider whether and how it might be taken. Even if, as I argued in Chapter Nine, this tendency can be overdone, its uncommonness is refreshing. And often it is fruitful.

And so we come to communitarian-liberalism. As we saw in the last chapter, Selznick does not vaunt collectivities as ultimate moral subjects but, on the contrary, insists that they must always be appraised in terms of their effects on individuals. He doesn't scoff at rights and liberties, indeed values them highly. He doesn't denigrate liberal institutional protections, separations, checks, balances, but emphasizes their importance. He is committed to the role of reason in public affairs. He puts a premium on tolerance, as a public virtue and a private one as well. The list of liberal values to which he subscribes is long.

Communitarian liberalism, then, is to be achieved without sacrifice of core liberal values, indeed would be incomplete and pernicious without them. The aim is "to amend liberalism, not to reject it . . . Nevertheless, the communitarian amendments are not minor, and they claim coherence."[7] In Selznick's view, liberals tend to underrate the conditions, particularly sociological conditions, on which the reliable attainment of liberal values depends. Many single-mindedly, sometimes simple-mindedly, overrate the sufficiency of those values for a good life, or even a good polity. They fail to recognize the extent to which communitarian values serve to enrich, rather than subvert, liberal elements of a well-ordered polity; indeed, they do so even when in tension with liberal tendencies, not merely when they accord with them. And liberals often lack imagination of the ways in which and the extent to which a narrowly individualistic liberalism can threaten social goods and of the ways these threats can arise, often from too much of a good thing rather than from obviously bad things.

A communitarian liberal view, by contrast, must supplement "liberal myopia"[8] with a more ample appreciation of the communitarian *supports* necessary to sustain liberal values in good shape; communitarian *supplements* without which liberal values are not enough; and the ways in which the goods of community can be *endangered* by hyperliberal excess—not because it is liberal but because it is hyper: "The main target of communitarian criticism is intellectual and practical excess. Good ideas are put forward without proper regard for limiting conditions, competing principles, and informing contexts."[9] Some of this excess can be traced back to the logic of liberal philosophy. More often, Selznick believes, it is a temptation generated by the liberal ethos[10] that comes to surround the tradition and forms what I have called its grain.

This is the case because the typical liberal social imaginary treats lightly the importance of core attachments, of particularity, of social rootedness, and of many other sources of guidance and well-being to which communitarians draw attention. Liberals often have an inadequate understanding of, maybe they just push to the side and ignore, some of the elementary conditions of social living, still more of flourishing, even understanding. Without due acknowledgment of these, however, liberal philosophy is likely to be impoverished, and the liberal polity is likely to suffer as well. Partly these inadequacies stem from an inadequate sociology, already apparent in the most common of liberal presuppositions, among them those about the preeminence of reason and individual choice in a moral life.

JUDGMENTS AND PREJUDGMENTS

In his short essay "What Is Enlightenment?" Kant answered thus: "man's release from his self-incurred tutelage," which in turn was his "inability to make use of his understanding without direction from another." The release, put simply, consisted in thinking for yourself. That is *thinking* and *for yourself*. Both elements mattered to Kant and have mattered to generations of liberals.[11] Custom, tradition, authority, religion, and so on, which had guided the unenlightened for so many generations, were rejected both because they were derived from, and imposed by, others present and past, and therefore not exercises of our *autonomy*, and because they substituted for the exercise of individual reason, rather than stemming from it. The motto he attributed to the Enlightenment, and which he adopted, was *sapere aude*, dare to know; "Have courage to use your own reason."

The Enlightenment didn't have it all its own way. Compare Kant with Edmund Burke's famous peaen to

> untaught feelings . . . prejudices . . . We are afraid to put men to live and trade each on his own private stock of reason; because we suspect that this stock in each man is small, and that the individuals would do better to avail themselves of the general bank and capital of nations, and of ages . . . of ready application in the emergency; it [prejudice] previously engages the mind in a steady course of wisdom and virtue, and does not leave the man hesitating in the moment of decision, skeptical, puzzled, and unresolved. Prejudice renders a man's virtue his habit; and not a series of unconnected acts. Through just prejudice, his duty becomes a part of his nature.[12]

This passage can jar a modern reader and, for all I know, Burke's own readers. It confronts the pejorative overtones that the term "prejudice" has today, with an evocation of its etymology as prejudgment: We need lots of the latter, so we are wrong to condemn the former. What Kant insists on as the distinctive human virtue—the autonomous exercise of individual reason—is what Burke is skeptical about. And *skeptical* is a key word in this context. Skeptics of this sort are not confident of the ability of individual reason to guide us unaided through the ways of the world or to lead us to our own benefit. They don't believe we're that smart.

Their thinking goes roughly like this: Existing values, cultures, traditions, institutions, practices, help us make our way in a world so complex and fraught with risk and uncertainty that we need all the help we can get. They embody preformed responses to recurrent problems and circumstances. They enable some things and disable others. They are often the products of long histories, embedded in everyday ways of thinking, behaving, valuing, and, yes, prejudices. They are repositories of congealed knowledge, meaning, value, and, on occasion, wisdom; familiar and, if we are lucky, good—anyway, good enough. Those who deny or ignore them are bound to get a lot of things wrong and waste a lot of time in the bargain.

Consider the observation of the English philosopher, A. N. Whitehead: "Operations of thought are like cavalry charges in a battle—they are strictly limited in number, they require fresh horses, and must only be made at decisive moments."[13] Cavalry charges might be fine things in their place, the thought seems to be, but armies routinely need much else. And so do we all. We too depend on many things besides conscious thought, among them habits, customs and, again, prejudices.

The difference between Kant and Burke is primarily an *evaluative* one: Is a moral judgment based on individual reasoning likely to be sounder than one founded in prejudice? But the matter goes deeper than matters of taste and choice. There is a sociology here. Selznick quotes Durkheim's observation that "a society without prejudices would resemble an organism without reflexes."[14] Indeed, there is a sense in which sociology has no other subject than prejudice. What, after all, is socialization about? Filling us up with *prejudgments*, that is quite literally prejudices, on which we depend and without which we would be helpless or harmful or both, in any society. These prejudgments have precisely the characteristics that Kant distrusted—we don't invent them, and we don't think our way to them—but we are and need to be full of them. And when a sociologist talks of socialization, she[15] doesn't think societies have a *choice* whether to do it or not: All societies do it, and no society can do without it. And so we're all programmed with prejudices. If they come to irk us, we can struggle against them, even reject them, but we have to deal with them, and the proportion most of us reject or even think about is relatively small. Our cavalries charge only on occasion.

There is simply no way out of it and no simple way round it. Prejudices inform our every reasoning, give us the topics we are concerned with, the questions we ask, the answers we are likely to find satisfactory, the horizons within which we reason.[16] They might limit what we can understand, but equally they inform our understanding, provide resources, latent knowledge and meaning, paradigms, and so on. Other times, other places, other prejudices; never no prejudice.

So we have two sorts of arguments for not condemning prejudice, one evaluative—reason *shouldn't* be our sole guide in living a life—and a second psychological or sociological—reason *isn't* our sole guide and, like it or not, our psyches and societies being as they are, it *can't* be. Selznick knew both arguments. He doesn't make the analogy with his own discussions of the constraining but also enabling consequences of institutionalization, but it is there to be made.

In *The Moral Commonwealth*, Selznick criticizes the freestanding, project-making, individual of liberal construction, whose autonomous and rational moral *choices* are to be secured and facilitated, so long as they do not interfere with those of other autonomous moral choice makers. Selznick's "implicated selves" also make moral choices, but that is not all they do, nor all that qualifies their actions as moral.

That is not to say that blind unreason is to be preferred to enlightened reason or even that convention is preferable to critical morality. Selznick is well aware of the reasons that people condemn many prejudices such as racism, and he shares the antipathy. He is unpersuaded, however, that an evil prejudice is evil simply because it is not the product of freestanding reason. It is evil because it is evil, however it is come to. Provenance is not a self-evident mark against an inherited judgment (nor for that matter is evil redeemed because one has thought about it).

It is true that those who begin with evil prejudices and never rethink them end up with evil prejudices, but that is not an argument for starting from nowhere, which, in any event, one never does or can. The problem with prejudiced bigots is not that they begin with prejudices because we all do that. It is rather the *way* bigots believe, the way their prejudices envelop their thought, that matters. People "blinded by prejudice" don't merely prejudge, as we all do; don't just rely on things other than reason, as we all do; don't even just think badly of people without sufficient evidence. Most of us do that too. They do so in a way that is not *reflexive* about their prejudices. They have no wish, or no ability, to take any distance from them, to try to uncover them, to interrogate them, to confront them with experience, dialogue, criticism, and revision. They are incapable of taking a posture that is at once both rooted and reflexive. Such a posture acknowledges that we never start nowhere but recommends, in classic pragmatist fashion, that we always be open to reflecting on our starting points and to finishing somewhere else. Hence the last words of Selznick's discussion of the moral person, who "ultimately . . . must be, as Walt Whitman wrote in Stanza 4 of *Song of Myself,* 'both in and out of the game and watching and wondering at it.'"[17]

IMPLICATED SELVES

According to Selznick, an adequate moral or political philosophy must rest on an adequate sociological appreciation of the extent to which our "selves" are always "implicated" in larger connections. Such an appreciation will recognize, for example, as John Stuart Mill failed to, that harm about which members of a community might rightly be concerned can extend beyond what is "near at hand":

> A community may properly be concerned about injury to the moral order . . . Liberty itself would be at risk, for it requires public nurture and support. We cannot defend a culture of liberty without asking what it requires to survive and flourish.[18]

Moreover, an adequate moral sociology should affect not merely one's appreciation of the *sources* of moral achievement, the *etiology* of social, and with it moral, competence, but also of its character and reach:

> We are responsible for our *selves,* but the self as a biological and social formation is decisively affected by circumstances not chosen. Among these are memberships in family and community. A received identity has much to offer: inner coherence, security, self-esteem. Although people often detach themselves from their roots and try to send down new ones, the difficulties are great and the costs are high.[19]

Family and community can be understood literally here, but they also are examples of those crucial core relationships discussed in Chapter Ten. The significance of these suggests a need for connections, and criteria of moral judgment and guidance, that are at once supraindividual but also less than universal, that grow from local soil and take heed of local terrain; that are, in this sense, particular. The tension between universals and particulars is thus central to Selznick's understanding of the moral life, and with it, political life. Indeed universal/particular represents one of those "polarities" of which Cohen wrote, in relation to which good sense involves "showing how they involve each other."

UNIVERSAL AND PARTICULAR

A sociologically grounded morality, then, must include and register what is close, particular, contingent, inherited, unthought; not merely what is universal, timeless, born of axioms, and delivered by logic. And yet modernity proliferates universalistic tendencies and proclivities, not least in moral thought. Modern liberals are accustomed to judge according to universalizable, impersonal, criteria: those of justice, not of love; civility, not piety. The significance of fixed statuses and status obligations recedes, open and fluid identities and attachments abound, and liberals applaud.

And yet the cultural attachments that most mold our lives are rooted in particulars, even if their *assessment* will often involve universals. Particularity, and the *"bounded* altruism"[20] that accompanies attachment to it, are important ingredients of moral actions and judgments themselves; they generate conventional morality, and that is usually a good place to start, if not to end. Selznick respects the expansive reach of liberal claims; indeed he views them as "more distinctively human"[21] than attachment to kith and kin, which is common enough among mammals. Liberal reflection seeks to rise above the common vices of parochialism, ethnocentrism, moralized intolerance, and their associated and parallel forms of hostility and exclusiveness. These evils of parochialism must, therefore, "be disciplined by a universalist ethic."[22] In early modernity such an ethic, developed largely by liberals, preliberals and protoliberals, was rightly seen as a key to liberation from the imprisoning closeness of religions and relatives, a source of individual freedom and a new opening to "the embrace of strangers."[23]

However, Selznick worries that modern universalism tends often to be both overly abstract and insecure. Abstraction has the virtue of disinterestedness and frees us from parochialism. On the other hand, it depersonalizes, often it dehumanizes, the objects of moral concern and thins and weakens the moral texture of our engagement with them and with others. Thus, Selznick recalls Mrs. Jellyby of Dickens's *Bleak House*, who

> practiced what Dickens called "telescopic philanthropy." She was indifferent to the chaos in her household and to the welfare of her husband and children. All her philanthropic energies were directed to furthering the prosperity of an African people who lived on the left bank of the Niger. . . .
>
> Telescopic philanthropy is still philanthropy, which is much better than nothing from a moral point of view, and can often be justified. But charity begins at home.[24]

An associated difficulty with a morality of abstract rules is that it gives short shrift to context. The human condition is a context, in that there are certain needs, satisfactions, and values generated simply by being human and living in the world. But most of our contexts are more close grained than that, and much that matters to us has to be understood in relation to them. Those contexts in turn are made up of institutions, practices, roles, expectations that are particular and that differ. The values generated by family life are not the same as those of an army, or not at least a good family, a successful army—and different contexts, different histories, different cultures, different families.

This does not mean that anything goes; common humanity remains, and criticism cannot simply be disarmed by parochialism, all the more because conventional morality, what we imbibe from others' prejudgments, has plenty of characteristic failings, among them incoherence, naivete, lack of adaptiveness to change, and parochialism.[25] Critical morality is, then, indispensable and must often call in aid universal values. We can never take "this is the way we do things here" as a conversation stopper. But it is not a bad way to start a conversation, and it needs to *be* a conversation, not a monologue or an ex cathedra pronouncement. It does well to start from Hegelian reflection on "social practice and belief" rather than Kantian autogeneration of universal moral laws.[26] Universalist enthusiasm can easily become hubris in this field. Reflective morality must often transcend contexts, but only after sensitive exploration of them. It requires openness to plurality, specific textures, thick understandings. Contexts need to be specified and the values appropriate to them analyzed; "Not all values are appropriate to all settings. To understand the conditions of appropriateness is part of the theory."[27]

Moreover, it is easier to fashion general rules for distant rather than close relations and harder to be universalist about moral aspirations than about baselines, at least if one's ideals are to take on rich and specific texture. Rights, for example, might still be an indispensable safety net for close relations that fail, such as broken marriages, and *universal* rights for injuries that will damage anyone who suffers them, but we do better if we don't fall into the net. Moreover, in circumstances, whether intimate or more impersonal, where aspirations are key:

> A morality of aspiration is not easily captured or readily cabined by rules and systems. Parents are required by law to care for their children, but beyond a minimum the level and quality of care are unspecified. A political constitution must state clearly how long a government may remain in office and how its successors are to be chosen, but its larger ideals may well be stated only as abstract concepts.[28]

Selznick is a theorist of complex and delicate balances, as we have often seen, and those between the claims of particularity and universality, fidelity to and transcendence of contexts, and, as we will see in a moment, piety and civility are among the ones he considers with most care. Not piety *or* civility, universality *or* the claims of locality, but *and*. Just as bigoted partisanship would overturn the scales in one direction, so too can enthusiastic universalism, in the other. Recall that what we have in common "*includes the particularity of cultural experience.*"[29] The trick is not "to presume an ethos of universalism" but rather to "appreciate and respect diversity without embracing a radical relativism."[30]

No one should be denied human rights[31] or other universal values, grounded in careful assessment of human needs, particularly for survival but also to some extent for flourishing. Indeed, the fight for them is among the great fights. Yet there are many circumstances where moral judgment and discrimination need to draw on other, richer, subtler, more nuanced, conceptual resources, drenched in local knowledge, long alive to local hopes and fears. The ability to hold onto two such truths at once is a salutary aspect of Selznick's enterprise—for it is not universal.

CIVILITY AND PIETY

In his first book, *The Division of Labor in Society*, Durkheim famously suggested that all societies depend on adequate forms of social integration but that premodern and modern societies differ radically in their form of integration, of solidarity. That of the former was "mechanical," a kind of social glue generated by and itself generating likeness, similarity of values, activities, beliefs, fears, myths, identities. Breach of norms involves passionate reaction because all are offended. Modern societies, with their extensive divisions of labor, changefulness, and variety, cannot survive this way; there is not enough likeness to go around. Instead they must develop relations of a different, "organic" kind among their many, varied, and interdependent parts. Modern solidarity is generated precisely by the interdependence on which a radical division of labor rests and lubricated by a different sort of connection, which does not involve repressing deviance in the name of shared values and taboos. Rather, it has the task of smoothing routine social interaction, often among strangers, repairing damaged social parts and putting them back in place. The former, the glue, fuses; the latter connects; the former is associated with communal passion and heat; the latter, lubricant, stays cool: Infraction is not a pretext for outrage but an occasion for readjustment and repair.

Selznick acknowledges this distinction and the many others like it—for example, Ferdinand Tönnies's *Gemeinschaft* and *Gesellschaft*, Sir Henry Maine's status and contract—and draws on them, but again only as qualified by the principle of polarity. His "piety" is related to the first item in each pair, "civility" to the second, and it is true that there are more sources of the former in premodern society and of the latter in modernity. However, a modern society in good order depends on having an adequate supply and complementary arrangement of the "two sources of moral integration [that] compete for pre-eminence as foundations of community: civility and piety. Civility governs diversity, protects autonomy, and upholds toleration; piety expresses devotion and demands integration."[32]

Selznick acknowledges that "modern thought is not comfortable with the idea of piety. The democratic and secular person is likely to associate it with sanctimonious devotion to ritual and uncritical subordination to religious authority."[33] He knows the discomfort and appreciates why it is felt, but not every form of piety is sanctimonious and uncritical. On the contrary, piety in the sense he understands it is "an aspect of human nature, a reflection of the need for coherence and attachment,"[34] rooted in "a sense of connectedness or common mooring."[35] We have need of both.

As we have seen, not all that counts in our lives is or should be entirely a matter of free, unsentimental decision. Nor is a society in good shape when individuals show no concern for their fellows; no loyalty to those with whom their lives have been organically intertwined, such as children and parents; no commitment to any entity larger than themselves but smaller than the world; no sense of obligation in relation to any of the preceding. Communitarians defend what Selznick elsewhere calls "the virtues of particularism. These virtues include loyalty and piety, especially accepting responsibility for children, parents, and others to whom we owe special obligations. Particularism arises from the experience of connectedness, which makes us aware that we are implicated selves, bound up with lives that we have created and that have created us."[36]

Piety is a matter more of feelings than ideas, though "the feelings are not irrational."[37] They remind us that we are connected with what (and who) went before us and succeeds us. Patriotism, for example, is "capable of creating a potent union of self and place, self and history . . . extends the reach of fellowship, enlarges the meaning of self-interest, and reinforces morality by securing it to a particular heritage."[38] These are all important sources of stability, continuity, and connection in our lives. But if these are virtues, they come with attendant vices, "corrupt forms that resist criticism, condemn apostasy, and create outcasts; that are self-righteous, intolerant, and unforgiving. This darker aspect of piety undercuts its moral worth. Therefore we need a complementary principle of order—the principle of civility."[39]

The concept of civility addresses the *texture* or *quality*—as distinct from merely the *existence*—of relations among citizens. Relations, particularly among nonintimates, are *civil*, in an old and large conception, where they are

> guided by the distinctive virtues of public life. These include, especially, moderation in pursuit of one's own interests, and concern for the common good. More particularly, civility signals the community's commitment to dialogue as the preferred means of social decision.
>
> Thus civility presumes diversity, autonomy, and potential conflict . . . In civility respect, not love, is the salient value.[40]

There are many different sorts of society and many different types of relationships within any particular society. Only some are civil, and perhaps only some should be. There are also fine relationships for which civility is not enough: love, for example. So civility cannot be the limit or whole of one's social ideals, merely a crucial element of a society in which one pursues and is drawn by other values as well. Moreover, civility is a matter of degree. That is true both of societies compared overall—some exhibit more civility than others—and in different domains—different sectors of a society are more or less civil than others. And because civility is not all one wants in a society, more is not always better: A purely civil society might be suffocatingly proper and solipsistically unattached. Still, though many societies exist with less, a modern society will not flourish without underpinnings for, and practices of, civil interaction.

In *civil* societies,[41] routine nonpredatory social relations can occur among nonintimates, which neither depend on love or deep connection nor—as is common in uncivil conditions—are fractured by their absence, and replaced by suspicion, hostility, hatred, or simple fear. Cool, civil connections are not the only ones that occur nor should they be, but in the public realm the possibility of such connections is key. People have familial, ethnic, religious, linguistic, attachments that often matter to them greatly and that differ; but they don't kill for them. Nor is it a realistic expectation that they might.

Civil relationships are not especially close, and they are not hot like love and hatred. They are the character of relationships among members of healthy voluntary associations, not of close families, on the one hand, nor of opposed troops, on the other. The opposite of my friend is not automatically my enemy but, say, my acquaintance or colleague or neighbor. I can do business with that person, and I do not necessarily betray anyone by doing so.

Civility is not one of those ideals that quickens the pulse. It might, however, steady it. Some of our most fulfilling relationships must be on the way out, if all we can say is that they are civil. A healthy society supplements and enriches civility in all sorts of ways. But a civil platform is a secure place to stand, a baseline social virtue, infinitely preferable to its historically conjoined "other"—fanaticism[42]—as it is to routine hatred, suspicion, hostility, and vengefulness.

Attachment to civility in public space is what distinguishes a *liberal* communitarian from other, among them pernicious, types. Communal attachments have many attractions, and a life devoid of any is likely to be arid and lonely. However, dense communities commonly also have characteristic vices. They often exact a terrible price for nonconformity; they are *illiberal* about controversy.

Notwithstanding these apparent, and real, contrasts, however, one should not imagine that civility is at one freezing pole of a contrast where love is at some distant simmering remove, with nothing to connect them. For, in line with his constant insistence that the demands of baselines lend themselves to enrichment by those of flourishing, Selznick sees in civility richer possibilities also. Bare civility is better than incivility, but it can be better than it is, without suddenly being love. It might, however, start to move in that direction; for ultimately, according to Selznick, the two ends of civility and piety approach each other. The approach occurs thus:

> civility and piety are by no means wholly antagonistic. Respect is not love, but it strains toward love as it gains substance and subtlety. Rudimentary respect is formal, external, and rule-centered—founded in fear of disruption and lack of cooperation. The corresponding civility can be chilly indeed, as some connotations of "being civil" suggest. An important change occurs when respect is informed by genuine appreciation for the values at stake in communication and good order.
>
> . . . In truly civil communication, for example, something more is required than self-restraint and taking turns. An effort must be made really to listen, that is, to understand and appreciate what someone else is saying. As we do so we move from arm's-length "inter-action" to more engaged "interaction." We discover and create shared meanings; the content or substance of the discussion becomes more important than the form. The outcome is often a *particular* community of discourse and a *unique* social bond. A foundation is laid for affection and commitment. In this way piety fleshes out the bare bones of civility. . . . When it is thus open to the claims of piety, civility shows its human face.[43]

Civility without piety, then, can be a thin and bloodless avoidance of responsibility, responsiveness, or commitment; piety without civility a source of exclusivist, narrow-minded parochialism, full of jingoistic mythology, hatreds, and fears. A salutary combination of civility and piety does not come easily and is not always easy to maintain. Among other things, a communitarian liberal sees *institutions of law and justice* as crucial in support of both.

LAW, JUSTICE, COMMUNITY

We saw in the last chapter that "strong communities are *institution-centered*." This is particularly important where the complex balances required of *liberal* communities are to be maintained. Such a community requires an institutional architecture that distributes power, channels it, coordinates it, restrains it, but does not emasculate it. It must defend individuals, while at the same time enabling pursuit of the common good, enable people to choose to interact civilly rather than rapaciously or fearfully. It must also connect with local sources of piety and affection.

Thin and Thick

It is common today to contrast "thin," typically procedural, accounts of moral and political ideals, such as morality, justice, democracy, and the rule of law, with "thick," normatively demanding ones. Social scientists usually favor the (more measurable) former, and philosophers the normatively more richly endowed latter. Typically, Selznick wants them both.

Justice narrowly conceived, as a protection, source of restraint, anchored in what we can rely on rather than what we might hope for, is necessary to ensure secure baselines for a well-arranged community. Such baselines, in the now familiar way Selznick thinks of them, are an indispensable part, but should not be the limit, of our ambitions or endeavors. A community is more secure to the extent that it has such foundations, but foundations are not usually where we stop building. A communitarian liberal will value liberal foundations for themselves and what they protect but also for what they enable. That, ideally, is a well-ordered and flourishing liberal community.

Selznick considers sympathetically Stuart Hampshire's argument for moral realism in relation to justice: "Justice is best conceived as a negative virtue: 'One has to ask, in a Hobbesian spirit, what it prevents rather than what it engenders.'"[44] Hobbes, of course, was preoccupied with that question, and his answers, Selznick concedes, though generated by "a fairly narrow conception of what self-interest entails," are powerful. They make "a great deal of sense—so long as we have in mind a threshold or baseline morality, and insofar as we postulate a fairly narrow conception of what rational self-interest entails":[45]

> It does not follow, however, that the promise of justice is necessarily circumscribed by these motivations and urgencies. When we look beyond its rudimentary forms, we see that justice does more than enforce minimal requirements of order and cooperation. *The process of doing justice stimulates moral and legal development.* . . .
>
> Thus justice has a vital part to play, not only in the bare survival of moral systems, but in their flourishing as well. The struggle for justice has its own dynamic and reaches well beyond restraint of domination . . .
>
> If we reduce justice to a negative virtue or to a way of achieving minimal cooperation, we lose a great deal of its resonance and promise. We fail to garner the psychological and intellectual benefits that come from receiving justice and doing justice. Most important, we miss the full contribution justice can make to the enrichment and enlargement of community.[46]

Again, in the notorious debates between natural lawyers and legal positivists, for example, the latter are right to say of law that it has no *necessary* connection with morals. There are plenty of immoral laws and legal orders. But sociologically that is an uninteresting point to make. Necessity is rare in social arrangements. However, continuity, affinity, and inclination are less rare, and law has many nonaccidental continuities and affinities with, and inclinations toward, morality. This point, more concerned with latency and significance than necessity, is crucial:

> Both sides have failed to see that the connection between law and justice is variable and probabilistic, but not adventitious. There is *inclination* but not *necessity* . . .
>
> The affinity of law and justice is neither necessary nor happenstance. It is not necessary because many contingencies and obstacles can intervene, notably the use of law as an instrument of domination. It is not happenstance because the quest for justice "under law" and through law occurs for sound and recurrent reasons. Many human communities have discovered that legal rules and standards are effective devices for instituting fairness and correcting the abuse of power. This experience suggests that the moral worth of law has an underlying basis, a basis that must be sought in the nature of human personality and in the continuities of social organization.[47]

In modern societies, law and justice do not merely block unwanted intrusion; they also facilitate connection between self and other, civility and piety, liberty and community. On the one hand, the connection between civility and the rule of law, conceived as a source of reliable *restraint* on arbitrary exercise of power, is patent. Routine civility among citizens, as its absence in so much of the world reveals, is not a natural, still less inevitable, offspring of human propensities or social interaction. It depends significantly on the existence and adequacy of supporting and sustaining frameworks, central among them political and legal institutions capable of curbing many of the harms people are liable to suffer or inflict where such restraints are weak. One thing such institutions have to manage to do routinely, and be widely understood to do, is limit caprice and arbitrariness in the exercise of power of all sorts. Thus a civil society depends on powerful institutionalised restraints, and thus too "justice *begins* as a principle of restraint,"[48] its realism is attuned to "what we can *rely on* to mitigate oppression and win cooperation."[49]

Civil society and the rule of law go well together, Selznick insists, and he says nothing to slight the significance of the rule of law as a source of restraint. On the contrary, in *The Moral Commonwealth* far more clearly and unambiguously than in *Law and Society in Transition*, he patiently and repeatedly insists on the need for power to tame power and, to that end, for relatively but seriously autonomous legal institutions. However, his ambitions reach further, and so, he believes, do those of the rule of law.

One starts with Hobbes, to ensure that the threat from others is constrained. One moves to Locke to extend that restraint to the state itself. And there is further still to go, for there are reasons both of developmental logic and moral ambition that explain why "although justice *emerges* as a response to practical urgencies, it *eventuates*, under appropriate conditions, in ideas and practices that are subtler and more value-laden."[50]

Many of these "subtler" ideas and practices have to do with the communitarian and integrative functions that Selznick sees law performing, when at its best. Where law achieves these results, and of course this too will be a matter of varying degrees, we have an example of a legal order deeply "imbricated," as E. P. Thompson has observed,[51] in civil society.

Repressive, arbitrary, purely instrumental law is a predominantly state-centered matter, but the rule of law in this integrative sense is something quite else. It is, ideally and to differing extents in practice, not just a wall separating one from the other, not merely a club wielded by one against the other, but more like a bridge between state and society, pylons firmly planted on both sides of the divide, traffic flowing in both directions, and steady, unfearful, and productive interaction occurring between persons on both sides. Or so it is when the rule of law is a living presence in society, part of the cultural understandings of everyday life, part of the frame that bounds what is doable and even thinkable. When that happens, law is what Habermas has called an "institution" of the everyday life world itself, available to citizens as a resource and protection in their relations with the state and with each other. It is not a mere "medium" for the transmission of power.[52]

Throughout Selznick's chapter on communitarian justice, themes that emerged in earlier work are enlisted to display the communitarian strain in legal orders. And that it often *is* a strain Selznick does not doubt, even if—as difficult as it might often be to reconcile tendencies in tension—he leaves no doubt that it is a strain worth enduring, even provoking. In any event, it is commonly unavoidable, built in, for as he explains:

> in many societies, law is a mainstay of cultural identity. It is also the bridge between justice and community. Law pours content into abstract principles of justice; gives them a distinctive configuration; binds them to a special ethos

and a special history. This process is marked by an inescapable tension. Every legal order is to some extent a reflex of power and domination, yet every legal order has some commitment to principles of justice. How that tension is resolved is a key to the construction of moral communities.[53]

Though natural lawyers exaggerate in claiming a *necessary* connection between law and morality, they are right to "stress the *continuities* of institutional and moral life, including the continuities of legal and moral responsibility. In this view, the blurring of institutional boundaries is a necessary and desirable part of moral ordering."[54] Moreover, this blurring is not merely a moral choice that natural lawyers happen to have made; it is an insight, indeed a communitarian insight. For the "most important contribution of natural-law doctrine is its affirmation of community":

> The doctrine presumes that every legal order has an implicit constitution. Beyond the specifics of positive law are the *premises* of the legal order, to which appeal can be made in the name of justice and community. The premises create legitimate authority; they are the source of civic obligation. The duty of officials and citizens to obey the law is grounded on the implicit constitution, which in turn presumes community membership. At bottom, fidelity to law is fidelity to community.[55]

Responsive Law

In this context, we return to responsive law, viewed less now as an alternative to the liberal rule of law than as another, more advanced, more community-connected, face of it. There is much more acknowledgment here than in *Law and Society in Transition* that something other than legitimacy is at stake in preservation of legal autonomy, and there is as before recognition that legal responsiveness, and the mixed legal/political/administrative institutions that best exemplify it, might threaten legal integrity. On the other hand, for reasons now familiar, "the very stability of the rule of law, where that has been achieved, makes possible a still broader vision and a higher aspiration."[56]

Rather than contrast autonomous and responsive law as though they represented two different kinds of legal order, Selznick now sees one as the basis and the other an enrichment of the rule of law. Indeed, there are familiar Selznickian grounds for connecting the two:

> we cannot really separate the negative and positive aspects of the rule of law. Indeed it would be highly unsociological to try to do so, for we would then miss the moral and institutional dynamics which create demands for justice, and which induce rulers to accept responsibility.[57]

Justice, we learn, "requires a responsive legal order,"[58] one that is "more problem-centered than rule-centered, more persuasive than coercive," less interested in going by the book than in achieving successful results, in favor of "maximum feasible *self*-regulation" over heavy-breathing bureaucratic oversight, but always warily so: "Deference is unjustified if the institution in question has little or no potential for self-regulation."[59] While presuming autonomy, responsive law "looks to the *partnership* of courts, legislatures, and executive agencies," on the principle that:

> In the contemporary situation, separation of spheres is no longer the key to political wisdom. The community needs all the help it can get, from institutions capable of making up for one another's deficiencies. Without yielding the principle of checks and balances, of power taming power, the system must be open to new ways of infusing public policy with direction and commitment. For this we need cooperation and complementarity, not distance and division.[60]

Partnership, finally, is appropriate not only among official agencies but between them and organs of the wider community. Thus, Selznick again revisits legal pluralism, which—not yet under that name—had been the subject of *Law, Society, and Industrial Justice*. This has both a positive and a normative component. The plurality of legal or lawlike orders is a fact, as that book showed, and as a great deal of legal pluralist writing has confirmed. However, Selznick not only believes that legal pluralism *is* the case but that there are grounds to suggest that it *should be* the case:

> Law is more just when it springs from the character and condition of the people and when it is administered with due regard for the integrity of practices and the autonomy of groups. Thus responsiveness calls for respect as well as outreach: respect for ordinary people and their legitimate expectations; for the complex texture of social life; for the activities on which prosperity depends; for the actual and potential 'living law' of private associations.[61]

In John Braithwaite's terms, which Selznick would doubtless endorse (and that were in part influenced by him):

> The most crucial determinant of the quality of justice in societies is neither the quality of their state justice system nor the quality of the culture of justice in private dispute resolution; it is the relationship between the two. When citizens are imbued with a culture of justice learned in part from a principled law that filters down to them (and that law is shaped by the principles that bubble up from their indigenous deliberation of disputes), when weaknesses of indigenous disputing can be remedied by legal enforcement of rights, then justice has the deepest meaning.[62]

RIGHTS

Liberals old and new value rights. Indeed they treasure them. Rights, for one of the most influential American liberals of the second half of the twentieth century, Ronald Dworkin, are "trumps." A liberal, on this view "takes rights seriously." Indeed, on this view, that is what it means to be a liberal.

Selznick takes rights seriously too. However, moral seriousness requires that a lot besides individual rights needs to be taken seriously as well. In by now predictable fashion, he believes liberals tend to take rights too exclusively seriously and in doing so underrate other aspects of a moral life in society that are also important, but either neglected by them, like responsibilities, or denied, like the common good. This is a high price to pay for what he criticizes as a "rights-*centered*" vision of morality. Rights-centered liberals indulge in the common error of allowing too much of a good thing to "trump" too many other good things.

As he so often finds partisans of good things doing, Selznick believes that liberals tend to overplay their hand. They too often succumb to "the lure of absolutes"[63] in their appraisal of their basic values, such as rights and liberties; too rarely take into account differences among *kinds* of rights; and competitions—with other rights but with other moral claims as well— too frequently assume that to establish someone has a right or liberty is to end discussion, rather than, as Selznick believes it often should be, just to begin it. Even if a liberal under challenge might argue that there are resources within liberal theory to resist absolutist temptations, the liberal ethos makes such temptations enduringly alluring.

A central theme of so much of Selznick's writing has been the importance of responsibility for and to others, and, closely connected with that, responsiveness as well. These are crucial dimensions of the moral competence of individuals, as of institutions and communities. Morally competent actors take responsibilities seriously; not exclusively but seriously. It is also crucial that these actors, in their particular contexts and circumstances, with particular responsibilities, connections, duties, be prepared to ask not merely whether they have a right to X, but whether it is right for them to have it, demand it, think only of it; whether assertion of it conflicts with their other commitments and responsibilities; whether there are contexts in which it is more appropriate to insist on it, and others where it is in bad taste or worse. Rights-centered liberals have a tendency to lessen

the significance of these sorts of questions, he believes; not necessarily because the logic of their position drives them there but rather because an
overemphasis on individuals and rights goes with the liberal ethos.

Ethos is a good word here, not only to capture something larger in
the liberal tradition than the strict force of argument but also to point to
some of what is at stake in a communitarian concern for the "social fabric."
Modern forms of relationship are not necessarily *incompatible* with a sense
of responsibility; the "market mentality" is not unable to accommodate
philanthropy and other gestures of supraindividual concern. But an ethos
in which responsibilities are overshadowed by rights and cooperation by
self-interest narrowly conceived is one in which something communitarians consider central is likely to be slighted, weakened, eroded, if not
erased: concern for the common good.

THE COMMON GOOD

If liberals tend to absolutize individuals and their rights, they tend to rela-
tivize, or reject out of hand, notions of "the common good." Plagued as it
is with the "sez who?" problem, the very conception seems to many liberals to smack of collectivism, reification, and other vices that liberals spend
much of their time strenuously seeking to avoid. I too have questioned
Selznick's assumption that it is always available to be found.

Selznick agrees that there is no axiomatic route to the common good;
"Instead, the common good is known in an untidy way, the only way we
learn from experience."[64] And yet liberals "make the common good even
more uncertain and difficult to grasp than it has to be. This uncertainty
gives license to ignore, or be indifferent to, what we owe to others and the
needs we share."[65] Alternatively, it makes it impossible to judge among different claims of good, imagining that everyone's claim is equally worthy of
regard. Nevertheless:

> We should not confuse the fact that we sometimes need to grit our teeth in the
> face of evil, resisting the impulse to censor, with the idea that any conception
> of the good, whatever its impulse, form, or consequence, is a welcome contri-
> bution to diversity. When neo-Nazis demonstrate in hateful ways, it is not re-
> spectful tolerance that restrains us. It is a well-founded fear of slippery slopes.
> To protect ourselves from ourselves we need hard rules, especially rules that
> curb official coercion. But a claim to respect must find its warrant in some-
> thing more than self-assertion.[66]

Even liberals who insist on governments limiting themselves to protecting "the right" while individuals choose "the good," cannot do without at least sub rosa appeals to the latter.[67] Instead of acknowledging this, however, the liberal favors state neutrality, a doctrine that Selznick readily concedes "makes sense for a broad range of decisions, particularly in a community that celebrates private initiative and personal autonomy."[68] On the other hand, taken literally it abandons concern for the "*kind* of community"[69] we belong to, "imperils confidence in many public objectives whose implementation must limit personal choice,"[70] and exacerbates the atomistic tendencies that, even without it, modernity generates.

By contrast, Selznick's closing chapter explores some of the moral responsibilities of a well-ordered and democratic commonwealth; one committed to the belief that "reflection and dialogue address the goodness of our lives, not only the more limited objective of keeping a society from falling apart."[71] These responsibilities rest on "our understanding of what [people] need to sustain their dignity and integrity as persons,"[72] a goal shared with liberals but with foundations that, he insists, are deeply communitarian. For a lot of what people need has to do with community; democracy itself "flourishes when it is part of, and sustained by, an appropriate way of life";[73] "Citizenship cannot flourish—the call to deliberation will not be heard—if the main sources of personal responsibility are attenuated or lost."[74]

The state is responsible for communal well-being, and this will include responsibility for the health of the community, for the capacity of its members to act responsibly in relation to each other and to the state itself, for "the strength and resilience of social life . . . the quality of life and the integrity of our institutions."[75] Not every well-intended measure of state intervention has borne this in mind:

> *Social* democracy is not necessarily *communal* democracy. Social democracy may or may not embrace concern for the vitality of community. It may be strongly individualist and statist. The programs of the welfare state are mainly designed to serve individual needs. Guided by principles of equality and personal autonomy, they display only passing concern for the integrity and well-being of groups and institutions, that is, for the spontaneous arrangements of civil society. As government moves in to supplement (and replace) private ordering, the fabric of community is weakened. . . .
>
> Like the market so prized by classical liberals, the welfare state easily becomes a bloodless repository of moral virtue. One grinds out exchanges; the other grinds regulations.[76]

The moral to draw is not the libertarian one that government should largely stay out of communal affairs; that way would be simply to abandon concern for extraindividual sources of human flourishing and to overlook "the principle that individual choice, to be fully rational, requires a supportive institutional context."[77] Nor is it that state power should be so checked and balanced that it is prevented from doing good, in order that it cannot do ill;[78] for there is a lot for states to do. One needs a state "committed to defining and furthering the common good" that is at the same time strong enough to do what it must and restrained enough not to be able to do what it must not. The trick is to recognize the difference and find ways to institutionalize it.[79]

That institutionalization must respect the classical liberal premise of individual moral primacy while also recognizing the reality, in their consequences, of the communities to which individuals belong. The moral contribution of those communities is *tested* by what they contribute to individual lives, but their shaping reality is not *reducible* to those lives. It has a significance, "a vivid reality,"[80] of its own.

Like the organizations Selznick studied in the 1940s and 1950s, and the corporations he explored in *Law, Society, and Industrial Justice*, our communities provide contexts of both survival and flourishing in our lives. Few of us are likely to flourish as individuals if those communities do not sustain and facilitate the social, economic, political, and spiritual conditions in which individuals can do well. That these are complex conditions, and flourishing a complex state of affairs, emerges from every one of the 538 pages of *The Moral Commonwealth*. That they are valuable, and worth our every effort to secure, is another message that emerges from those same pages.

Do we have any assurance that they will be secured? Not really. Do we have reason to persevere in trying to secure them? Yes:

> The feeling is one of "hopeful sadness." We have to do the best we can but we're not sure we will succeed. . . . I have to say communitarian liberalism is going against the stream, the other pressures are extraordinary. You're not sure you're going to conquer but you might do better than you think.[81]

In his biography of Dewey, Alan Ryan remarks on the fact that, soon after his death in 1952, "He exemplified the 'philosopher as sage,' and by the 1950s that was old hat. Modern philosophers had become technically sophisticated about what they were doing and in the process had become reluctant to risk themselves over much of the philosophical landscape."[82] Dewey's reputation has revived somewhat in recent years, but the point remains.

Like Dewey, Selznick lived and wrote for a very long time. His "sage-like" propensities developed inversely to the direction of his profession.[83] As he grew older, his work conformed less and less to the tight contours of the disciplines he had both inhabited and influenced. And while his work was always distinctive, his themes became larger and his ambitions more "visionary" than is common in the academy and indeed than was characteristic of his earlier work. He also hoped they might reach intelligent nonspecialists and engage them in "public philosophy," a form of reflection that "speaks to matters of public concern and serves as a source of insight and judgment."[84]

The richness, span, sensibility, and magisterial quality of this later work have been very attractive to some, including me. It drew not merely on professional accomplishment but on a long life of intellectual reflection. Not everyone was so charmed, however. One critic, full of praise for the reach, erudition, and complexity of this deep distillation of and reflection on pragmatic themes, thinks its very strengths undermine it as a contribution of or to pragmatism:

> Because of its coverage, this book is a relatively abstract and acontextual work about the importance of pragmatism and context. The form of the work, in other words, is in tension with its content—almost as though the ghost of Immanuel Kant, rejected in substance, still controls the form that a grand work of theory must take.[85]

If allegiance to a creed is what matters, this might be an important criticism, but given the many noncreedal virtues of the book, which Williams stresses, an outsider such as I can remain unperturbed.

However, other academic readers, even friends and admirers of Selznick, were impatient with the style and character of the enterprise as it developed in his later years. They took it to be a falling off: too vague, cloudy, hortatory, abstract, not empirical enough for the sociologists, not analytically sharp enough for the philosophers. Where was the novelty, where the rigor, bite, edge?

There is something in this sort of criticism, and perhaps it is why books of his later sort come less commonly from distinguished academic thinkers than they once did. But it is not an accident or an unproblematic sign of progress that a great deal of modern social science deals rigorously with topics smaller in every sense than Selznick's, some so small as to be hardly visible.

There is much to be gained when a scholar of distinction seeks to distill what he has learned and reflected deeply on and extend his reach, in the way Selznick was determined to do, particularly in *The Moral Commonwealth* but also in the later more autumnal distillations, *The Communitarian Persuasion* and *A Humanist Science*. My own view is that any loss of bite or "rigor," in the modern behavioralist senses of these terms, is more than compensated for by the largeness, fineness, and richness of the enterprise, taken both retail in those works and wholesale in the oeuvre as a whole. This is all the more true because, in his later works as indeed always with Selznick, one senses that one is in the hands of a wise, humane, erudite, sane, and deeply reflective guide. *His* concerns are not small. They may not always be our own, we needn't follow him everywhere, but it is hard not to learn from him.

Missing What Matters

In the introduction to this book, I suggested that Selznick was interesting not merely for his particular subjects and what he had to say about them, or his informing discipline(s) and what he contributed to it or them, but for distinctive aspects of his ways of thought, his moral-intellectual character and sensibility. The book has largely followed his subjects and the order in which he took them up, with matters of the latter sort being discussed as they emerged in the writings. I conclude by drawing a few of them together.

The fox knows many things, we are told, but the hedgehog knows one big thing. Isaiah Berlin famously draws from this ancient and somewhat delphic pronouncement a contrast between two casts of mind separated, he suggests, by "a great chasm." Hedgehogs "relate everything to a single central vision, one system less or more coherent or articulate, in terms of which they understand, think and feel." Foxes, by contrast, "pursue many ends, often unrelated and even contradictory, connected, if at all, only in some *de facto* way, for some psychological or physiological cause, related by no moral or aesthetic principle."[1]

Because chasms are what dichotomies do, as Selznick might have observed, once thus enunciated and set against each other the space between these two ways of thinking does seem large, perhaps unbridgeable. In fact, however, some of the most interesting thinkers occupy it. Less aimless than foxes, less Procrustean than hedgehogs, they are alive to tension, variety, incommensurability in the world, and yet their thought has coherence, if often of a complex sort. Indeed Berlin himself is one such: He writes about everything,[2] but there are clear and recurrent overarching concerns.

Selznick is another. Someone who skimmed his works could easily con-clude that he was a particularly energetic and omnivorous fox, for he pops up in so many fields. However, if the thought of foxes might be supposed less complex and interconnected than that of hedgehogs, Selznick is no ordinary fox.

But then he is not an ordinary hedgehog either. Unlike many famous intellectual hedgehogs, among them some who influenced him, Selznick's intellectual character is not Procrustean or reductionist; anything but. If anything, it is more like his ideal community—unity of unities, full of di-versity within but not atomistic or unconnected. While a close community of hedgehogs is an uncomfortable, prickly, thought, and it is hard to envis-age what a marriage between hedgehog and fox would be like, it might at least be expected to exhibit that tolerance for ambiguity that Selznick so commended and incarnated. And, if Selznick might be said to have con-summated such a marriage, what, to conclude, are some of its distinctive features?

As we have seen, apart from his sociology text, each of Selznick's books before *The Moral Commonwealth* had a specific institution or class of institutions as its subject and became famous and influential specifi-cally for its interpretation of that subject. Thus, the TVA was the epony-mous subject of his first book, communist organizational strategy of his second, administrative leadership of his third, regulation of labor rela-tions of his fourth, transformations in modern law of his fifth. Even *The Moral Commonwealth*, with its wide scope, erudition, and ambition, was a contribution to a specific, if large, theme: the challenges to and sources of moral competence of persons, institutions and communities. *The Communitarian Persuasion* was a continuation of that theme. *A Humanist Science* sought specifically to defend his version of sociological ecumen-ism. Of course, one learns a lot about these specific subjects from these works. And yet, as Nonet stressed and many have felt, something else was always going on. And so it was.

One source of this overflow was his "generalizing impulse." *TVA* was never just about the TVA; *The Organizational Weapon* not just about com-munists; *Leadership in Administration* not just about how to get ahead in business; *Law, Society, and Industrial Justice* not—spectacularly not—just about industry and employment; and so on. This lent depth, richness, and complexity to each of his works, as it does to the whole. In Selznick's case especially, it is a mistake to take the title of any particular work as a sum-mation of its significance or implications. There is always more than one might expect inside: more themes, more arguments, and also more than themes and arguments.

One source of connection between these elements, of course, was the underlying and linking problematic of so much of Selznick's work, the fate and conditions for realization of values in the world. We are invited to treat these as central problems and to learn to be alert—scientifically alert—to "recurrent sources of vitality and decay." Where such matters arise in standard-issue social science, by contrast, they too often do so coyly, sotto voce, even clandestinely. Selznick's work is refreshing for its absence of apology about these matters, as well as for the reflexive and sustained thoughtfulness that he brings to them.

Now if one is interested in the play of values in the world, this leads to a certain paradox of the modern academy. Philosophers, particularly moral philosophers, say a lot about values, and much of it is very clever. But what do philosophers know? They live in the world, it's true, talk about it often enough, and the modern analytical kind are skilled in carving up—occasionally filleting to perfection—what other philosophers and even ordinary folk say about it. But actually to *study* it? That, many of them proudly say and display, is not their business. Sociologists by contrast are paid to study it, and one thing social science could bring to the study of values in the world is acknowledgment of fact, contingency, and variation. Such acknowledgment is to Selznick a hallmark of social science, but again sociologists are not likely to bestow it too closely on phenomena such as values, that they "handle gingerly and view with alarm." Even if this coyness is overcome, sociology is not a good source of principled reflectiveness on the evaluation of values, which is where philosophy has something to say. Yet some social phenomena are in lousy shape, some in good, some in excellent. Which are what, and how would we know? Many social scientists have thought this has nothing much to do with them.

Selznick disagreed. Like Roger Cotterrell calling for a renewed sociology of morality,[3] which he would have welcomed, Selznick wished to redirect or augment the attentions of sociology to questions of value. More than that, he believed that this engagement should draw on an uncommon range, variety, and richness of intellectual resources, from the social sciences, humanities, particularly philosophy and history and, on occasion, from world religions.

The integrations Selznick favors reflect the spaciousness of his concerns and the breadth of what he finds useful and interesting. They also connect with a central feature of his academic temper—a combination of distinguished disciplinary pedagogy and institution building with skepticism about the point and worth of disciplinary apartheid, or purity, for its own sake.

In *A Humanist Science* Selznick recalled that the sharp disciplinary distinctions that mean so much in the modern academy had no hold on its greatest ancestors, discussion of whom enriches that book, and more profoundly *The Moral Commonwealth*. Though he respected the disciplines, the training and skills they generated, and the results they reached, and clear though it is that he is by formation and intellectual character a sociologist, he lamented what he called the "rampant multiculturalism in academic life":[4]

> The disciplines to which many of us have devoted our lives, into which we have socialized our students, have unfortunately become intellectual islands. These islands have their own jargon, their own culture, their own paradigms, their own ways of thinking. These self-reproducing disciplines have often stood in the way of serious engagement with major issues.

He favored following where the problem led, rather than where the discipline dictated. I return to this point in a moment.

Apart from matters of themes and approach, I have claimed, Selznick's writings reflect and express a characteristic intellectual and moral sensibility—above all, scrupulous and nuanced; judicious and thoughtful. These may not always be virtues; one might be *too* balanced. However, there are worse ways to be.

He had an almost allergic response to shrill rhetorical heightening of the dramatic in social life. Apart from anything else, it wasn't his style. Tolerance for ambiguity allows that social life will be full of tensions and ambiguities. These might not be resolved any time soon, or perhaps any time at all, but that doesn't necessarily make them inexorable, unsustainable contradictions. We often just need to work out how to live with them, not ditch one option because there's another.

I argued in Chapter Nine that this tendency might make it hard to recognize real zero-sum encounters where they occur. At times, though he always allows for such things in principle, he seems to sideline them in practice. And given his determination to assist social "reconstruction," that might have become a systematic bias. Still, the opposite bias is very common, and Selznick's sensibility is a corrective, perhaps a useful prejudice in the sense discussed in Chapter Eleven.

A person of Selznickian sensibility will be sensitive to empirical variation and crucial distinctions; be alert to the significance of qualifying adjectives as much as reifying nouns; be aware that very little that matters in social life is "nothing but . . . ," or apt to be successfully resolved by a choice between all and nothing; avoid the pseudo-drama of so many ideological confrontations; be suspicious of a quick fix; avoid intellectual habits that dim one's vision, even if they might quicken one's pulse.

Virtues, we learn to recognize, are typically mixed with corrupting vices; vices often have redeeming virtues. It is rare that we can soar over life's predicaments as the crow flies, but that doesn't mean we're stranded; we should endeavor to navigate as best we can. If some aspects of modernity give us reason for "hopeful sadness," as Selznick had suggested to me, both the adjective and the noun matter. There are sources of hope as well as of sadness; sometimes they're the same; sometimes one generates the other. Neither should be thought a priori to cancel the grounds of the other.

Sensibility too is evident in Selznick's treatment of other thinkers. He disagreed with many, often strongly but rarely polemically or even harshly. *The Moral Commonwealth* is a large and intricate mosaic of refined appreciations of thinker after thinker, from each of whom he sought to extract something valuable as he gently distinguished their views from his own. This exemplifies more than a style, unless in the sense that *"le style c'est l'homme même."*

Of course this rich stream of reflection did not all happen at once. It is a long story, which a couple of Selznick's own concepts might illuminate. I began this conclusion by suggesting that, although Selznick had written on many subjects, he is as much hedgehog as fox, that is to say, a systematic thinker rather than merely a scurrier in unrelated directions. That is true, and it speaks to the coherence of the work, but it is not enough to say, for two reasons.

First, it doesn't give sufficient weight to the amount of *development* in his thought. Selznick had long believed that persons, institutions, social orders are subject to development, which is not merely change. It is more, because there is *direction*, at least potentially, to that change. Part of understanding is to seek the particular character of that development, to try to uncover its direction and, recognizing that little is inevitable in social life, to reveal its implicit dynamics, the dispositions embedded within it, the "incipient," "emerging," even if "inchoate" seeds of what is to come in what already is; whether it be postbureaucratic forms in bureaucracy, responsive law in autonomous law, institutions in what begin as mere organizations. However plausible this might be of institutions, it applies well to Selznick's own thought and to that of other strong thinkers. They are often usefully read backwards, as it were, so that one finds fully formed the meaning of much that went before in germ, the tendency of which might not have been apparent when it first appeared, even to its author.

This is one of the things that raises Selznick's work, as an achievement, from simple coherence to integrity, a concept he had long used and theorized. For if his preoccupations, immediate aims, subjects, and, indeed, sensibility have impressive continuities, they are also impressively various and subject to change. The coherence of his thought is complex, not that of someone with just one thing to say. After all, the thoughts of someone who keeps repeating himself might be called coherent. They are—it is!—certainly consistent, but that would not necessarily be praiseworthy—unless it was a very *big* thing being repeated. Nor is simple consistency always a virtue. Trivial consistencies are commonplace, and consistent folly is also not rare. Selznick's coherence was not of those sorts.

Integrity might well spur a change of mind or heart. It might indeed be a *mark* of integrity to be open to change, even of some of one's deepest convictions. This, presumably, is the point of the famous response attributed to Keynes, when once accused of inconsistency: "When the facts change, I change my mind. What do you do, sir?"

In this, Selznick was with Keynes. He kept returning to a number of related and large themes, to do with the fate of ideals in the world, especially in the modern world, and particularly to do with the workings of large institutions, among them bureaucracies and law. But he also kept thinking and rethinking his views, refining them, elaborating them, exploring them in different contexts. The scope of his interests, the focus of his passions, his particular judgments, and his public mood and posture changed considerably over the years; for what was constant in his work was not a particular set of conclusions but the integrity with which he approached a significant range of problems.

Integrity, of course, is a significant term of art in Selznick's thought, applied to institutions, persons, and communities. It is also an aspect of his intellectual character. At one point in *The Moral Commonwealth*, he quotes a passage from Bernard Williams about personal integrity. Integrity on this understanding presumes that:

> the person in question has, as seriously as possible, tried to think about the standards or the fundamental projects which are sustaining him or her. If he has done that and if, in the light of the thought he has displayed there, he comes out and does say, this is what I do most fundamentally believe in, and

this is what I am going to do, then that person is displaying integrity, even though you do not agree with whatever it is that is sustaining him.[5]

That gets it just about right.

I conclude with a question. If there are any distinctive virtues in Selznick's style of thinking, how likely are they to be fostered, indeed found, in the contemporary academy?[6]

At the start of this book I mentioned that Selznick, like many leading thinkers of his generation, was intellectually formed without as well as within academic disciplines. This partly accounts for the nature and range of the questions he thought important to ask, what he thought useful in answering them, and the answers he came to give. Even within the academy, he wrote as an intellectual, informed by and responsive to what he studied there, but not only that. He felt free to draw on the full palette of resources available to that type, not merely those licensed to disciplined professionals. Indeed, in a revealing interview with sociology graduate students at Berkeley, he explained that one reason he entered sociology was the idea that it "was a house that had and would have many mansions, that it would be possible to be a rather free roving intellectual and follow one's own bent without being too constrained by the necessities of the more tightly organized disciplines."[7]

The house he entered has been remodeled and vastly expanded. An enormous number of rooms have been added, and occupancy has soared. However, expectations of proper behavior have changed. Unlike Selznick's generation, the professional formation for those who have entered it in recent years is more commonly the primary, often the only, intellectual formation available. This has consequences. Most contemporary social scientists command a more limited span; indeed, more commonly it is not theirs to command. The discipline dictates the range, and these disciplinary dictates are not becoming more ecumenical, to use Selznick's word, over time. For such a mind, "humanist science" can be only a contradiction, not a goal.

Of course such expansiveness as Selznick pursued exacts a fee. It is hard to accomplish successfully, which might be why it is not often tried. As scholarship burgeons and becomes ever more technically driven and accomplished, the more one tries to keep up with, the harder it is not to be left behind. Amateurishness beckons. Even if it is avoided the effort is not always welcomed, both because the range of professionally acceptable questions gets narrower, ways of investigating them more subject to professional dictate, and acceptable ways of answering them too are, with all Foucaultian resonances of the word, ever more disciplined. Apart from intrinsic intellectual pressures in this direction, institutional and competitive demands in the contemporary "education sector" also encourage a narrowing of focus and forms of self-protection like those called, in another profession under pressure, "defensive medicine." Like so many clichés, that about knowing ever more about ever less reflects real developments.

We admire for good reason the power of modern specializations, the skill involved, and the intellectual rewards to be gained. But, as some will acknowledge, all this cleverness frequently comes at a price in terms of, among other things, intellectual and moral spaciousness and largeness and significance of concern. Not every stride made by specialization and expertise can sensibly be regarded as progress. Their rigors are not always as attractive as they can be impressive. Questions posed diminish in significance, while ways of answering them become ever more sophisticated; we are cleverer about how to explore, less interesting about what.

Apart from what people come to do, there is a eugenic aspect to this: what intellectual categories and talents come to be bred in and out of an increasingly specialized and technicized world is a question deserving scientific scrutiny itself. Perhaps this is what Max Weber had in mind when he foreshadowed for the "last man" of our cultural development, the potential triumph of "specialists without spirit, sensualists without heart; this nullity imagines that it has attained a level of civilization never before achieved."[8] Perhaps too it explains his alleged retort to a complaint that he ventured beyond his field: "I am not a donkey, and I don't have a field."

Perhaps these trends are unavoidable, perhaps they should be applauded, but they also have a price. Whatever the limits of Selznick's enterprise and the inadequacies of this account of it, I hope they might at least remind readers of some of the virtues of such determined and sober spaciousness, reach, and integrity as he displayed; also of what might be lost when they are systematically, even proudly, reduced, and when methods replace problems as agenda setters. Perhaps "remind" is too optimistic a word here. Social scientists under a certain age may have rarely encountered such virtues, let alone imagined that a card-carrying social scientist might hazard to exhibit them, still less believe that they are central to his and their common vocation. Selznick's work is rich evidence for just such a quaint belief.

Reference Matter

Notes

INTRODUCTION

1. Philippe Nonet, "Technique and Law," in Robert Kagan, Martin Krygier, and Kenneth Winston, eds., *Legality and Community: The Legacy of Philip Selznick* (Lanham, MD: Rowman & Littlefield, 2002), 50.

2. Philip Selznick, *TVA and the Grass Roots. A Study in the Sociology of Formal Organizations* (Berkeley: University of California Press, 1949; reissued in paperback with a significant new preface by Harper & Row, New York, in 1966 and republished in paper and on Kindle, with a new foreword by Jonathan Simon, by Quid Pro Quo, LLC, in 2011).

3. Selznick, *The Organizational Weapon. A Study of Bolshevik Strategy and Tactics* (Santa Monica, CA: RAND Corporation, 1952). Reissued with a new preface by Free Press, Glencoe IL, 1960, Kindle edition forthcoming with a new foreword by Martin Krygier, with Quid Pro Quo, LLC, in 2012.

4. Selznick, *Leadership in Administration. A Sociological Interpretation*, (New York: Harper & Row, 1957). Reissued with new preface by University of California Press, Berkeley, 1984.

5. Leonard Broom and Philip Selznick, *Sociology: A Text with Adapted Readings* (New York: Harper & Row, 1955; 7th edition, 1981).

6. Selznick, "Sociology and Natural Law," *Natural Law Forum* 6 (1961): 84–108.

7. Selznick, *Law, Society, and Industrial Justice* (New York: Russell Sage Foundation, 1969).

8. Selznick, *Law and Society in Transition. Toward Responsive Law*, (New York: Harper Torch Books, 1978). New edition with introduction by Robert A. Kagan, New Brunswick, NJ: Transaction Publishers, 2001.

9. Selznick, "Jurisprudence and Social Policy: Aspirations and Perspectives," *California Law Review*, 68 (1980), 208.

10. Selznick, *The Moral Commonwealth. Social Theory and the Promise of Community*, (Berkeley: University of California Press, 1992).

11. Selznick, *The Communitarian Persuasion*, (Washington, DC: Woodrow Wilson Center, 2002).

12. Selznick, *A Humanist Science. Values and Ideals in Social Inquiry*, (Stanford, CA: Stanford University Press, 2008).

13. Selznick, *The Moral Commonwealth*, ix.

14. Ibid., x.

15. Selznick, *A Humanist Science*, 4.

16. Ibid., 5.

17. Kenneth Winston, remarks at memorial service for Philip Selznick, January, 20, 2011.

18. One work of legal philosophy that compares his concept of ideals with that of the German legal philosopher Gustav Radbruch is Sanne Taekema, *The Concept of Ideals in Legal Theory* (The Hague: Kluwer Law International, 2002). There is also a collection of essays in honor of Selznick that discusses various aspects of his thought: *Legality and Community*, note 1 in this chapter.

19. Both definitions are taken from the *Oxford English Dictionary*, 2nd edition.

20. They also influenced two of my other books, even their titles: *Between Fear and Hope: Hybrid Thoughts on Public Values* (Sydney: ABC Press, 1997); and *Civil Passions* (Melbourne: Black Inc., 2005).

CHAPTER ONE

1. Kim Lane Scheppele, "The Passing of a Generation," *Law & Courts* 20, 2 (Spring 2010), 6.

2. Philip Selznick in Joseph Dorman, *Arguing the World: The New York Intellectuals in Their Own Words* (Chicago: University of Chicago Press, 2001), 46. This is the text of a PBS film of that title, directed by Joseph Dorman and exploring the early careers of Daniel Bell, Nathan Glazer, Irving Howe, and Irving Kristol. Selznick appears in the film.

3. Seymour Martin Lipset, "Out of the Alcoves," *The Wilson Quarterly* 23 (1990), 85.

4. Douglas G. Webb, "Philip Selznick and the New York Sociologists," paper presented at the Annual Convention of the Canadian Historical Association, Ottawa, Ontario, June 9–11, 1982, 9.

5. Trotsky took the characterization from the historian N. N. Sukhanov. Stalin was often underestimated by those he later destroyed. Sukhanov was arrested in 1930, confessed to mythical crimes in a show trial in 1931, was later accused of further crimes, and was shot in 1940, the same year that Trotsky was assassinated. He was rehabilitated in 1992.

6. The idea of a concept "with a social theory built into it" is that of my former doctoral supervisor, Eugene Kamenka. For more on the development of "bureaucracy" as one such, see my chapters 2 to 4 of Eugene Kamenka and Martin Krygier, eds., *Bureaucracy: The Career of a Concept* (London: Edward Arnold), 1979; and "Marxism and Bureaucracy. A Paradox Resolved," *Politics* 20, 2 (1985), 58–69.

7. The argument is elaborated at greatest length in Leon Trotsky, *The Revolution Betrayed* (London: New Park Publications, 1973; originally published in 1936).

8. Constance Ashton Myers, "American Trotskyists: The First Years," *Studies in Comparative Communism* X, 1 & 2 (1977), 146–147. See, further, Myers, *The Prophet's Army: Trotskyists in America, 1928–1941*, Contributions in American History, 56 (Westport, CT: Greenwood Press, 1977), chapter 8.

9. S. M. Lipset, "Steady Work: An Academic Memoir," *Annual Review of Sociology* 212 (1996), 5.

10. Guenther Roth, "The Historical Relationship to Marxism," in Reinhard Bendix and Guenther Roth, *Scholarship and Partisanship: Essays on Max Weber* (Berkeley: University of California Press, 1971), 248.

11. See Robert Michels, *Political Parties: A Sociological Study of the Oligarchical Tendencies of Modern Democracy*. Eden and Cedar Paul, trans. (New York: The Free Press, 1962. Originally published 1911), 50.

12. His enthusiasm did not last, however. He ended his life a supporter of Mussolini.

13. Michels, *Political Parties*, 62.

14. Ibid., 79. Cf. 147: "The concentration of power in those parties which preach the Marxist doctrine is more conspicuous than the concentration of capital predicted by Marx in economic life."

15. Ibid., 365.

16. Ibid., 111, and similarly 170. Though Max Weber agreed with Michels on a great deal, he disputed this assimilation of indispensability and power. A group, slaves for example, could be both indispensable and weak. See Max Weber, *Economy and Society*, volume III, Guenther Roth and Claus Wittich, eds., (New York: Bedminster Press, New York, 1968), 991.

17. Michels, *Political Parties*, 367.

18. Ibid., 72.

19. Ibid., 338–339. Cf. 190: "Mechanism becomes an end in itself."

20. Ibid., 334.

21. Martin Krygier, interview with Philip Selznick, January 4, 2002 (notes on file with author).

22. One of these, also a contributor, was the noted sociologist Lewis Coser, writing under the pseudonym "Louis Clair."

23. Philip Selznick, "Reply to Virgil J. Vogel," in "Exchange: Revolution Sacred and Profane," *Enquiry* 2, 3 (Fall 1945), 16.

24. Selznick, "The Dilemma of Social Idealism," *Enquiry* 1,1 (November 1942), no page number.

25. Michels, *Political Parties*, 206.

26. Later Selznick's objection is different, less that Michels spoke of human nature than that he said more than he needed to: "This proposition is not really necessary to his argument. He need only have postulated ordinary human desire for security, comfort, and status. These motivations, which are sufficiently powerful, and the recurrent phenomena to which Michels called attention—especially the prerogatives of office and the nature of rank-and-file participation—adequately explain the drift to oligarchy" (Selznick, *The Moral Commonwealth* [Berkeley: University of California Press, 1992], 245).

27. Selznick, "The Dilemma of Social Idealism."

28. Selznick, "On Redefining Socialism," *Enquiry* 1,5 (July 1943), 3.

29. See Selznick, "Dilemma of Social Idealism" and "The Iron Law of Bureaucracy," *Modern Review* (1950), 157–165.

30. Selznick, "The Iron Law of Bureaucracy," 165.

31. Ibid., 160.

32. Selznick, "Dilemma of Social Idealism" [no page number].

33. Selznick, "The Iron Law of Bureaucracy," 159.

34. Selznick, *The Moral Commonwealth*, 247–248.

35. Selznick, "Approach to a Theory of Bureaucracy," *American Sociological Review* 8 (1943), 49.

36. Ibid., 51.

37. Cf. ibid., 54.

38. Alvin Gouldner, "Metaphysical Pathos and the Theory of Bureaucracy," *American Political Science Review* 49, 2 (1955), 496–507. See Chapter 5 in this volume.

39. "An Oral History with Philip Selznick," conducted by Roger Cotterrell, January 2002, (Regional Oral History Office, Bancroft Library, University of California Berkeley, 2010), 9. Available at http://digitalassets.lib.berkeley.edu/roho/ucb/text/selznick_philip.pdf; http://law.berkeley.edu/selznick.htm. Excerpts from these interviews were published in "Selznick Interviewed. Philip Selznick in Conversation with Roger Cotterrell," (2004) 31 *Journal of Law and Society*, 291–317.

CHAPTER TWO

1. Shared with a number of other thinkers about dark times. See especially Judith Shklar, *Ordinary Vices* (Cambridge, MA: Harvard University Press, 1984), 5: "One begins with what is to be avoided." See too Avishai Margalit, *The Decent Society* (Cambridge, MA: Harvard University Press, 1996), 4: "There is a weighty asymmetry between eradicating evil and promoting good. It is much more urgent to remove painful evils than to create enjoyable benefits."

2. For a good account of the relationship between Dewey's thought and Selznick's, particularly on the nature of ideals but on many other matters as well, see Sanne Taekema, *The Concept of Ideals in Legal Theory* (The Hague: Kluwer Law International, 2002), chapters 5–7. Because she concentrates more on Selznick's later writings, and particularly *the Moral Commonwealth*, however, her Selznick is a sunnier, more optimistic fellow than I think his writings as a whole reveal him to be. In particular, the Michelsian and Niebuhrian strands in his thought get almost no attention. He is portrayed as a thinker who discerns only natural tendencies to good, whereas he insists that tendencies to good and to evil both have natural sources.

3. Cf. John Dewey, "Theory of Valuation," *International Encyclopedia of Unified Science*, II, 4 (1939), 27.

4. John Dewey, "The Nature of Aims," *Human Nature and Conduct* (New York: The Modern Library, 1930), 233.

5. Dewey, "Theory of Valuation," 35.

6. Dewey, "The Nature of Aims," 225.

7. Ibid., 232.

8. Dewey, *The Quest for Certainty*, Gifford Lectures 1929 (New York: G. P. Putnam's Sons, 1960), 279, 280.

9. Ibid., 280, 281.

10. Ibid., 281.

11. Both essays appeared in 1938. They are republished in Leon Trotsky, *Their Morals and Ours* (New York: Pathfinder Press, 1972).

12. Trotsky, *Their Morals and Ours*, 37.

13. Trotsky, "Means and Ends," *Their Morals and Ours*, 55.

14. Ibid., 54.

15. Selznick, "An Oral History with Philip Selznick," conducted by Roger Cotterrell, 2002, 8–9, available at http://digitalassets.lib.berkeley.edu/roho/ucb/text/selznick_philip.pdf; http://law.berkeley.edu/selznick.htm.

16. Well discussed in Daniel F. Rice, *Reinhold Niebuhr and John Dewey: An American Odyssey.* (Albany: State University of New York Press, 1993).

17. Reinhold Niebuhr, *Moral Man and Immoral Society* (New York: Charles Scribner's Sons, 1932), 23.

18. Dewey, *Reconstruction in Philosophy* (Boston: Beacon Press, 1959 [1920]), 95–96.

19. Niebuhr, *Moral Man and Immoral Society*, xv.

20. Ibid., 272.

21. See Niebuhr, *The Nature and the Destiny of Man. A Christian Interpretation*, vol. 2, "Human Destiny" (London: Nisbet & Co., 1943), 21.

22. Niebuhr, *The Nature and Destiny of Man*, vol. 1, "Human Nature" (London: Nisbet & Co., 1941), 117.

23. Gertrude Jaeger, "The Philosophy of the Once-Born," *Enquiry* 2, 1 (April 1944), 11.

24. See Chapter 9 in this volume.

25. Selznick, "Dilemma of Social Idealism," (first page). *Enquiry* 1,1 (November 1942), no page number.

26. Selznick, "Revolution Sacred and Profane," *Enquiry* 2,2 (Fall 1944), 18.

27. Selznick, "The Iron Law of Bureaucracy," *Modern Review* (1950), 162.

28. Ibid., 161.

29. Selznick, "Mr Selznick Replies [to Louis Clair]," *Enquiry* 1, 6 (November 1943), 11–12.

30. Selznick, "The Iron Law of Bureaucracy," 161.

31. Selznick, "Revolution Sacred and Profane," 11.

32. Ibid., 13.

33. Louis Clair (Lewis Coser), "A Radical in Retreat," *Enquiry* 1, 6 (November 1943), 3–8.

34. Ibid., 5.

35. Ibid., 8.

36. Virgil J. Vogel, "Exchange: Revolution Sacred and Profane," *Enquiry* 2, 3 (Fall 1945), 15.

37. Philip Sherman, "James Burnham's 'Managerial Revolution,'" *The Call*, May 17, 1941, 6; "James Burnham on Revolution," *The Call*, May 24, 1941, 6.

38. Selznick, "Dilemma of Social Idealism," 2nd page. Compare George Orwell: "Burnham has probably been more right than wrong about the present and

the immediate past. For quite fifty years past the general drift has almost certainly been towards oligarchy . . . Burnham sees the trend and assumes that it is irresistible, rather as a rabbit fascinated by a boa constrictor might assume that a boa constrictor is the strongest thing in the world." ("James Burnham and the Managerial Revolution," in *The Collected Essays, Journalism and Letters of George Orwell, vol. IV*, Sonia Orwell and Ian Angus, eds. [London: Secker & Warburg], 176.)

39. Selznick, "The Iron Law of Bureaucracy," 157.

40. Ibid., 161.

41. Ibid., 162.

42. Selznick, "Revolution Sacred and Profane," 14–15.

43. Selznick, "On Redefining Socialism," *Enquiry* 1, 5 (July 1943), 6.

44. Selznick, "Mr Selznick Replies [to Louis Clair]," 12.

CHAPTER THREE

1. Webb, "Philip Selznick and the New York Sociologists," paper presented at the Annual Convention of the Canadian Historical Association, Ottawa, Ontario, June 9–11, 1982, 18.

2. Selznick, "An Approach to a Theory of Bureaucracy" *American Sociological Review* 8 (1943), 47–54; "Foundations of the Theory of Organization," *American Sociological Review* (1948), 25–35.

3. Selznick, *Leadership in Administration*, (New York: Harper & Row, 1957). Reissued with new preface by University of California Press, Berkeley, 1984, v.

4. Selznick, "A Theory of Bureaucratic Behavior," unpublished copy on file with Martin Krygier.

5. Charles H. Page, *Fifty Years in the Sociological Enterprise: A Lucky Journey* (Amherst: University of Massachusetts Press, 1982), 91.

6. See especially Robert Merton, "Bureaucratic Structure and Personality," *Social Forces* 18 (1940), 560–568, and, later, the co-edited *Reader in Bureaucracy* (New York: Free Press, 1952), which contains two excerpts from *TVA*.

7. It is not clear to what extent the group actually existed *as* a group. See Charles Crothers, "The Dysfunctions of Bureaucracies: Merton's Work in Organizational Sociology," in Jon Clark, Celia Modgil, and Sohan Modgil, eds., *Robert K. Merton: Consensus and Controversy* (London: The Falmer Press, 1990), 212.

8. Martin Krygier, interview with Philip Selznick, March 2003 (notes on file with author).

9. U.S. Congress, *House Document 15*, 73d Cong., 1st sess., 1933, quoted in *TVA and the Grass Roots* (New York: Harper & Row, 1966), 5; and *The Moral Commonwealth* (Berkeley: University of California Press: 1992), 339.

10. *TVA*, 5.

11. Ibid., 6.

12. For a taste of Lilienthal's rhetoric, see *TVA: Democracy on the March* (New York: Harper & Brothers, 1944; Twentieth Anniversary edition, 1953).

13. Charles Perrow, *Complex Organizations. A Critical Essay*, 3rd ed. (New York: Random House, 1986), 160.

14. Selznick, *The Moral Commonwealth*, 339.

15. "An Oral History with Philip Selznick," conducted by Roger Cotterrell, 2002, Regional Oral History Office, Bancroft Library, University of California Berkeley, 2010, 9. Available at http://digitalassets.lib.berkeley.edu/roho/ucb/text/selznick_philip.pdf, 31–32.

16. Merton famously wrote "The Unanticipated Consequences of Social Action," *American Sociological Review* 1 (1936), 894–904. However, Selznick did not recall this as his inspiration. He acknowledged great scholarly debts to Merton, particularly to the *character* of his intellectual engagement, as a scholar and a teacher. However,

> I don't think he had much to do with the framework of the argument. I did use the term "unanticipated consequences". . . . in my first outline, I used a little different phrase, a phrase that really came out of my Marxist background. I talked about "objective consequences," not unintended consequences. And then, I think partly because I really was—kind of [out] of a respect for Merton, because I knew he had done that—I softened it to unanticipated consequences.
> COTTERRELL: So it was a kind of close relative of latent functions?
> SELZNICK: Yes, right. But in the Marxist circles that I lived in for a couple of years, the phrase "objective consequences" was very, very, very current. It also meant consequences are objective in the sense that you didn't intend them, but they flowed from the logic of whatever you were doing, so that people would say—when they had had an argument with somebody . . . "Objectively, you're a class enemy" or "You're serving the purposes of the class enemy," things like that.
> I don't think it would be truthful to say that Bob had any particular influence on the argument. I'm sure that he helped a lot with clarifying various bits and pieces here and there. (Selznick oral history, 35–36. Similarly, see Martin Krygier, interview with Philip Selznick, January 4, 2002 [notes on file with author].)

17. Selznick, *TVA and the Grass Roots*, 9.

18. Lilienthal, quoted in Selznick, *TVA*, 28.

19. Statement by Authority in Senate Hearings (1940), quoted by Selznick in *TVA*, 32.

20. Ibid., 37.

21. Ibid., 217.

22. Institutions created by grants of federal land to the states, which could sell or develop it to establish colleges specializing in agriculture, science, and engineering.

23. Selznick, *The Moral Commonwealth*, 340.

24. Selznick, *TVA*, 13.

25. Ibid., 259.

26. Ibid., 15.

27. Ibid., 262.

28. Ibid., 55.

29. Ibid.

30. Ibid., 137–138.

31. R. G. Tugwell and E. C. Banfield, "Grass Roots Democracy?—Myth or Reality?," *Public Administration Review* 10, 1 (1950), 51.

32. Selznick, *TVA*, 73.

33. Ibid., 262.

34. Ibid., 181.

35. Ibid., 181.

36. Ibid., 263.

37. Selznick, *The Moral Commonwealth*, 341.

38. Selznick, *TVA*, 220.

39. Ibid., 48.

40. Ibid., 263.

41. Ibid., 265–266.

42. Selznick, "An Approach to a Theory of Bureaucracy"; and "The Iron Law of Bureaucracy" *Modern Review* (1950), 157–165.

43. Selznick, *TVA*, 9.

44. Preface to the 1966 Torchbook edition of *TVA*, ix–xi, see Chapter 5 in this volume. And see Seymour Martin Lipset, introduction to Michels, *Political Parties*: "Selznick's work, which has been among the most influential in the field of organizational analysis, in large measure began with an effort to systematize and extend Michels' insights into the source of deviations from professed norms." Roberts Michels, *Political Parties: A Sociological Study of the Oligarchical Tendencies of Modern Democracy*. Eden and Cedar Paul, trans. (New York: The Free Press, 1962. Originally published 1911), 25. Crothers notes of Merton that, "although he had earlier read Michels, he had found his causal [*sic*] style of presentation alienating, and thus he did not evoke Michels while developing his perspective on organizations. He only re-read Michels in the mid- or later 1940s at the instigation of some of his own students," *op. cit.*, 225. Those students were probably Selznick and Lipset.

45. Preface to the 1966 Torchbook edition, ix–x.

46. Ibid., 7.

47. Martin Krygier, videotaped interview with Philip Selznick, 7 January, 2002; available at http://law.berkeley.edu/selznick.htm

48. The book is not concerned, except incidentally, with the *exercise* of power by communist parties but with strategies for gaining it.

49. Selznick, *The Organizational Weapon*, 12.

50. Ibid., 17.

51. Selznick, *Leadership in Administration*, 48.

52. Selznick, *The Organizational Weapon*, xii.

53. Ibid., xii.

54. Ibid., 22.

55. Ibid., 20.

56. Ibid., 4.

57. Ibid., 113.

58. Ibid., xiv.

59. Ibid., xiii.

60. Ibid., 26.

61. Ibid., 54.

62.

What is really urgent is that the other left-wing movements *compete for the same social base* as do the communists. . . . It is here that the party is most vulnerable, for without its base it is nothing. He who can expose the party before the *relevant* public—the labor movement and liberal opinion—is therefore its main and intolerable enemy.

This is not a matter of emotional response but of the hard coin of politics. Programmatically, the communists may declare that the "bankers and bosses" or the "imperialists" are the enemy. But these forces do not challenge the communists at the source of power. (Ibid., 226–227)

63. Cf. ibid., 163.
64. See, for example, ibid., 64.
65. Ibid., 65.
66. Ibid., 57.
67. Ibid., 59.
68. Ibid., 8. Cf. "An Oral History with Philip Selznick," 46: "I'll give you something I heard recently about the Mormons. Somebody was saying about the young Mormons who were sent out as missionaries, the important influence is not so much the converts that they get, but the way this activity influences the missionaries themselves. These young people, having been involved for two years in this kind of activity, are now, themselves, ineradicably fixed as Mormons. So there is that dynamic that all organizations have to take into account—what I called at one point the internal relevance of apparently external activity."
69. Ibid., 244.
70. Ibid., 39.
71. Ibid., 44.
72. Ibid., 47.
73. Ibid.
74. Ibid., 81.
75. Ibid., 88–89.
76. Ibid., 178.
77. Ibid., 164.
78. A large part of which also appeared in Selznick, "Institutional Vulnerability in Mass Society," *American Journal of Sociology* 56 (July 1951), 320–331.
79. Selznick, *The Organizational Weapon*, 276.
80. Ibid., 280–281.
81. Ibid., xvii.
82. Barrington Moore, "Review," *American Political Science Review* 46 (1952), 875.
83. Selznick, *The Organizational Weapon*, 313–314.
84. Ibid., 16.
85. Ibid., 332–333.
86. In an unpublished paper, "Sociological Inquiry and the Logic of Means," first written in 1954 or 1955, then rediscovered by its author and reproduced in 1962 (on file with Martin Krygier).
87. Perrow, *Complex Organizations*, 159.

CHAPTER FOUR

1. Hugh Heclo, "The Statesman: Revisiting *Leadership in Administration*," in Robert Kagan, Martin Krygier, and Kenneth Winston, eds., *Legality and Community: The Legacy of Philip Selznick* (Lanham, MD: Rowman & Littlefield, 2002), 296.

2. Ibid.

3. Weber became far more central to Selznick's thinking and writing later. See *Law, Society, and Industrial Justice*, (New York: Russell Sage Foundation, 1969), esp. at 75–82. And see *The Moral Commonwealth*, (Berkeley: University of California Press, 1992), 273–280.

4. See Robert Merton, "Bureaucratic Structure and Personality," (first published 1940) in *Social Theory and Social Structure* (New York: The Free Press, 1968, enlarged edition), 249–260.

5. Philippe Nonet and Philip Selznick, *Law and Society in Transition*, (New Brunswick, NJ: Transaction Publishers, 2001) 14.

6. Max Weber, *Economy and Society*, vol. III, Guenther Roth and Claus Wittich, eds. (New York: Bedminster Press, New York, 1968), 975.

7. Ibid.

8. Ibid., 959.

9. Ibid., 987–988.

10. Weber, "Parliament and Government in a Reconstructed Germany," Appendix II, in *Economy and Society*, vol. III, 1404.

11. Ibid.

12. See Weber, "Politics as a Vocation," in *From Max Weber* (London: Routledge and Kegan Paul, 1970), 95; and "Parliament and Government in a Reconstructed Germany," esp. at 1403–1405, "The Political Limitations of Bureaucracy."

13. He was particularly influenced by Chester I. Barnard. See especially *The Functions of the Executive* (Cambridge, MA: Harvard University Press, 1938).

14. Selznick, "Approach to a Theory of Bureaucracy," *American Sociological Review* 8 (1943), 50. My italics.

15. Ibid.

16. Selznick, *Leadership in Administration* (Berkeley: University of California Press, 1984), 92.

17. He refers to and draws on predecessors in "An Approach."

18. Ibid., 47.

19. Ibid., 48.

20. Ibid., 49.

21. Selznick, "Foundations of the Theory of Organization," *American Sociological Review* 13 (1948), 23–35. 25. Citations in this and the next paragraph are all to p. 25.

22. Ibid., 27. Citations in this paragraph are all to this page.

23. See Barnard, *The Functions of the Executive*, and, on this point, W. Richard Scott, "Symbols and Organizations: From Barnard to the Institutionalists," in Oliver E. Williamson, ed., *Organization Theory: From Chester Barnard to the Present and Beyond* (New York: Oxford University Press, 1990), 38–41.

24. Ibid., 32.

25. "Foundations of the Theory of Organization," 35.

26. See *TVA*, 59.

27. Selznick, *Leadership in Administration*, 17.

28. "I did not mean to deny the prevalence or importance of other institutionalizing processes, including the creation of a formal structure, the emergence of informal norms, selective recruiting, administrative rituals, ideologies, and much

else that results from a special history of goal seeking, problem solving, and adaptation" ("Institutionalism 'Old' and 'New,'" *Administrative Science Quarterly* 41 [1996], 271).

29. Selznick, *The Moral Commonwealth*, 233.

30. Selznick, *Leadership in Administration*, 7.

31. Ibid.

32. Ibid., 16. Cf. *The Moral Commonwealth*, 232: "The underlying reality—the basic source of stability and integration—is the creation of social entanglements or commitments. Most of what we do in everyday life is mercifully free and reversible. But when actions touch important issues and salient values or when they are embedded in networks of interdependence, options are more limited. Institutionalization constrains conduct in two main ways: by bringing it within a normative order, and by making it hostage to its own history." And see *Law, Society, and Industrial Justice*, 44.

33. Selznick, *Leadership in Administration*, 93–94.

34. Ibid., 27.

35. Ibid., 5.

36. Ibid., 6.

37. Selznick, *Law, Society, and Industrial Justice*, 44.

38. Selznick, *Leadership in Administration*, 21.

39. Ibid., 8.

40. Ibid., 13.

41. Ibid., 6.

42. Ibid., 100.

43. Ibid., 65.

44. Ibid., 60.

45. Ibid.

46. Ibid., 16.

47. Ibid., 3.

48. Ibid., 27.

49. Ibid., 34.

50. Ibid., 35.

51. Selznick, "Foundations of the Theory of Organizations," 30.

52. Selznick, *Leadership in Administration*, 40.

53. Selznick, *The Moral Commonwealth*, 321.

54. Selznick, *Leadership in Administration*, 139–140.

55. Ibid., 140.

56. Ibid., 70.

57. Ibid., 28.

58. Ibid., 26.

59. Ibid., 47.

60. Ibid., 45.

61. Ibid., 74.

62. Ibid., 79.

63. Ibid., 135–136.

64. Ibid., 141.

65. Ibid., 79

66. Ibid., 81.
67. Ibid., 103.
68. Ibid., 119.
69. Ibid., 125–126.
70. Ibid., 124–125.
71. Ibid., 126–127.
72. Ibid., 143.
73. Ibid., 149.
74. See www.angelfire.com/nj3/leadership/FinalPaper.html.
75. Selznick, *Leadership in Administration*, ix.
76. Ibid., 1.
77. Ibid., 1–2.
78. Ibid., 37.
79. Note that this phrase is only a slight, but significant, alteration of the ambition Selznick attributes to the Communist Party: "*to turn members of a voluntary association into disciplined and deployable political agents.*"
80. Ibid., 61.
81. Heclo, op. cit., 296–297.
82. Ibid., 299.
83. Selznick, *Leadership in Administration*, 65.
84. Ibid., vii.
85. Selznick, "The Ethos of American Law," in Irving Kristol and Paul Weaver, eds., *The Americans: 1976* (Lexington, MA: Lexington Books, 1976), 229.

CHAPTER FIVE

1. See James J. Chriss, "Alvin W. Gouldner and Industrial Sociology at Columbia University," *Journal of the History of the Behavioral Sciences* 37, 3 (2001), 241–259.
2. Alvin Gouldner, "Metaphysical Pathos and the Theory of Bureaucracy," *American Political Science Review* 49, 2 (1955), 496–507.
3. Ibid., 498.
4. Ibid., 507.
5. Ibid., 503.
6. Ibid., 505–506.
7. See Judith Shklar, "The Liberalism of Fear," in Judith Shklar and Stanley Hoffman, eds., *Political Thought and Political Thinkers* (Chicago: University of Chicago Press, 1998), 9.
8. "Dilemma of Social Idealism," *Enquiry* 1,1 (November 1942), [no page number].
9. Cf. "An Oral History with Philip Selznick," conducted by Roger Cotterrell, 2002, 34; available at http://digitalassets.lib.berkeley.edu/roho/ucb/text/selznick_philip.pdf; http://law.berkeley.edu/selznick.htm:

> Most people did not really take the point of view that I did—I think, a somewhat more balanced view—because even in those early days, I said something like this: . . . Actually, it was in an article I did about Michels. I said, well, the logic of this is . . . you can't say, "Who says organization says oligarchy." That's nonsense. I mean, empirically. It

doesn't always happen. What you've got to say is that this tendency to create a self-perpetuating leadership and similar things is something that will happen if you allow organizations to follow the line of least resistance.

So I was saying what you learn from all this is something about the problematics of social life, the kinds of dangers that arise that we have to be ready to deal with. You have to understand what can take place. I didn't really mean to communicate what Al Gouldner called a "metaphysical pathos." I thought that was silly. I could understand why he might come to that conclusion, but I was not really saying that democracy was impossible or anything like that. I wasn't repeating Michels. Michels said, "The waves of history break ever on the same shoals" and so on and so forth.

I wasn't saying that; I was just saying that these are the problems of life, of organization, and we have to be prepared to meet them, and that shouldn't keep us from seeing the positive side of things. I was willing to see the positive side of the TVA.

10. Selznick, *The Moral Commonwealth*, (Berkeley: University of California Press, 1992), 182.

11. Selznick, *TVA*, x, quoted in Chapter Three, n.45, of this volume.

12. Sheldon Wolin, *Politics and Vision: Continuity and Innovation in Western Political Thought* (Princeton, NJ: Princeton University Press, 1960; expanded edition 2004).

13. Ibid., 4.

14. Ibid., 281.

15. Ibid., 327.

16. Ibid., 328.

17. Ibid., 329.

18. Ibid., 336.

19. Ibid., 369.

20. Ibid., 369–370.

21. Ibid., 383.

22. Ibid., 377.

23. Ibid., 383.

24. Ibid., 384.

25. Ibid., 385.

26. Ibid., 387.

27. Ibid., 388.

28. Selznick, "Rejoinder to Wolin," in Amitai Etzioni, ed., *A Sociological Reader on Complex Organizations*, 2nd edition (New York: Holt, Rinehart and Winston, 1969), 149–154.

29. Ibid., 150.

30. Ibid.

31. Ibid.

32. Ibid., 151.

33. Ibid., 152.

34. Ibid., 153.

35. Ibid., 154.

36. See Blandine Kriegel, *The State and the Rule of Law* (Princeton, NJ: Princeton University Press, 1995).

CHAPTER SIX

1. Martin Krygier, videotaped interview with Philip Selznick, January 8, 2002; available at http://law.berkeley.edu/selznick.htm.

2. Martin Krygier, interview with Philip Selznick, March 2003 (notes on file with author).

3. Chester Barnard, *The Functions of the Executive* (Cambridge, MA: Harvard University Press, 1938), xxx.

4. Ibid., xxix.

5. Eugen Ehrlich, *Fundamental Principles of the Sociology of Law* (Cambridge, MA: Harvard University Press, 1936), xv; now reissued, with a new introduction by Klaus Ziegert (New Brunswick, NJ: Transaction Publishers, 2002), lviv.

6. Selznick, "Sociology of Law," in Robert K. Merton et al., eds., *Sociology Today: Problems and Prospects* (New York: Basic Books, 1959), 118–119.

7. See Selznick, "Sociology of Law," *The Encyclopedia of Philosophy*, vol. 7 (London: Macmillan, 1967), 478–480; Selznick, "The Sociology of Law," *The International Encyclopedia of the Social Sciences*, vol. 9 (New York: Macmillan, 1968), 50–59.

8. Selznick, "Sociology of Law," in Merton, 116.

9. See Gertrude Jaeger and Philip Selznick, "A Normative Theory of Culture," *American Sociological Review* (October 1964), 653–669.

10. Lon Fuller, *The Morality of Law* (New Haven, CT: Yale University Press, 1969), 123.

11. Selznick, "Review of *The Morality of Law*," *American Sociological Review* 30 (1965), 947.

12. See Chapter Nine in this volume.

13. Fuller "disliked the phrase 'law and society.' He objected to the 'and' as a distancing imagery; it seemed to counterpose what should be understood as wholly intermingled. We may not wish to indulge that bit of purism, but the point is well taken" (Selznick, "Jurisprudence and Social Policy: Aspirations and Perspectives," *California Law Review* 68 [1980], 216). Cf. Lon L. Fuller, "Some Unexplored Social Dimensions of the Law," in Arthur E. Sutherland, *Path of the Law from 1967* (Cambridge, MA: Harvard University Press, 1968), 57: "By speaking of law *and* society we may forget that law is itself a part of society, that its basic processes are *social* processes, that it contains within its own internal workings social dimensions worthy of the best attentions of the sociologist."

14. *Encyclopedia of Philosophy*, 478.

15. Ibid., 479.

16. Selznick, "Jurisprudence and Social Policy: Aspirations and Perspectives," 218–219.

17. *Encyclopedia of Philosophy*, 479; and see *Encyclopedia of the Social Sciences*, 51.

18. *Encyclopedia of Philosophy*, 479.

19. Cf. "An Oral History with Philip Selznick," conducted by Roger Cotterrell, 2002, 9; available at http://digitalassets.lib.berkeley.edu/roho/ucb/text/selznick_philip.pdf; http://law.berkeley/selznick.htm. 108:

> I'm not sure I understand exactly why, but I've been in recent years uncomfortable with the word "legality." I know it was used, and I didn't want to object to it when Bob Kagan and Ken Winston and Martin put together this book on *Legality and Community*.

I thought it would be obnoxious of me to say, "Well, I really don't like that word any more." But, in fact . . . I did say legality or the rule of law. Well, why didn't I just say the rule of law? I suppose I was trying to suggest that we're talking about law plus values.

20. Selznick, "Sociology of Law," in Merton, 126–127.

21. In 1969 the *Forum* was renamed the *American Journal of Jurisprudence*.

22. See Selznick, "A Case for Legal Naturalism: 'Sociology and Natural Law' Revisited," *Polish Sociological Review* 3, 131 (2000), 268.

23. Much of Selznick's essay and "Sociology of Law" from the *International Encyclopedia of the Social Sciences* appear reworked as the opening chapter, "Law, Society, and Moral Evolution," of *Law, Society, and Industrial Justice*.

24. H. L. A. Hart, "Positivism and the Separation of Law and Morals," *Harvard Law Review* 71 (1958), 593–629; Lon L. Fuller, "*Positivism* and Fidelity to Law—A Reply to Professor Hart," *Harvard Law Review* (1958), 630–671. For a recent discussion of contemporary bearings of this debate, see Peter Cane, ed., *The Hart-Fuller Debate in the Twenty-First Century* (Oxford, UK: Hart Publishers, 2010).

25. Hart, *The Concept of Law* (Oxford, UK: Clarendon Press, 1961); 2nd edition with a posthumously published postscript, 1994.

26. Reprinted with a comment by Ernest Nagel, rejoinder by Fuller, and reply to the rejoinder by Nagel, in the 1958 and 1959 volumes of the *Natural Law Forum*.

27. *Harvard Law Review* 83 (1970), 1474–1480), and "A Case for Legal Naturalism . . ." n. 22 *supra*.

28. *Harvard Law Review* 83 (1970), 1477–1478.

29. Selznick, "Sociology and Natural Law," 84.

30. Ibid., 85.

31. Ibid.

32. Ibid., 86.

33. Selznick, *The Moral Commonwealth*, 21.

34. For a reprise of Dewey's arguments, and a critique that Selznick would find congenial, of Richard Rorty's relativist remake of Dewey, see Hilary Putnam, *The Collapse of the Fact/Value Dichotomy and Other Essays* (Cambridge, MA: Harvard University Press, 2002). And see Chapter Nine in this volume.

35. See "A Normative Theory of Culture." Later still he came to prefer the term *humanist science*.

36. Selznick, "Sociology and Natural Law," 86.

37. Ibid. Compare Morris Cohen, in *Reason and Nature*, 2nd edition (Glencoe, IL: Free Press, 1953), at 346: "If we keep in mind both the historic and the teleologic aspect of social life, we see an interaction and a mutual dependence between the descriptive and the normative, between the actual historic cause and the ideal demands of a given system."

38. Selznick, "Sociology and Natural Law," 86–87.

39. Ibid., 87.

40. Selznick, *Law, Society, and Industrial Justice*, 10.

41. Selznick, "Sociology and Natural Law," 90.

42. Ibid., 87.

43. Selznick, *The Moral Commonwealth*, xiii.

44. Selznick, "Sociology and Natural Law," 87–88. For his own attempt to develop an alternative to the prevailing social science conception of culture, see

Gertrude Jaeger and Philip Selznick, "A Normative Theory of Culture," *American Sociological Review* 29 (1964), 653–669.

45. "Sociology and Natural Law," 88. Selznick reiterates these examples and some of these points in his reply to Donald Black's critical review of *Law, Society, and Industrial Justice*, critical above all because of the melding of facts and values in that book. See Chapter Nine in this volume.

46. Ibid., 90.

47. Selznick, "The Dialectic of Fact and Value: Foundations of a Humanist Social Science," Bernard Moses Memorial Lecture, University of California, Berkeley, February 21, 1973, ms. p. 12.

48. Selznick, "Sociology and Natural Law," 88, 90.

49. Selznick, "Jurisprudence and Social Policy: Aspirations and Perspectives," 215.

50. On Durkheim as a sociologist of morals, with ambitions that often put one in mind of Selznick, see Roger Cotterrell, "Durkheim on Justice, Morals and Politics," in Cotterrell, ed., *Emile Durkheim: Justice, Morality and Politics*, (Farnham, UK: Ashgate, 2010), xi–xxiv.

51. Selznick, "Sociology and Natural Law," 91.

52. Ibid., 91.

53. Selznick, *Law, Society, and Industrial Justice*, 4. Cf. *The Moral Commonwealth*, 358.

54. Selznick, *Law, Society, and Industrial Justice*, 5.

55. Selznick, "Sociology and Natural Law," 91.

56. Selznick, "Review of *Morality of Law*," 947.

57. Selznick, "Sociology and Natural Law," 95.

58. Ibid., 100.

59. Ibid., 98.

60. Ibid., 94.

61. Ibid., 95.

62. Selznick, *Law, Society, and Industrial Justice*, 13.

63. See my "Hart, Fuller and Law in Transitional Societies," in Peter Cane, ed., *The Hart-Fuller Debate in the Twenty-First Century*, 114–120.

64. Selznick, "Sociology and Natural Law," 96.

65. Ibid., 97–98. I have sought to explore this theme in "Thinking Like a Lawyer," in Wojciech Sadurski, ed., *Ethical Dimensions of Legal Theory* (Amsterdam: Rodopi, 1991), 67–90.

66. "Sociology and Natural Law," 99.

67. Ibid., 98.

68. Ibid., 98–99.

69. Ibid., 100.

70. Selznick, "A Case for Legal Naturalism," 271.

71. Selznick, "Rejoinder to Donald Black," *American Journal of Sociology* 78 (1973), 1268.

72. Selznick, "Sociology and Natural Law," 101.

73. Ibid.

74. Ibid.

75. Ibid., 103.
76. *International Encyclopedia of Social Sciences*, 58.

CHAPTER SEVEN

1. Selznick, Reply to Glazer, *Commentary* 39:3 (1965), 80. The last two sentences do not appear in the version published in *Commentary*. They can be found in the version reprinted in Seymour Martin Lipset and Sheldon S. Wolin, eds., *The Berkeley Student Revolt* (New York: Doubleday-Anchor, 1965), 303.
2. Ibid., 82.
3. Ibid., 83.
4. Glazer, Reply to Selznick, *Commentary* 39:3 (1965), 85.
5. Martin Krygier, videotaped interview with Philip Selznick, January 9, 2002; available at http://law.berkeley.edu/selznick.htm.
6. Nathan Glazer, "What Happened at Berkeley," *Commentary* 39:1 (1965), 47.
7. Martin Krygier, videotaped interview with Philip Selznick, January 8, 2002, available at http://law.berkeley.edu/selznick.htm.
8. Ibid.
9. Martin Krygier, videotaped interview with Philip Selznick, January 9, 2002, at http://law.berkeley.edu/selznick.htm. Selznick expressed similar views to Roger Cotterrell, though he stressed continuities somewhat more. See "An Oral History with Philip Selznick," conducted by Roger Cotterrell, 2002, 9; available at http://digitalassets.lib.berkeley.edu/roho/ucb/text/selznick_philip.pdf; http://law.berkeley/selznick.htm.
10. Annual Report of the Center for the Study of Law and Society, July 1961–June 1962, 1.
11. Martin Krygier, videotaped interview with Philip Selznick, January 9, 2002; available at http://law.berkeley.edu/selznick.htm.
12. Selznick, op. cit., 52.
13. Although, see Franz L. Neumann, *The Rule of Law* (Leamington Spa, UK: Berg, 1986), and other works from associates of the Frankfurt School, particularly Otto Kirchheimer. See also Vilhelm Aubert, *In Search of Law* (Totowa, NJ: Barnes & Noble, 1984).
14. Cf. Martin Krygier, "The Rule of Law. Legality, Teleology, Sociology," in Gianluigi Palombella and Neil Walker, eds., *Relocating the Rule of Law* (Oxford, UK: Hart Publishing, 2009), 45–69.
15. Selznick, *Law, Society, and Industrial Justice*, 1.
16. Ibid., 37.
17. Ibid., 36.
18. Ibid., 41.
19. Ibid., 38.
20. Ibid., 46.
21. Ibid., 44
22. Ibid., 45.
23. Ibid.
24. Ibid.

25. Ibid., 63. (Similar conclusions were reached independently by Ian Macneil, writing on the "relational" theory of contract. As Macneil later observed:

> So plainly obvious were the things I was writing during those seven years [1967–1974] that I was sure someone would beat me to the exposition of a fairly comprehensive relational contract theory. My selfish concern escalated no end when sometime in 1973 I came across Selznick (1969). There it was! At least, there it almost was because Selznick focused largely on labor relations, with only casual attention to contractual relations generally. ("Reflections on the Relational Theory," in *The Relational Theory of Contract* [London: Sweet & Maxwell, 2001], 291–292)

26. Ibid., 60.

27. Ibid., 63.

28. Ibid., 67.

29. Ibid.

30. Ibid., 70–71.

31. Ibid., 63.

32. Ibid., 71-72.

33. Selznick, "Review of *The Morality of Law*," 947. Cf. Fuller, *The Morality of Law*, 129.

34. See Martin Krygier, "Law and the State," *Encyclopedia of Law and Society: American and Global Perspectives*, vol. 3 (Thousand Oaks, CA: Sage, 2007), 1431–1434.

35. Selznick, "Sociology and Natural Law," at 84.

36. I have particularly in mind Malinowski, Ehrlich, and Petrażycki, the first two subjects of the Austro-Hungarian Empire, the third of the Russian. Selznick knew Malinowski's writings, though I do not know that he was influenced by them, and he was well acquainted with Ehrlich's major book, which he frequently cited.

37. *Law, Society, and Industrial Justice*, 34, quoting Ehrlich, *Fundamental Principles of the Sociology of Law*, (Cambridge, MA: Harvard University Press, 1936), xv.

38. See esp. David Nelken, "Law in Action or Living Law? Back to the Beginning in Sociology of Law," *Legal Studies* 4 (1984), 157–174.

39. "I think the point is that he and I shared a sociological perspective. I don't think that his writings were a big influence on me but it was helpful to refer to him as someone who expressed the significance of a sociological perspective for jurisprudence." (Personal correspondence, May, 21, 2007).

40. Selznick, *Law, Society, and Industrial Justice*, at 4.

41. Ibid., 7.

42. Ibid., 8. Italics in original. Ehrlich was more skeptical of the value of that "funded experience."

43. Selznick, "Sociology and Natural Law," 84.

44. Selznick, *Law, Society, and Industrial Justice*, 14.

45. Ibid., 17.

46. Ibid., 7.

47. Selznick, "The Sociology of Law," *International Encyclopedia of Social Science*, 55.

48. Ibid., 56.

49. Selznick, *Law, Society, and Industrial Justice*, 33.

50. Ibid.

51. Marc Galanter, "Justice in Many Rooms: Courts, Private Ordering, and Indigenous Law," *Journal of Legal Pluralism* 19 (1981), 1–47, at 20.

52. Selznick, *The Moral Commonwealth*, 266. This says nothing about whether the claim is objectively rightful, but "only that it is *accepted* as such."

53. See Philippe Nonet and Philip Selznick, *Law and Society in Transition: Toward Responsive Law* (New York: Harper Torch Books, 1978). New edition with introduction by Robert A. Kagan (New Brunswick, NJ: Transaction Publishers, 2001), 10.

54. Selznick, *Law, Society, and Industrial Justice*, 8.

55. Ibid., 35.

56. Ibid., 8.

57. Ibid., 9.

58. Ibid.

59. Ibid., 18.

60. Ibid.

61. Weber, *Economy and Society*, vol. 2, 687.

62. Martin Krygier, videotaped interview with Philip Selznick, January 10, 2002; available at http://law.berkeley.edu/selznick.htm.

63. Selznick, *Law, Society, and Industrial Justice*, 38–39.

64. Ibid., 30. The point is repeated in *The Moral Commonwealth*, 272. And see ibid., 269.

65. Selznick, *Law, Society, and Industrial Justice*, 30.

66. Selznick, *International Encyclopedia of the Social Sciences*, 55.

67. Selznick, *Law, Society, and Industrial Justice*, 18–19.

68. Ibid., 21.

69. Ibid., 23.

70. Ibid., 25.

71. Ibid.

72. Ibid.

73. Ibid., 25–26.

74. Ibid., 28.

75. Ibid., 31.

76. "My view of law and authority has certainly benefited from the stirrings of the sixties, especially on the campuses, where there has been a quest for enlarged student rights and for the reconstruction of authority," (Preface, v).

77. Ibid., 29.

78. Ibid.

79. Ibid., 32–33.

80. Ibid., 75.

81. Ibid., 77.

82. Ibid., 82.

83. Ibid., 80.

84. Ibid., 81.

85. Ibid., 82.

86. Ibid., 82–83.

87. Ibid., 84.

88. Ibid., 92.

89. Ibid., 93.

90. Ibid., 95.

91. Ibid., 115.

92. Ibid., 100.

93. Ibid., 102.

94. Ibid., 117.

95. Ibid., 115.

96. Ibid., 117.

97. Philip Pettit, *Republicanism* (Oxford, UK: Oxford University Press, 1999).

98. Selznick, *Law, Society, and Industrial Justice*, 117.

99. Ibid.

100. Ibid., 118.

101. Ibid., 154. The last sentence, as Selznick well knew, inverts Engels's promise that under communism the government of men would give way to the administration of things.

102. Ibid., 155.

103. Ibid., 178.

104. Ibid., 182.

105. Ibid., 243.

106. Selznick, "Legal Institutions and Social Controls," *Vanderbilt Law Review* 17 (1963), 89.

107. Selznick, "American Society and the Rule of Law," *Syracuse Journal of International Law and Commerce* 33 (2005), 37.

108. Compare Selznick, "Legal Institutions and Social Controls," 87–90.

109. *Law, Society, and Industrial Justice*, 246.

110. Ibid.

111. Ibid., 259.

112. Ibid., 271.

113. Ibid., 272.

114. Ibid., 249.

115. Ibid., 256.

116. Ibid., 250.

117. Ibid., 273.

118. Ibid., 276.

119. Ibid., 275.

120. Ibid., 273.

121. Ibid., 275.

122. See Lauren B. Edelman and Mark C. Suchman, "Introduction: The Interplay of Law and Organisations," in Suchman and Edelman, eds., *The Legal Lives of Private Organizations* (Aldershot, UK: Ashgate, 2007), xii.

123. See, for example, Malcolm M. Feeley, "Law, Legitimacy, and Symbols: An Expanded View of Law and Society in Transition," *Michigan Law Review* 77 (1979), 901; Erhard Blankenburg, "The Poverty of Evolutionism: A Critique of Teubner's Case for 'Reflexive Law,'" *Law and Society Review* 18 (1984), 281–284.

124. See Stephen M. Bainbridge, "Employee Involvement Postcollective Bargaining," in Robert Kagan, Martin Krygier, and Kenneth Winston, eds., *Legality*

and Community: The Legacy of Philip Selznick (Lanham, MD: Rowman & Little-field, 2002), 203–218.

125. See Marc Hertogh, "The Living *Rechtstaat*, A Bottom-Up Approach to Legal Ideas and Social Reality," in Wibren van der Burg and Sanne Taekema, eds., *The Importance of Ideals* (Brussels: P.I.E.—Peter Lang, 2004), 75–95.

126. Donald Black, "Review of *Law, Society, and Industrial Justice*," *American Journal of Sociology* 78 (1972), 714: "This book may even add to the progress of . . . a trend Lon Fuller once described as 'creeping legalism.' Selznick both celebrates the trend and applies sociology to its advance."

127. Lon L. Fuller letter to Philip Selznick, January 12, 1972:

> If I have one fundamental criticism it is that in dealing with institutional procedures (such as adjudication) your thesis assumes a kind of continuum, and that one can be "adjudicative" in one's approach to a problem in varying degrees. Or again, it assumes that procedures of decision and authoritative direction can be "legalized" along a kind of continuum, with no clear stopping places en route.
>
> Coupled with this is a tendency to disregard the costs of judicialization and legalization. . . . There is, in the book, little sense of dilemma and none of tragic choice. . . .
>
> I have been suggesting that your book does not recognize sufficiently the costs and disadvantages of legalization and judicialization. . . . processes have an internal integrity that cannot be violated without damage to their moral efficacy. Plainly this is true of contracts, elections and deciding issues by lot. I think it is also true of adjudication. . . .
>
> I am disturbed by what seems to be a too free-wheeling disposition toward the internal integrity of adjudicative forms.

128. See Lauren B. Edelman, "Legality and the Endogeneity of Law," in Robert Kagan, Martin Krygier, and Kenneth Winston, eds., *Legality and Community: The Legacy of Philip Selznick* (Lanham, MD: Rowman & Littlefield, 2002), 201.

129. "The Statesman: Revisiting *Leadership in Administration*," in *Legality and Community*, 296–297.

CHAPTER EIGHT

1. Martin Krygier, videotaped interview with Philip Selznick, January 9, 2002; available at http://law.berkeley.edu/selznick.htm.

2. Selznick, "Jurisprudence and Social Policy: Aspirations and Perspectives," *California Law Review* 68 (1980), 207.

3. Report to Sanford Elberg, Dean of the Graduate Division, University of California, Berkeley (August 23, 1974), 2.

4. John Philip Reid, *Rule of Law* DeKalb: Northern Illinois University Press, 2004), 12.

5. Henry Bracton, *On the Laws and Customs of England, vol. 2*, translated and edited by Samuel E. Thorne (Cambridge, MA: Harvard University Press, 1968), 305–306, quoted in ibid., 11.

6. See also Gerald Postema, *Bentham and the Common Law Tradition* (Oxford, UK: Clarendon Press, 1989).

7. See Judith N. Shklar, "Political Theory and the Rule of Law," in Shklar, *Political Thought and Political Thinkers*, 24; Joseph Raz, "The Rule of Law and its Virtue," in *The Authority of Law* (Oxford, UK: Clarendon Press, 1979), 228;

and discussion in Martin Krygier, "Rule of Law," forthcoming in A. Sajó and M. Rosenfeld, eds., *Oxford Companion to Comparative Constitutional Law* (Oxford, UK: Oxford University Press, 2011).

8. Selznick, *The Moral Commonwealth* (Berkeley: University of California Press, 1992), 174. This formulation goes back a long way in Selznick; cf. "On Redefining Socialism," *Enquiry* 1, 5 (July 1943), 9: "The redefinition of socialism must base itself solidly upon the explicit recognition and understanding of this fundamental principle of social life: *only power can check power* . . . The efficacy of the principle that only power checks power, and only power can be relied upon to maintain liberty, is evident in the experience of all groups organized formally or informally or informally for social action."

9. Ibid., 289.

10. Ibid., 464.

11. Selznick, Annual Report of the Center for the Study of Law and Society, July 1961–June 1962, 3–4.

12. Ibid., 6.

13. Philippe Nonet and Philip Selznick, *Law and Society in Transition* [hereafter abbreviated as *LST*], (New York: Harper Torch Books, 1978). New edition with introduction by Robert A. Kagan (New Brunswick, NJ: Transaction Publishers, 2001), 3.

14. Ibid., 3.

15. Ibid., 8.

16. Ibid., 18.

17. Ibid., 3.

18. Ibid., 6–7.

19. Ibid., 17.

20. See Roberto Mangabeira Unger, *Law in Modern Society* (New York: Basic Books, 1976); and Eugene Kamenka and Alice Erh-Soon Tay "Beyond Bourgeois Individualism—The Contemporary Crisis in Law and Legal Ideology," in Eugene Kamenka and R. S. Neale, eds., *Feudalism, Capitalism and Beyond* (Canberra and London: ANU Press, 1975), 126–144. There are differences between these typologies but significant affinities, of content and of purpose, as well.

21. *LST*, 12.

22. Ibid., 13.

23. Hart, *The Concept of Law* (Clarendon Press: Oxford, 1961; 2nd edition with a new postscript, 1994), 13–17.

24. Cf. Martin Krygier, "*The Concept of Law* and Social Theory," *Oxford Journal of Legal Studies* 2.2 (1982), 155–180.

25. *LST*, 3–4.

26. See Herbert Packer, "Two Models of the Criminal Process," *University of Pennsylvania Law Review* 113 (1964), 1–68, on tensions between "due process" and "crime control" models of and in criminal law.

27. *LST*, 17.

28. Ibid., 18–20.

29. Ibid., 23.

30. Stephen Holmes, "Cultural Legacies or State Collapse?," public lecture no. 13, delivered at Collegium Budapest, November 1995, 38.

31. *LST*, 24.

32. Ibid., 14.

33. Ibid., 14.

34. See my "The Grammar of Colonial Legality: Subjects, Objects, and the Australian Rule of Law," in Geoffrey Brennan and Francis G. Castles, eds., *Australia Reshaped: 200 Years of Institutional Transformation* (Cambridge, UK: Cambridge University Press, 2002), 220–260.

35. Unger, *Law in Modern Society*, 52–54.

36. *LST*, 34.

37. Ibid., 33.

38. Ibid., 34.

39. Cf. my "Virtuous Circles: Antipodean Reflections on Power, Institutions, and Civil Society," *Eastern European Politics and Societies* 11, 1 (Winter 1997), 36–88.

40. *LST*, 57.

41. Ibid., 52.

42. Ibid., 46.

43. Ibid.

44. Selznick, "Legal Cultures and the Rule of Law," in Martin Krygier and Adam Czarnota, eds., *The Rule of Law after Communism* (Aldershot, UK: Ashgate, 1999), 21.

45. Selznick, "Sociology and Natural Law," *Natural Law Forum* 6 (1961): 84–108, at 103, quoted in Chapter Six of this volume at note 75:

> The ideal is to be realized in history and not outside of it. But history makes its own demands. Even when we know the meaning of legality we must still work out the relation between general principles and the changing structure of society. New circumstances do not necessarily alter principles, but they may and do require that new rules of law be formulated and old ones changed. In a system governed by a master ideal, many specific norms, for a time part of that system, may be expendable. The test is whether they contribute to the realization of the ideal.

46. See Chapter Eleven in this volume.

47. See my "Four Puzzles about the Rule of Law: Why, What, Where? And Who Cares?," in James Fleming, ed., *Getting to the Rule of Law*, Nomos (New York: New York University Press, 2011), 64–104.

48. *LST*, 53.

49. Ibid.

50. Ibid., 54.

51. Ibid.

52. See Tom Campbell, *The Legal Theory of Ethical Positivism* (Aldershot, UK: Dartmouth, 1996).

53. I have sought to elaborate some presuppositions of ethical positivism and develop a partly Selznick-derived critique of it, in "Ethical Positivism and the Liberalism of Fear," in Tom Campbell and Jeffrey Goldsworthy, eds., *Judicial Power, Democracy, and Legal Positivism* (Dartmouth, UK: Ashgate, 2000), 59–86.

54. *LST*, 55.

55. Ibid., 56.

56. Ibid., 56–57.

57. Ibid., 60.
58. Ibid., 70.
59. Ibid., 53
60. See Max Weber, *Economy and Society*, vol. 2 (New York: Bedminster Press, 1968), 848.
61. *LST*, 67.
62. Ibid., 71–72.
63. Ibid., 78–79.
64. Ibid., 79–80.
65. Ibid., 80.
66. Ibid., 82–83.
67. Ibid., 89.
68. Ibid., 100.
69. Ibid., 96.
70. Ibid., 104–105.
71. Ibid., 84.
72. Gunther Teubner, "Substantive and Reflexive Elements in Modern Law," *Law and Society Review* 17 (1983), 239–285. See also Erhard Blankenburg, "The Poverty of Evolutionism: A Critique of Teubner's Case for 'Reflexive Law,'" *Law and Society Review* 18 (1984), 273–289; and Gunther Teubner, "Autopoiesis in Law and Society: A Rejoinder to Blankenburg," *Law and Society Review* 18 (1984), 291–301.
73. *LST*, 108.
74. Selznick, *Leadership in Administration*, (New York: Harper & Row, 1957). Reissued with new preface by University of California Press, Berkeley, 1984, 62–63; 90–133.
75. *LST*, 110.
76. Peter Vincent-Jones, "Responsive Law and Governance in Public Services Provision: A Future for the Local Contracting State," *The Modern Law Review* 61 (1998), 365.
77. *LST*, 112.
78. Quoting Kenneth C. Davis, *Administrative Law Text* (St. Paul, MN: West Publishing, 1959), 30.
79. *LST*, 110.
80. See John Braithwaite, *Regulatory Capitalism: How It Works, Ideas for Making It Work Better* (Cheltenham, UK: Edward Elgar, 2008). See also Christine Parker, *The Open Corporation: Effective Self-Regulation and Democracy* (Cambridge, UK: Cambridge University Press, 2002).
81. David Nelken, "Is There a Crisis in Law and Legal Ideology?" *Journal of Law and Society* 9 (1982), 180.
82. Malcolm Feeley, "Law, Legitimacy, and Symbols: An Expanded View of Law and Society in Transition," *Michigan Law Review* 77 (1979), 902. See also Erhard Blankenburg, "The Poverty of Evolutionism."
83. See note 20 in this chapter. See, too, Geoffrey de Q. Walker, *The Rule of Law, Foundation of Constitutional Democracy* (Melbourne, Australia: Melbourne University Press, 1988); and Brian Tamanaha, *Law as a Means to an End: Threat to the Rule of Law* (Cambridge, UK: Cambridge University Press, 2006). For a good

survey and discussion of this line of argument, see Brendan Edgeworth, *Legal Modernity and Postmodernity* (Aldershot, UK: Ashgate, 2003), chapter 4.

84. See Friedrich von Hayek, *Law, Legislation and Liberty* (Chicago: University of Chicago Press, 1973 [vol. 1]; 1974 [vol. 2]; 1979 [vol. 3]).

85. Unger, *Law in Modern Society*, 195, 197.

86. Kamenka and Tay, "Beyond Bourgeois Individualism," 135.

87. Cf. Antonin Scalia, "The Rule of Law as a Law of Rules," *University of Chicago Law Review* 56 (1989), 1175–1188.

88. Joseph Raz, *Practical Reason and Norms* (London: Hutchinson, 1975), 35–48.

89. *LST*, 74–76.

90. Nevertheless, his affection and admiration for Selznick continued. See "Technique and Law." in Robert Kagan, Martin Krygier, and Kenneth Winston, eds., *Legality and Community: The Legacy of Philip Selznick* (Lanham, MD: Rowman & Littlefield, 2002), 49–66.

91. Philippe Nonet, "In the Matter of *GREEN v. RECHT*," *California Law Review* 75 (1987), 363, 364.

92. Nonet, op. cit., 464.

93. *LST*, 82.

94. Ibid., 83.

95. Ibid., 85.

96. Ibid., 101.

97. Ibid., 102.

98. Ibid., 102–103.

99. Ibid., at note 62.

100. Ibid., 103.

101. Ibid., 77–78.

102. Selznick, *The Moral Commonwealth*, 335.

103. Ibid., xiii.

104. *LST*, 76.

105. Selznick, "Legal Cultures and the Rule of Law," 34.

106. Selznick, *The Moral Commonwealth*, 439.

107. *LST*, 116.

108. Selznick, *The Moral Commonwealth*, 336.

109. Selznick, *Leadership in Administration*, 126–127.

110. Selznick, *The Moral Commonwealth*, 464.

111. *LST*, 116.

112. Selznick, "Legal Cultures and the Rule of Law," 30.

113. *LST*, 67.

114. Ibid., 64.

115. See Selznick, *The Moral Commonwealth*, 436–437.

116. Selznick, "Legal Cultures and the Rule of Law," 26.

117. Ibid., 27.

118. See Eugene Bardach and Robert Kagan, *Going by the Book* (Philadelphia: Temple University Press, 1982). See also Carol Heimer, "The Routinization of Responsiveness: Regulatory Compliance and the Construction of Organizational

Routines," *American Bar Foundation Working Paper* No. 9801, 6, 7; and John Braithwaite and Valerie Braithwaite, "The Politics of Legalism: Rules versus Standards in Nursing-Home Regulation," *Social and Legal Studies* 4 (1995), 336–337.

CHAPTER NINE

1. Philippe Nonet, "For Jurisprudential Sociology," *Law & Society Review* 10 (1976), 529, 537.

2. Austin Sarat, "Donald Black Discovers Legal Realism: From Pure Science to Policy Science in the Sociology of Law," *Law and Social Inquiry* 14 (1989), 766.

3. See Donald J. Black, "Review of *Law, Society, and Industrial Justice*," *American Journal of Sociology* 78 (1972), 709–714.

4. Ibid., 709.

5. Ibid.

6. Ibid., 714.

7. Ibid., 712.

8. Ibid., 714.

9. See Black, "The Boundaries of Legal Sociology," *Yale Law Journal* 81 (1971–1972), 1086–1100.

10. Ibid., 1090.

11. Black, "Review," 714.

12. Black, "*Boundaries*," 1091.

13. Philip Selznick, "Rejoinder to Donald T. Black," *American Journal of Sociology* 78 (1973), 1266.

14. Philip Selznick, rejoinder at 1266–1267.

15. Ibid, 1268.

16. See Gabriel Abend, "Two Main Problems in the Sociology of Morality," *Theory and Society* 37 (2008), 87–125, for a good survey of philosophical approaches and their bearing on sociology.

17. See Sarat, "Donald Black Discovers Legal Realism."

18. See, for example, the glowing tributes to his "pure sociology" in the, special issue of *Contemporary Sociology* 31 (2002) devoted to it.

19. Philip Selznick, "The Dialectic of Fact and Value: Foundations of a Humanist Social Science," (unpublished Bernard Moses Memorial Lecture, February 17, 1973. On file with the author), 12.

20. See "the entanglement of fact and value," in Hilary Putnam, *The Collapse of the Fact/Value Dichotomy and Other Essays* (Cambridge, MA: Harvard University Press, 2002), 28–45.

21. Hilary Putnam, *Pragmatism: An Open Question* (Oxford, UK: Blackwell, 1985), 16–17.

22. Hilary Putnam and Ruth Anna Putnam, "Dewey's *Logic:* Epistemology as Hypothesis," in Hilary Putnam, *Words and Life* {Cambridge, MA: Harvard University Press, 1994), 200.

23. Richard Rorty, *Consequences of Pragmatism* (Minneapolis: University of Minnesota Press, 1982), 166.

24. Selznick, *The Moral Commonwealth* (Berkeley: University of California Press, 1992), 31. For views Selznick found congenial on these issues, see Charles

W. Anderson, "Pragmatism and Liberalism, Rationalism & Irrationalism: A Response to Richard Rorty," *Polity* 23 (1991), 357–371; and James Campbell, "Rorty's Use of Dewey," *Southern Journal of Philosophy* (1984) 22, 175–187.

25. Cheryl Misak, *Truth, Politics, Morality: Pragmatism and Deliberation* (London: Routledge, 2000), 54.

26. Ibid., 1. See also Ruth Putnam, "Democracy and Value Inquiry," in John R. Shook and Joseph Margolis, eds., *A Companion to Pragmatism* (Oxford, UK: Blackwell, 2006).

27. Misak, op.cit., 52.

28. Arthur L. Stinchcombe, "Review of Lawrence M. Friedman, *The Legal System* and Donald Black, *The Behavior of Law*," *Law & Society Review* 12 (1977), 131.

29. Albert Hirschman, "Morality and the Social Sciences," in Norma Haan, Robert N. Bellah, Paul Rabinow, and William M. Sullivan, eds., *Social Science as Moral Inquiry* (New York: Columbia University Press, 1983), 31.

30. Amartya Sen, *The Idea of Justice* (Cambridge, MA: Harvard University Press, 2009).

31. Sen, *On Ethics and Economics* (Oxford, UK: Blackwell, 1987), 89. Cf. Hilary Putnam, "Fact and Value in the World of Amartya Sen," in *The Collapse of the Fact/Value Distinction and Other Essays* (Cambridge, MA: Harvard University Press, 2002).

32. See H. L. A. Hart on the need for an analyst to understand the "internal point of view" of legal subjects (*The Concept of Law* [Oxford, UK: Clarendon Press, revised edition 1994]).

33. "An Oral History with Philip Selznick," conducted by Roger Cotterrell, 9; available at http://digitalassets.lib.berkeley.edu/roho/ucb/text/selznick_philip.pdf; http://law.berkeley/selznick.htm. 33. See too Selznick, *The Organizational Weapon, The Organizational Weapon. A Study of Bolshevik Strategy and Tactics* (Glencoe, IL: Free Press, 1960; Kindle edition forthcoming with a new foreword by Martin Krygier, with Quid Pro Quo, LLC, in 2012), x.

34. Selznick, "The Dialectic of Fact and Value," 2. See Cohen, *Reason and Nature*, 165–168.

35. James B. Rule, *Insight and Social Betterment* (New York: Oxford University Press, 1978), 16.

36. Ibid., 17.

37. Ibid., 108–109.

38. A similar point is made in general terms by Blankenburg, "The Poverty of Evolutionism: A Critique of Teubner's Case for 'Reflexive Law,'" *Law and Society Review* 18 (1984), 273–289, about the slippages in evolutionary accounts that transfer from individual to social development.

39. Martin Krygier, videotaped interview with Philip Selznick, January 18, 2002; available at http://law.berkeley.edu/selznick.htm.

CHAPTER TEN

1. Cited in Raimond Gaita, *A Common Humanity: Thinking about Love, Truth, and Justice* (London: Routledge, 2000), 16.

2. Charles Taylor, *Modern Social Imaginaries* (Durham NC: Duke University Press, 2004), 1.

3. Selznick, *The Moral Commonwealth*, (Berkeley: University of California Press, 1992), 4.

4. Ibid.

5. Ibid., 5–6.

6. Ibid., 8.

7. Ibid., 13–14.

8. Ibid., 17.

9. Ibid., 19.

10. Ibid., 29.

11. Ibid., 133.

12. See Chapter Four of this volume.

13. *The Moral Commonwealth*, 207.

14. Quoted from John Dewey, *The Quest for Certainty*, Gifford Lectures, 1929 (New York: G. P. Putnam's Sons, 1960), 260; Dewey's emphasis.

15. Selznick, *The Moral Commonwealth*, 33.

16. Ibid., 35.

17. Selznick, *Leadership in Administration*, (New York: Harper & Row, 1957). Reissued with new preface by University of California Press, Berkeley, 1984, 119; quoted in Chapter Four of this volume at note 68.

18. Selznick, *The Moral Commonwealth*, 35–36.

19. Ibid., 243. Cf. Selznick, "The Ethos of American Law," in Irving Kristol and Paul Weaver, eds., *The Americans: 1976* {Lexington, MA: D .C. Heath and Co, 1976), 213: "The person is the touchstone of worth and all institutions are to be judged by what they cost in human terms, and by what they can do to help people get on with the business of living."

20. *The Moral Commonwealth*, 244, n26.

21. Ibid., 244. See also Selznick, *A Humanist Science* (Stanford, CA: Stanford University Press, 2008), 60: "Personal and institutional virtues have closely similar functions and require analogous resources of reflection and control."

22. Selznick, *The Moral Commonwealth*, 29.

23. Ibid., 101.

24. Ibid., 119.

25. Ibid., 120.

26. Selznick, "The Dialectic of Fact and Value" (unpublished Bernard Moses Memorial Lecture, February 17, 1973. On file with the author), 15.

27. See particularly Selznick, "A Normative Theory of Culture," *American Sociological Review* 29 (1964), 653–669.

28. Martin Krygier, interview with Philip Selznick, March 2003 (notes on file with author). Cf. "Sociology and Natural Law," *Natural Law Forum* 6 (1961): 94, and *The Moral Commonwealth*, 100.

29. *The Moral Commonwealth*, 123.

30. Selznick, "Normative Theory of Culture," 660.

31. Selznick, *The Moral Commonwealth*, 395.

32. Ibid., 133.

33. Ibid., 102–103.

34. José Ortega y Gasset, *History as System* (New York: W. W. Norton, 1941), 217; quoted in Selznick, *The Moral Commonwealth*, 121.

35. Joseph de Maistre, *Oeuvres Complètes de J. De Maistre* (Lyon: Librairie Generale Catholique et Classique 2e Tirage, Emmanuel Vitte, Directeur, 1891), vol. 1, 74.

36. Selznick, *The Moral Commonwealth*, 95.

37. Ibid., 124.

38. Ibid., 123.

39. Martha Nussbaum, "Capabilities and Human Rights," *Fordham Law Review* 66 (1997), 286.

40. Nussbaum, "Human Functioning and Social Justice: In Defense of Aristotelian Essentialism," *Political Theory* 20 (1992), 207–208.

41. Selznick, *The Moral Commonwealth*, 38.

42. Clifford Geertz, "The Impact of the Concept of Culture on the Concept of Man," in *The Interpretation of Cultures* (New York: Basic Books, 1973), 43.

43.

I am a Jew. Hath not a Jew eyes? hath not a Jew hands, organs, dimensions, senses, affections, passions? fed with the same food, hurt with the same weapons, subject to the same diseases, healed by the same means, warmed and cooled by the same winter and summer as a Christian is? If you prick us do we not bleed? if you tickle us do we not laugh? if you poison us, do we not die? and if you wrong us, shall we not revenge? If we are like you in the rest, we will resemble you in that. (Shakespeare, *The Merchant of Venice*, III. i. 56–76)

44. For a profound evocation and characterization of the indecencies of humiliation, see Avishai Margalit, *The Decent Society* (Cambridge, MA: Harvard University Press, 1996). See also Raimond Gaita, *A Common Humanity*.

45. Selznick, *The Moral Commonwealth*, 9.

46. Alexander Goldenweiser, *Anthropology* (New York: Crofts, 1937), 125, cited in Selznick, *The Moral Commonwealth*, 98.

47. Ibid., 96.

48. Ibid., 148.

49. Ibid., 150.

50. Ibid., 138.

51. Ibid., 157.

52. Ibid., 149.

53. Ibid., 150.

54. Ibid., 151.

55. Ibid., 160.

56. Ibid., 150.

57. Ibid., 175.

58. Ibid., 208.

59. Ibid., 172.

60. Gertrude Jaeger, "The Philosophy of the Once-Born," *Enquiry* 2, 1 (April 1944), 11–16.

61. Selznick, *The Moral Commonwealth*, 31.

62. Ibid., 175.

63. Ibid., 182.

64. Ibid., 151–152.
65. Ibid., 124.
66. Ibid., 183.
67. See ibid., 201ff.
68. Ibid., 205.
69. Ibid., 212.
70. Ibid., 208–209.
71. Ibid., 212, 213.
72. Ibid., 216.
73. Ibid., 219.
74. Ibid., 221.
75. Ibid., 222.
76. Ibid., 191.
77. Ibid., 184.
78. Ibid., 193.
79. For example, William Kornhauser, *The Politics of Mass Society* (London: Routledge & Kegan Paul, 1965).
80. Selznick, "Institutional Vulnerability in Mass Society," *American Journal of Sociology* 56 (1951): 330.
81. Selznick, "A Normative Theory of Culture," 658.
82. "Traditional man can sometimes escape the tyranny of kings, but only at the cost of falling under the tyranny of cousins, and of ritual." Ernest Gellner, *Conditions of Liberty* (Harmondsworth, UK: Penguin, 1994), 7.
83. Selznick, *The Moral Commowealth*, 193.
84. Ibid., 232.
85. Selznick, *The Communitarian Persuasion* (Washington, DC: Woodrow Wilson Center, 2002), 98.
86. Selznick, *The Moral Commonwealth*, 235.
87. Ibid., 237.
88. Ibid.
89. Ibid., 242–243.
90. Ibid., 247. See Chapter Two in this volume.
91. Ibid., 242.
92. Ibid., 248.
93. Ibid., 249.
94. Ibid., 330.
95. Ibid., 250.
96. Selznick, *The Communitarian Persuasion*, 87.
97. Selznick, *The Moral Commonwealth*, 281.
98. Ibid., 279.
99. Ibid., 254.
100. Ibid., 250.
101. Ibid., 257.
102. Ibid., 258.
103. Ibid., 263.
104. Ibid., 264.
105. Ibid., 289.

106. Ibid.
107. Ibid., 290.
108. Ibid.
109. Ibid., 295.
110. Ibid.
111. Ibid., 297.
112. Ibid., 316.
113. Ibid., 319.
114. Ibid., 321.
115. Ibid., 322.
116. Ibid., 324.
117. Ibid., 331.
118. Ibid., 334.
119. Ibid., 335.
120. See Chapter Four in this volume.
121. Selznick, *The Moral Commonwealth*, 351–352.
122. See John Braithwaite, *Regulatory Capitalism* (Cheltenham, UK: Edward Elgar, 2008); and Christine Parker, *The Open Corporation*. (Cambridge, UK: Cambridge University Press, 2002).
123. Selznick, *The Moral Commonwealth,* 352, note 59.
124. Ibid., 347.
125. Ibid.
126. Ibid., 357.
127. See for example Michael Sandel, *Liberalism and the Limits of Justice* (Cambridge, UK: Cambridge University Press, 1982); Charles Taylor, "Atomism," in *Philosophy and the Human Sciences* (Cambridge, UK: Cambridge University Press, 19850, vol. 2, 187–210; and Alasdair MacIntyre, *After Virtue: A Study in Moral Theory* (London: Duckworth, 1981). For discussions, see Amy Gutmann, "Communitarian Critics of Liberalism," *Philosophy and Public Affairs* 14 (Summer 1985), 308–322; and Michael Walzer, "The Communitarian Critique of Liberalism," *Political Theory* 18 (1990), 6–23. For collections that include Selznick and speak to his themes, see Emilios A. Christodoulidis, ed., *Communitarianism and Citizenship* (Aldershot, UK: Ashgate, 1998); and Paul van Seters, ed., *Communitarianism in Law and Society* (Lanham, MD: Rowman & Littlefield, 2006).
128. See Walzer, "The Communitarian Critique of Liberalism."
129. This is not of course literally the case, since the "lettre" was coined in the nineteenth century, but he was way ahead of the revival of its currency.
130. Selznick oral history, 155–156.
131. Selznick, *The Moral Commonwealth*, 360–365.
132. Ibid., 358.
133. Ibid., 359.
134. Ibid., 360.
135. Ibid., 363.
136. Ibid., 368–369.
137. Selznick, *The Communitarian Persuasion*, 39.
138. Selznick, "Institutional Vulnerability in Mass Society," 324.
139. Selznick, *The Communitarian Persuasion*, 19.

140. Selznick, *The Moral Commonwealth*, 370–371.
141. Ibid., 360.
142. Ibid., 360.

CHAPTER ELEVEN

1. See Martin Krygier, videotaped interview with Philip Selznick, January 11, 2002; available at http://law.berkeley.edu/selznick.htm.
2. Selznick, *The Moral Commonwealth*, (Berkeley: University of California Press, 1992), 371.
3. Ibid., 373.
4. Ibid., 374.
5. Ibid., 386.
6. Or even more than two horns! See my "Conservative Liberal Socialism Revisited," *The Good Society* 11 1 (2002), 6–15; and "In Praise of Hybrid Thoughts," in *Between Fear and Hope. Hybrid Thoughts on Public Values* (Sydney: ABC Press, 1997).
7. Selznick, *The Communitarian Persuasion* (Washington, DC: Woodrow Wilson Center, 2002), 10.
8. Ibid., 56.
9. Ibid., 7.
10. Selznick, *The Moral Commonwealth*, 379.
11. See Jeremy Waldron, "Theoretical Foundations of Liberalism," *The Philosophical Quarterly* 37 (1987), 127–150. This section of my chapter draws on my "In Praise of Prejudice," *Best Australian Essays 2003* (Melbourne: Black Inc., 2003), 121–131.
12. Edmund Burke, *Reflections on the Revolution in France*, ed. with an introduction by Conor Cruise O'Brien (Harmondsworth: Penguin, 1969), 183.
13. A. N. Whitehead, *An Introduction to Mathematics* (New York: H. Holt & Co., 1911), 61.
14. Selznick, *The Moral Commonwealth*, 394.
15. This locution itself is already a somewhat self-conscious but—at least among Western academics—well-mobilized counterresponse to generations of socialization. In due course it might become unselfconscious, in which case we will all be socialized to do it, until the next challenge.
16. For an ontological version of this point, see Hans-Georg Gadamer, *Truth and Method* (New York: Crossroad, 1982).
17. Selznick, *The Moral Commonwealth*, 228.
18. Selznick, *The Communitarian Persuasion*, 57–59.
19. Selznick, *The Moral Commonwealth*, 397–398.
20. Ibid., 194.
21. Ibid.
22. Ibid., 205.
23. Ibid., 196.
24. Ibid., 201–202.
25. Ibid., 392–393.
26. See ibid., 397–398.

27. Selznick, "The Dialectic of Fact and Value," (unpublished Bernard Moses Memorial Lecture, February 17, 1973. On file with the author), 21.

28. Selznick, *The Moral Commonwealth*, 60.

29. Ibid., 102, quoted in Chapter Ten of this volume at note 33.

30. Selznick, "Legal Cultures and the Rule of Law," in Martin Krygier and Adam Czarnota, eds., *The Rule of Law after Communism* (Aldershot, UK: Ashgate, 1999), 32.

31. See my "Human Rights and a Humanist Social Science," in Christopher L. Eisgruber and András Sajó, eds., *Global Justice and the Bulwarks of Localism: Human Rights in Context* (Leiden: Martinus Nijhoff Publishers, 2005), 43–84.

32. Selznick, *The Moral Commonwealth*, 387.

33. Ibid.

34. Ibid.

35. Ibid., 388.

36. Selznick, "Social Justice: A Communitarian Perspective," *The Responsive Community* 6, 4 (Fall 1996), 23.

37. Selznick, *The Moral Commonwealth*, 388.

38. Ibid., 389.

39. Ibid., 390.

40. Ibid., 391.

41. See my *Civil Passions* (Melbourne: Black Inc., 2005).

42. See Dominique Colas, *Civil Society and Fanaticism* (Stanford, CA: Stanford University Press, 1997).

43. *The Moral Commonwealth*, 391–392.

44. Ibid., 429 (quoting Stuart Hampshire, *Innocence and Experience* [Cambridge, MA: Harvard University Press, 1989], 68.

45. Ibid., 430.

46. Ibid., 430–431.

47. Ibid., 444–445.

48. Ibid., 429.

49. Ibid., 429.

50. Ibid., 431.

51. E. P. Thompson, *Whigs and Hunters* (Harmondsworth, UK: Penguin, 1977), 261.

52. Jürgen Habermas, "Law as Medium and Law as Institution," in Günther Teubner, ed., *Dilemmas of the Welfare State* (Berlin: de Gruyter, 1986), 212.

53. Selznick, *The Moral Commonwealth*, 433–434.

54. Ibid., 436.

55. Ibid., 445.

56. Selznick, *The Moral Commonwealth*, 464.

57. Selznick, "Legal Cultures and the Rule of Law," 25.

58. Selznick, *The Moral Commonwealth*, 463.

59. Ibid., 470–471.

60. Ibid., 474.

61. Ibid., 469–470.

62. John Braithwaite, *Regulatory Capitalism* (Cheltenham, UK: Edward Elgar, 2008), 187–188; and "Homage to Selznick," ibid., at 162–163.

63. Selznick, *The Communitarian Persuasion*, 71ff.

64. Ibid., 139.

65. Ibid., 124.

66. Selznick, *The Moral Commonwealth*, 531.

67. Ibid., 381.

68. Ibid., 384.

69. Ibid., 382.

70. Ibid., 386.

71. Selznick, *The Communitarian Persuasion*, 125.

72. *The Moral Commonwealth*, 483.

73. Ibid., 502.

74. Ibid., 524.

75. Selznick, *The Communitarian Persuasion*, 53.

76. Selznick, *The Moral Commonwealth*, 512.

77. Ibid., 516.

78. Ibid., 535.

79. See my "The Good That Governments Do," in *Civil Passions*, 177–200.

80. Selznick, *The Moral Commonwealth*, 536.

81. Martin Krygier, interview with Philip Selznick, March 2003 (notes on file with author).

82. Alan Ryan, *John Dewey and the High Tide of American Liberalism* (New York: W. W. Norton & Co., 1995), 22.

83. However, recently prominent discussions of "public sociology" might suggest the situation is not stable. See, generally, the voluminous discussions of Michael Barawoy's 2004 ASA Presidential Address: For Public Sociology, and more particularly Paul van Seters, "From Public Sociology to Public Philosophy: Lessons for Law and Society," *Law and Social Inquiry* 35 (2010), 1137–1154.

84. Selznick, *A Humanist Science*, 129.

85. David C. Williams, "Pragmatism and Faith: Selznick's Complex Commonwealth," *Law and Social Inquiry* 19 (1994), 776.

CONCLUSION

1. Isaiah Berlin, *The Hedgehog and the Fox* (New York: Simon and Schuster, 1953), 1.

2. All the more posthumously, when nothing that he wrote seems likely to remain unpublished.

3. See editor's introduction to Roger Cotterrell, ed., *Emile Durkheim on Justice, Morals and Politics* (Farnham, UK: Ashgate, 2010), xiii:

> The *sociology of morality* is a term that, in relatively modern times, has seemed somewhat obsolescent. It has designated an absence—an intellectual space that, since the work of some nineteenth century pioneers, few have thought it appropriate to try to fill. . . . But at the beginning of the twenty-first century, the vacant space marked out for a sociology of morals is being seen increasingly as a place of loss—a void that needs to be filled."

4. See "Tribute to Amitai Etzioni by Philip Selznick;" 11th Annual Meeting on Socio-Economics, Madison, Wisconsin, July 9, 1999; available at www.sase.org/index.php?option=com_wrapper&Itemid=53.

5. Donald McDonald, "The Uses of Philosophy: An Interview with Bernard Williams," *The Center Magzine*, 49 (November 1983); available at www.uq.edu.au/~pdwgrey/web/res/bwilliams.usephil.html and quoted in Selznick, *The Moral Commonwealth* (Berkeley: University of California Press, 1992), 213.

6. In a way and not coincidentally, Kim Lane Scheppele, "The Passing of a Generation," *Law & Courts* 20, 2 (Spring 2010), 5–11, asks a similar question. My thought about this issue was partly sparked by her piece and our correspondence about it.

7. The interview is available at http://sociology.berkeley.edu/publicsociology/facultyvideos/oldseries/selznick/play.php.

8. Max Weber, *The Protestant Ethic and the Spirit of Capitalism* (London: Unwin, 1971), 182.

Index

Jurists: Profiles in Legal Theory

GENERAL EDITOR

William Twining

Hugh Baxter, *Habermas: The Discourse Theory of Law and Democracy*

Thomas Garden Barnes, Edited and with an Introduction by Allen D. Boyer, *Shaping the Common Law: From Glanvill to Hale, 1188–1688*

William E. Conklin, *Hegel's Laws: The Legitimacy of a Modern Legal Order*

Neil MacCormick, *H.L.A. Hart*, Second Edition

Wouter de Been, *Legal Realism Regained: Saving Realism from Critical Acclaim*

John Dinwiddy, Edited by William Twining, *Bentham: Selected Writings of John Dinwiddy*

Allen D. Boyer, *Sir Edward Coke and the Elizabethan Age*

Colin Imber, *Ebu's-su`ud: The Islamic Legal Tradition*

Edited by Robert W. Gordon, *The Legacy of Oliver Wendell Holmes, Jr.*